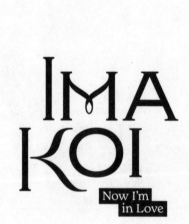

IMA KOI
Now I'm in Love

1

STORY & ART BY

Ayuko Hatta

CONTENTS

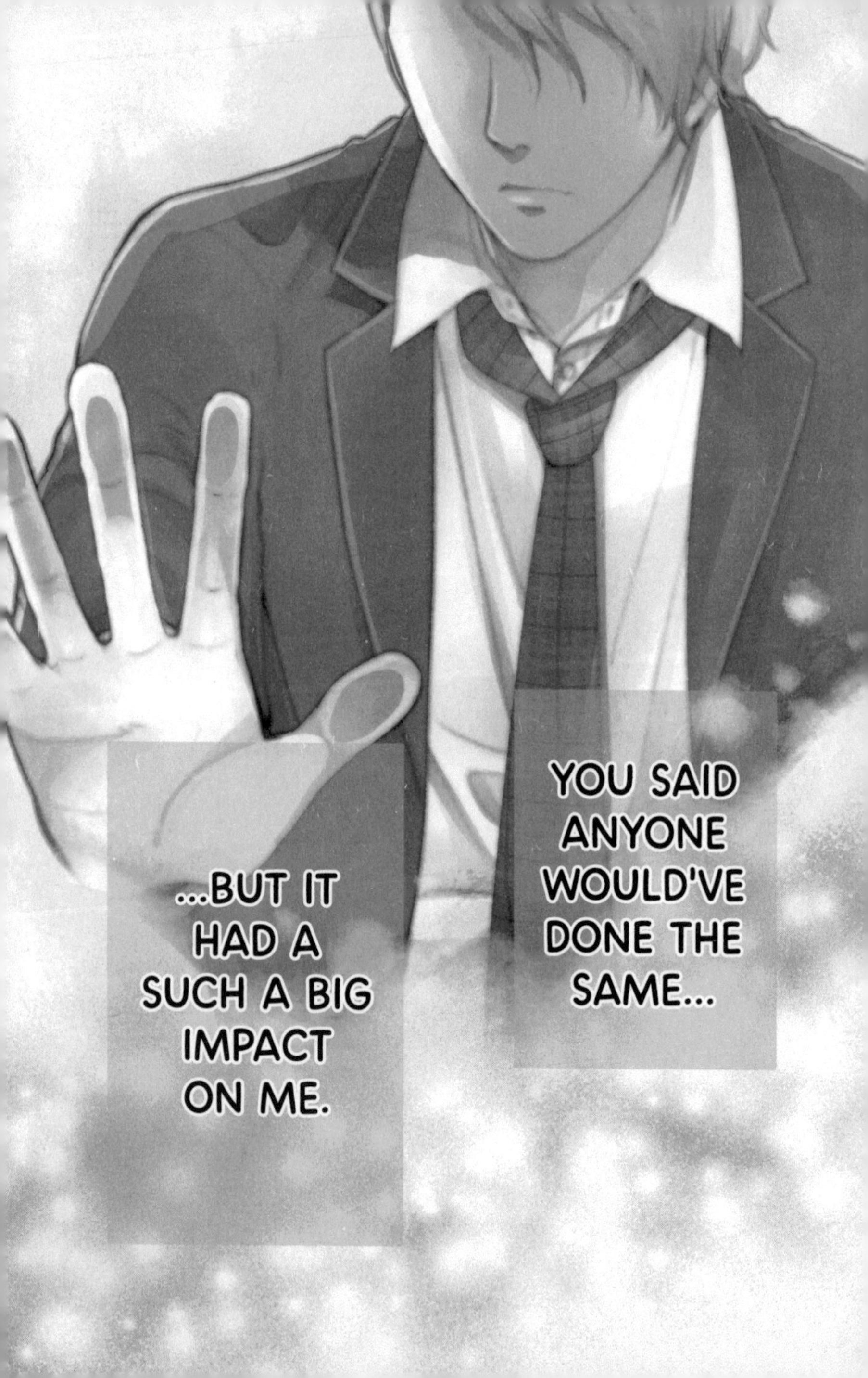
YOU SAID ANYONE WOULD'VE DONE THE SAME...
...BUT IT HAD A SUCH A BIG IMPACT ON ME.

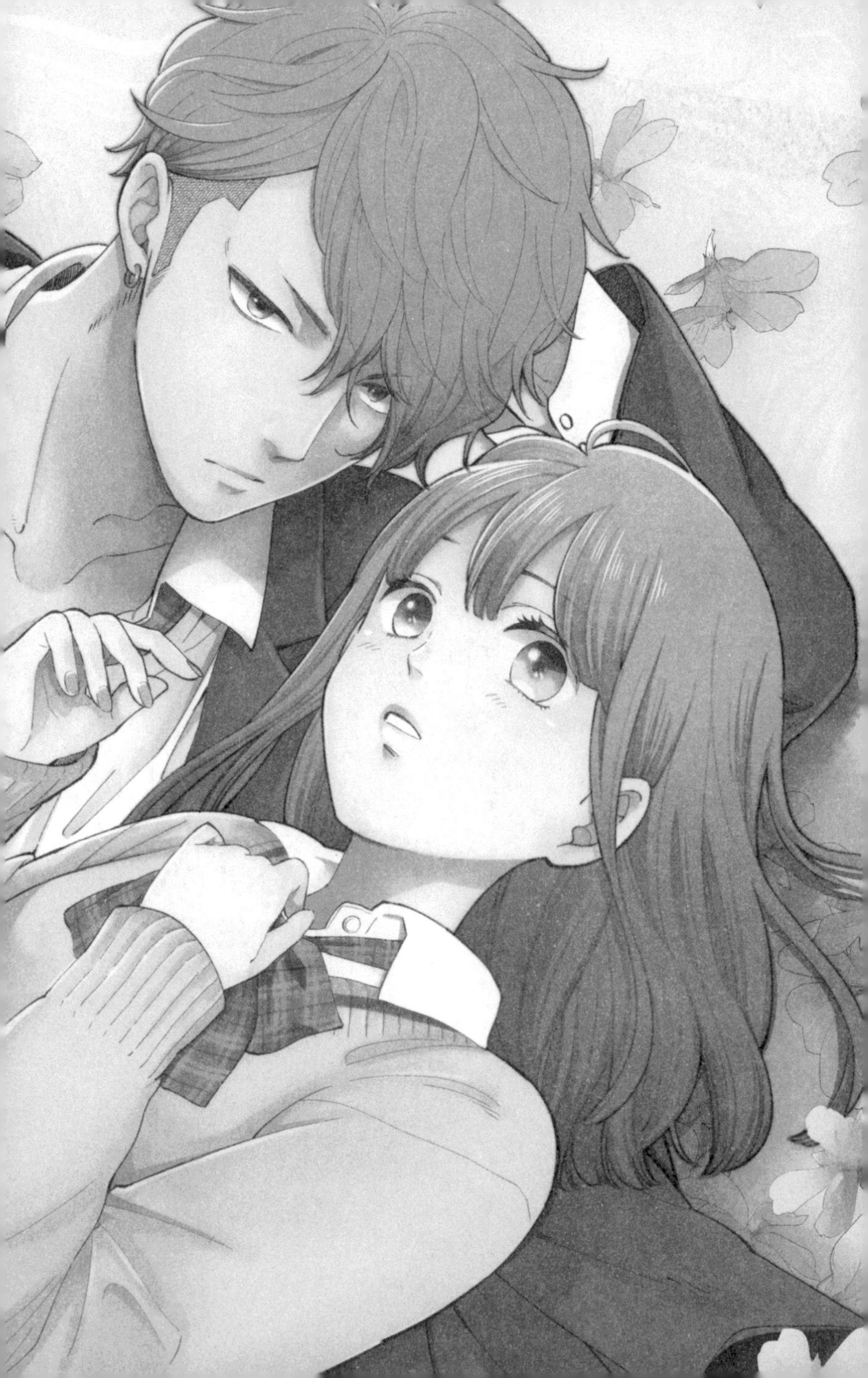

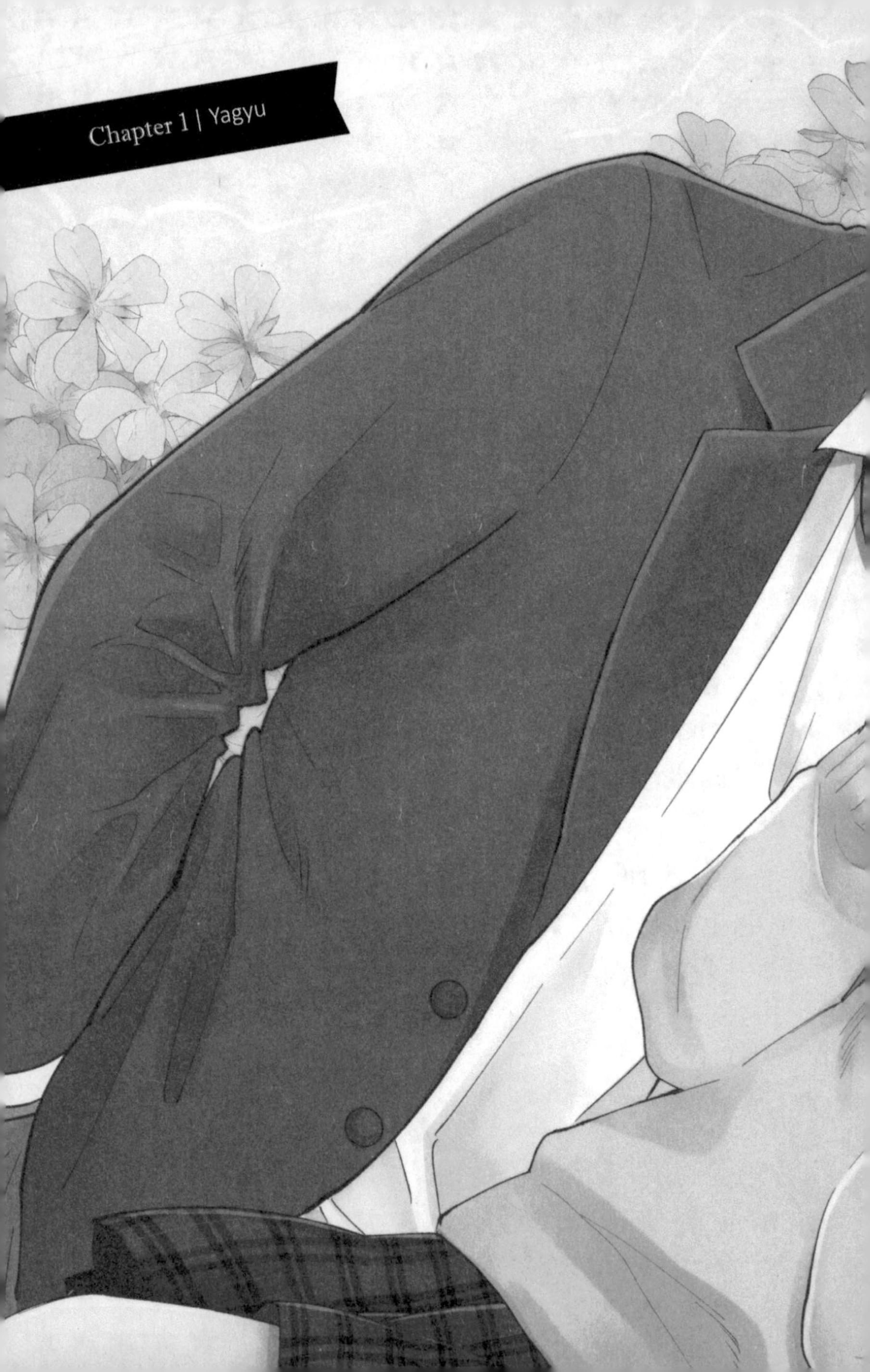
Chapter 1 | Yagyu

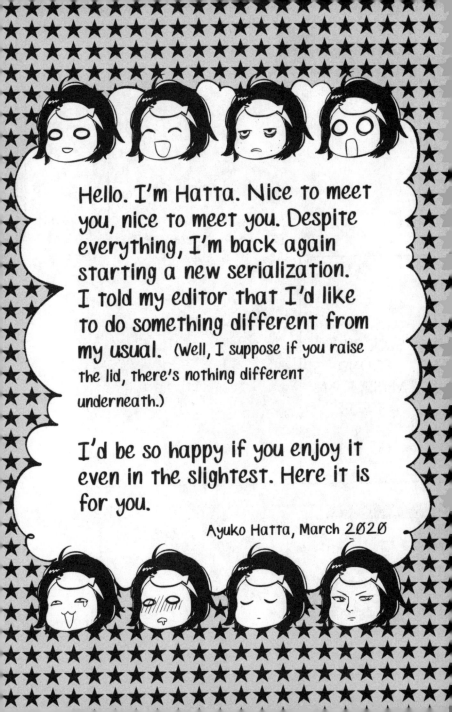

Hello. I'm Hatta. Nice to meet you, nice to meet you. Despite everything, I'm back again starting a new serialization. I told my editor that I'd like to do something different from my usual. (Well, I suppose if you raise the lid, there's nothing different underneath.)

I'd be so happy if you enjoy it even in the slightest. Here it is for you.

Ayuko Hatta, March 2020

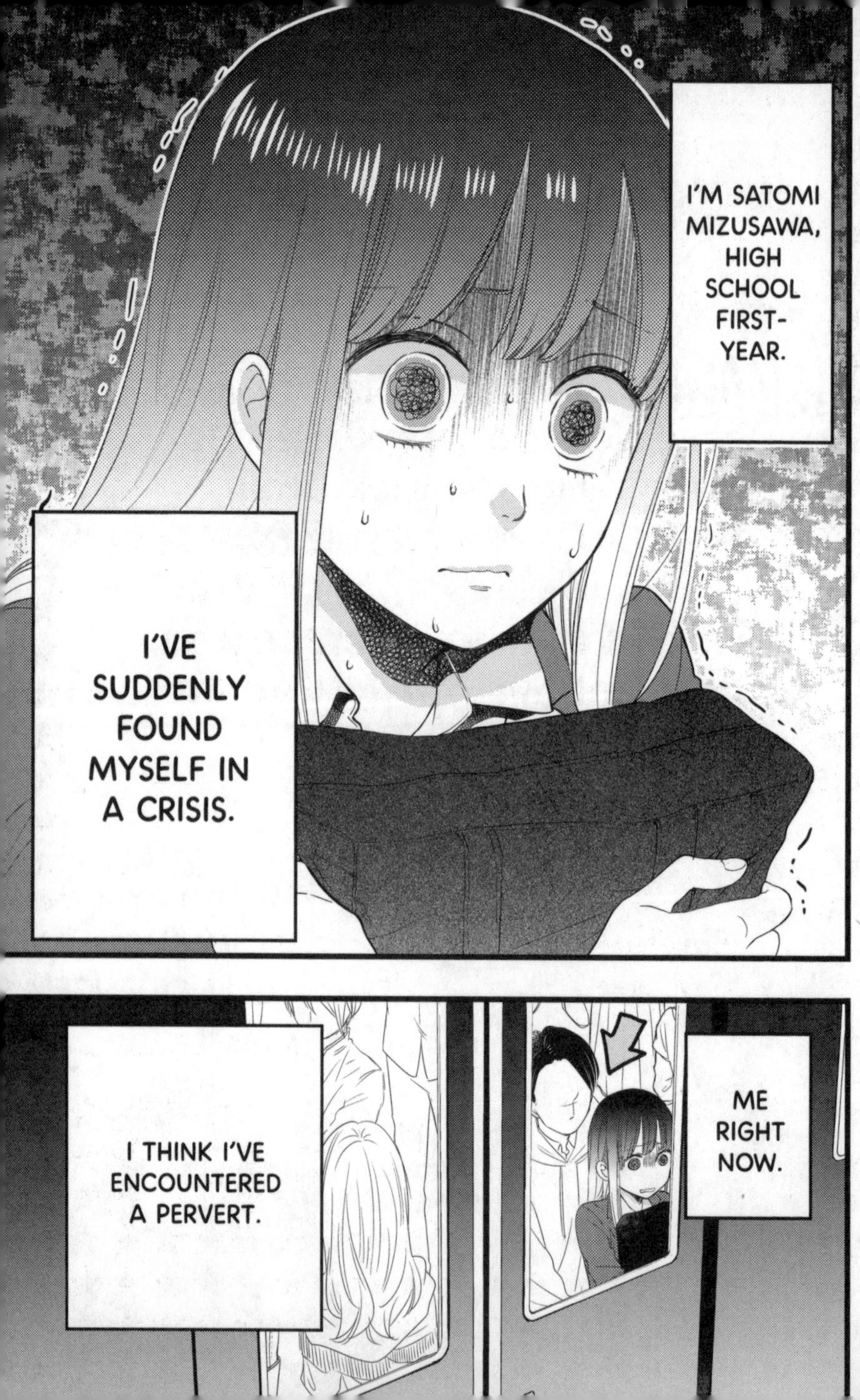
I'M SATOMI MIZUSAWA, HIGH SCHOOL FIRST-YEAR.
I'VE SUDDENLY FOUND MYSELF IN A CRISIS.
ME RIGHT NOW.
I THINK I'VE ENCOUNTERED A PERVERT.

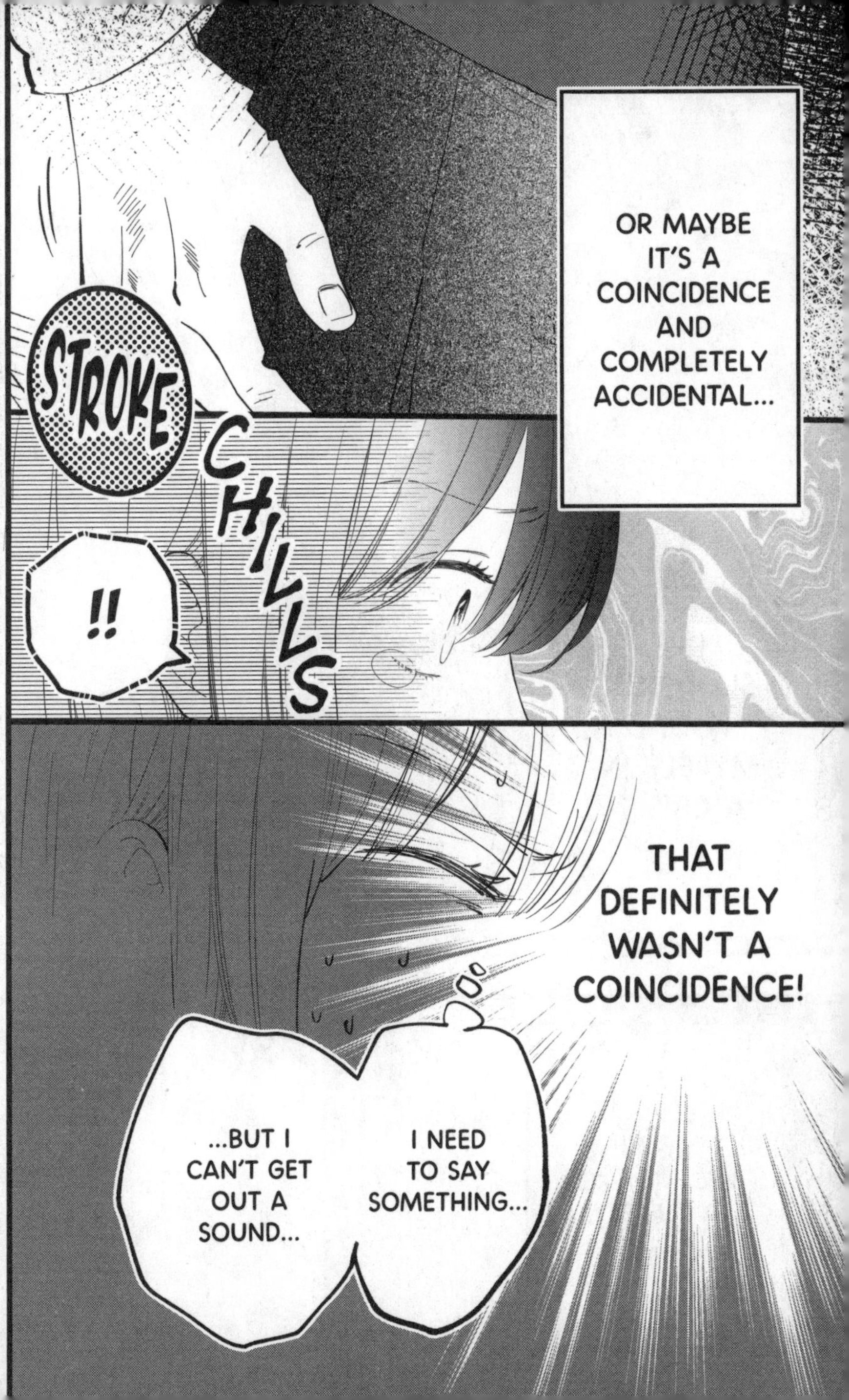
OR MAYBE IT'S A COINCIDENCE AND COMPLETELY ACCIDENTAL...
STROKE
CHILLS
!!
THAT DEFINITELY WASN'T A COINCIDENCE!
I NEED TO SAY SOMETHING...
...BUT I CAN'T GET OUT A SOUND...

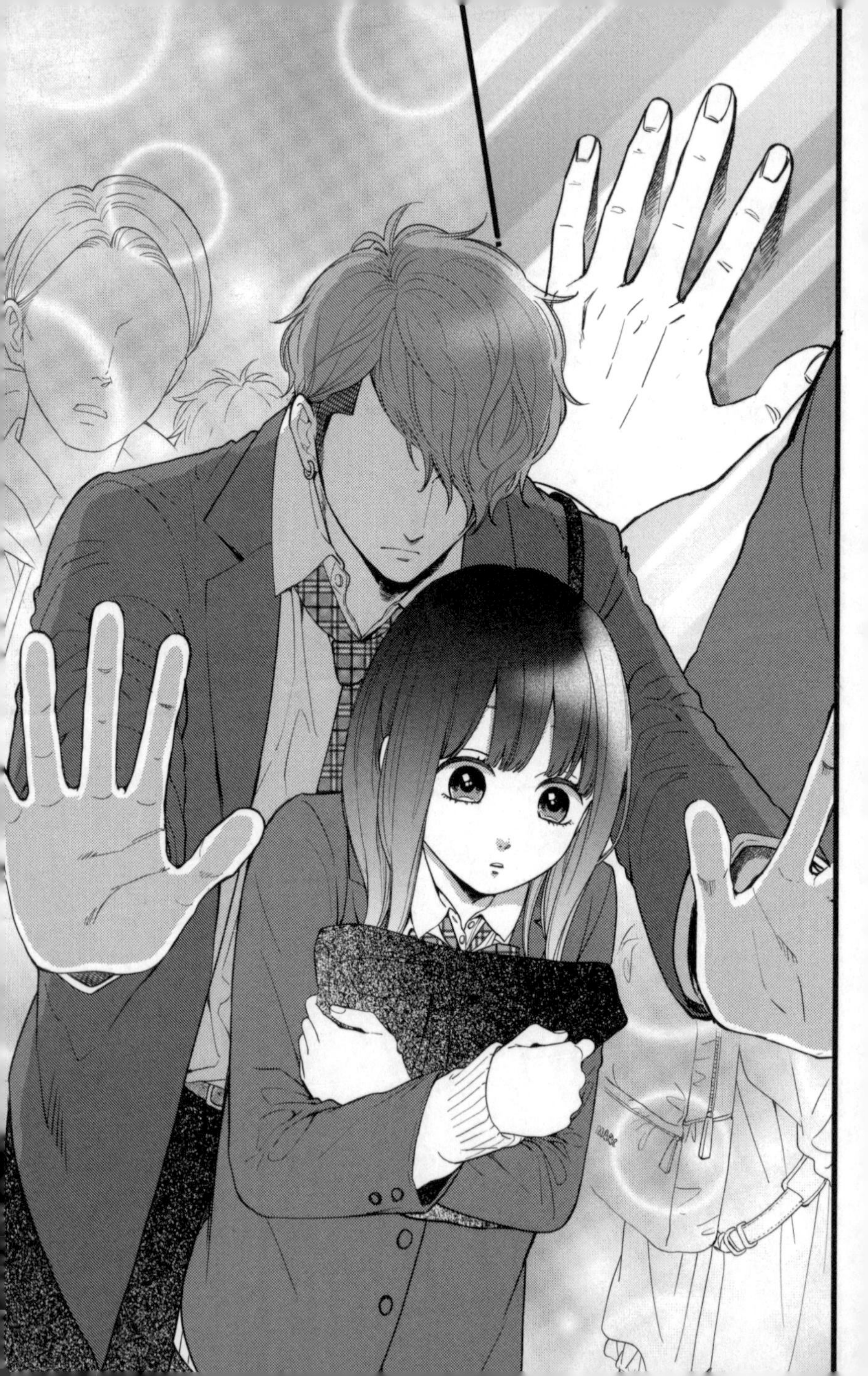

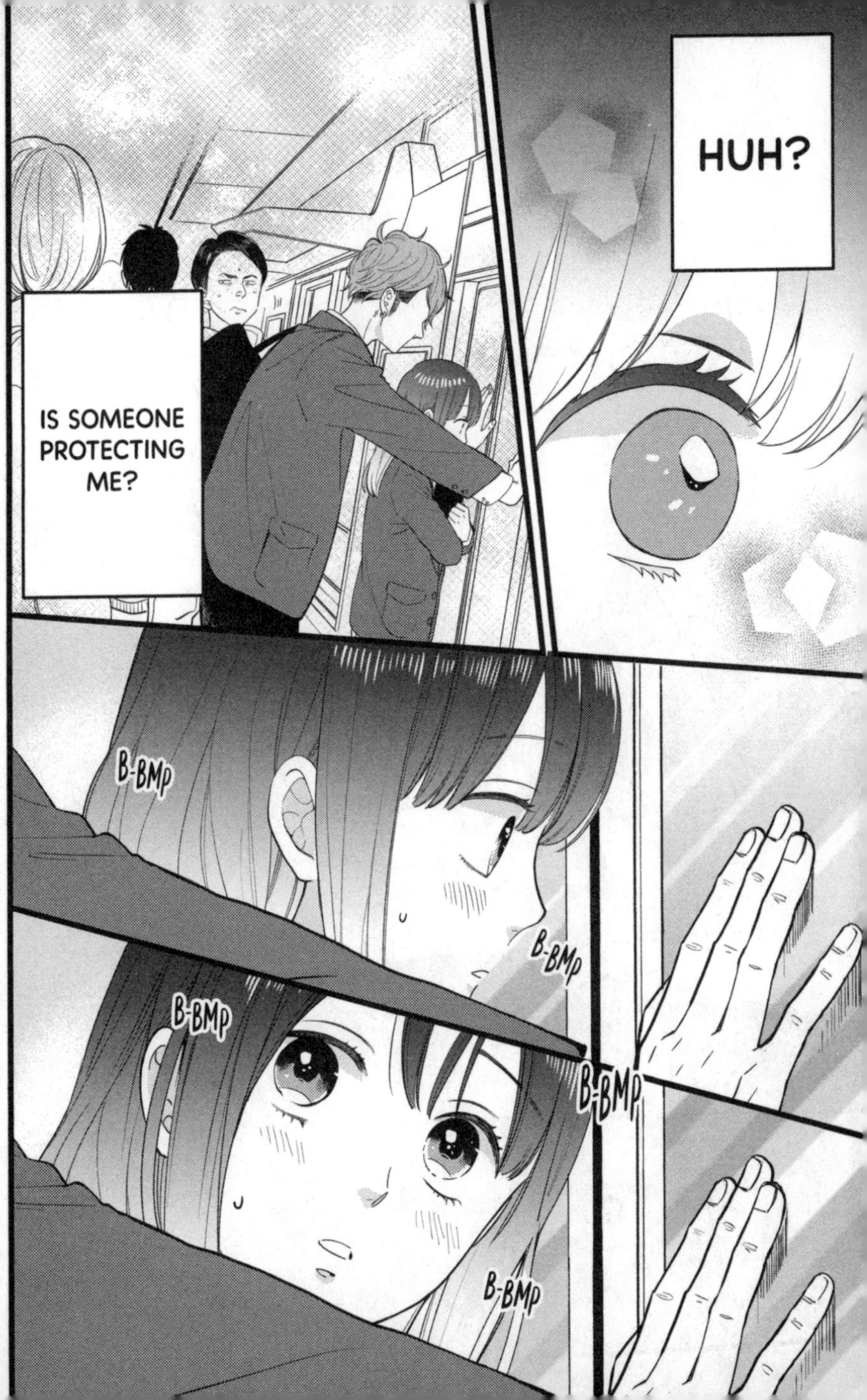
HUH?
IS SOMEONE PROTECTING ME?
B-BMP
B-BMP
B-BMP
B-BMP
B-BMP

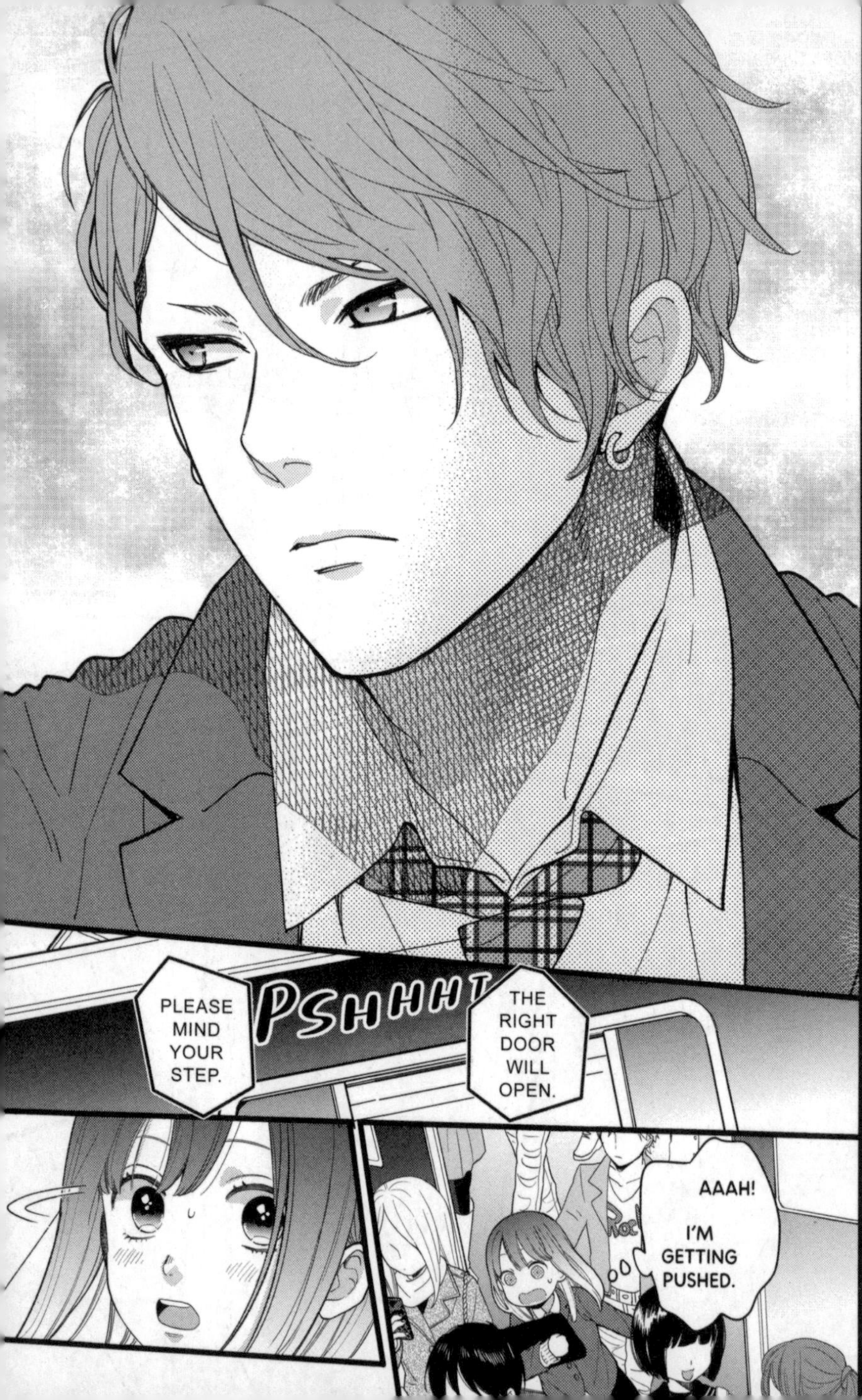
THE RIGHT DOOR WILL OPEN.
PSHHHT
PLEASE MIND YOUR STEP.
AAAH!
I'M GETTING PUSHED.

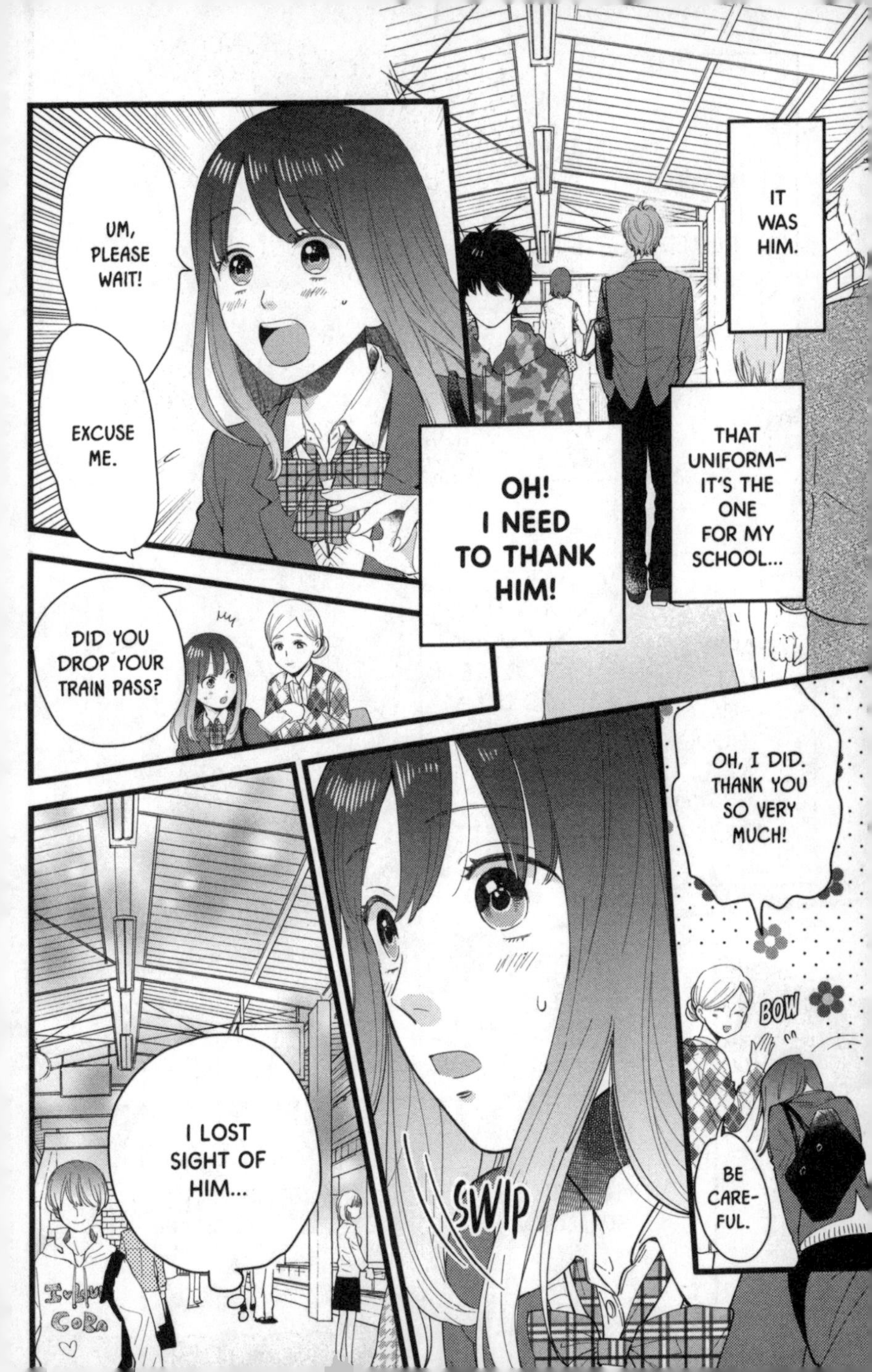
IT WAS HIM.
THAT UNIFORM—IT'S THE ONE FOR MY SCHOOL...
OH! I NEED TO THANK HIM!
UM, PLEASE WAIT!
EXCUSE ME.
DID YOU DROP YOUR TRAIN PASS?
OH, I DID. THANK YOU SO VERY MUCH!
BOW
BE CARE-FUL.
SWIP
I LOST SIGHT OF HIM...

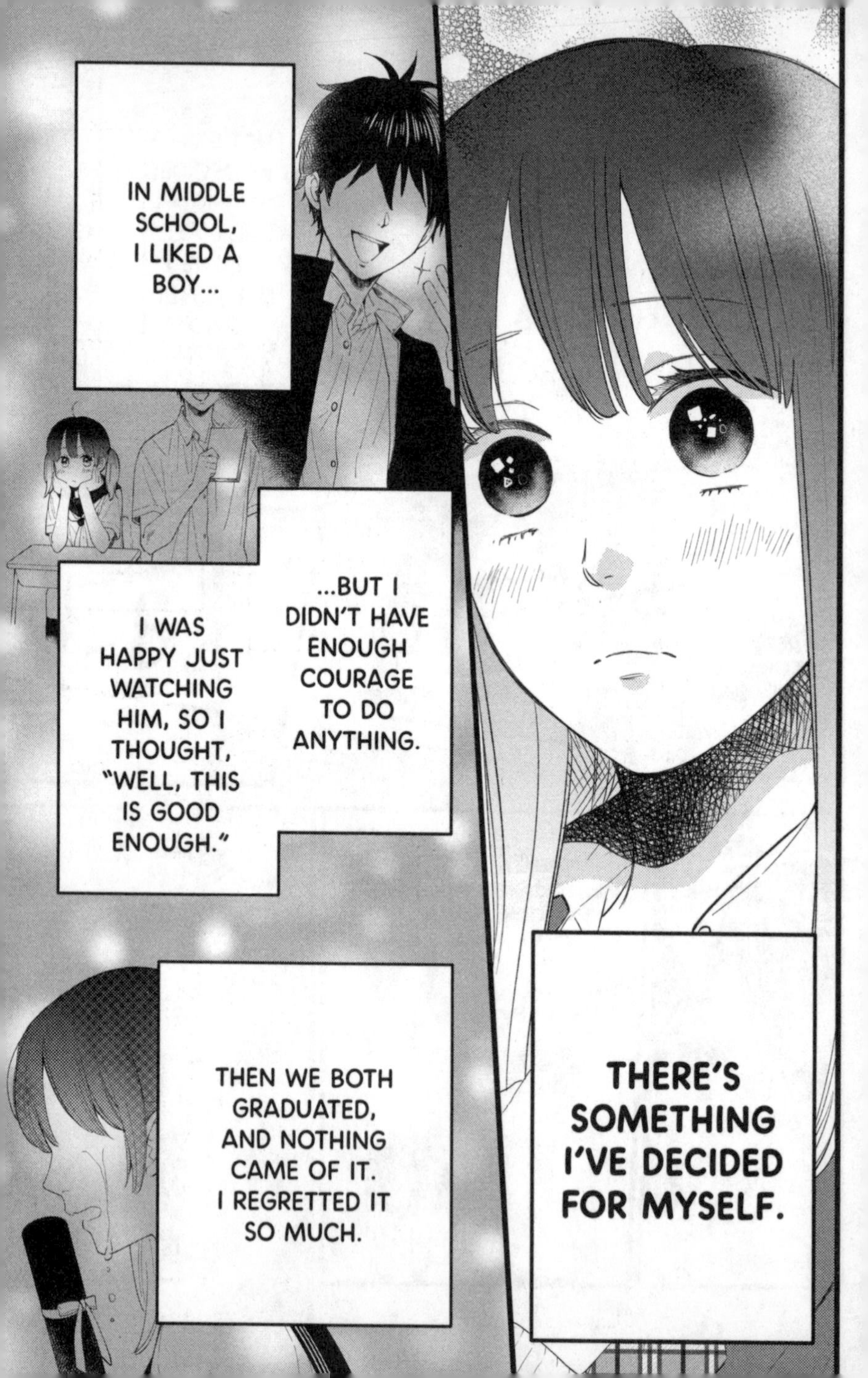
THERE'S SOMETHING I'VE DECIDED FOR MYSELF.
IN MIDDLE SCHOOL, I LIKED A BOY...
...BUT I DIDN'T HAVE ENOUGH COURAGE TO DO ANYTHING.
I WAS HAPPY JUST WATCHING HIM, SO I THOUGHT, "WELL, THIS IS GOOD ENOUGH."
THEN WE BOTH GRADUATED, AND NOTHING CAME OF IT. I REGRETTED IT SO MUCH.

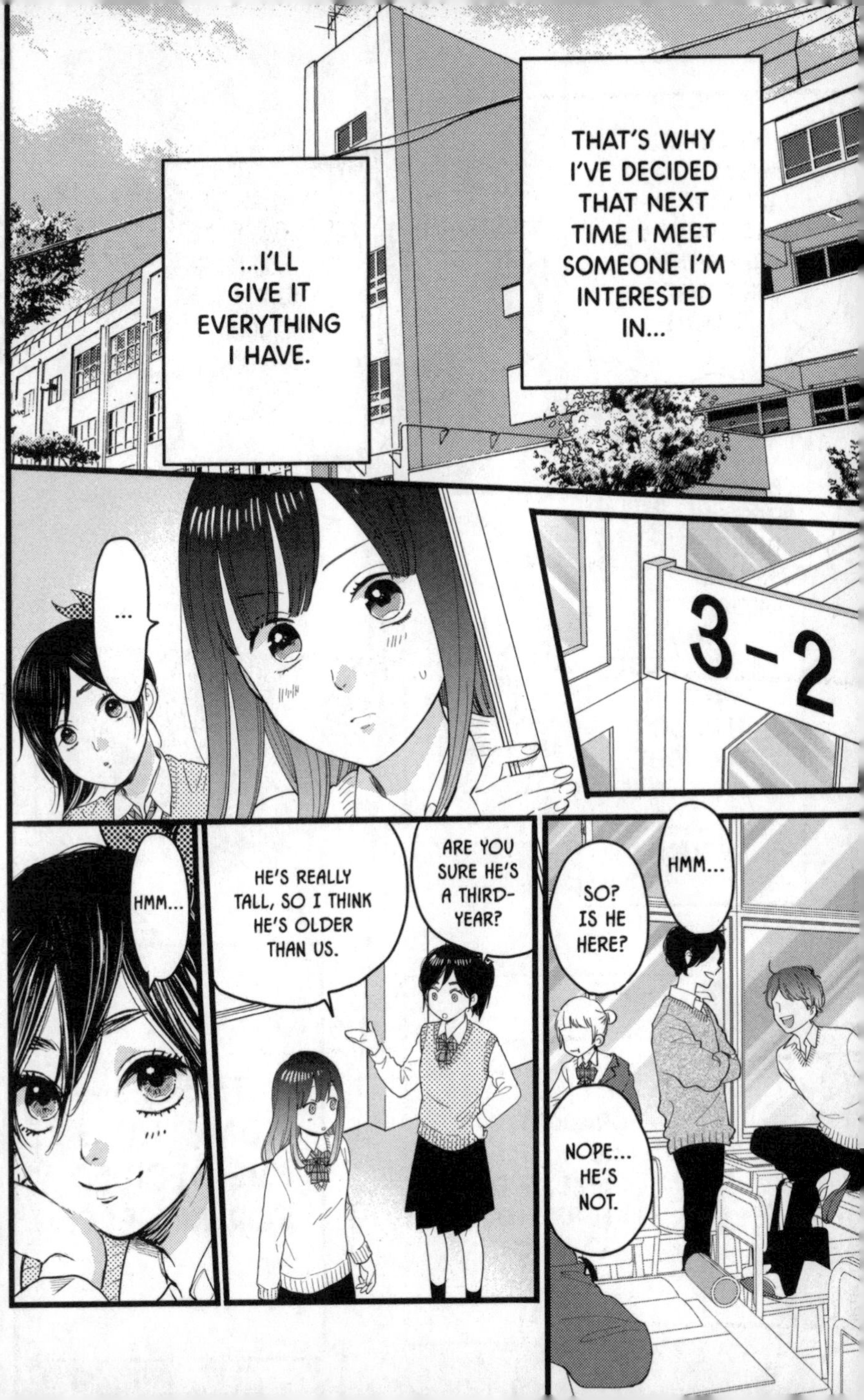
THAT'S WHY I'VE DECIDED THAT NEXT TIME I MEET SOMEONE I'M INTERESTED IN...
...I'LL GIVE IT EVERYTHING I HAVE.
3-2
...
HMM...
SO? IS HE HERE?
NOPE... HE'S NOT.
ARE YOU SURE HE'S A THIRD-YEAR?
HE'S REALLY TALL, SO I THINK HE'S OLDER THAN US.
HMM...

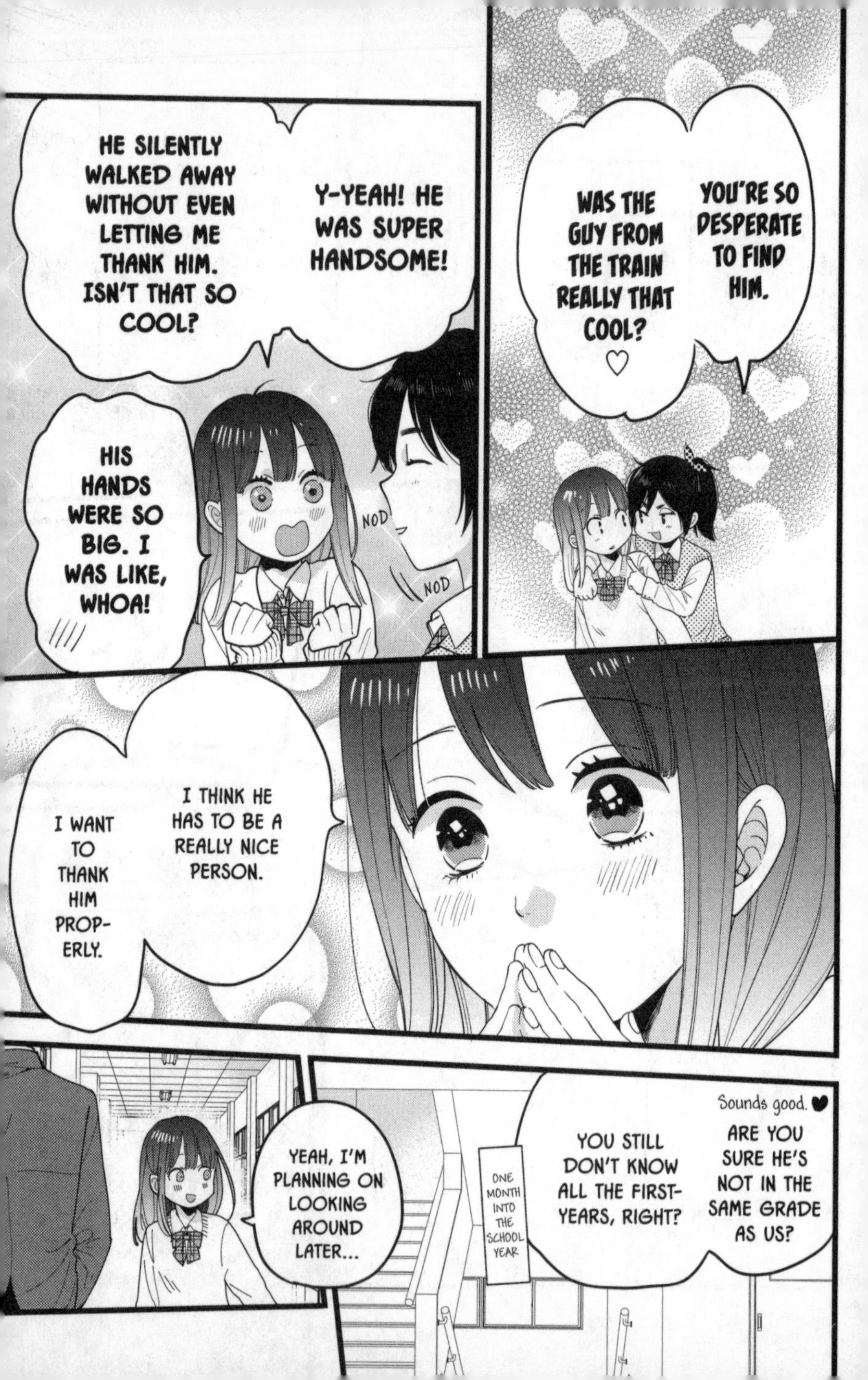
YOU'RE SO DESPERATE TO FIND HIM.
WAS THE GUY FROM THE TRAIN REALLY THAT COOL? ♡
Y-YEAH! HE WAS SUPER HANDSOME!
HE SILENTLY WALKED AWAY WITHOUT EVEN LETTING ME THANK HIM. ISN'T THAT SO COOL?
NOD
NOD
HIS HANDS WERE SO BIG. I WAS LIKE, WHOA!
I THINK HE HAS TO BE A REALLY NICE PERSON.
I WANT TO THANK HIM PROP-ERLY.
Sounds good. ♥
ARE YOU SURE HE'S NOT IN THE SAME GRADE AS US?
YOU STILL DON'T KNOW ALL THE FIRST-YEARS, RIGHT?
ONE MONTH INTO THE SCHOOL YEAR
YEAH, I'M PLANNING ON LOOKING AROUND LATER...

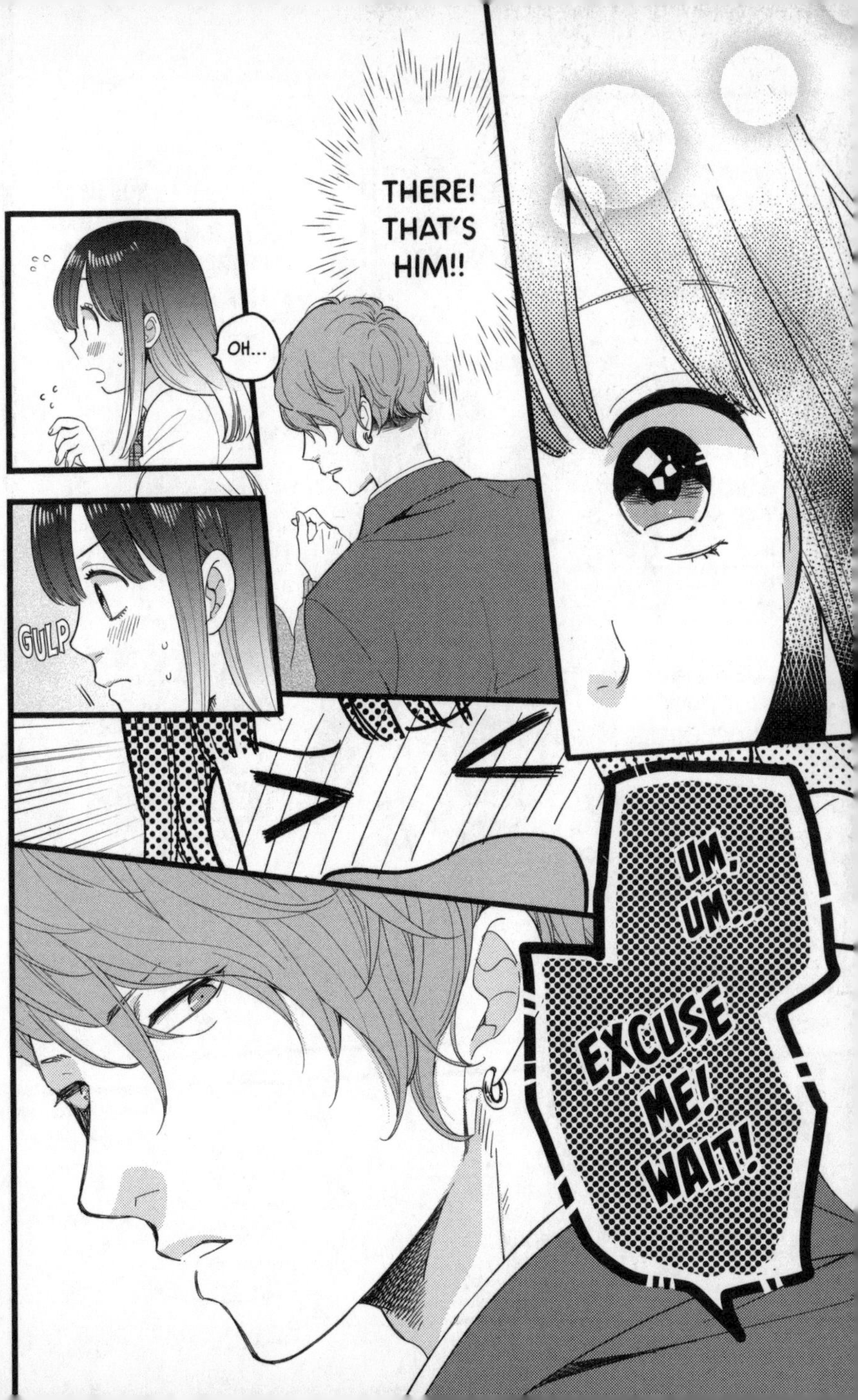
THERE! THAT'S HIM!!
OH...
GULP
UM, UM... EXCUSE ME! WAIT!

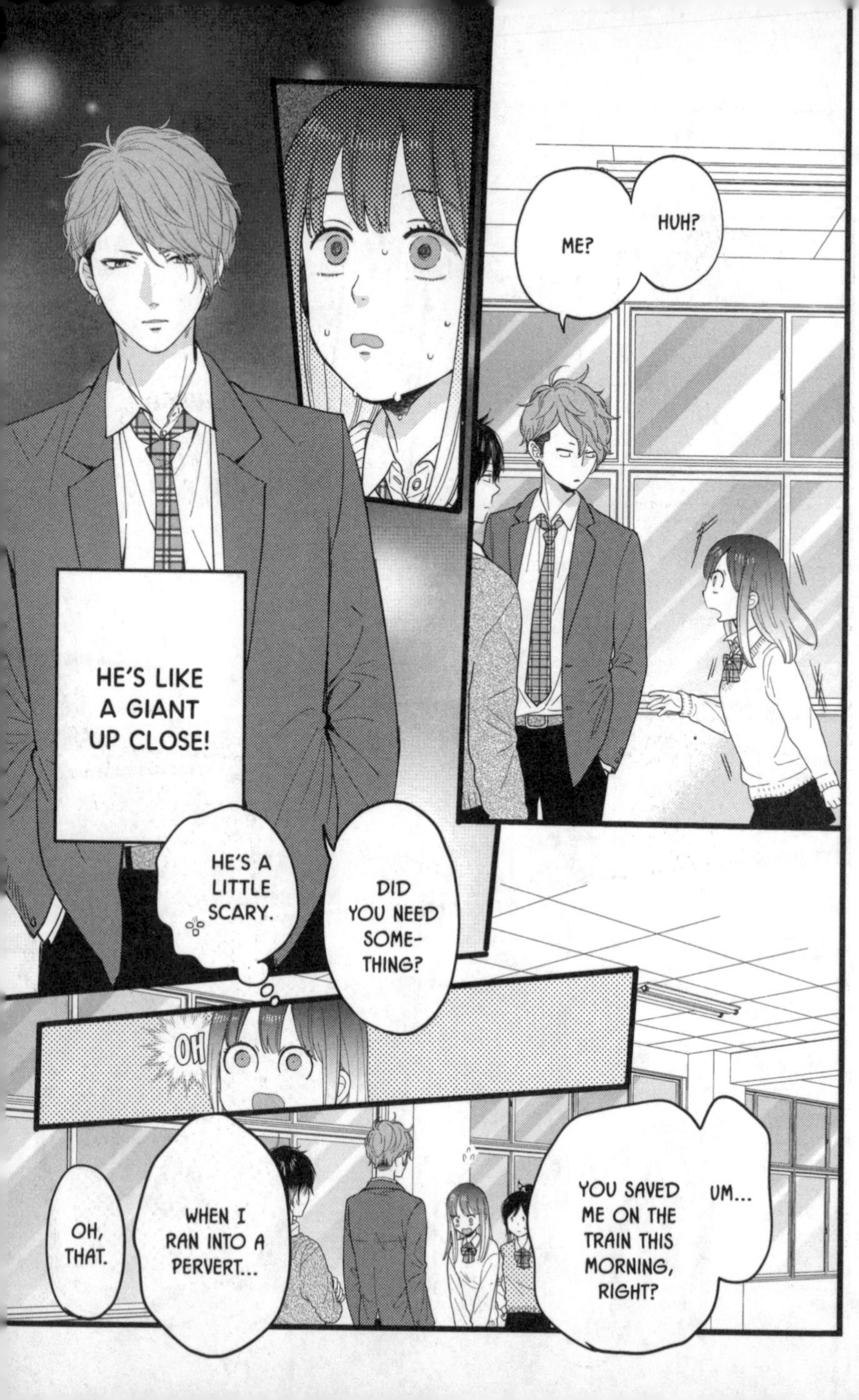
HUH?
ME?
HE'S LIKE A GIANT UP CLOSE!
DID YOU NEED SOMETHING?
HE'S A LITTLE SCARY.
OH
UM...
YOU SAVED ME ON THE TRAIN THIS MORNING, RIGHT?
WHEN I RAN INTO A PERVERT...
OH, THAT.

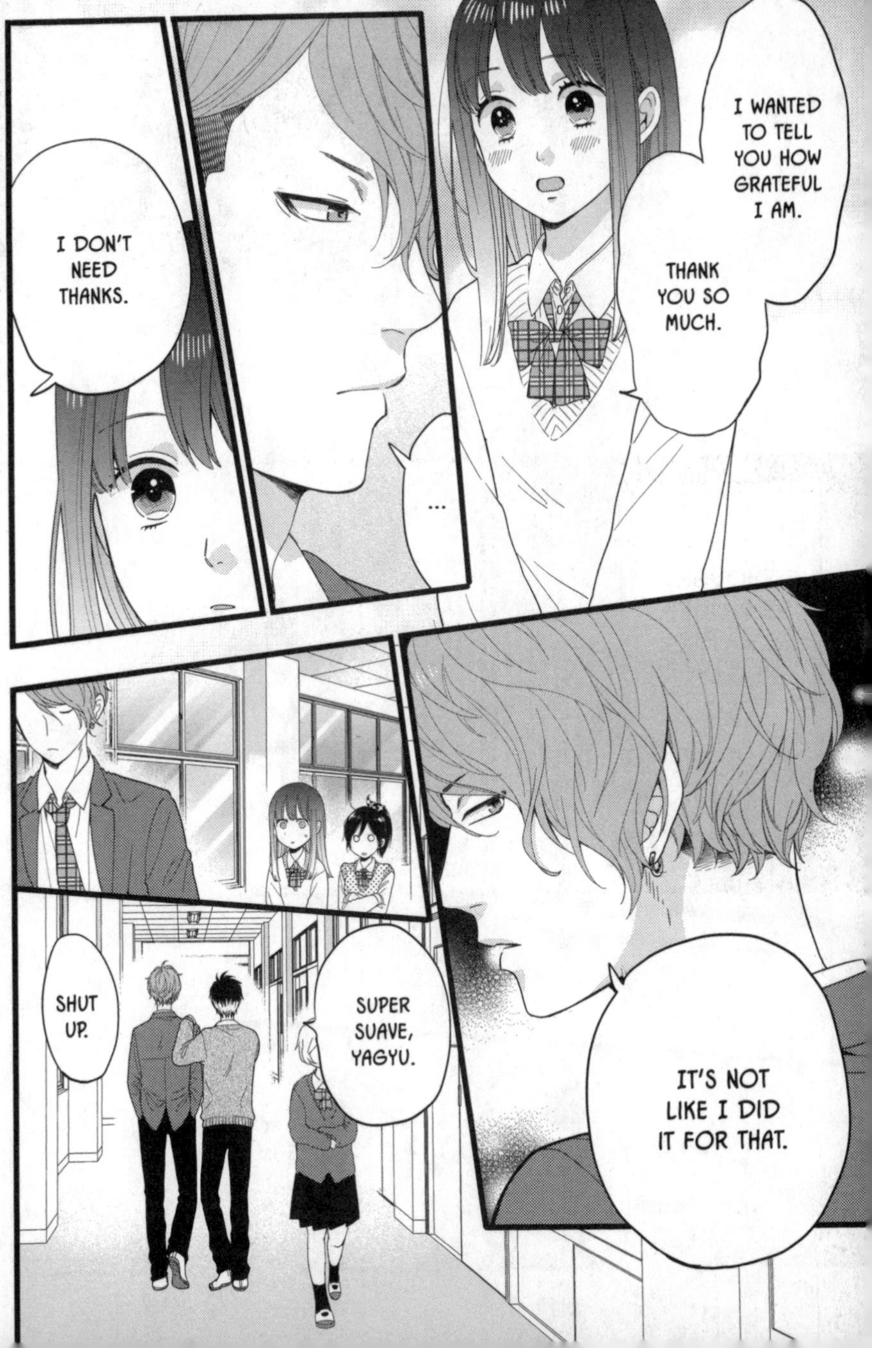
I WANTED TO TELL YOU HOW GRATEFUL I AM.
THANK YOU SO MUCH.
...
I DON'T NEED THANKS.
IT'S NOT LIKE I DID IT FOR THAT.
SUPER SUAVE, YAGYU.
SHUT UP.

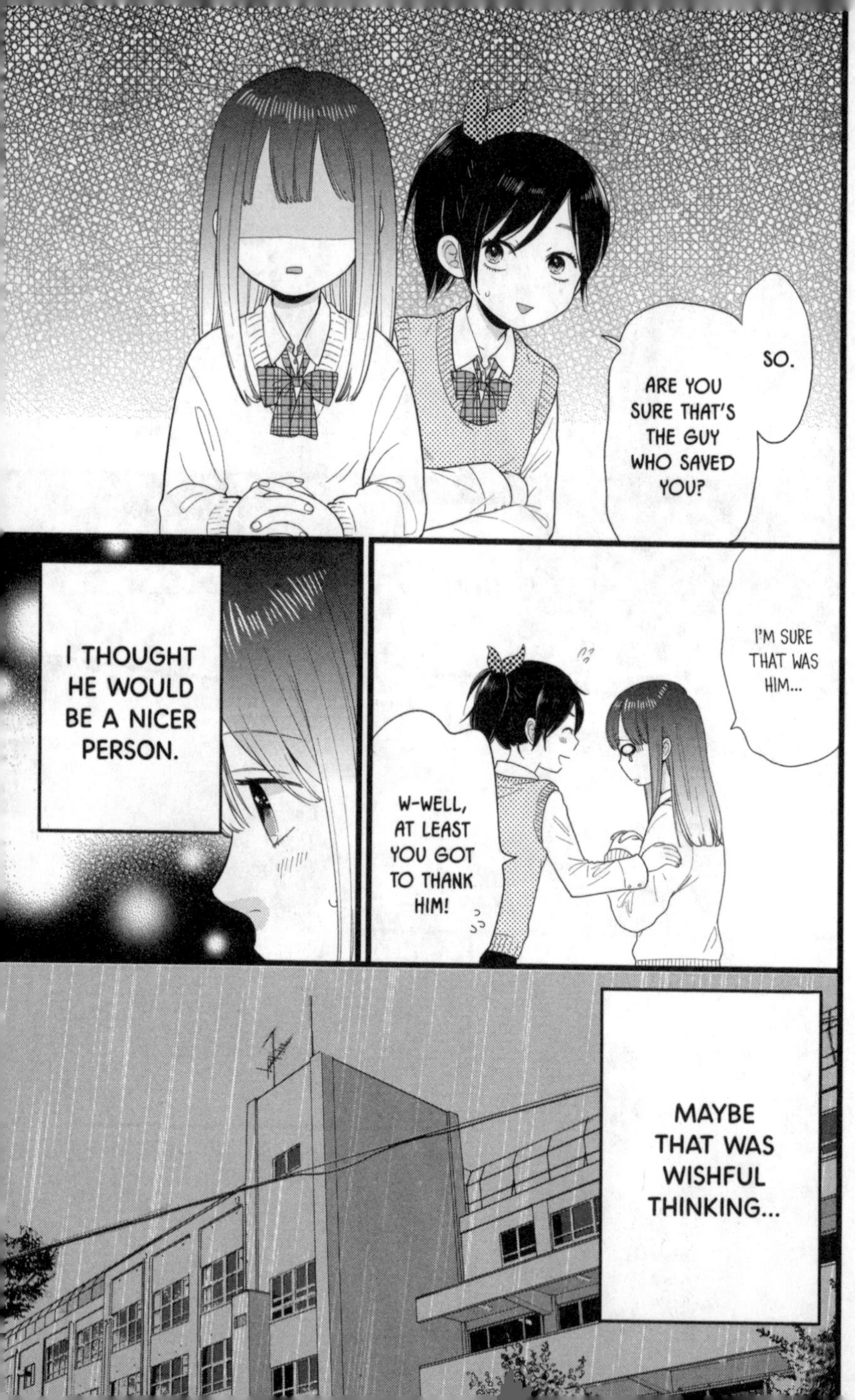
SO. ARE YOU SURE THAT'S THE GUY WHO SAVED YOU?
I'M SURE THAT WAS HIM...
W-WELL, AT LEAST YOU GOT TO THANK HIM!
I THOUGHT HE WOULD BE A NICER PERSON.
MAYBE THAT WAS WISHFUL THINKING...

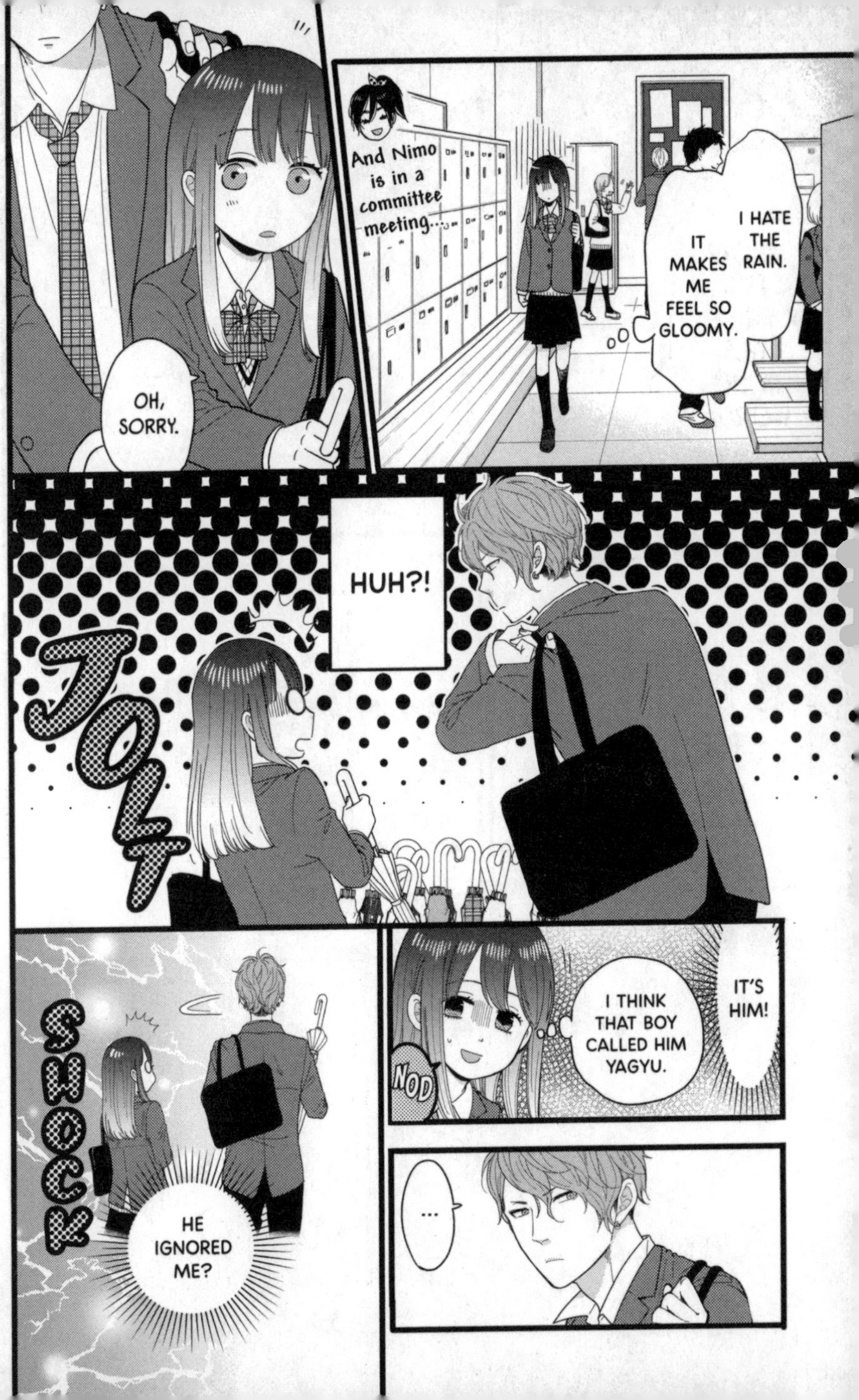
I HATE THE RAIN. IT MAKES ME FEEL SO GLOOMY.
And Nimo is in a committee meeting...
OH, SORRY.
HUH?!
JOLT
IT'S HIM!
I THINK THAT BOY CALLED HIM YAGYU.
NOD
...
SHOCK
HE IGNORED ME?

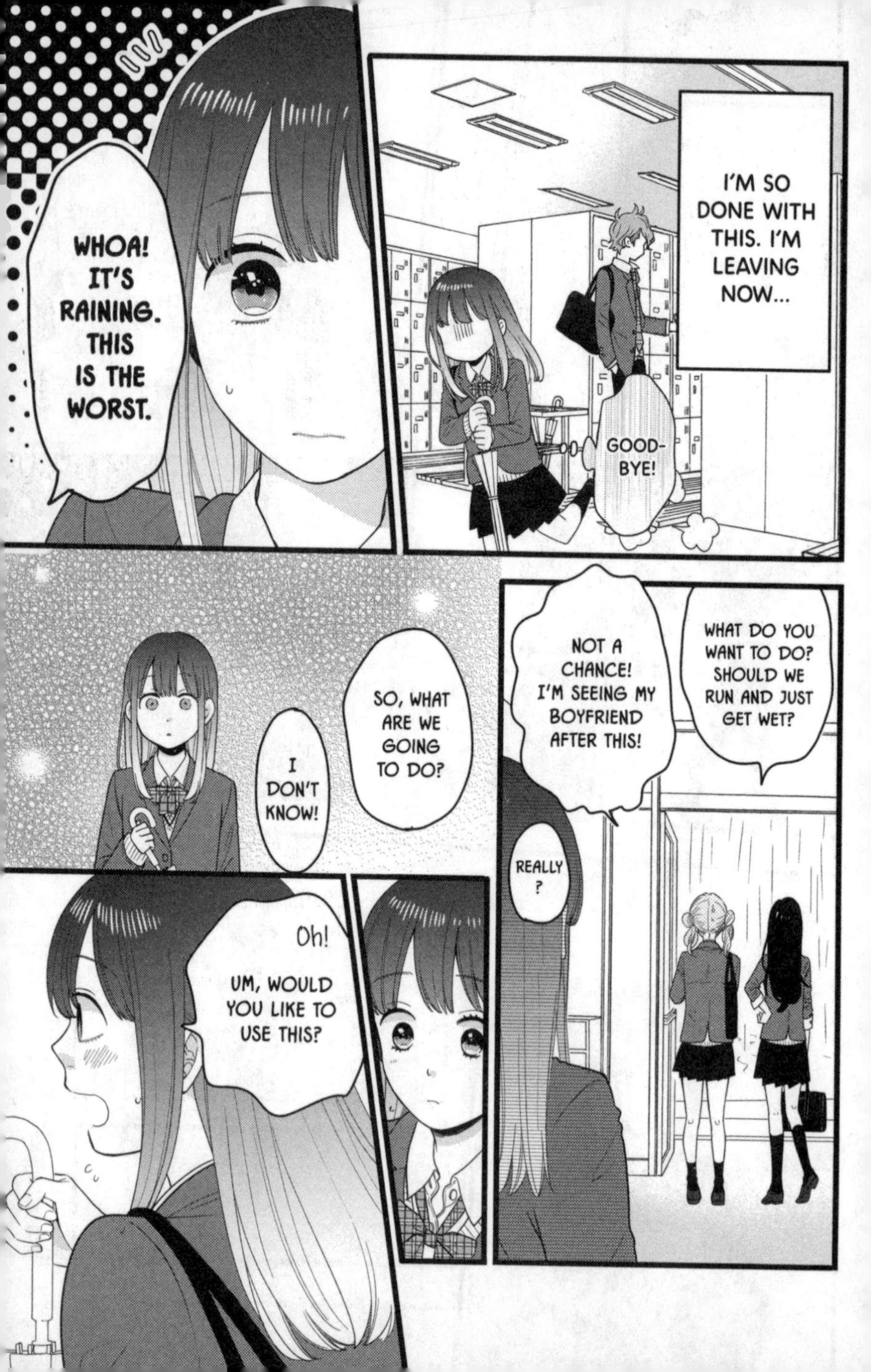
I'M SO DONE WITH THIS. I'M LEAVING NOW...
GOOD-BYE!
WHOA! IT'S RAINING. THIS IS THE WORST.
WHAT DO YOU WANT TO DO? SHOULD WE RUN AND JUST GET WET?
NOT A CHANCE! I'M SEEING MY BOYFRIEND AFTER THIS!
REALLY?
SO, WHAT ARE WE GOING TO DO?
I DON'T KNOW!
Oh!
UM, WOULD YOU LIKE TO USE THIS?

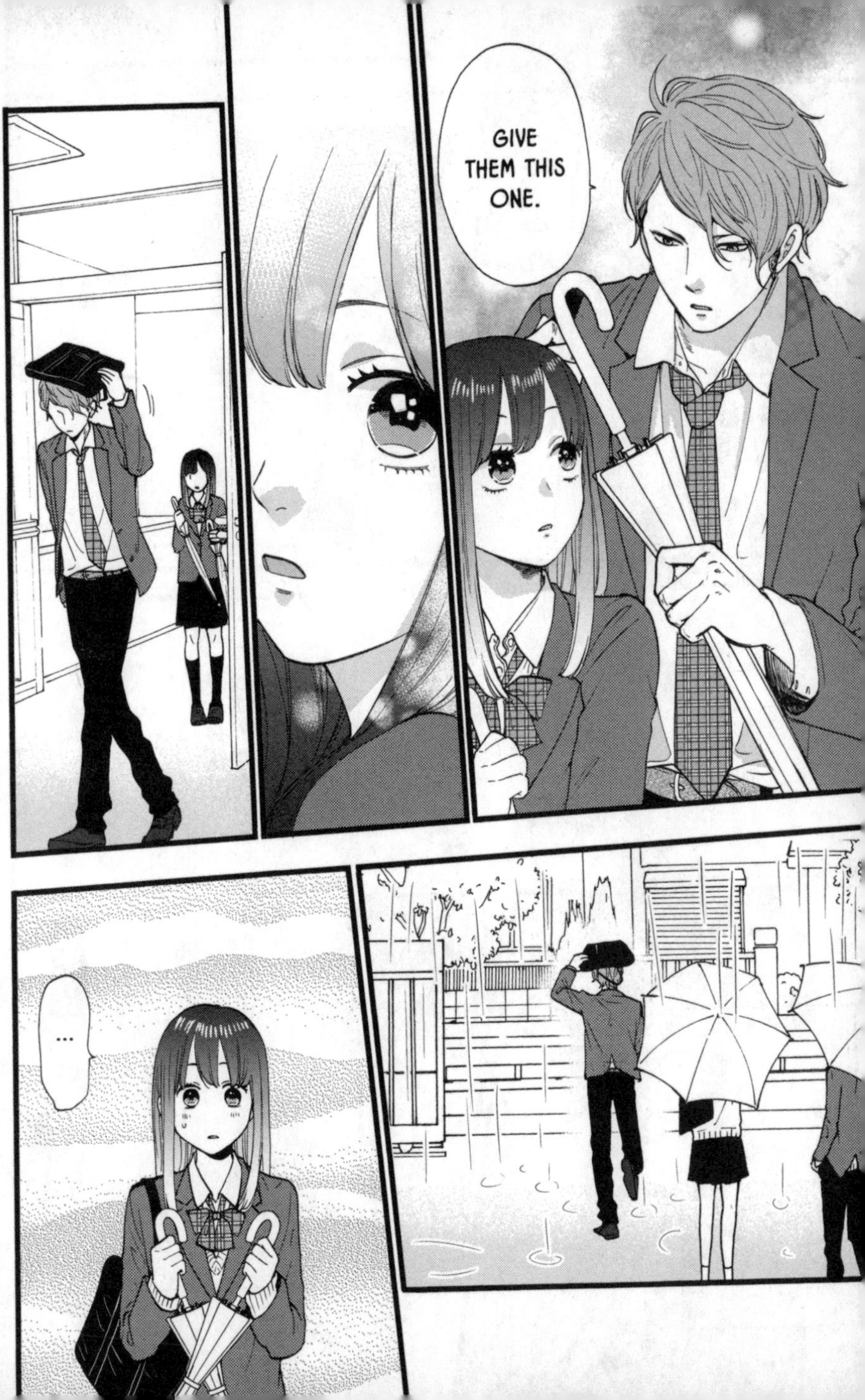
GIVE THEM THIS ONE.
...

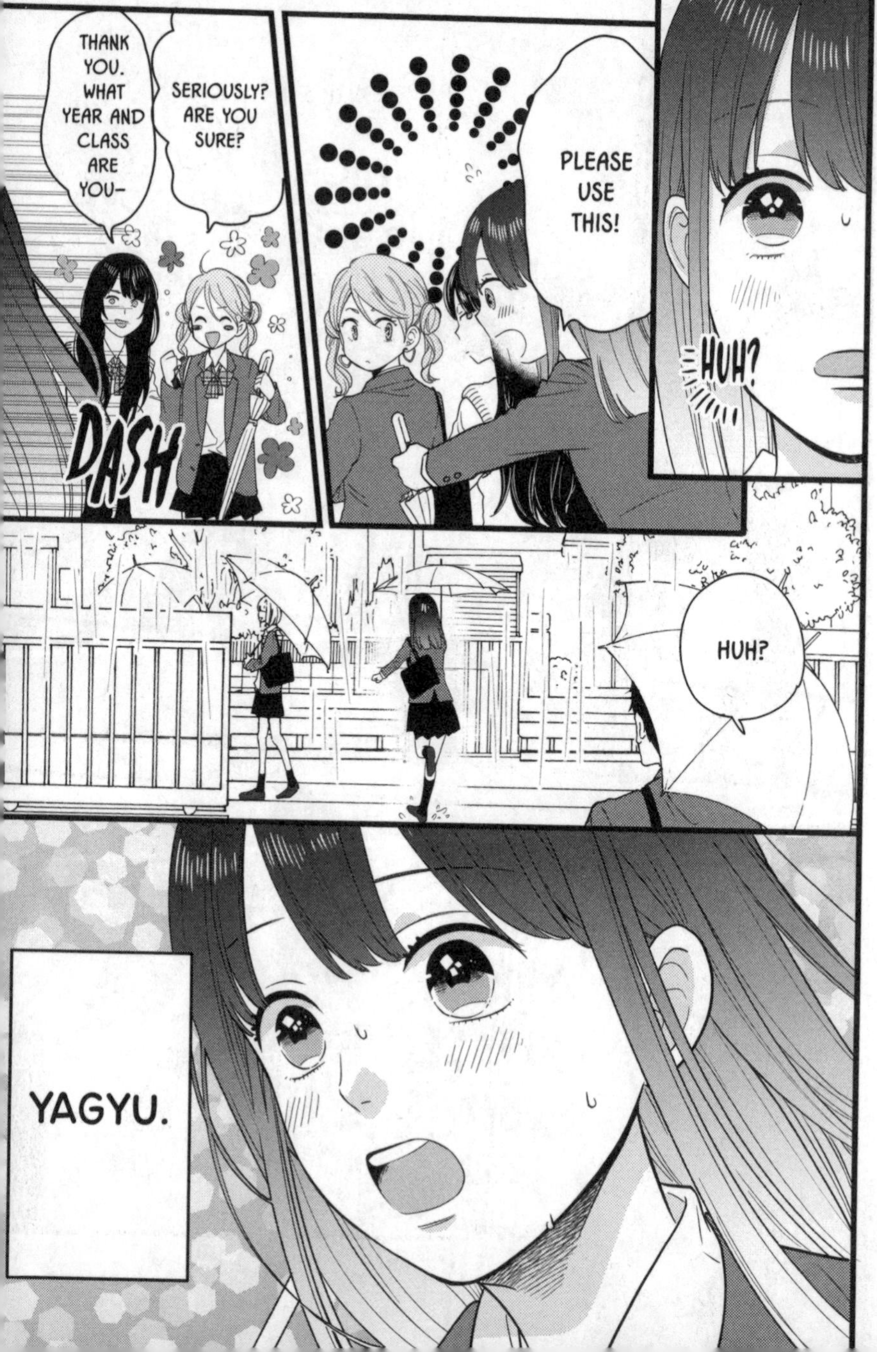
HUH?
PLEASE USE THIS!
SERIOUSLY? ARE YOU SURE?
THANK YOU. WHAT YEAR AND CLASS ARE YOU-
DASH
HUH?
YAGYU.

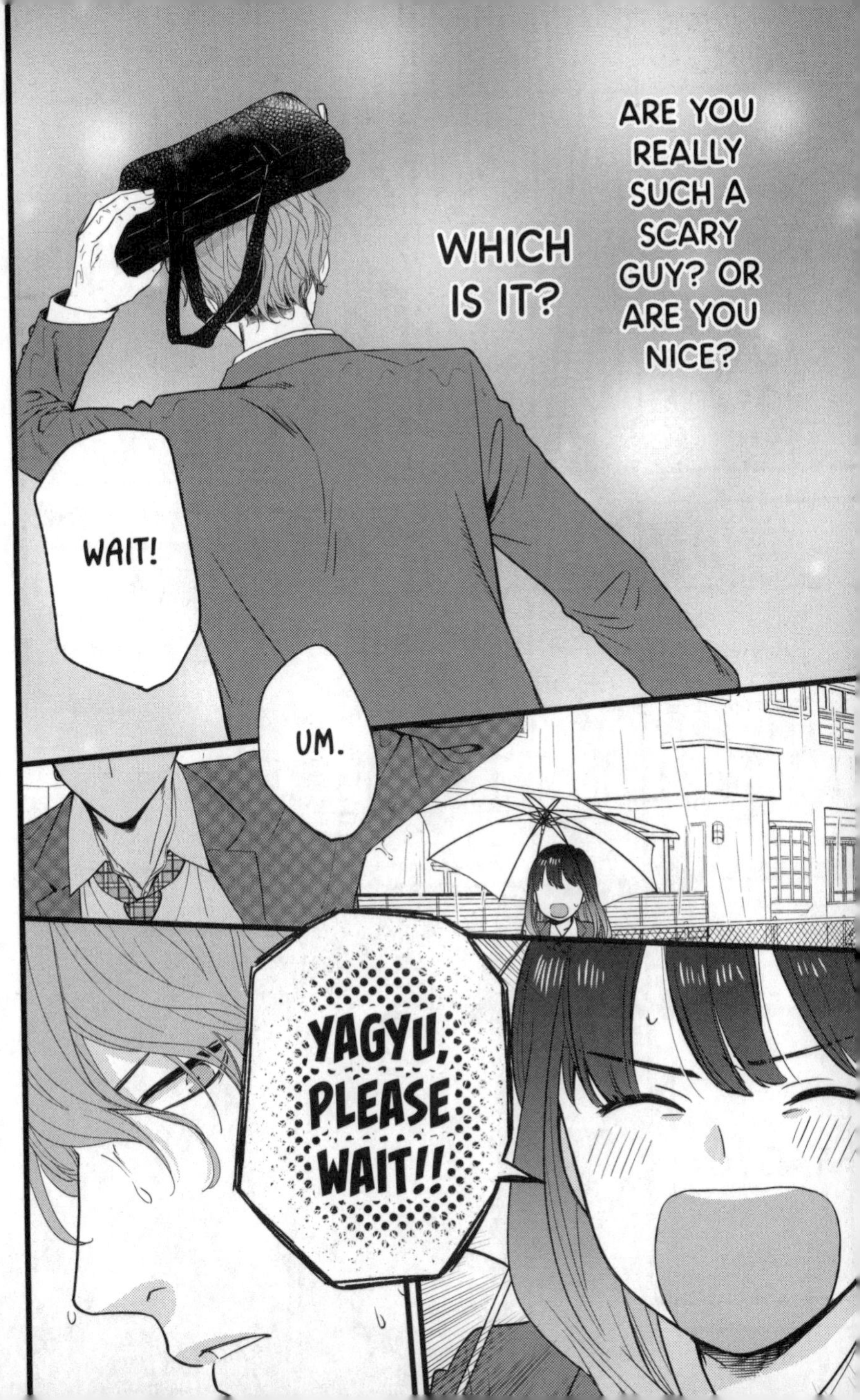
ARE YOU REALLY SUCH A SCARY GUY? OR ARE YOU NICE?
WHICH IS IT?
WAIT!
UM.
YAGYU, PLEASE WAIT!!

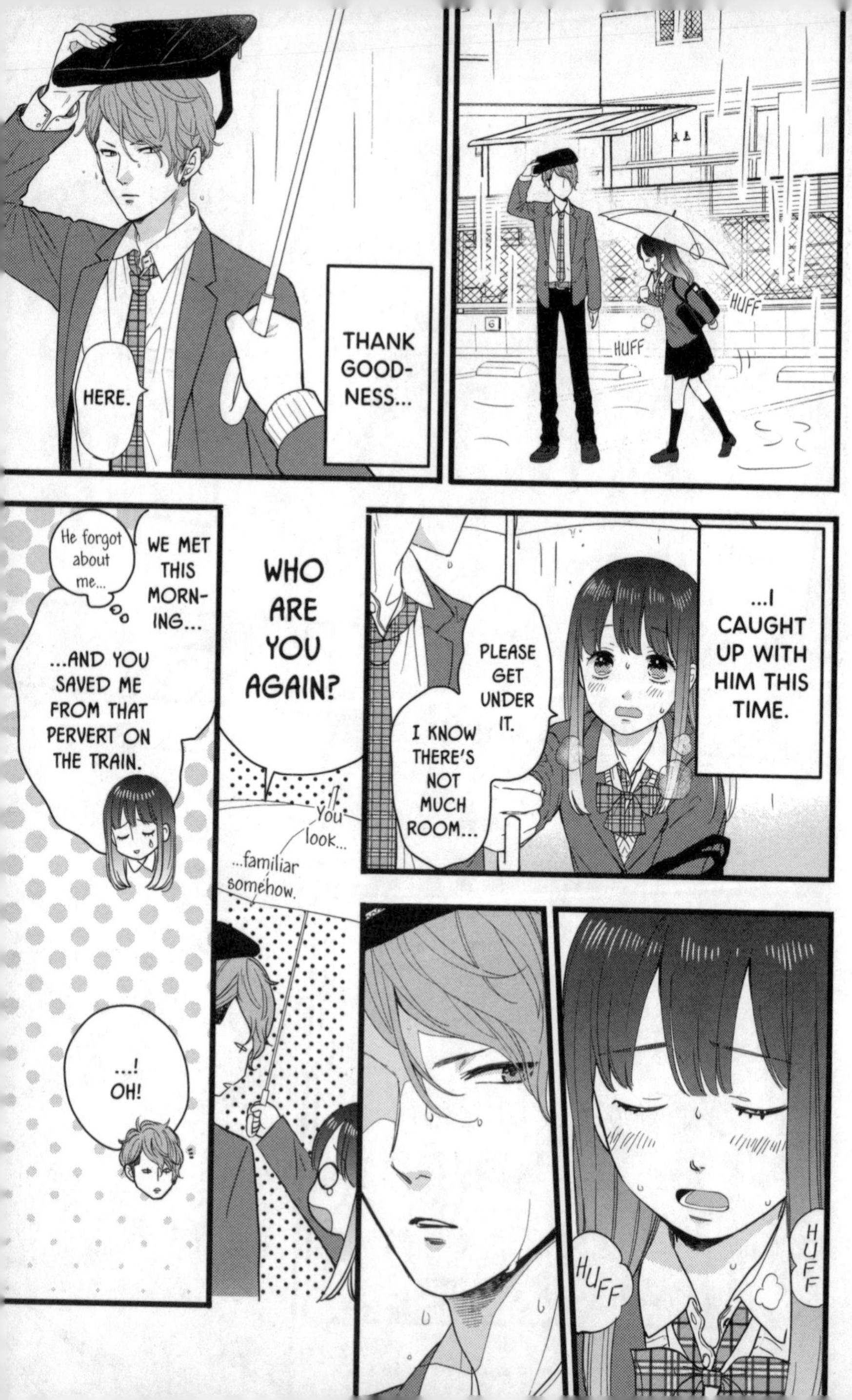
HUFF
HUFF
THANK GOOD-NESS...
HERE.
...I CAUGHT UP WITH HIM THIS TIME.
PLEASE GET UNDER IT.
I KNOW THERE'S NOT MUCH ROOM...
HUFF
HUFF
WHO ARE YOU AGAIN?
You look...
...familiar somehow.
WE MET THIS MORN-ING...
He forgot about me...
...AND YOU SAVED ME FROM THAT PERVERT ON THE TRAIN.
...! OH!

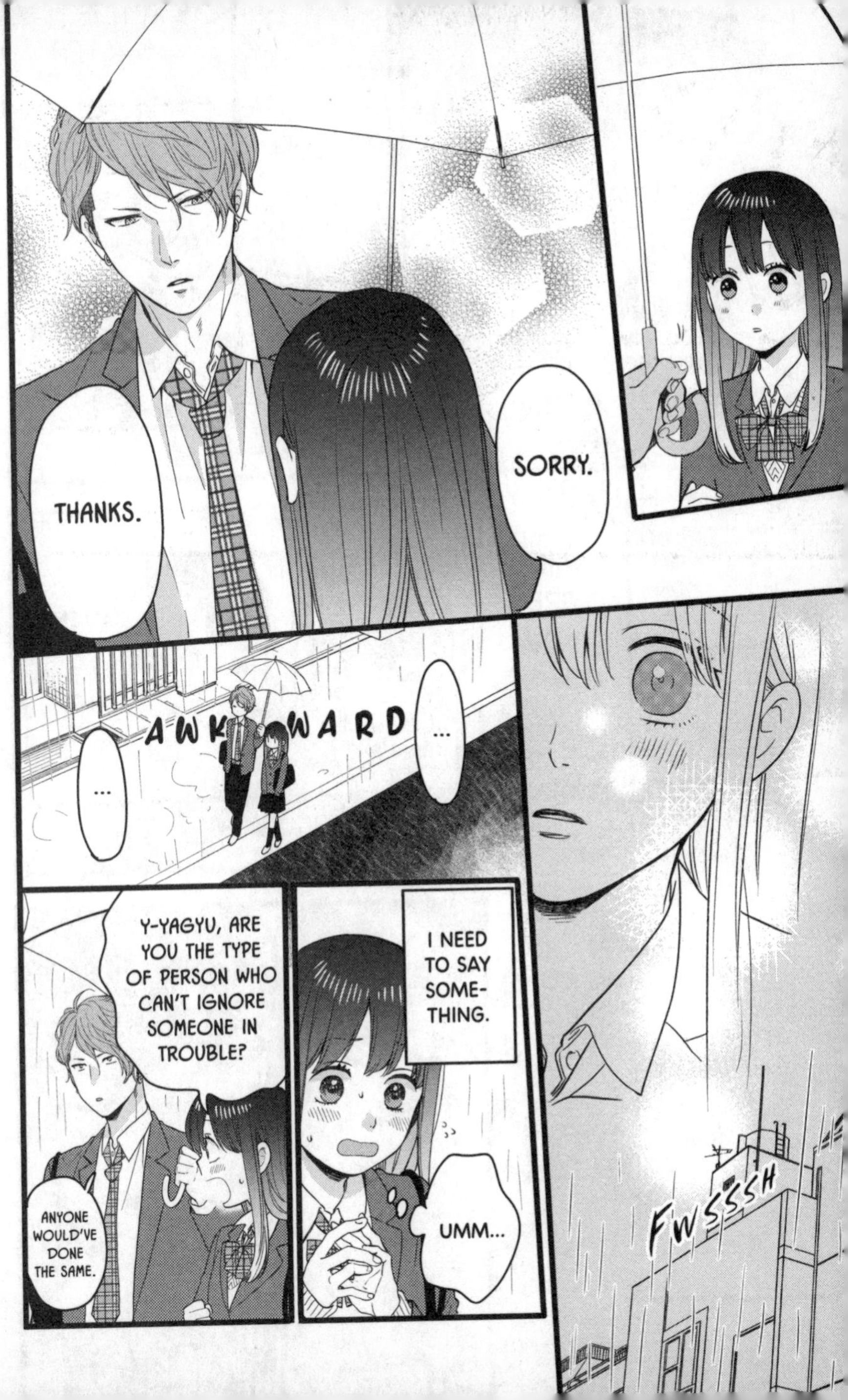
SORRY.
THANKS.
FWSSSH
...
AWKWARD
...
I NEED TO SAY SOME-THING.
UMM...
Y-YAGYU, ARE YOU THE TYPE OF PERSON WHO CAN'T IGNORE SOMEONE IN TROUBLE?
ANYONE WOULD'VE DONE THE SAME.

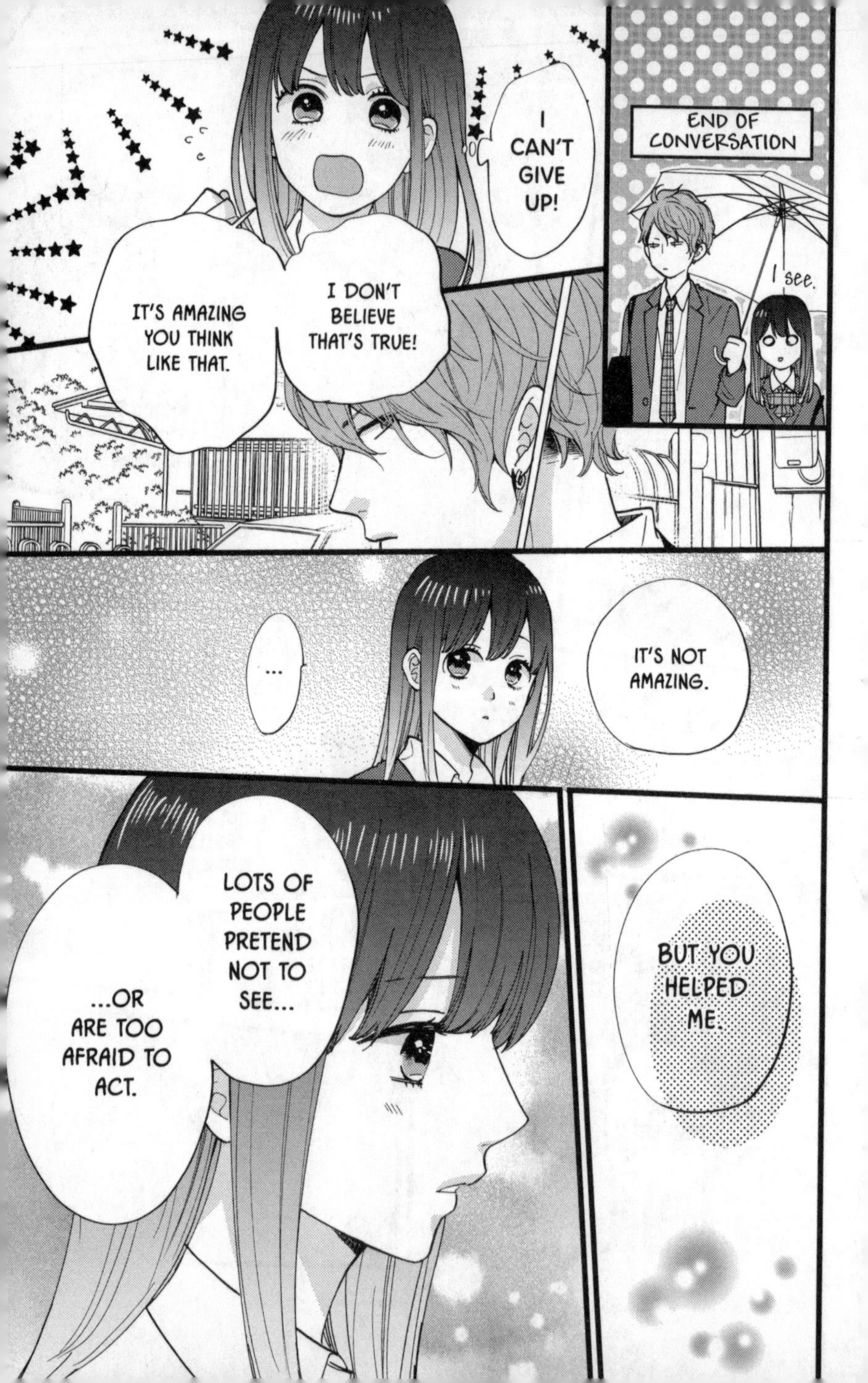
END OF CONVERSATION
I see.
I CAN'T GIVE UP!
I DON'T BELIEVE THAT'S TRUE!
IT'S AMAZING YOU THINK LIKE THAT.
IT'S NOT AMAZING.
...
BUT YOU HELPED ME.
LOTS OF PEOPLE PRETEND NOT TO SEE...
...OR ARE TOO AFRAID TO ACT.

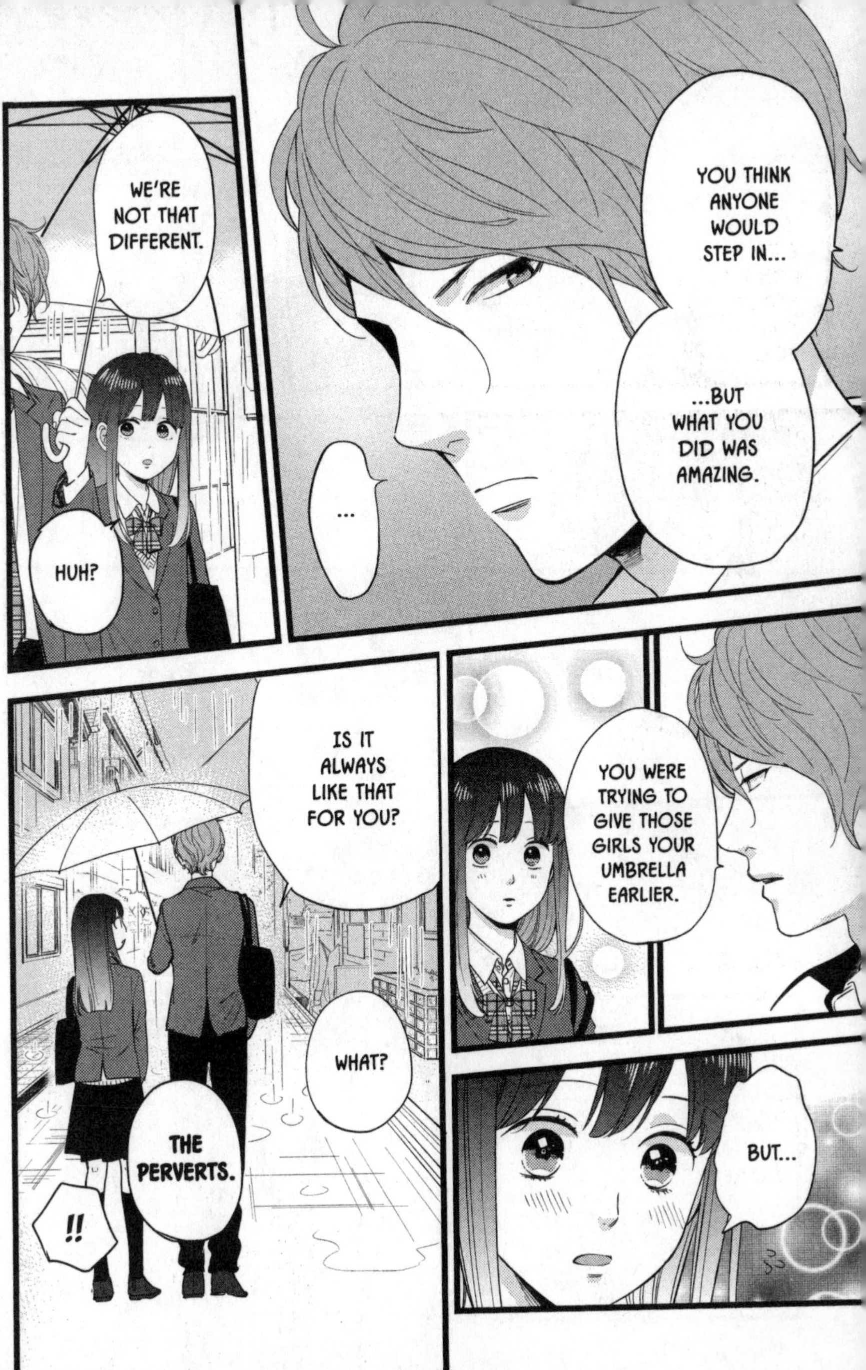
YOU THINK ANYONE WOULD STEP IN...
...BUT WHAT YOU DID WAS AMAZING.
...
WE'RE NOT THAT DIFFERENT.
HUH?
YOU WERE TRYING TO GIVE THOSE GIRLS YOUR UMBRELLA EARLIER.
BUT...
IS IT ALWAYS LIKE THAT FOR YOU?
WHAT?
THE PERVERTS.
!!

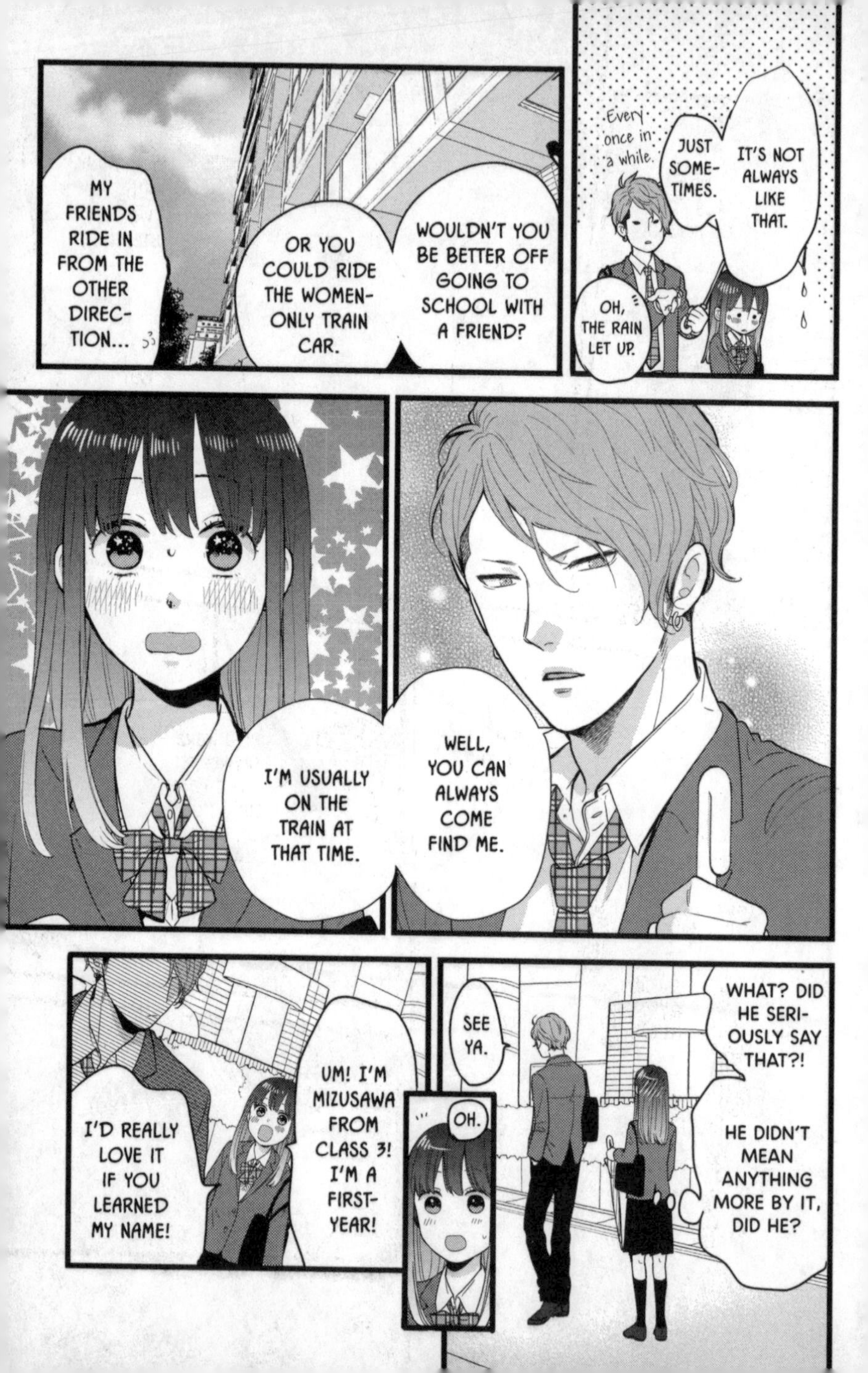
IT'S NOT ALWAYS LIKE THAT.
JUST SOMETIMES.
Every once in a while.
OH, THE RAIN LET UP.
WOULDN'T YOU BE BETTER OFF GOING TO SCHOOL WITH A FRIEND?
OR YOU COULD RIDE THE WOMEN-ONLY TRAIN CAR.
MY FRIENDS RIDE IN FROM THE OTHER DIREC-TION...
WELL, YOU CAN ALWAYS COME FIND ME.
I'M USUALLY ON THE TRAIN AT THAT TIME.
WHAT? DID HE SERI-OUSLY SAY THAT?!
HE DIDN'T MEAN ANYTHING MORE BY IT, DID HE?
SEE YA.
OH.
UM! I'M MIZUSAWA FROM CLASS 3! I'M A FIRST-YEAR!
I'D REALLY LOVE IT IF YOU LEARNED MY NAME!

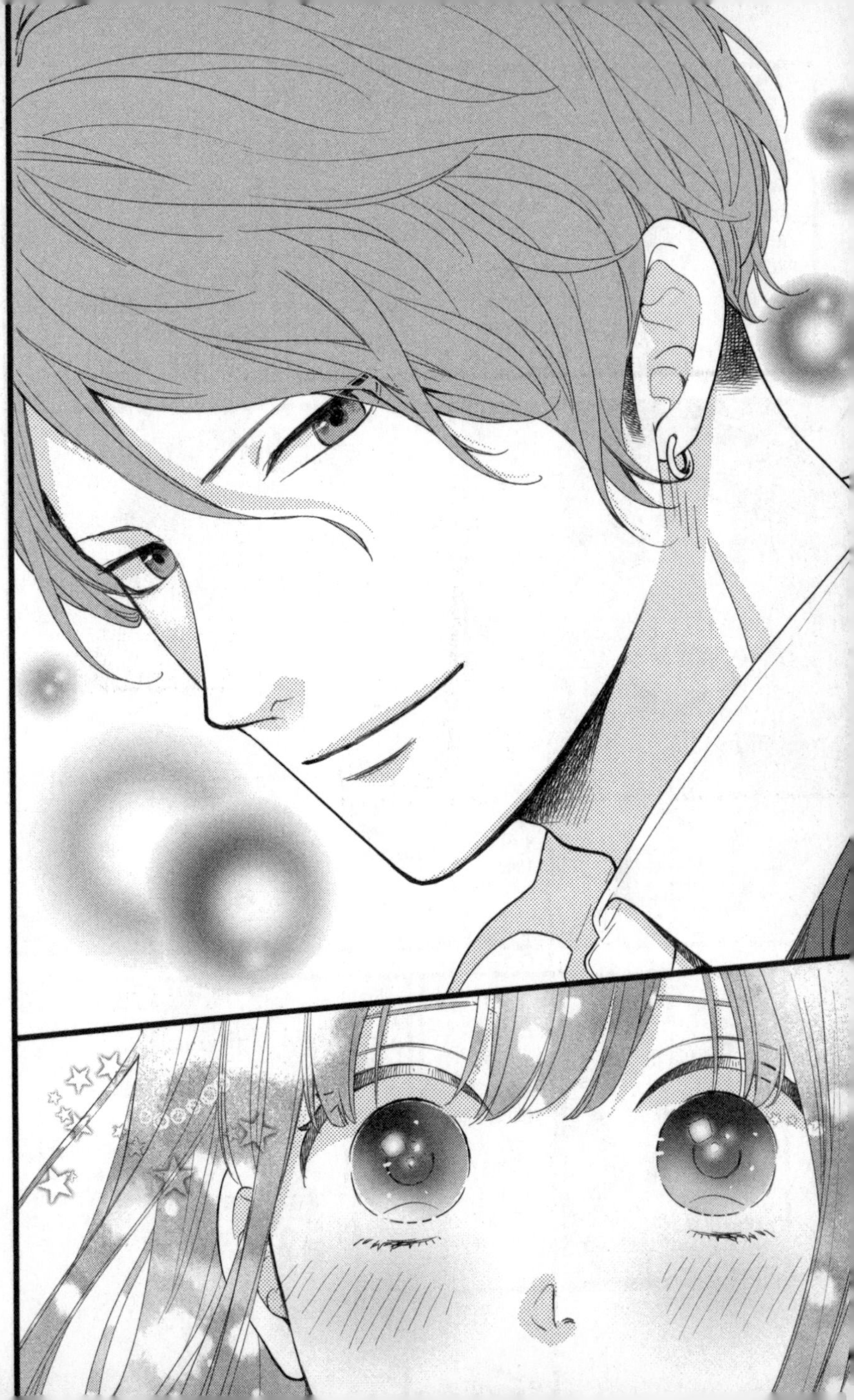

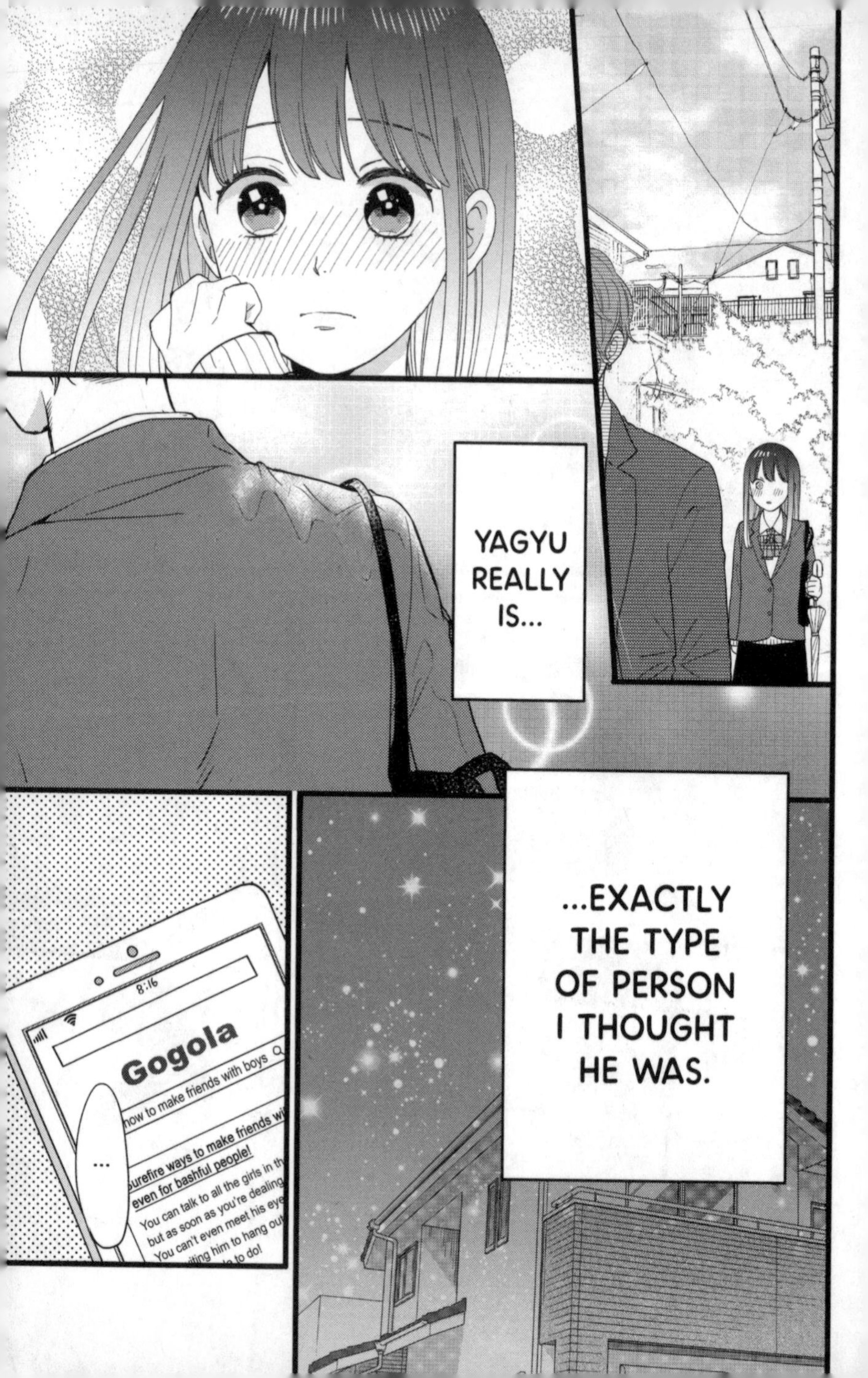
YAGYU REALLY IS...
...EXACTLY THE TYPE OF PERSON I THOUGHT HE WAS.
...
8:16
Gogola
how to make friends with boys
even for bashful people!
You can talk to all the girls in th
but as soon as you're dealing
You can't even meet his eye

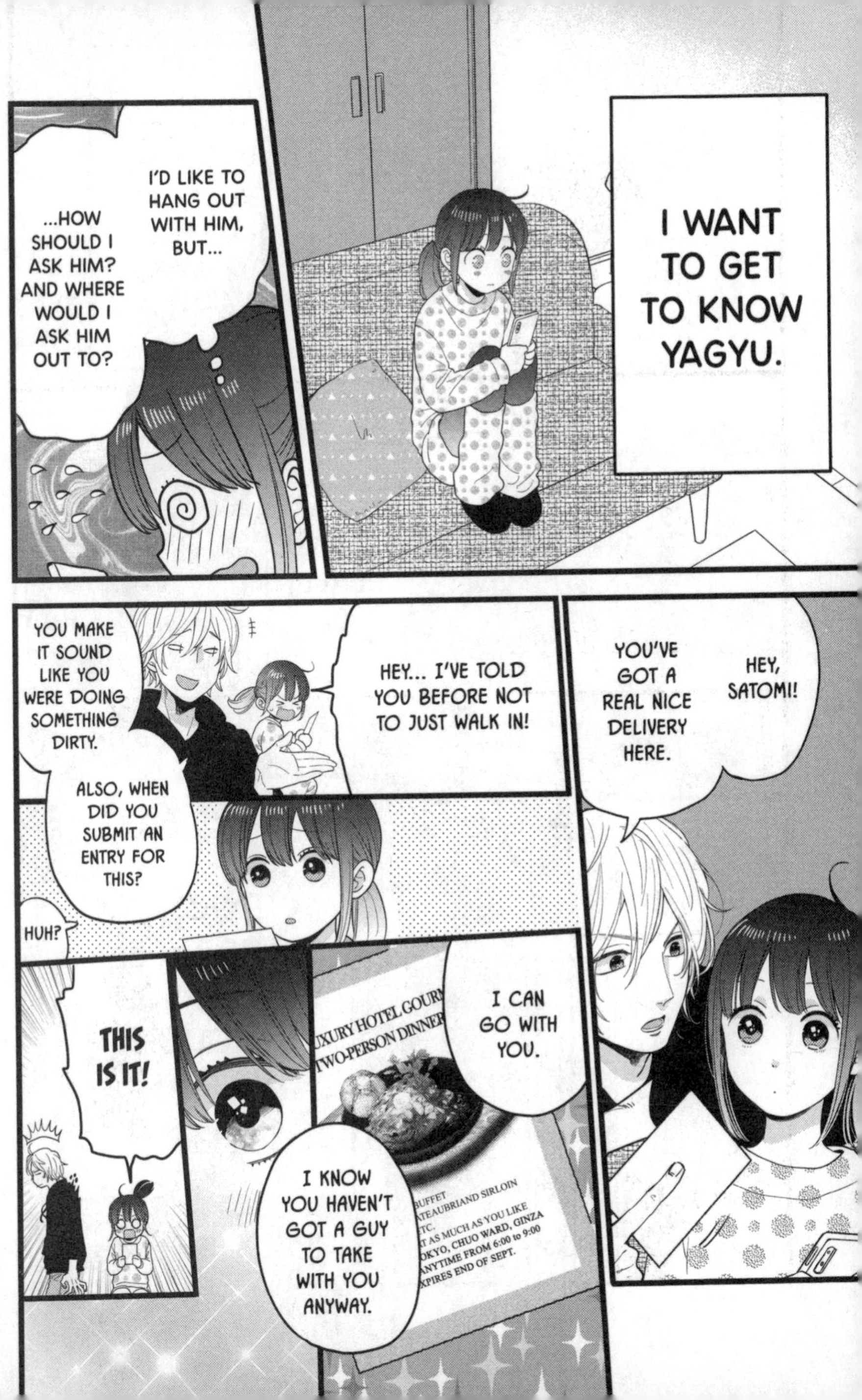
I WANT TO GET TO KNOW YAGYU.
I'D LIKE TO HANG OUT WITH HIM, BUT...
...HOW SHOULD I ASK HIM? AND WHERE WOULD I ASK HIM OUT TO?
HEY, SATOMI!
YOU'VE GOT A REAL NICE DELIVERY HERE.
HEY... I'VE TOLD YOU BEFORE NOT TO JUST WALK IN!
YOU MAKE IT SOUND LIKE YOU WERE DOING SOMETHING DIRTY.
ALSO, WHEN DID YOU SUBMIT AN ENTRY FOR THIS?
HUH?
I CAN GO WITH YOU.
BUFFET
ANYTIME FROM 6:00 to 9:00
I KNOW YOU HAVEN'T GOT A GUY TO TAKE WITH YOU ANYWAY.
THIS IS IT!

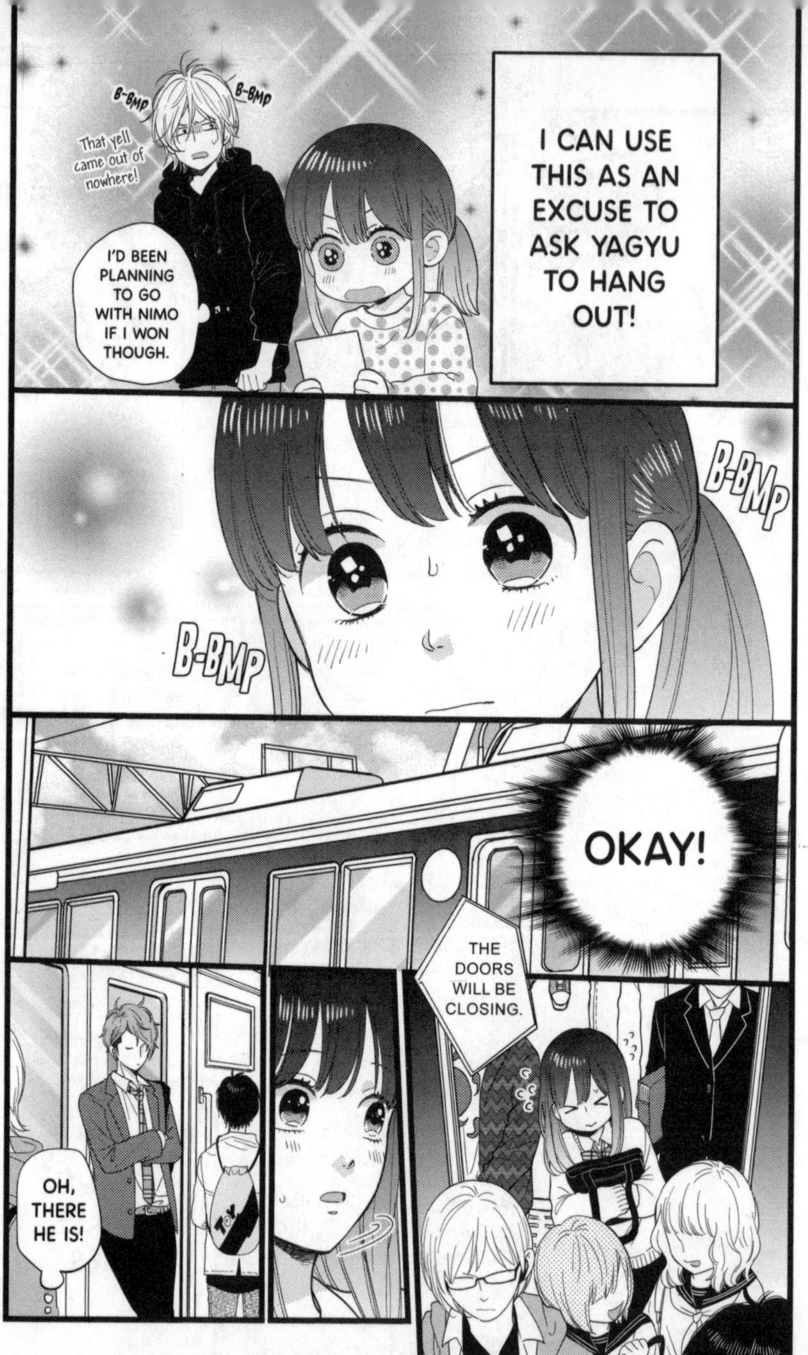
I CAN USE THIS AS AN EXCUSE TO ASK YAGYU TO HANG OUT!
B-BMP
B-BMP
That yell came out of nowhere!
I'D BEEN PLANNING TO GO WITH NIMO IF I WON THOUGH.
B-BMP
B-BMP
OKAY!
THE DOORS WILL BE CLOSING.
OH, THERE HE IS!

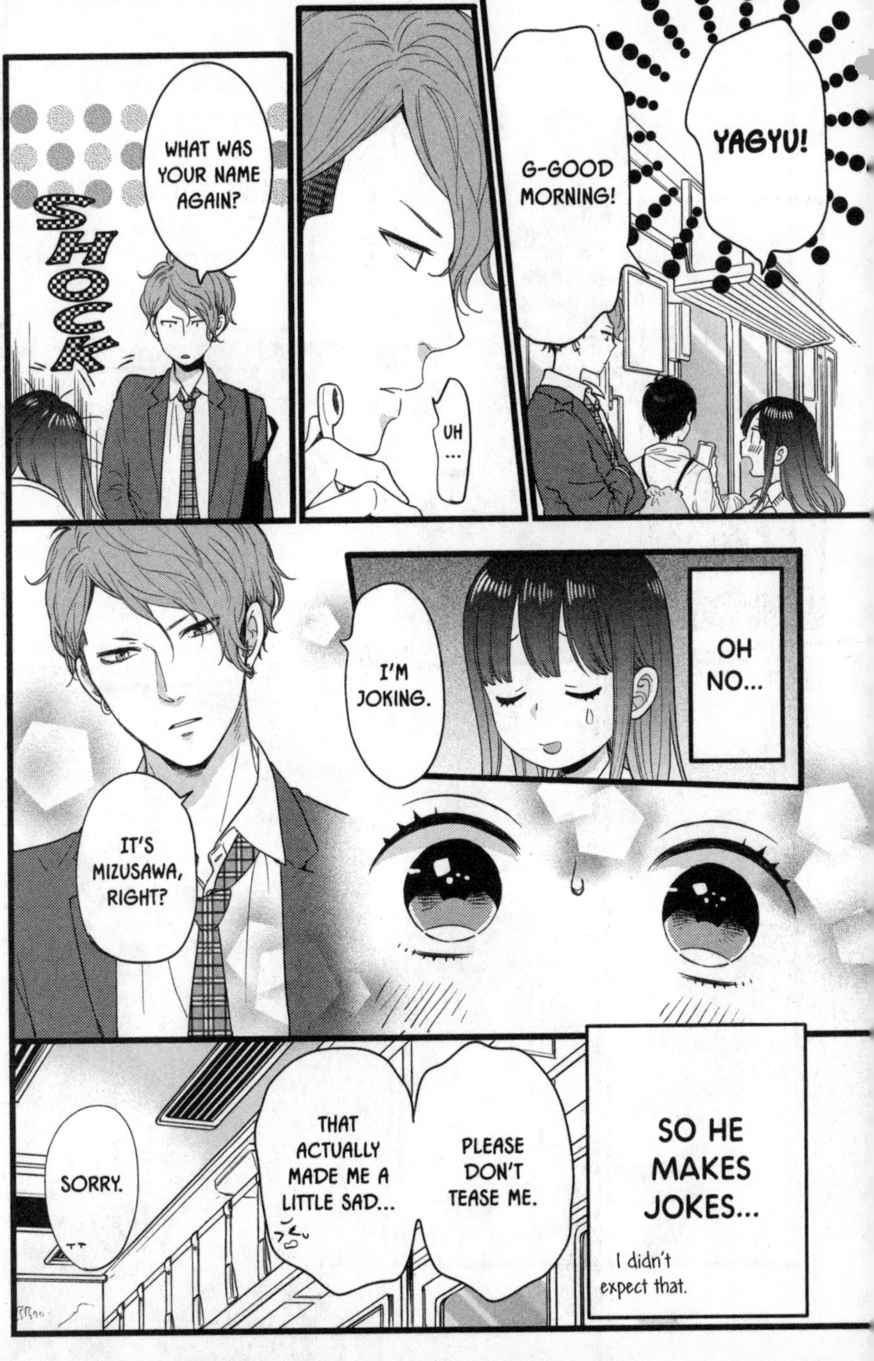
YAGYU!
G-GOOD MORNING!
UH ...
WHAT WAS YOUR NAME AGAIN?
SHOCK
OH NO...
I'M JOKING.
IT'S MIZUSAWA, RIGHT?
SO HE MAKES JOKES...
I didn't expect that.
PLEASE DON'T TEASE ME.
THAT ACTUALLY MADE ME A LITTLE SAD...
SORRY.

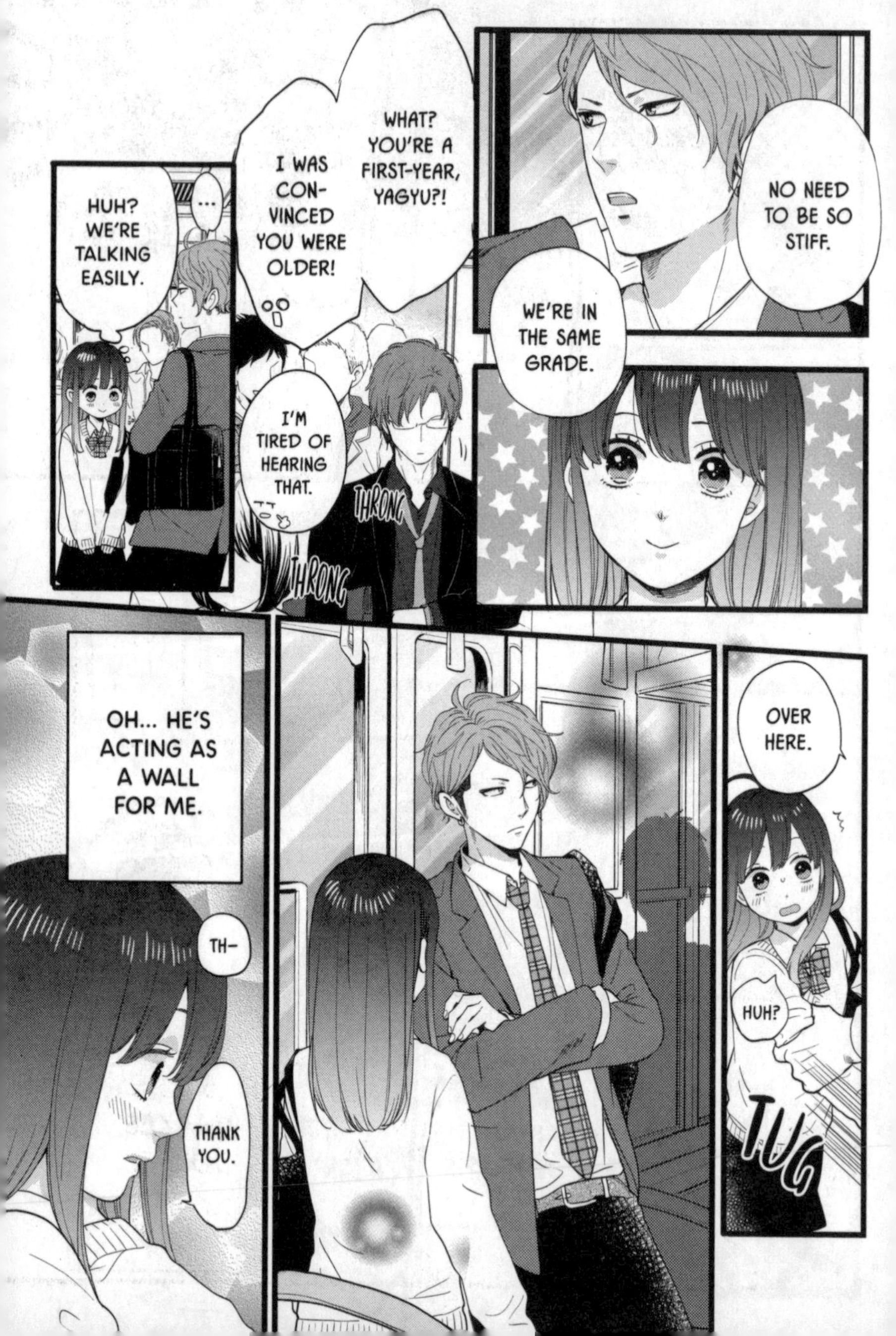
NO NEED TO BE SO STIFF.
WE'RE IN THE SAME GRADE.
WHAT? YOU'RE A FIRST-YEAR, YAGYU?!
I WAS CON-VINCED YOU WERE OLDER!
I'M TIRED OF HEARING THAT.
THRONG
THRONG
HUH? WE'RE TALKING EASILY.
...
OVER HERE.
HUH?
TUG
OH... HE'S ACTING AS A WALL FOR ME.
TH-
THANK YOU.

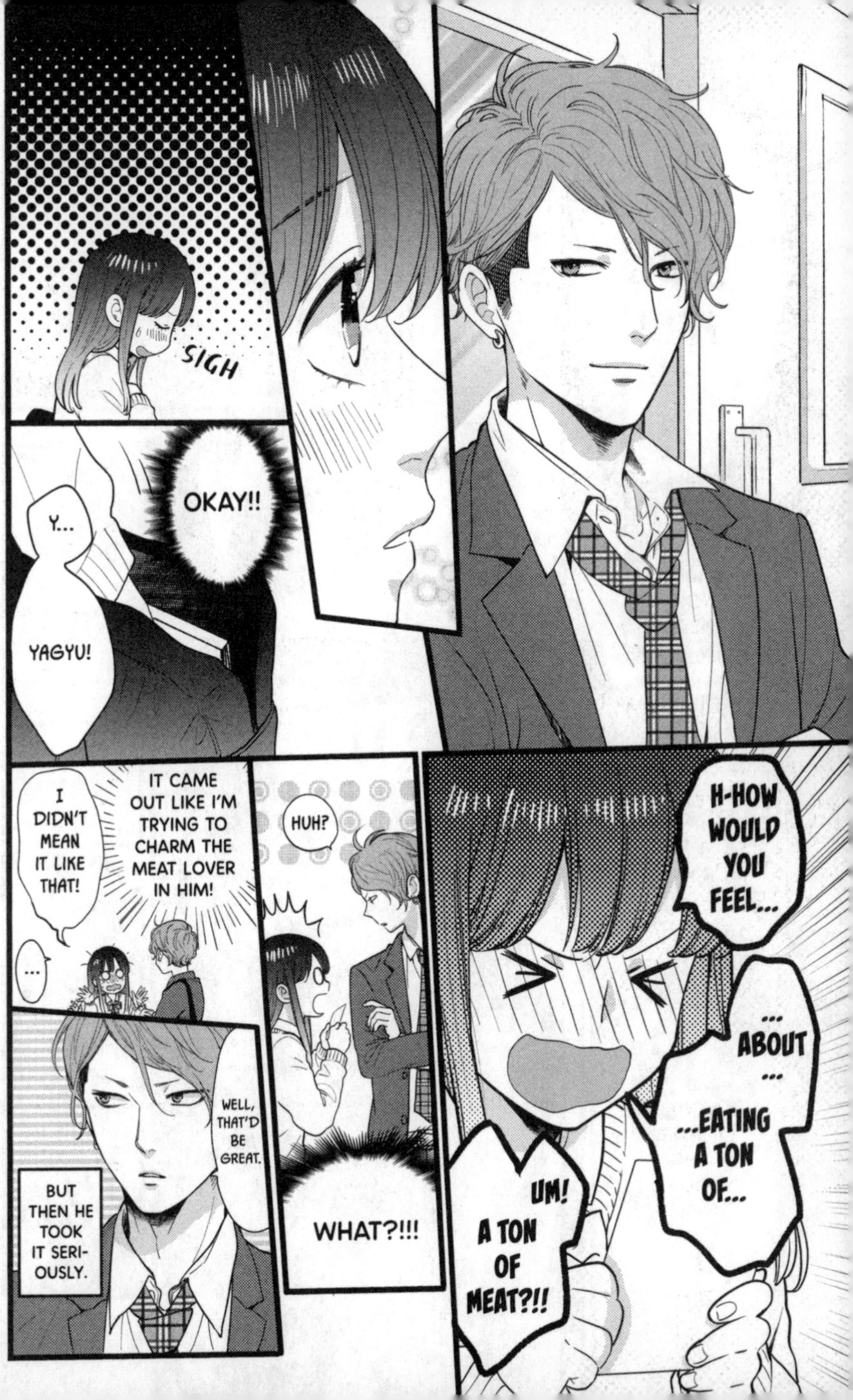
SIGH
OKAY!!
Y...
YAGYU!
H-HOW WOULD YOU FEEL...
...ABOUT...
...EATING A TON OF...
UM! A TON OF MEAT?!!
HUH?
WHAT?!!!
IT CAME OUT LIKE I'M TRYING TO CHARM THE MEAT LOVER IN HIM!
I DIDN'T MEAN IT LIKE THAT!
...
WELL, THAT'D BE GREAT.
BUT THEN HE TOOK IT SERI-OUSLY.

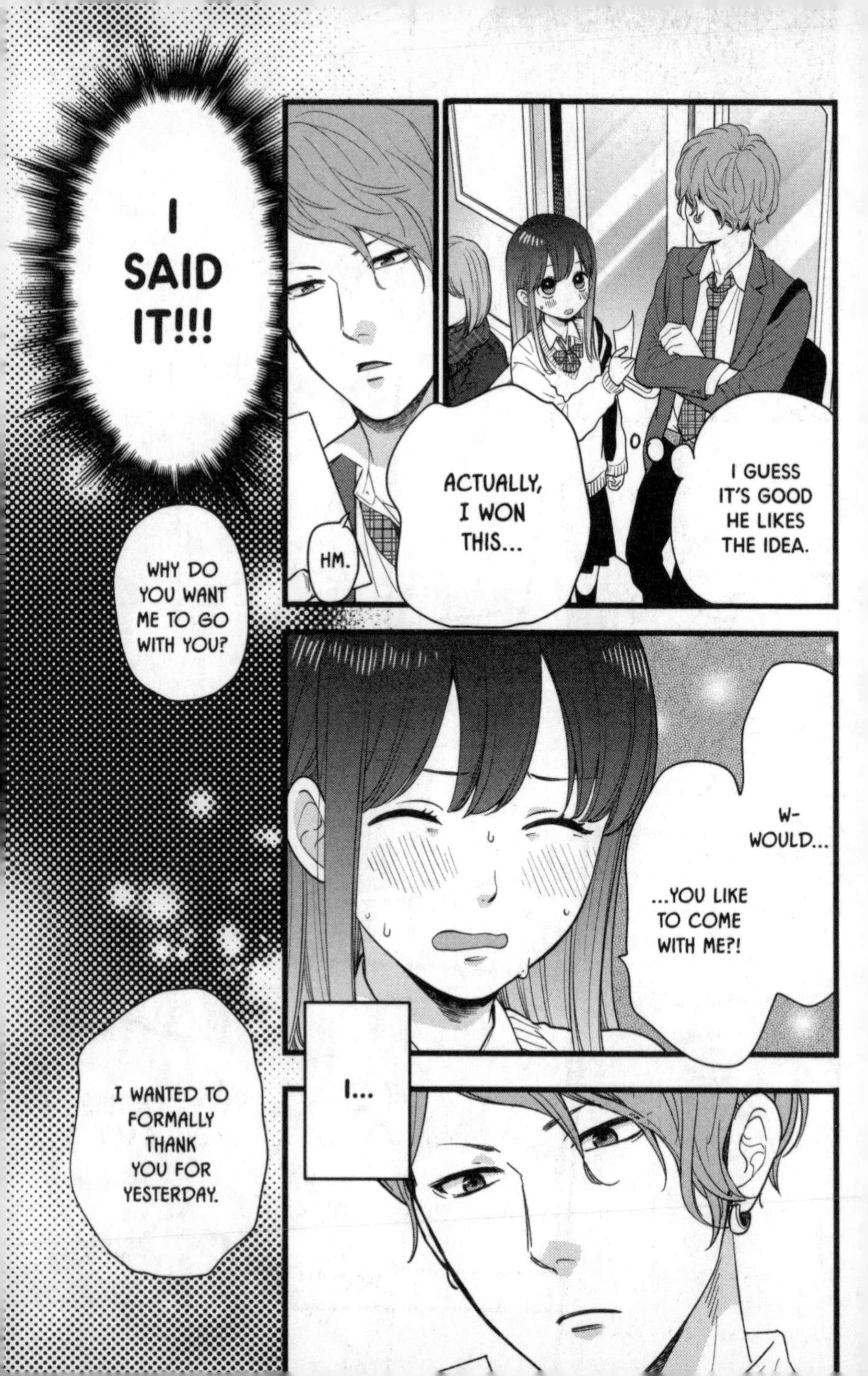
I GUESS IT'S GOOD HE LIKES THE IDEA.
ACTUALLY, I WON THIS...
HM.
W- WOULD...
...YOU LIKE TO COME WITH ME?!
I...
I SAID IT!!!
WHY DO YOU WANT ME TO GO WITH YOU?
I WANTED TO FORMALLY THANK YOU FOR YESTERDAY.

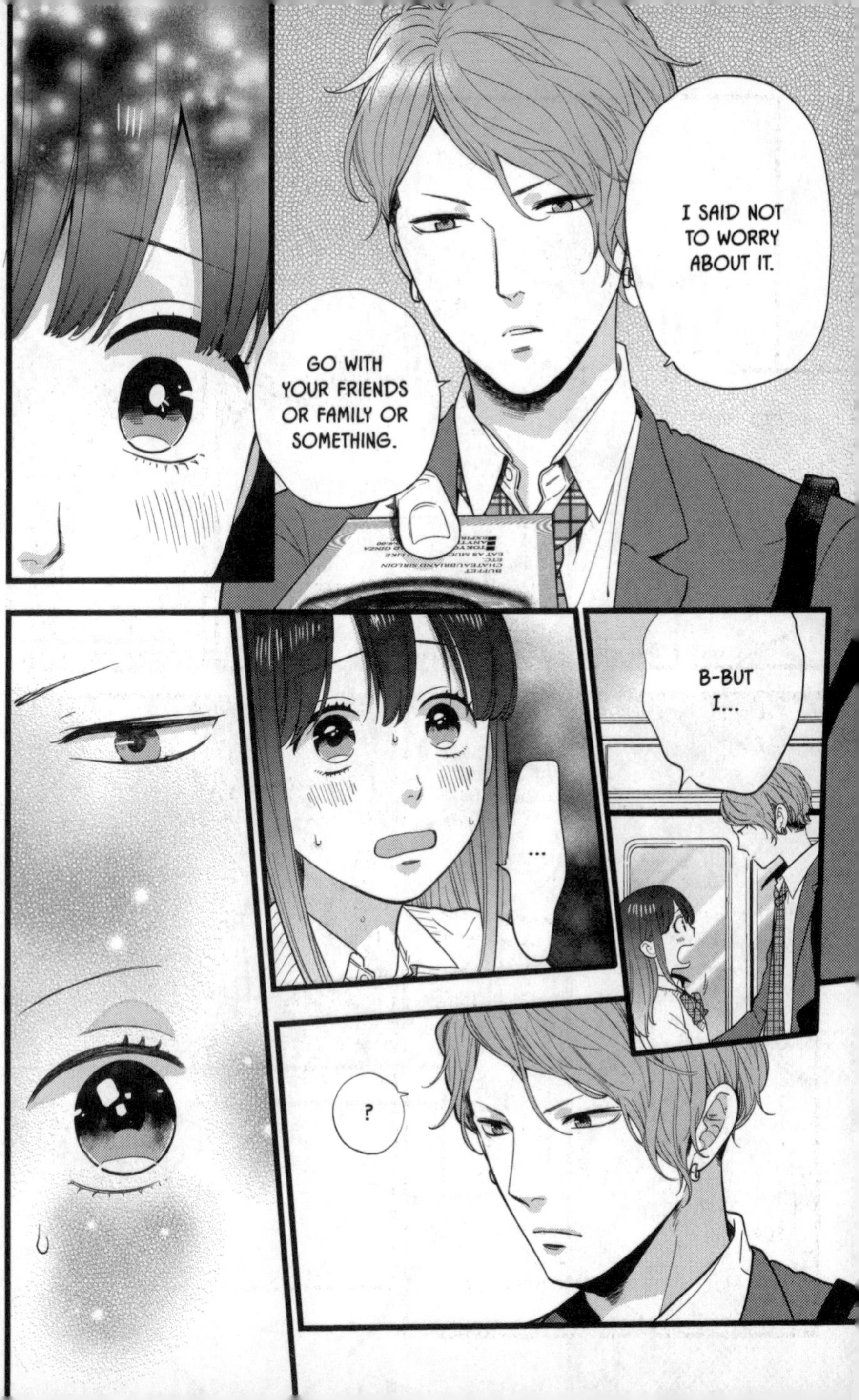
I SAID NOT TO WORRY ABOUT IT.
GO WITH YOUR FRIENDS OR FAMILY OR SOMETHING.
B-BUT I...
...
?

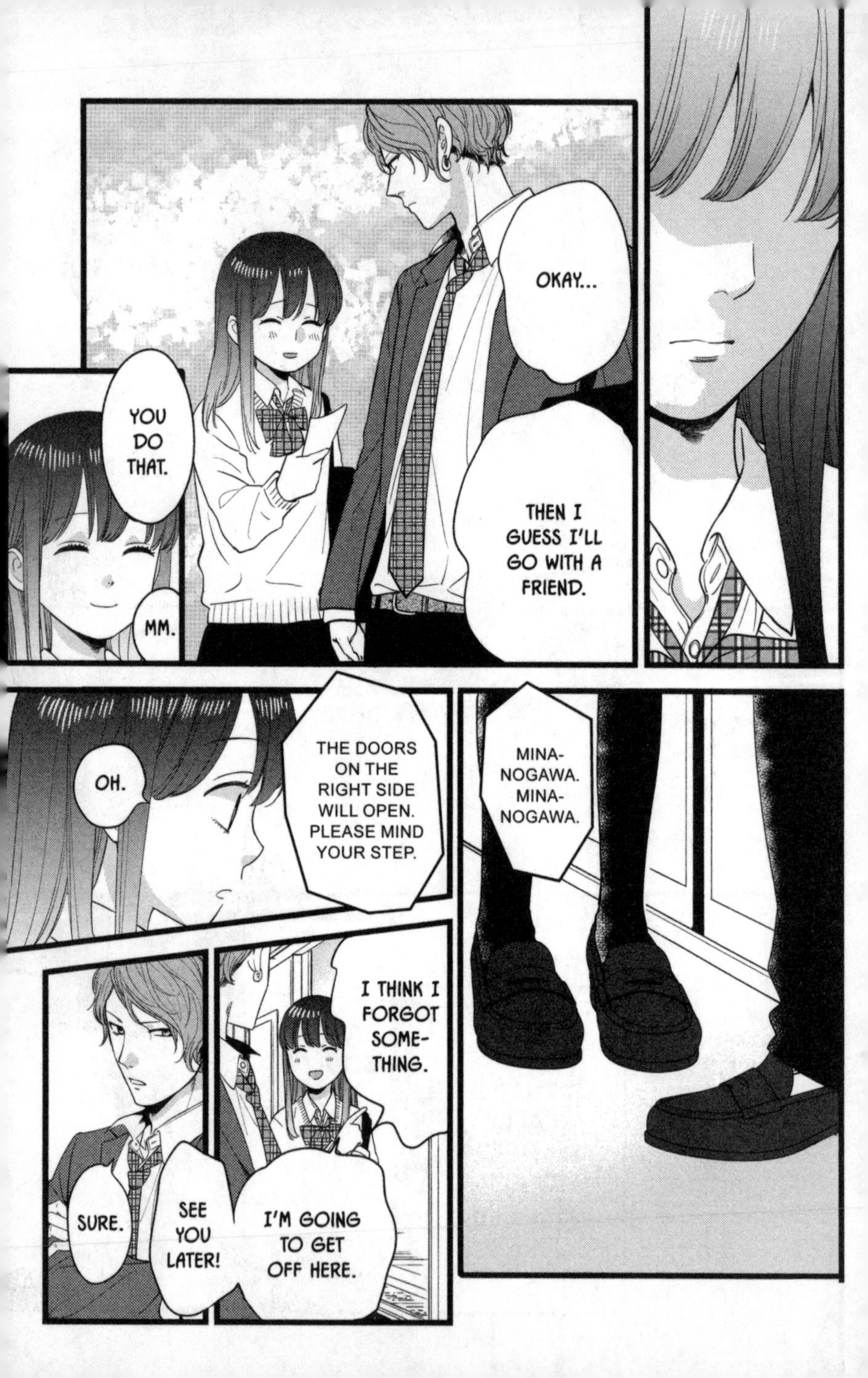
OKAY...
THEN I GUESS I'LL GO WITH A FRIEND.
YOU DO THAT.
MM.
MINA-NOGAWA. MINA-NOGAWA.
THE DOORS ON THE RIGHT SIDE WILL OPEN. PLEASE MIND YOUR STEP.
OH.
I THINK I FORGOT SOME-THING.
I'M GOING TO GET OFF HERE.
SEE YOU LATER!
SURE.

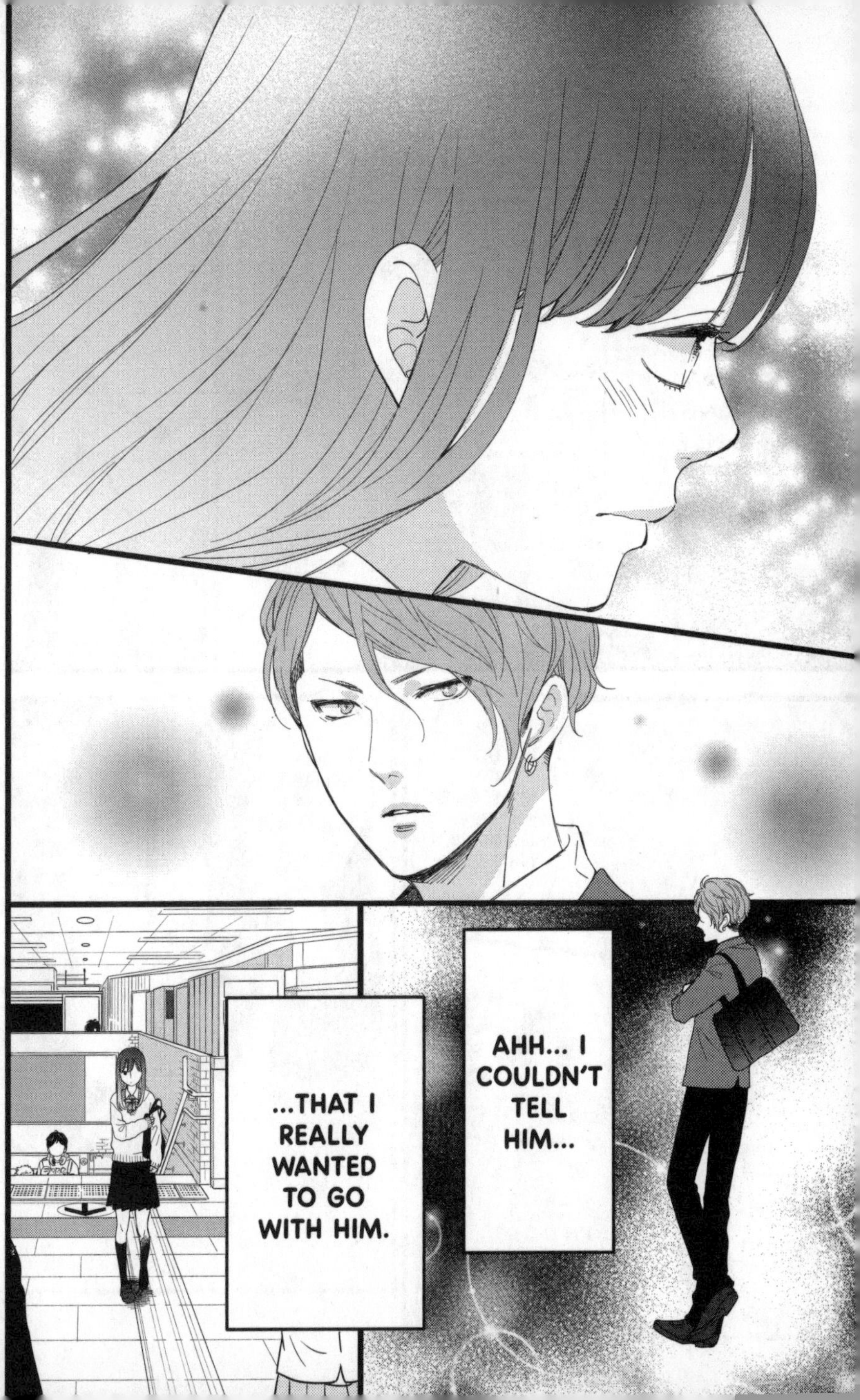
AHH... I COULDN'T TELL HIM...
...THAT I REALLY WANTED TO GO WITH HIM.

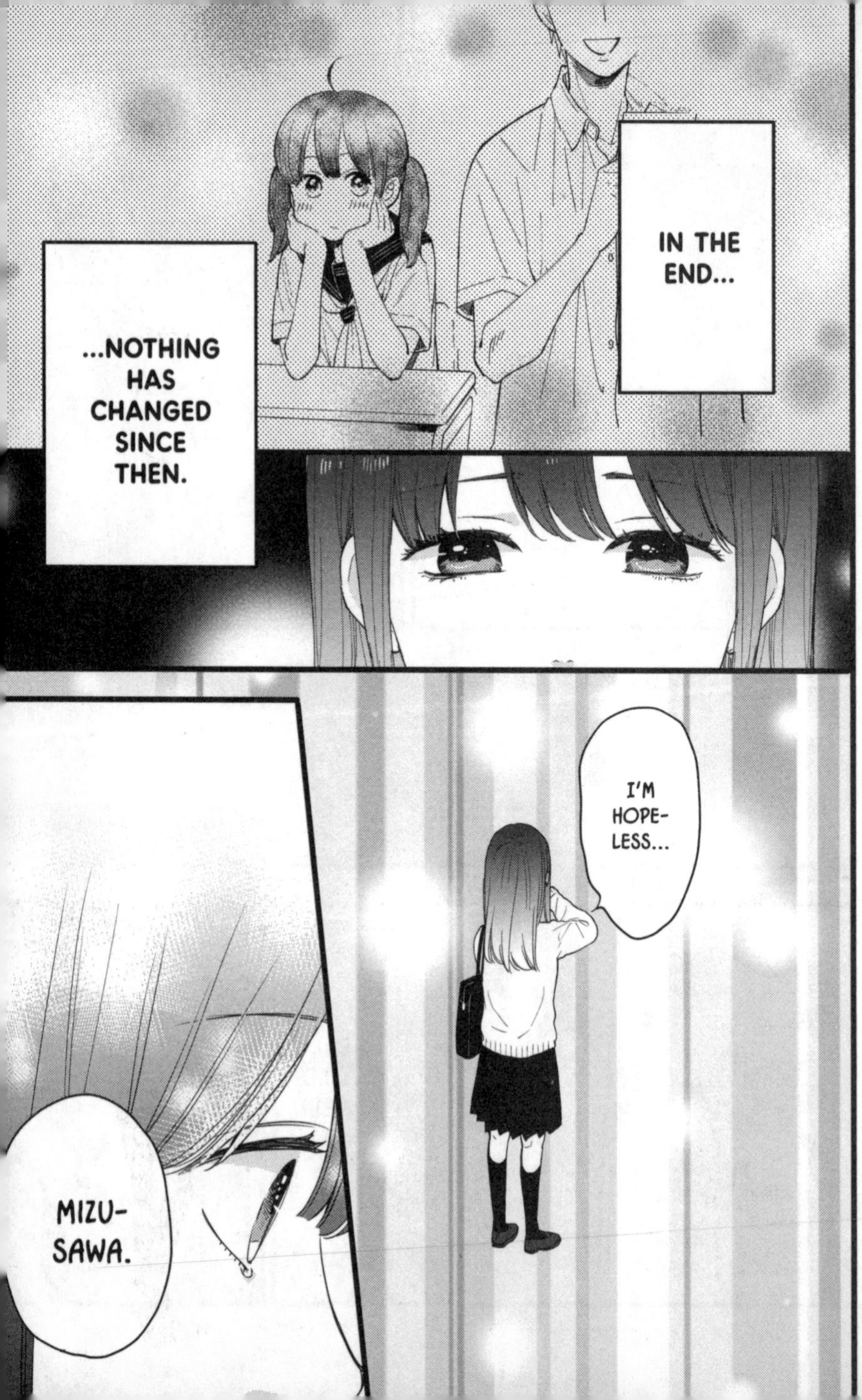
IN THE END...
...NOTHING HAS CHANGED SINCE THEN.
I'M HOPE-LESS...
MIZU-SAWA.

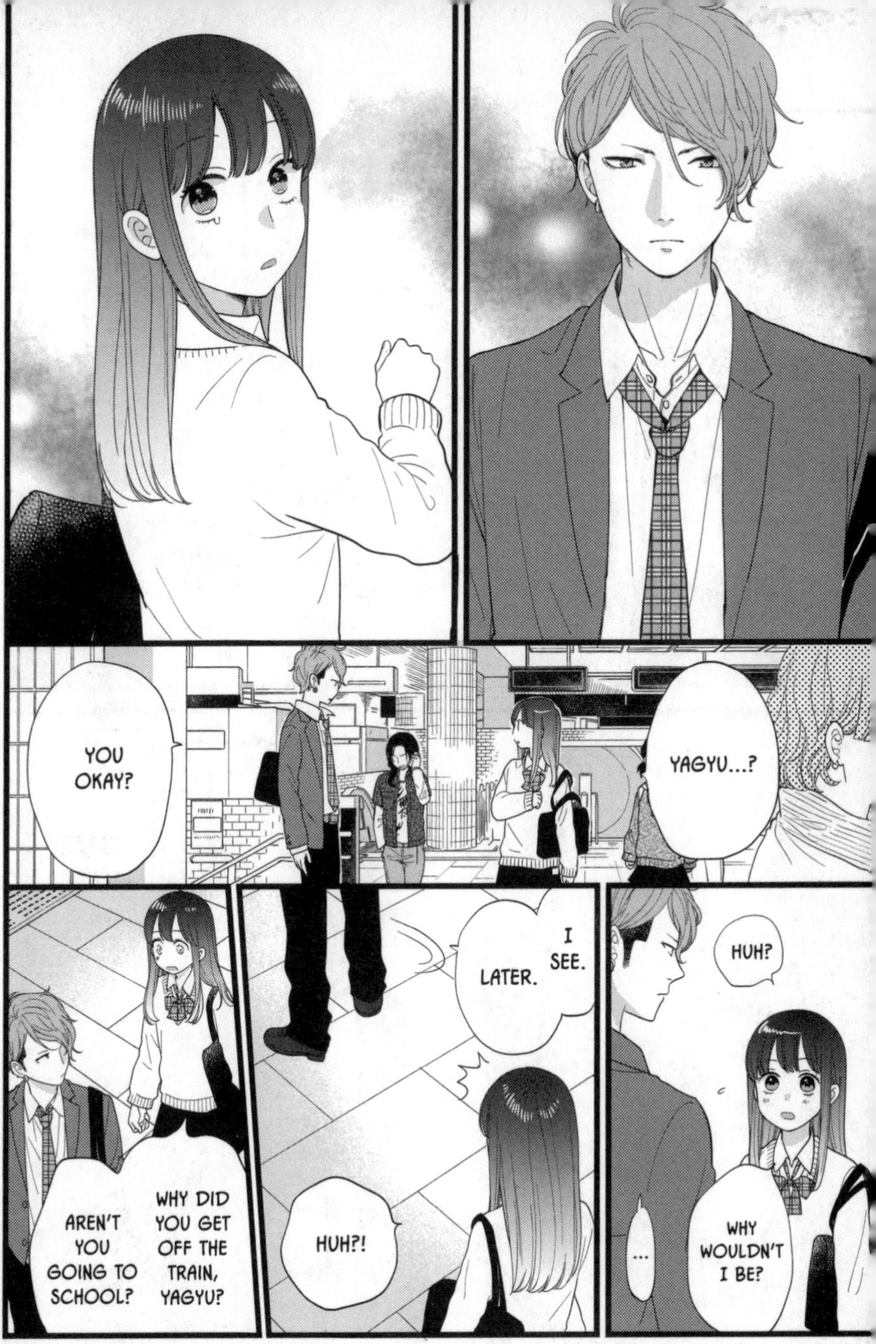
YAGYU...?
YOU OKAY?
HUH?
WHY WOULDN'T I BE?
...
I SEE.
LATER.
HUH?!
WHY DID YOU GET OFF THE TRAIN, YAGYU?
AREN'T YOU GOING TO SCHOOL?

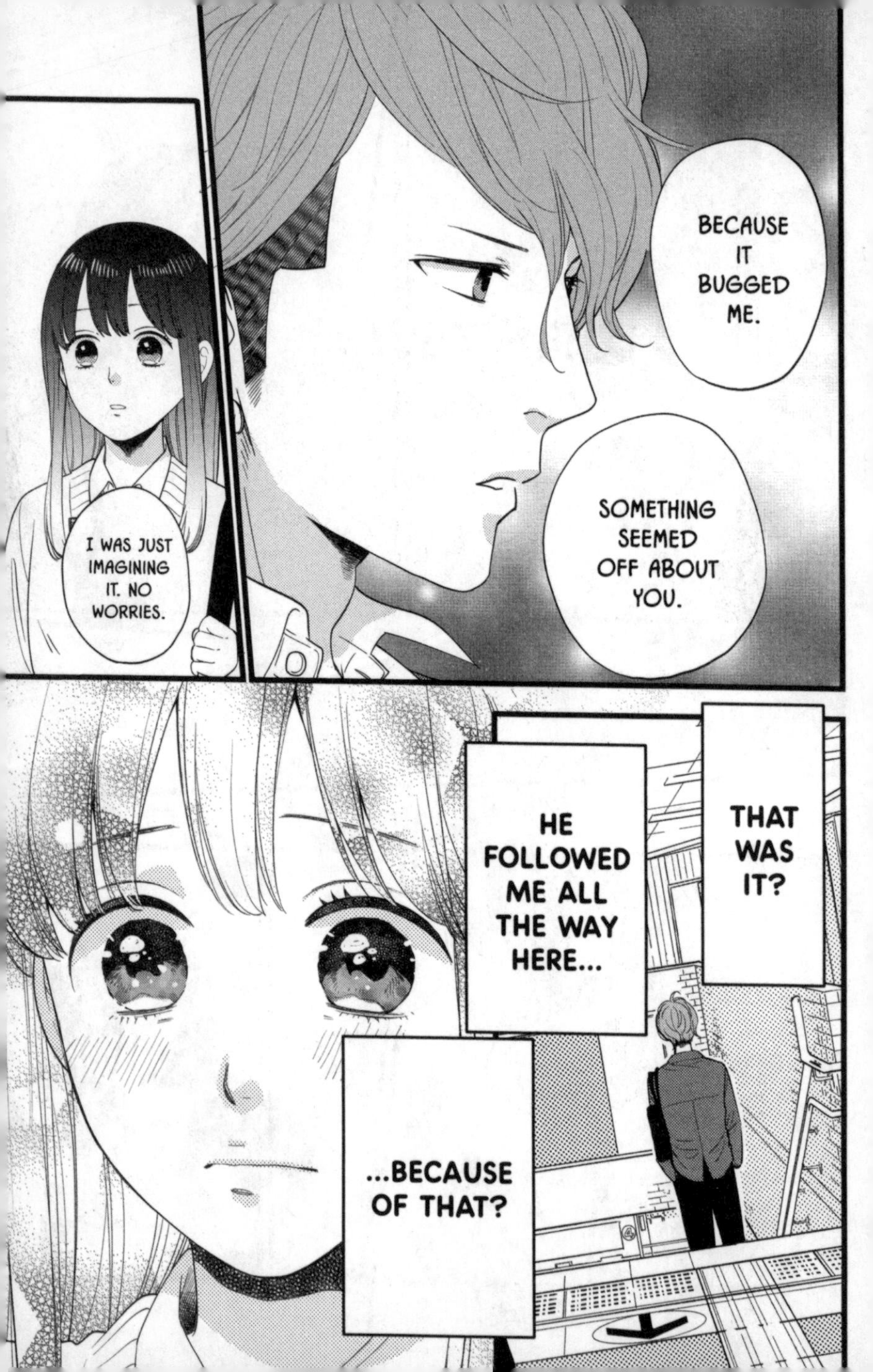
BECAUSE IT BUGGED ME.
SOMETHING SEEMED OFF ABOUT YOU.
I WAS JUST IMAGINING IT. NO WORRIES.
THAT WAS IT?
HE FOLLOWED ME ALL THE WAY HERE...
...BECAUSE OF THAT?

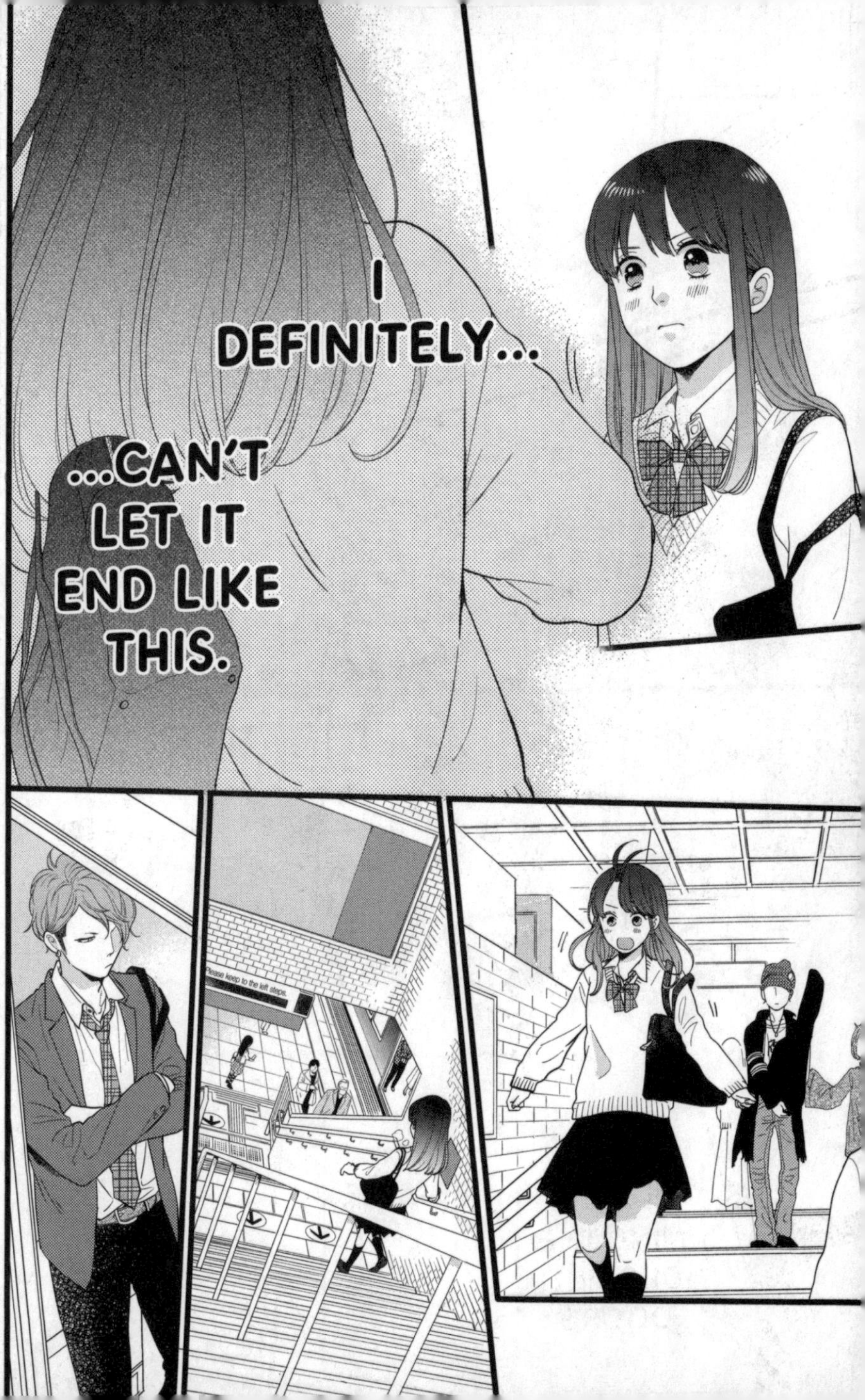
I DEFINITELY...
...CAN'T LET IT END LIKE THIS.
Please keep to the left steps.

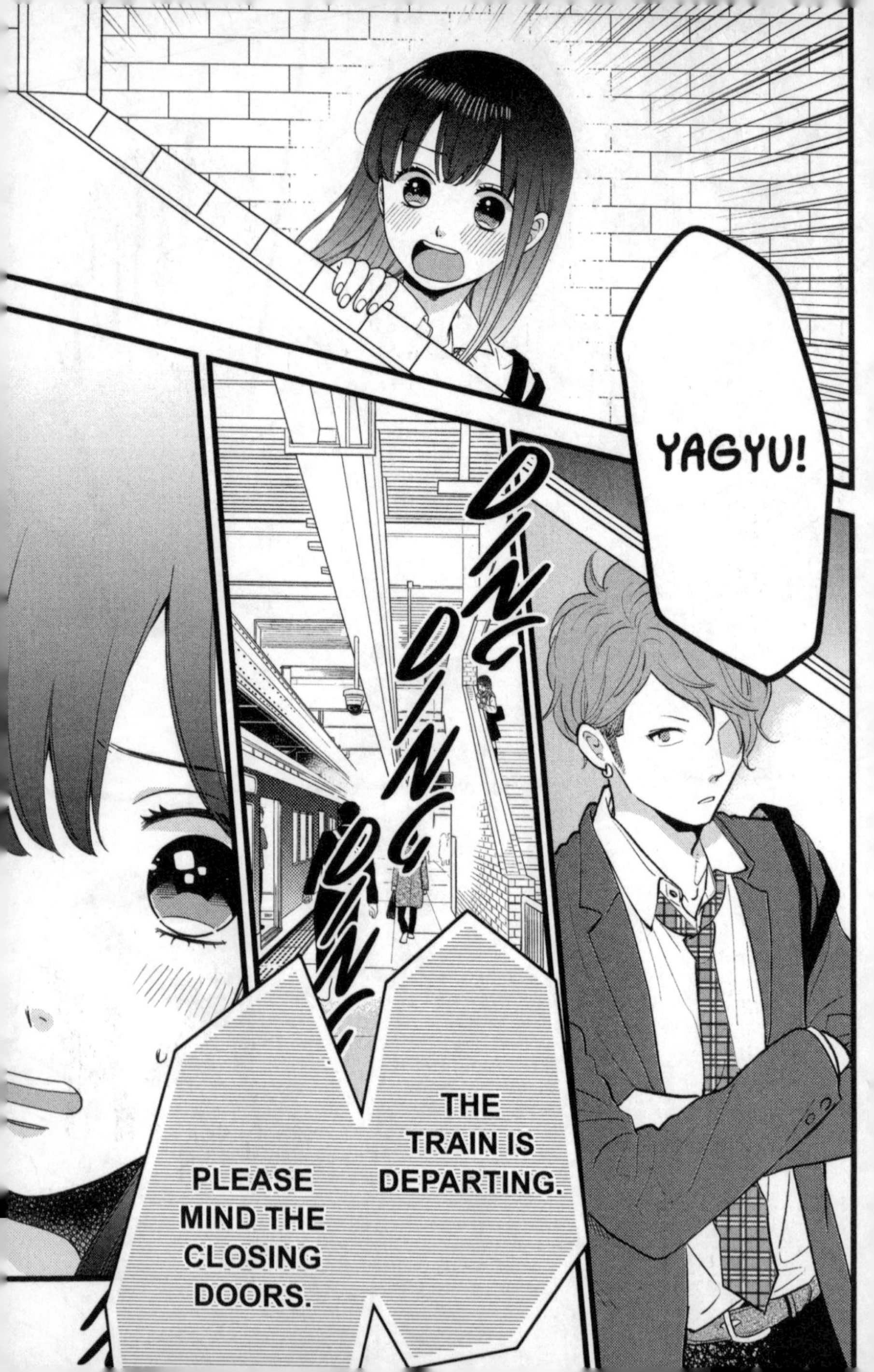
YAGYU!
DING DING DING DING
THE TRAIN IS DEPARTING.
PLEASE MIND THE CLOSING DOORS.

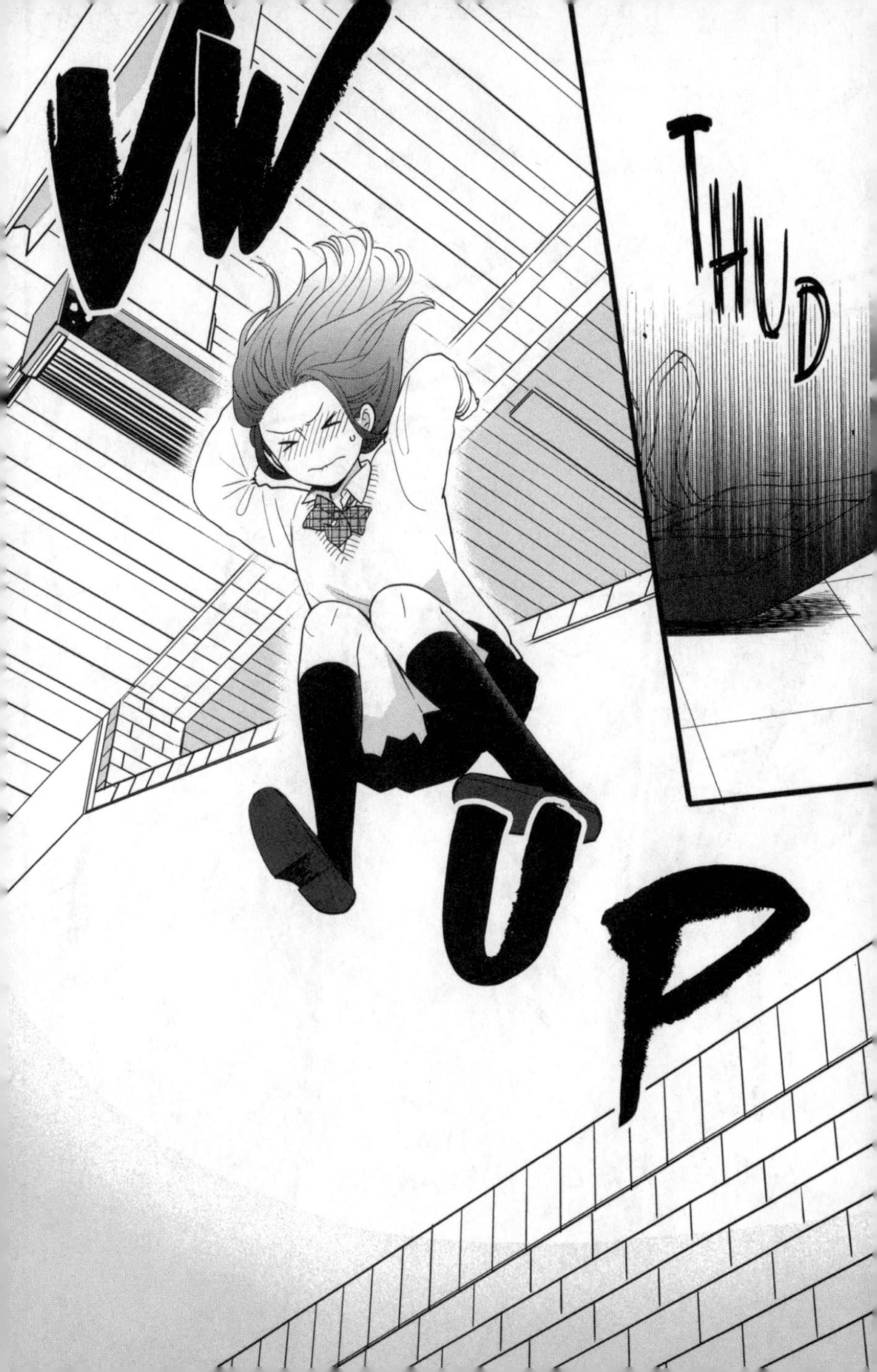
THUD
VWUP

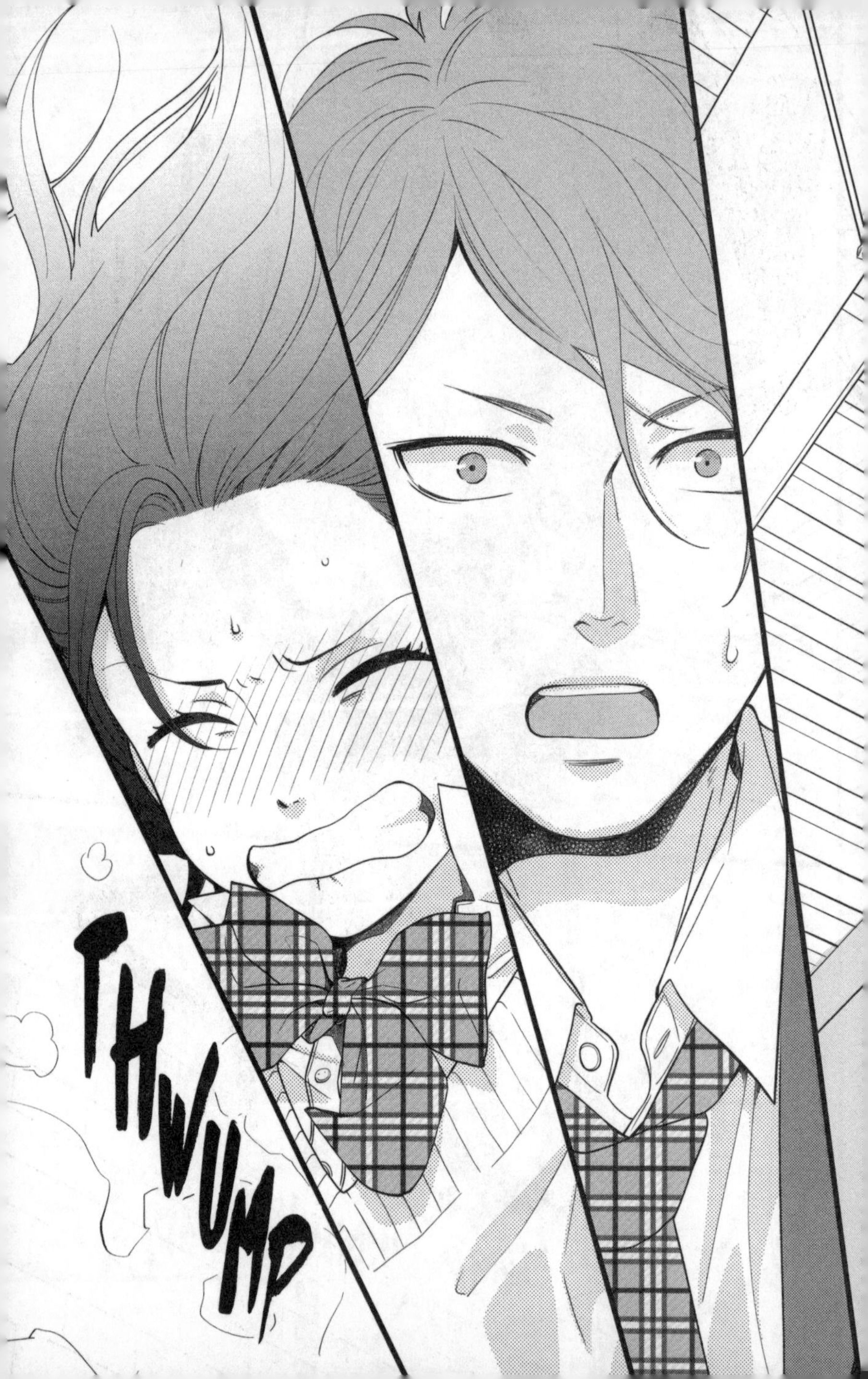
THWUMP

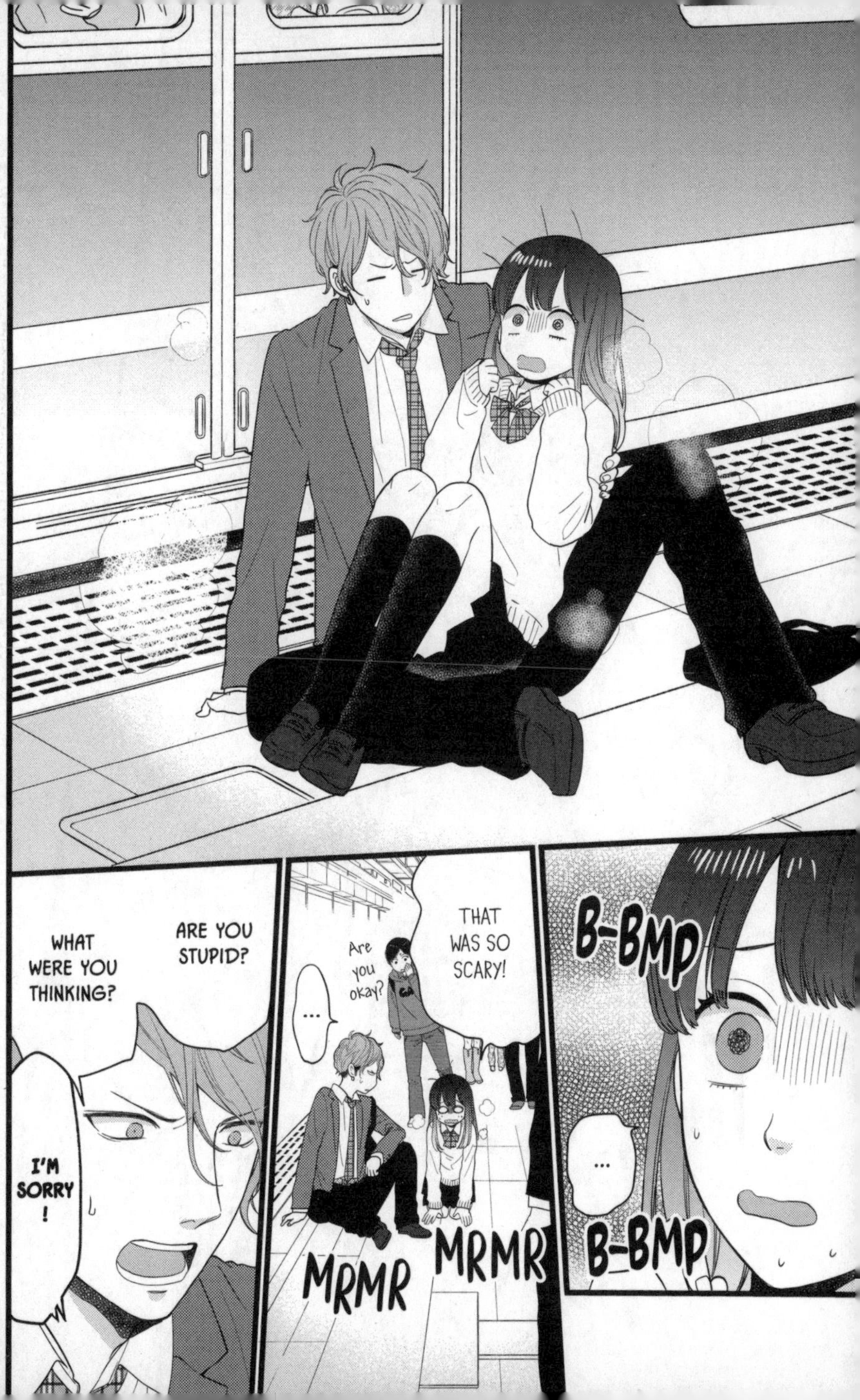
B-BMP
...
B-BMP
THAT WAS SO SCARY!
Are you okay?
...
MRMR
MRMR
ARE YOU STUPID?
WHAT WERE YOU THINKING?
I'M SORRY!

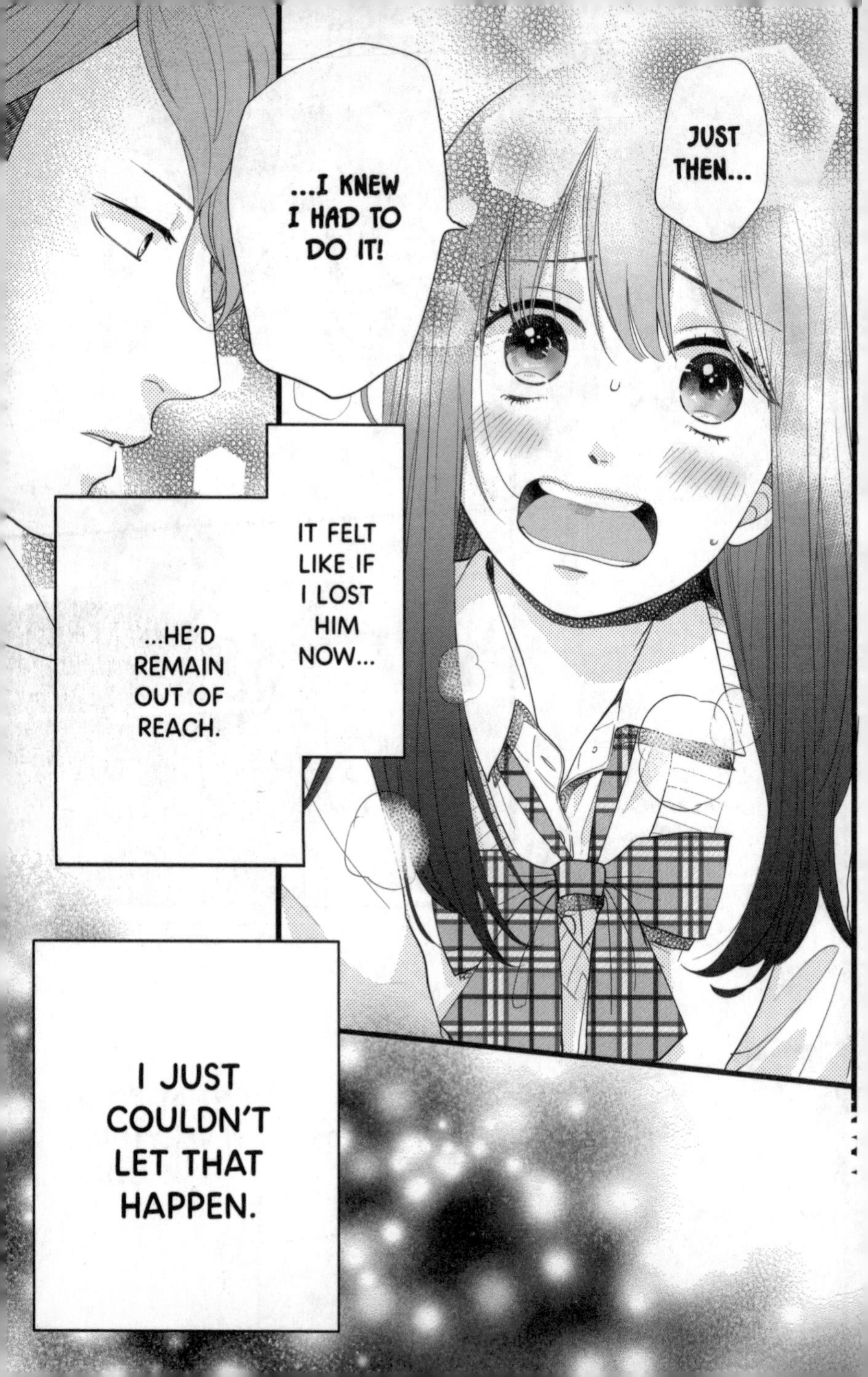
JUST THEN...
...I KNEW I HAD TO DO IT!
IT FELT LIKE IF I LOST HIM NOW...
...HE'D REMAIN OUT OF REACH.
I JUST COULDN'T LET THAT HAPPEN.

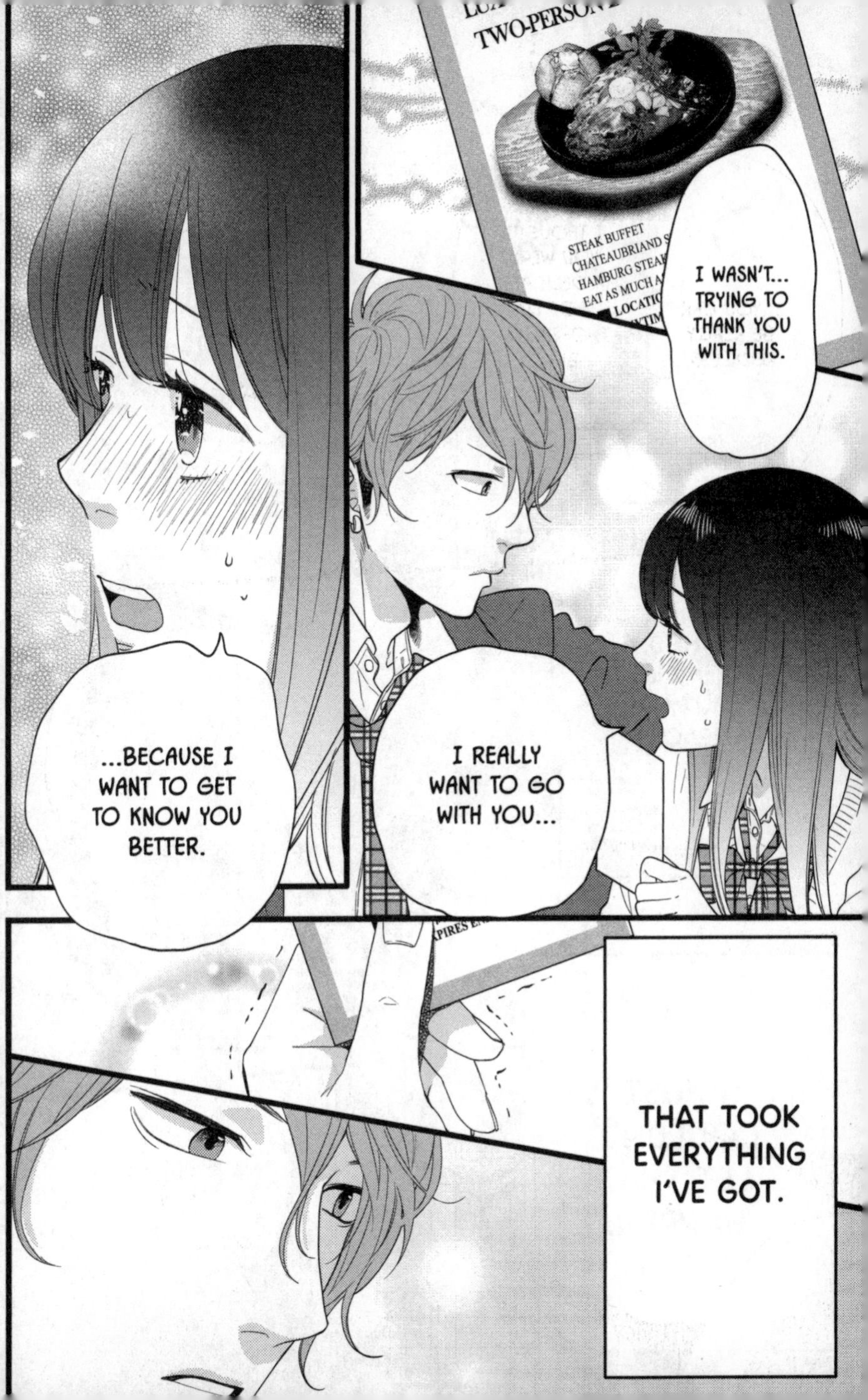
TWO-PERSON
STEAK BUFFET
I WASN'T... TRYING TO THANK YOU WITH THIS.
I REALLY WANT TO GO WITH YOU...
...BECAUSE I WANT TO GET TO KNOW YOU BETTER.
THAT TOOK EVERYTHING I'VE GOT.

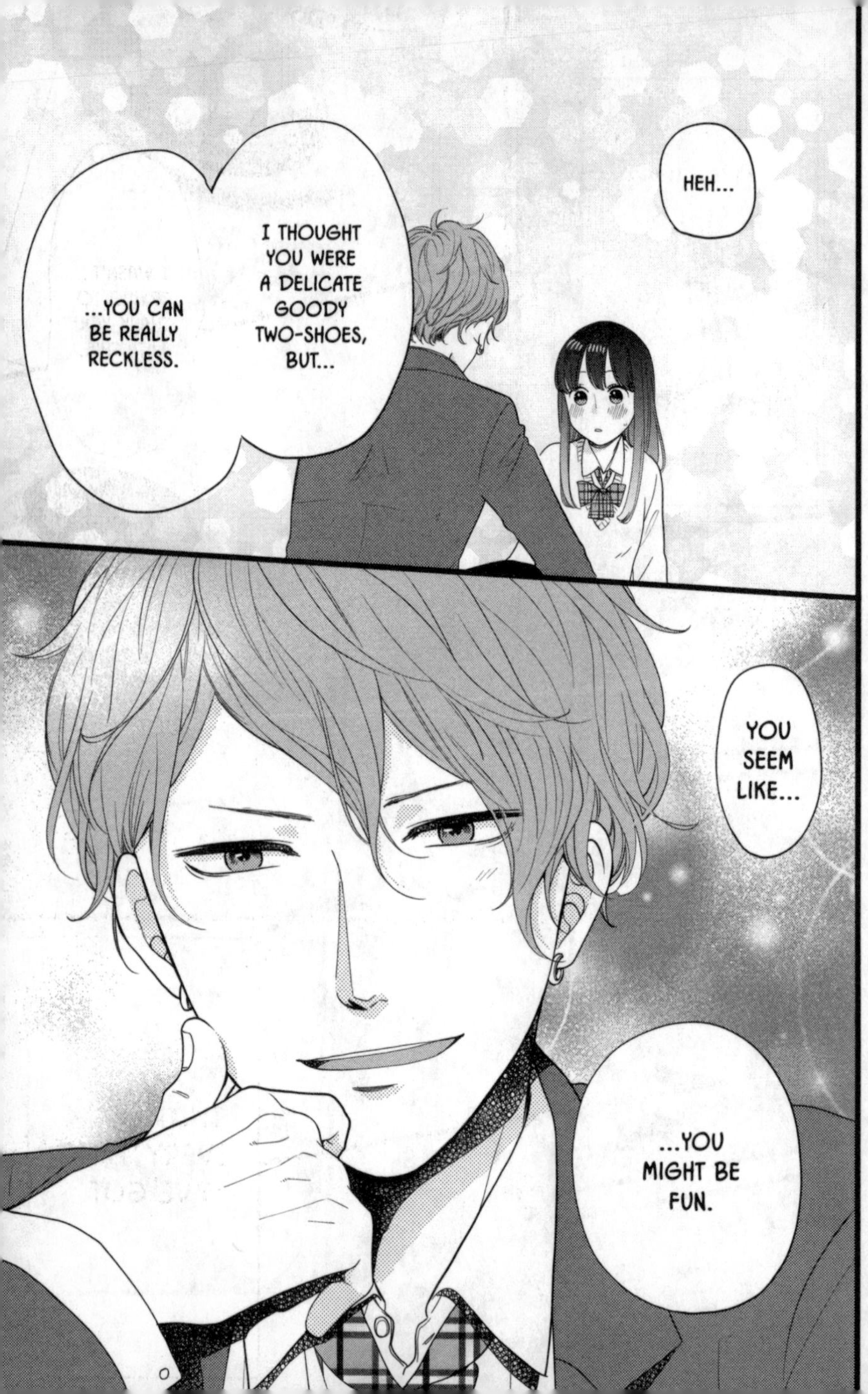
HEH...
I THOUGHT YOU WERE A DELICATE GOODY TWO-SHOES, BUT...
...YOU CAN BE REALLY RECKLESS.
YOU SEEM LIKE...
...YOU MIGHT BE FUN.

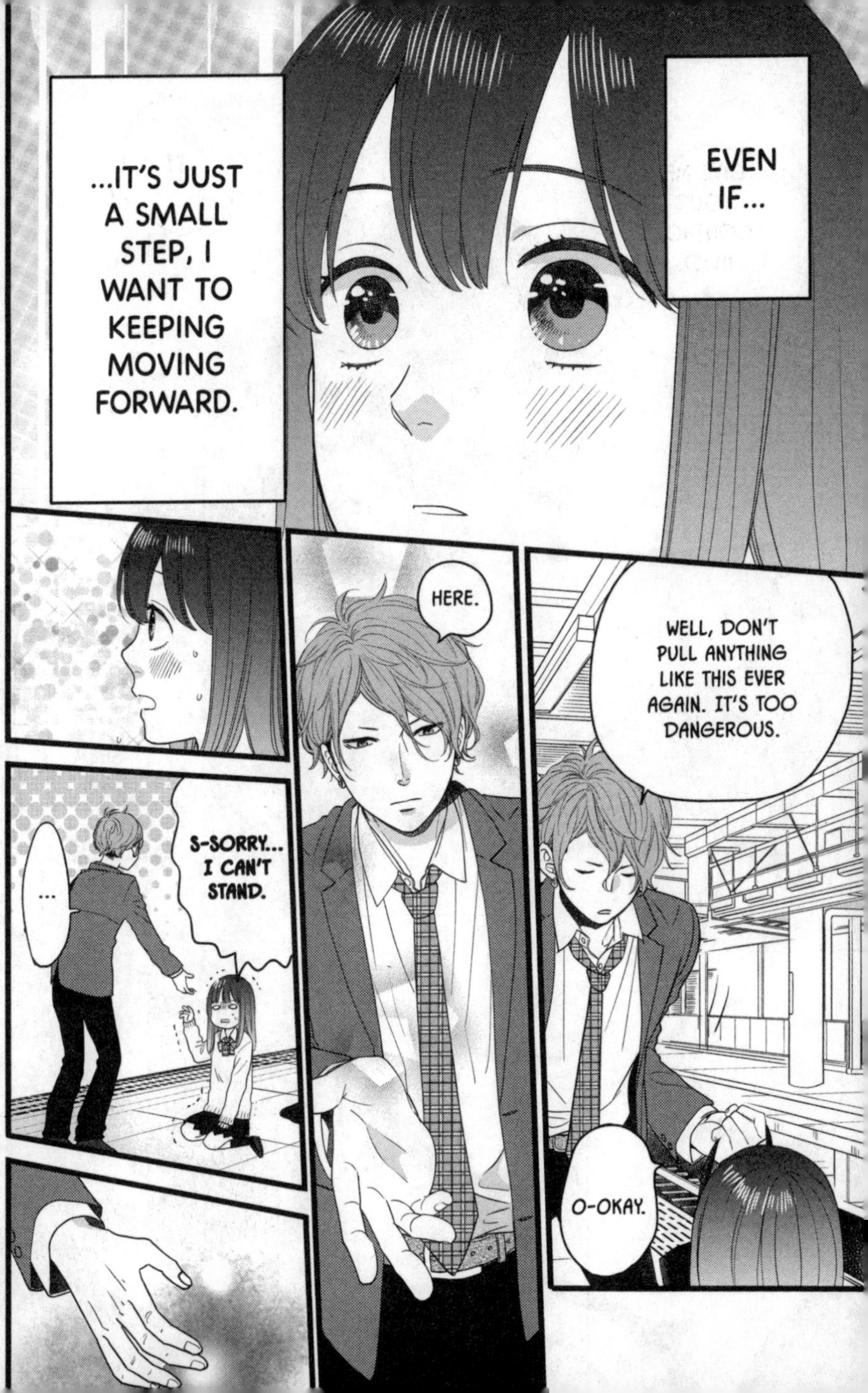
EVEN IF...
...IT'S JUST A SMALL STEP, I WANT TO KEEPING MOVING FORWARD.
WELL, DON'T PULL ANYTHING LIKE THIS EVER AGAIN. IT'S TOO DANGEROUS.
O-OKAY.
HERE.
S-SORRY... I CAN'T STAND.
...

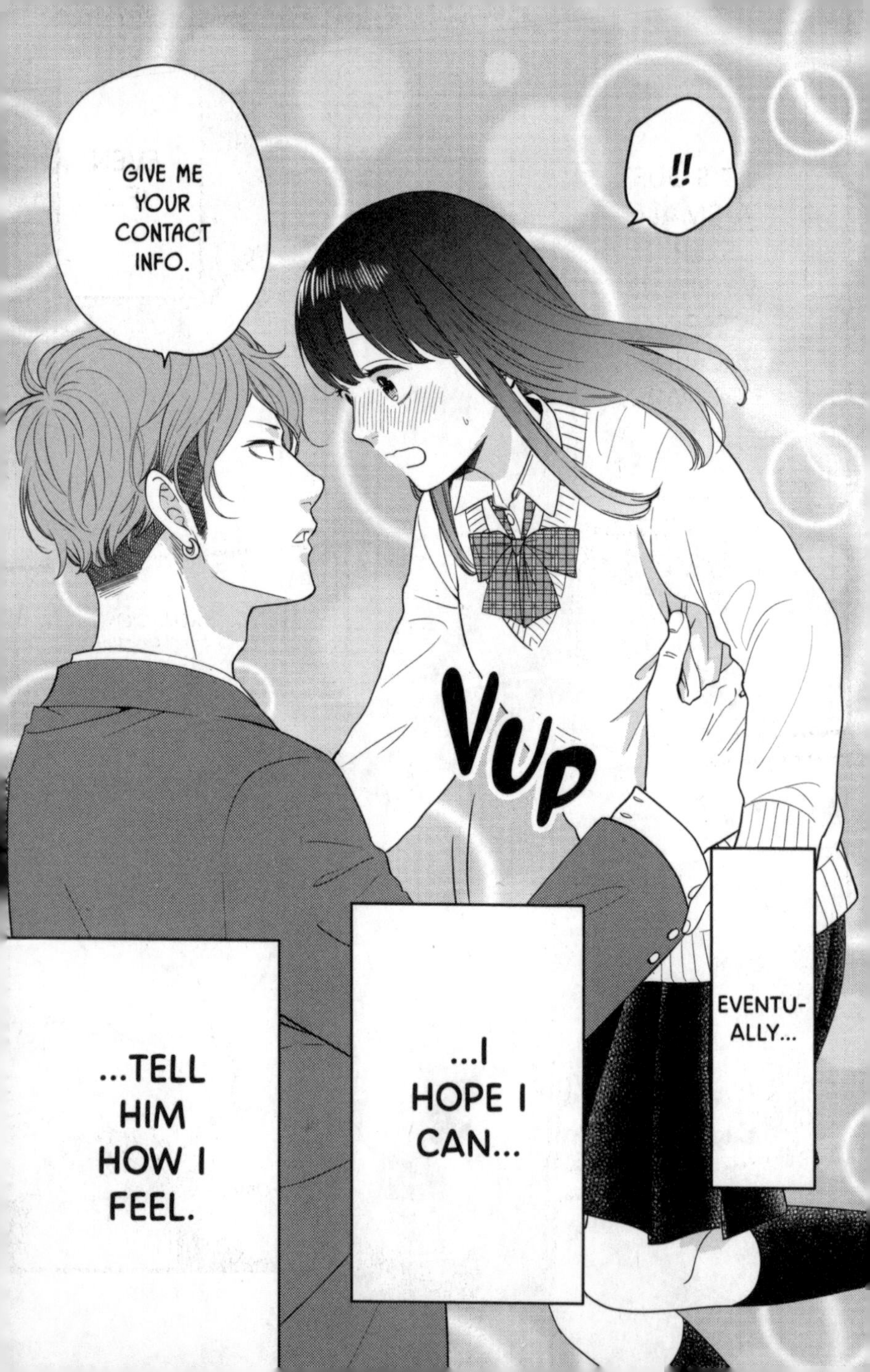
GIVE ME YOUR CONTACT INFO.
!!
VUP
EVENTU-ALLY...
...I HOPE I CAN...
...TELL HIM HOW I FEEL.

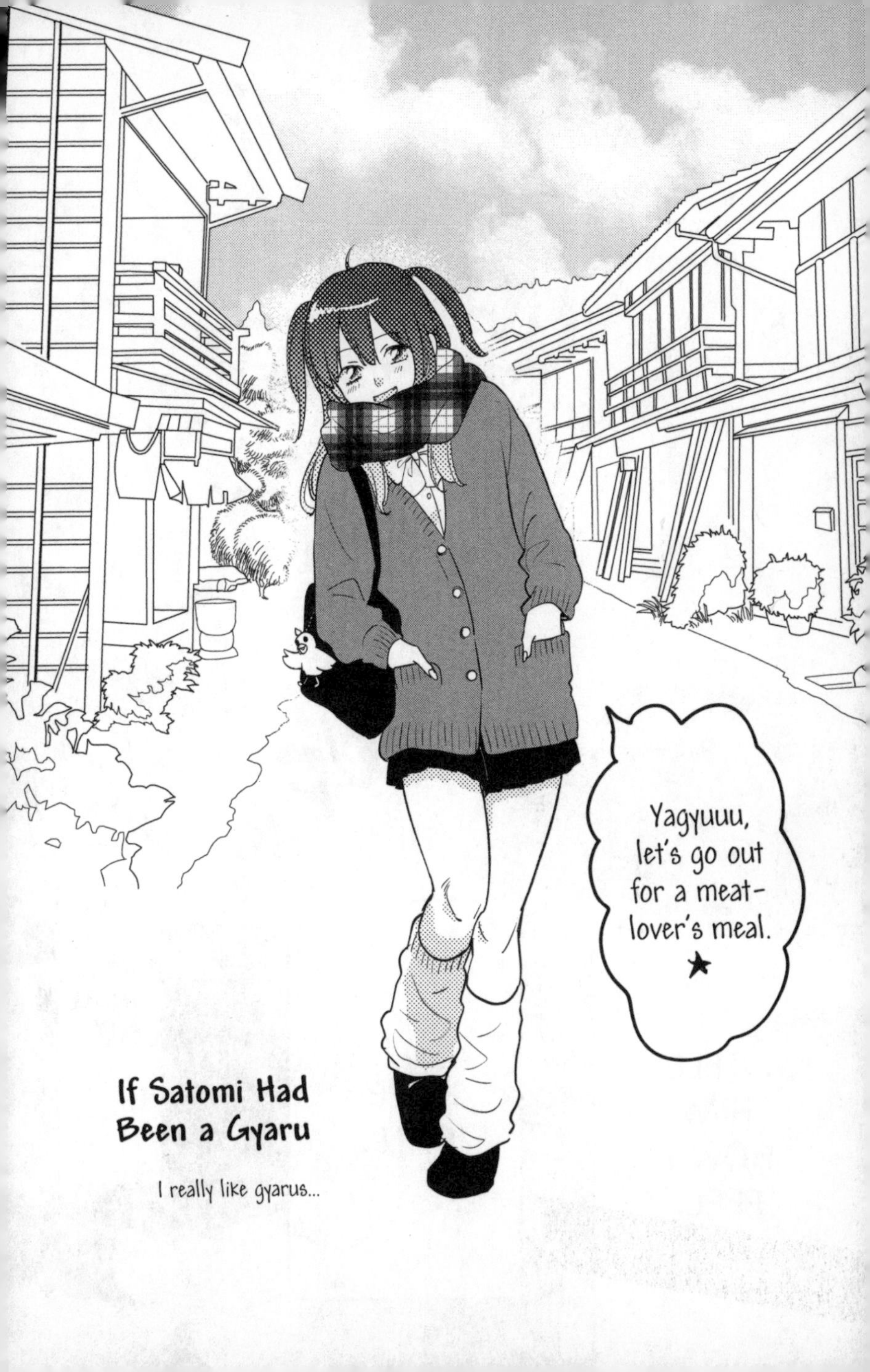
Yagyuuu, let's go out for a meat-lover's meal. ★
If Satomi Had Been a Gyaru
I really like gyarus...

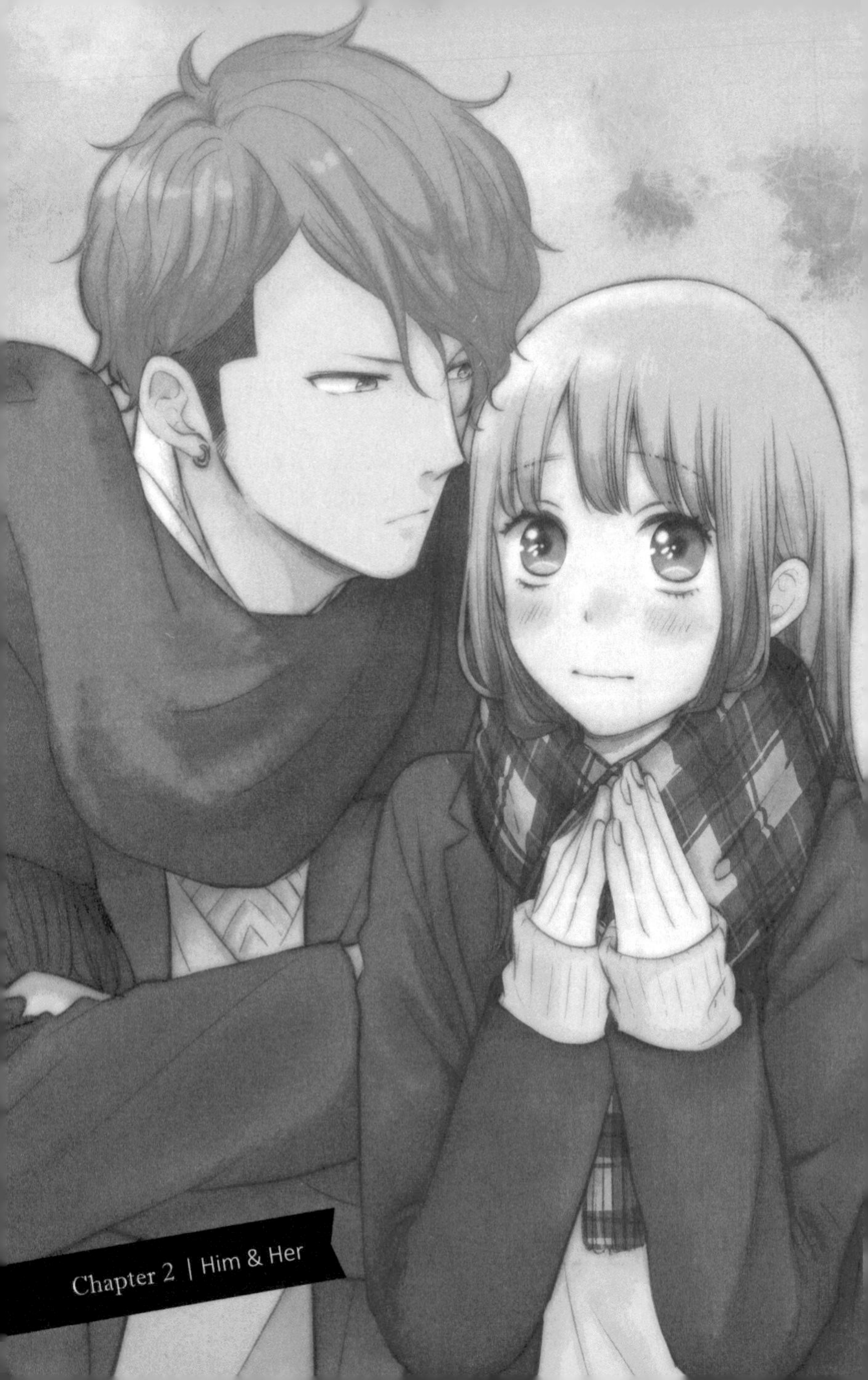

Chapter 2 | Him & Her

I drew this for the April 2020 issue of *Betsuma* as a color preview, but my deadline was the same day as my sister's surgery, so I remember I ended up drawing it while waiting in the hospital.
You really can use an iPad for everything.

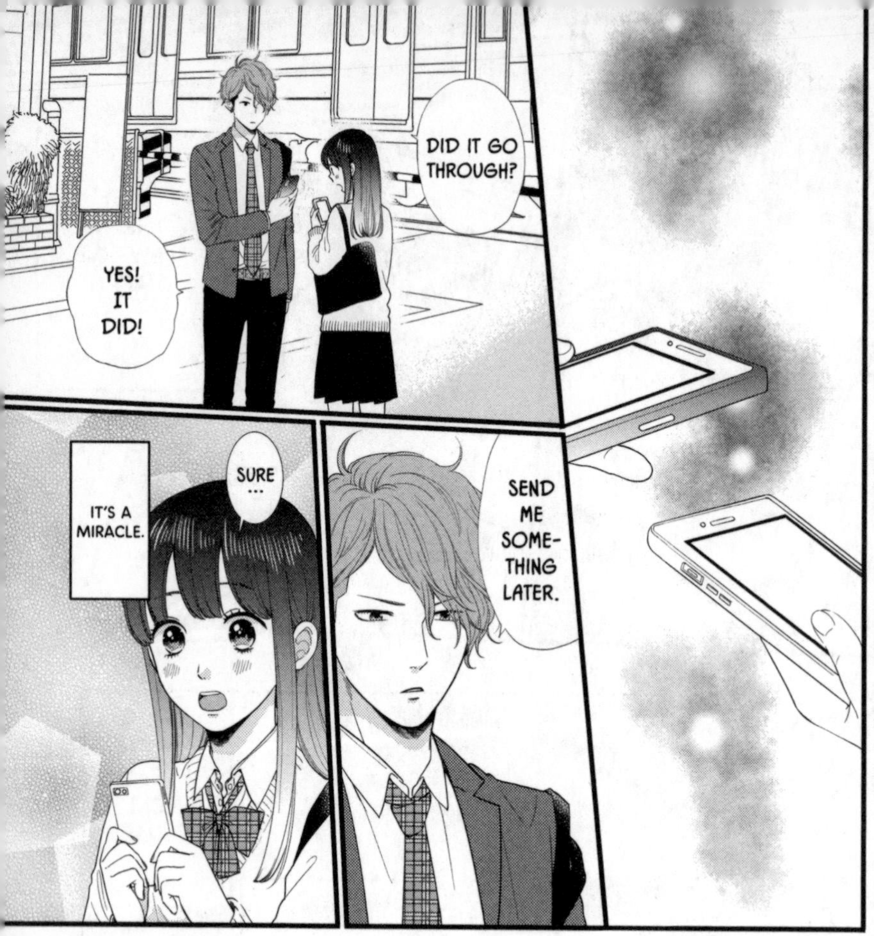
DID IT GO THROUGH?
YES! IT DID!
SEND ME SOME-THING LATER.
SURE...
IT'S A MIRACLE.

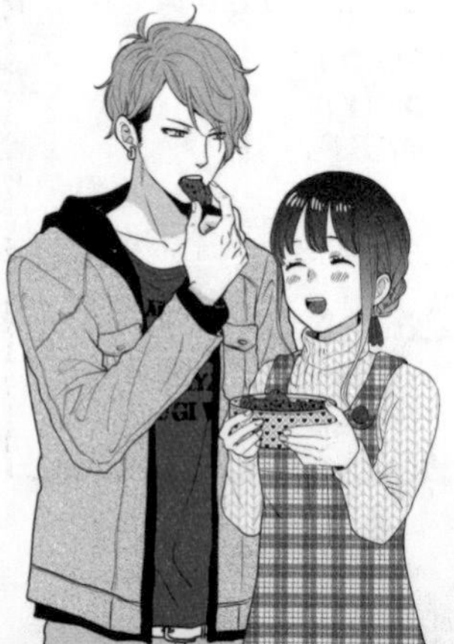

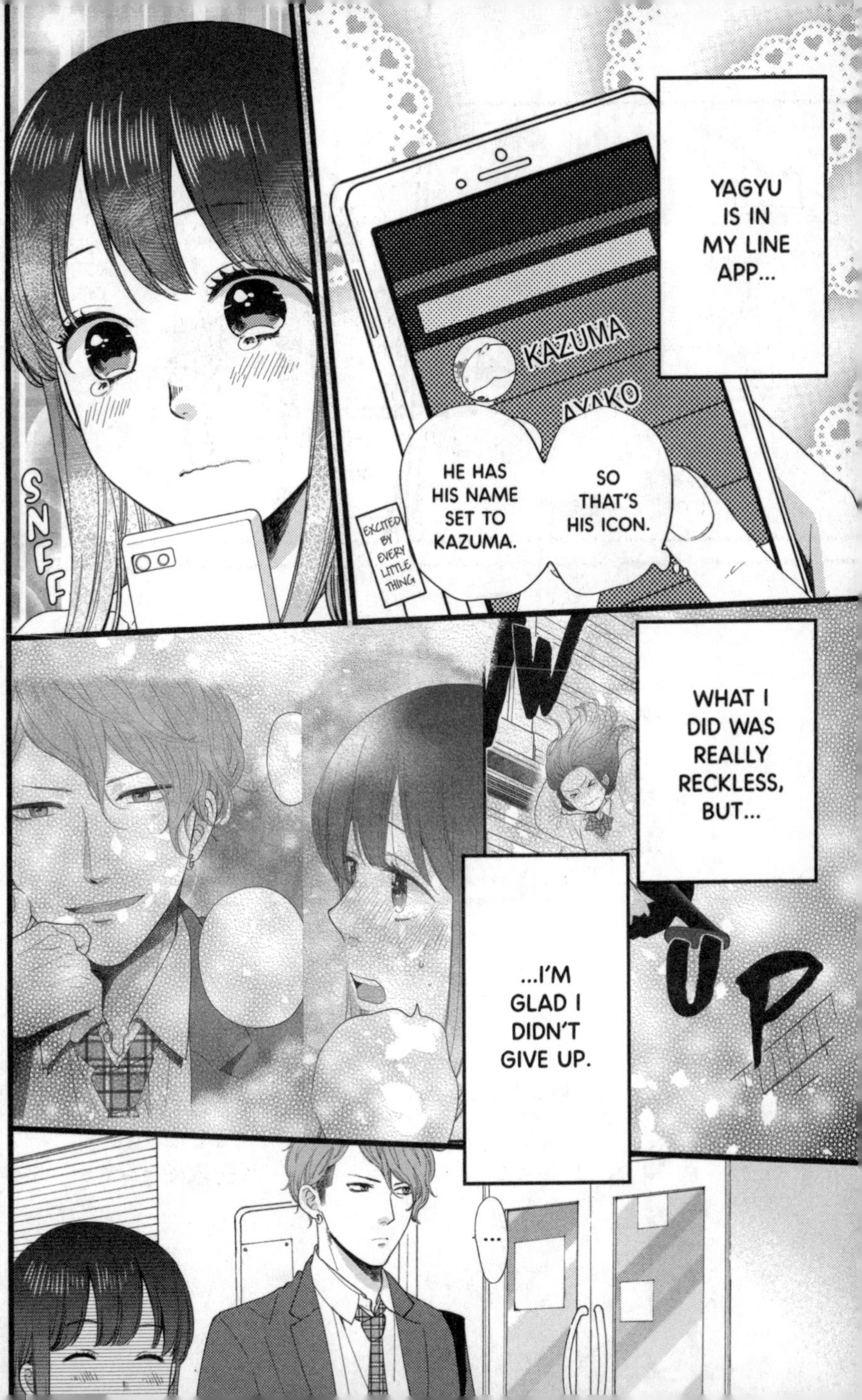
YAGYU IS IN MY LINE APP...
KAZUMA
AYAKO
SO THAT'S HIS ICON.
HE HAS HIS NAME SET TO KAZUMA.
EXCITED BY EVERY LITTLE THING
SNFF
WHAT I DID WAS REALLY RECKLESS, BUT...
...I'M GLAD I DIDN'T GIVE UP.
UP
...

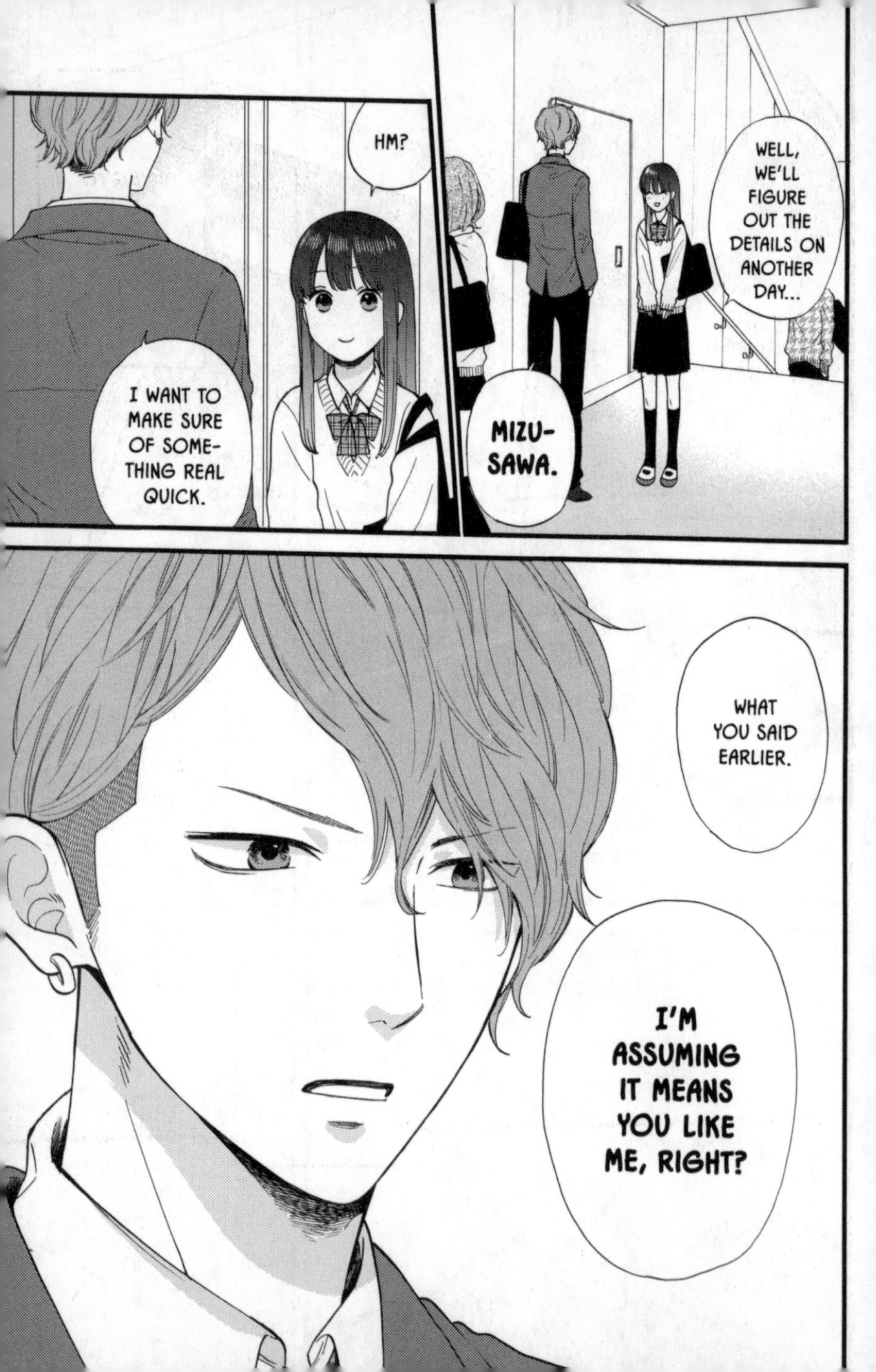
WELL, WE'LL FIGURE OUT THE DETAILS ON ANOTHER DAY...
MIZU-SAWA.
HM?
I WANT TO MAKE SURE OF SOME-THING REAL QUICK.
WHAT YOU SAID EARLIER.
I'M ASSUMING IT MEANS YOU LIKE ME, RIGHT?

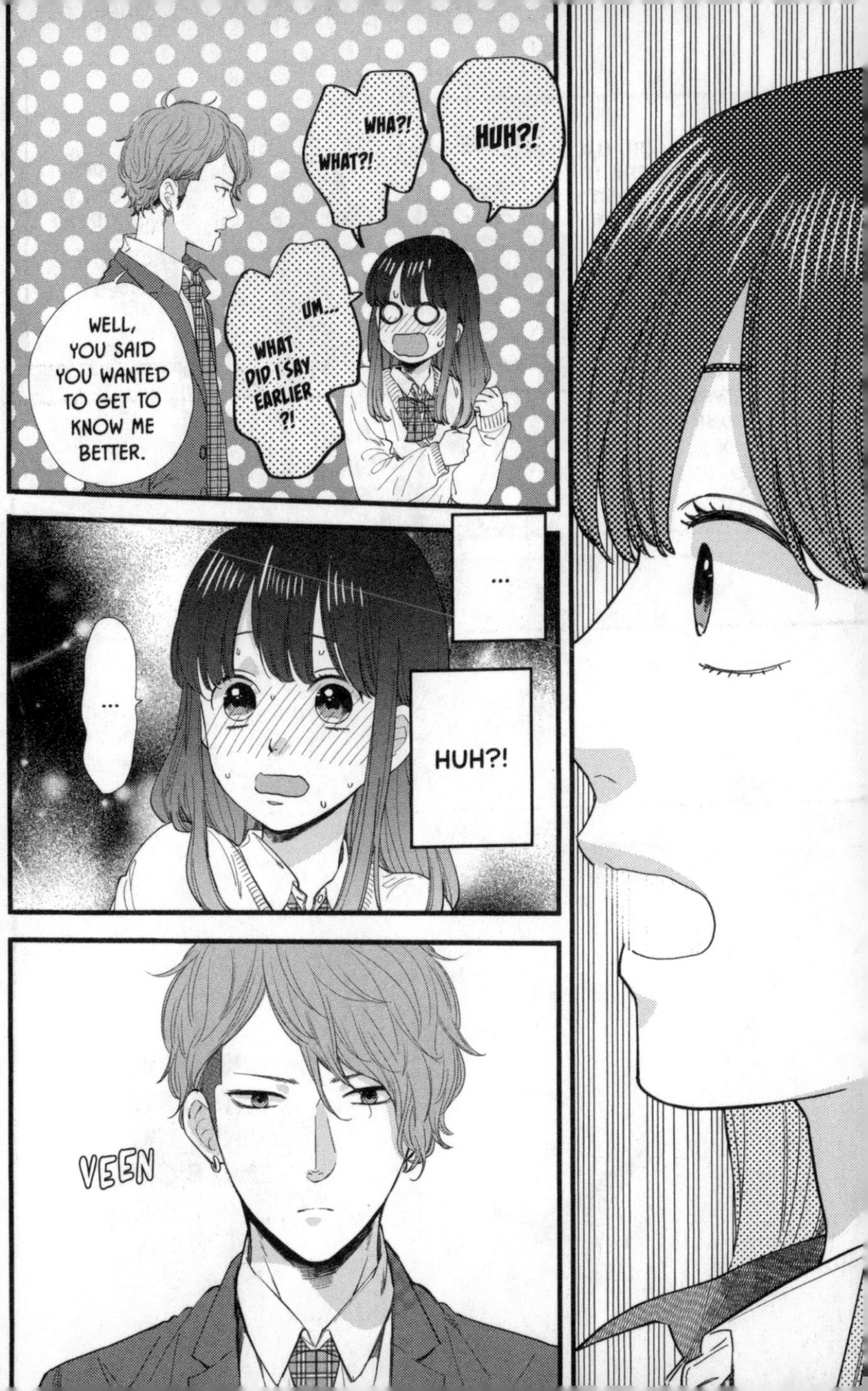
HUH?!
WHA?!
WHAT?!
UM... WHAT DID I SAY EARLIER?!
WELL, YOU SAID YOU WANTED TO GET TO KNOW ME BETTER.
...
HUH?!
...
VEEN

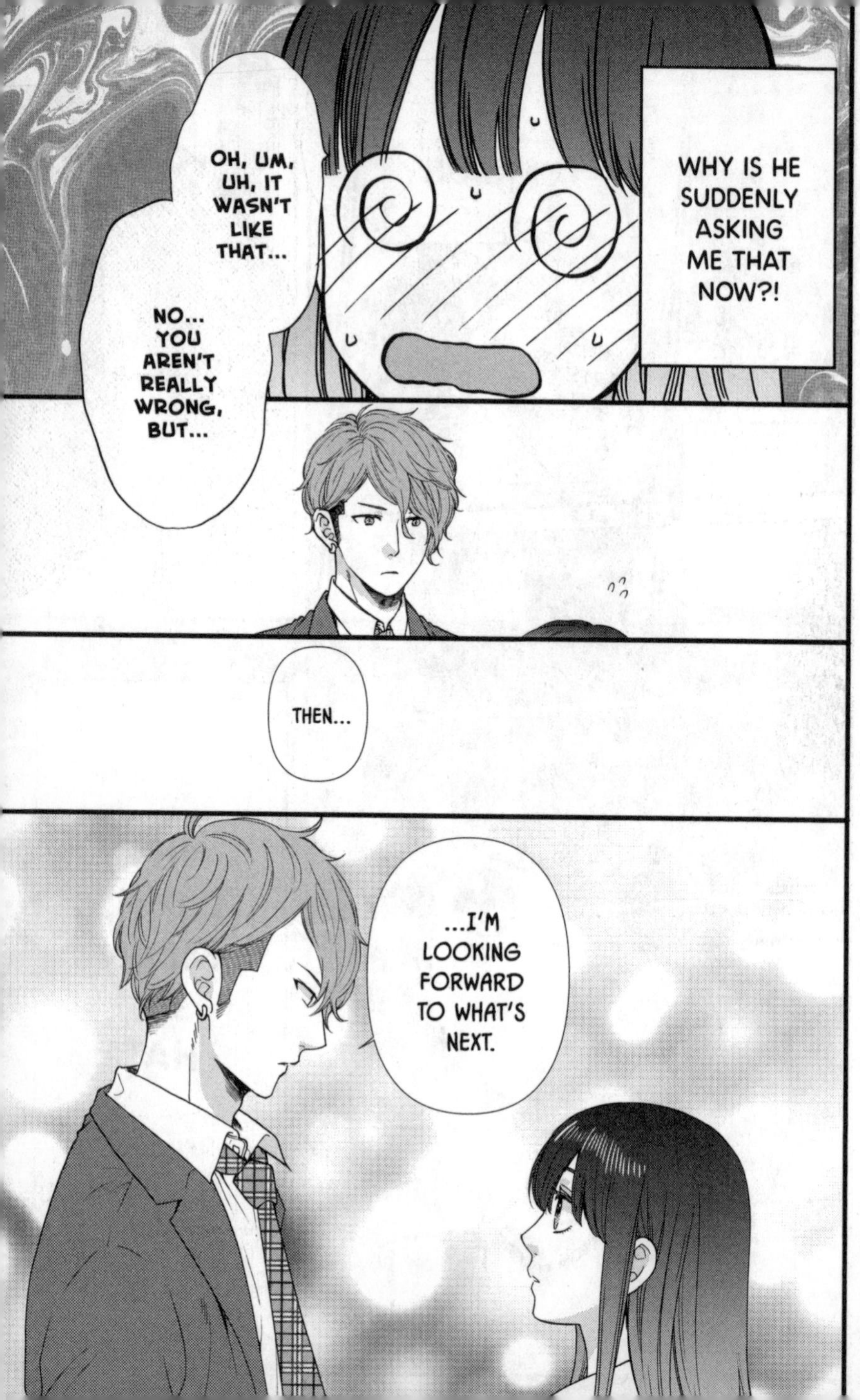
WHY IS HE SUDDENLY ASKING ME THAT NOW?!
OH, UM, UH, IT WASN'T LIKE THAT...
NO... YOU AREN'T REALLY WRONG, BUT...
THEN...
...I'M LOOKING FORWARD TO WHAT'S NEXT.

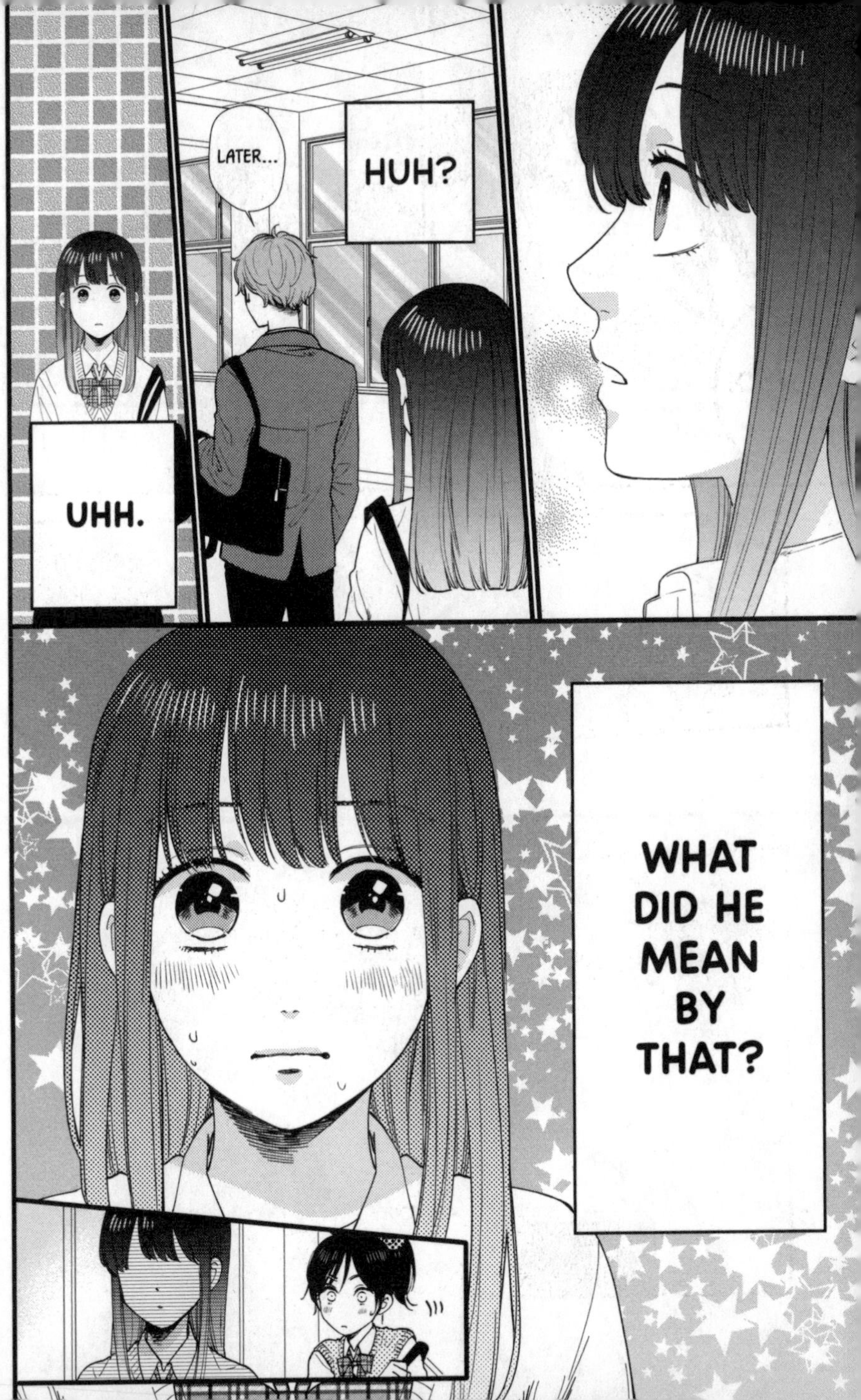
HUH?
LATER...
UHH.
WHAT DID HE MEAN BY THAT?

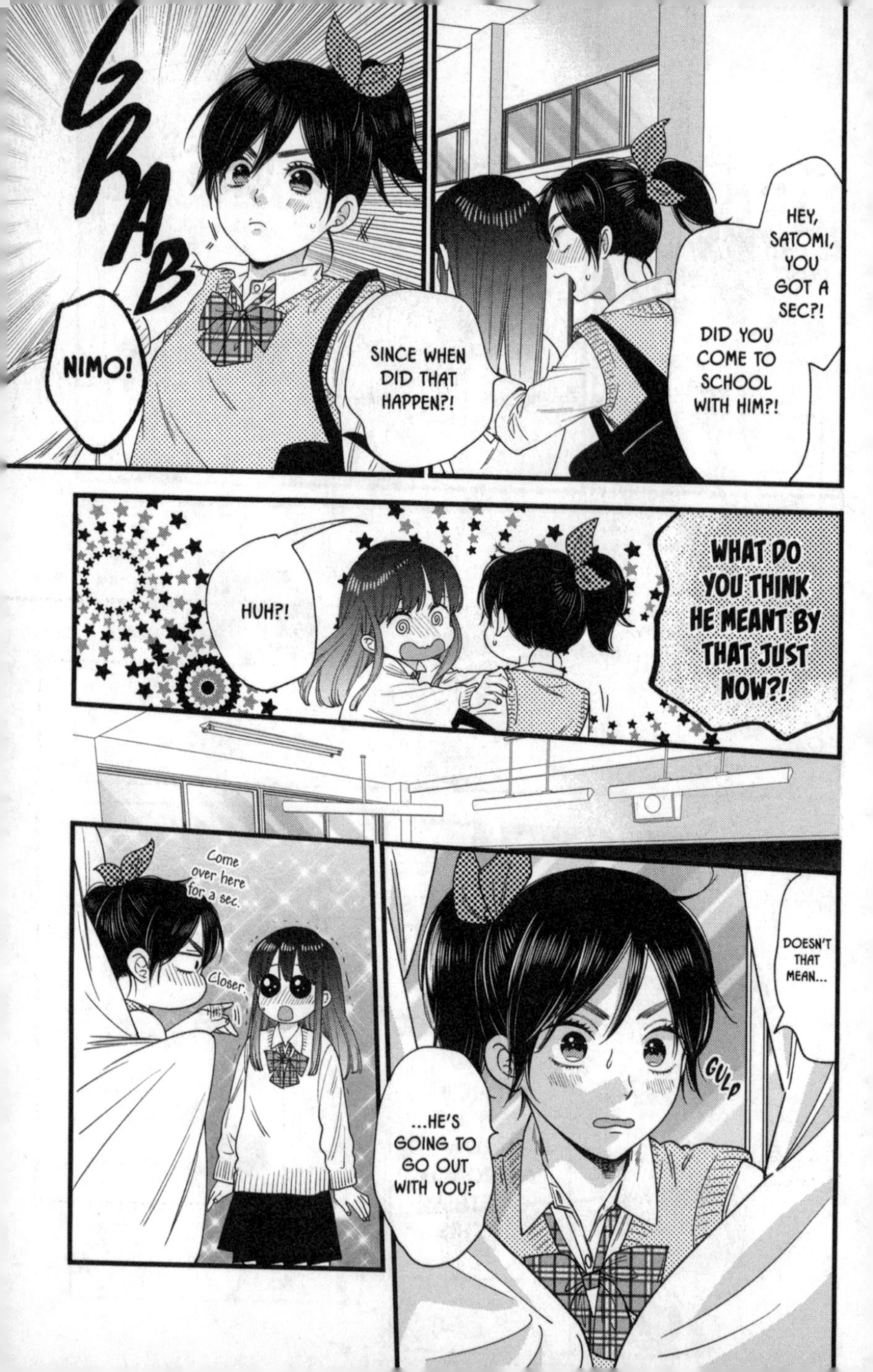
HEY, SATOMI, YOU GOT A SEC?!
DID YOU COME TO SCHOOL WITH HIM?!
SINCE WHEN DID THAT HAPPEN?!
GRAB
NIMO!
WHAT DO YOU THINK HE MEANT BY THAT JUST NOW?!
HUH?!
DOESN'T THAT MEAN...
GULP
...HE'S GOING TO GO OUT WITH YOU?
Come over here for a sec.
Closer.

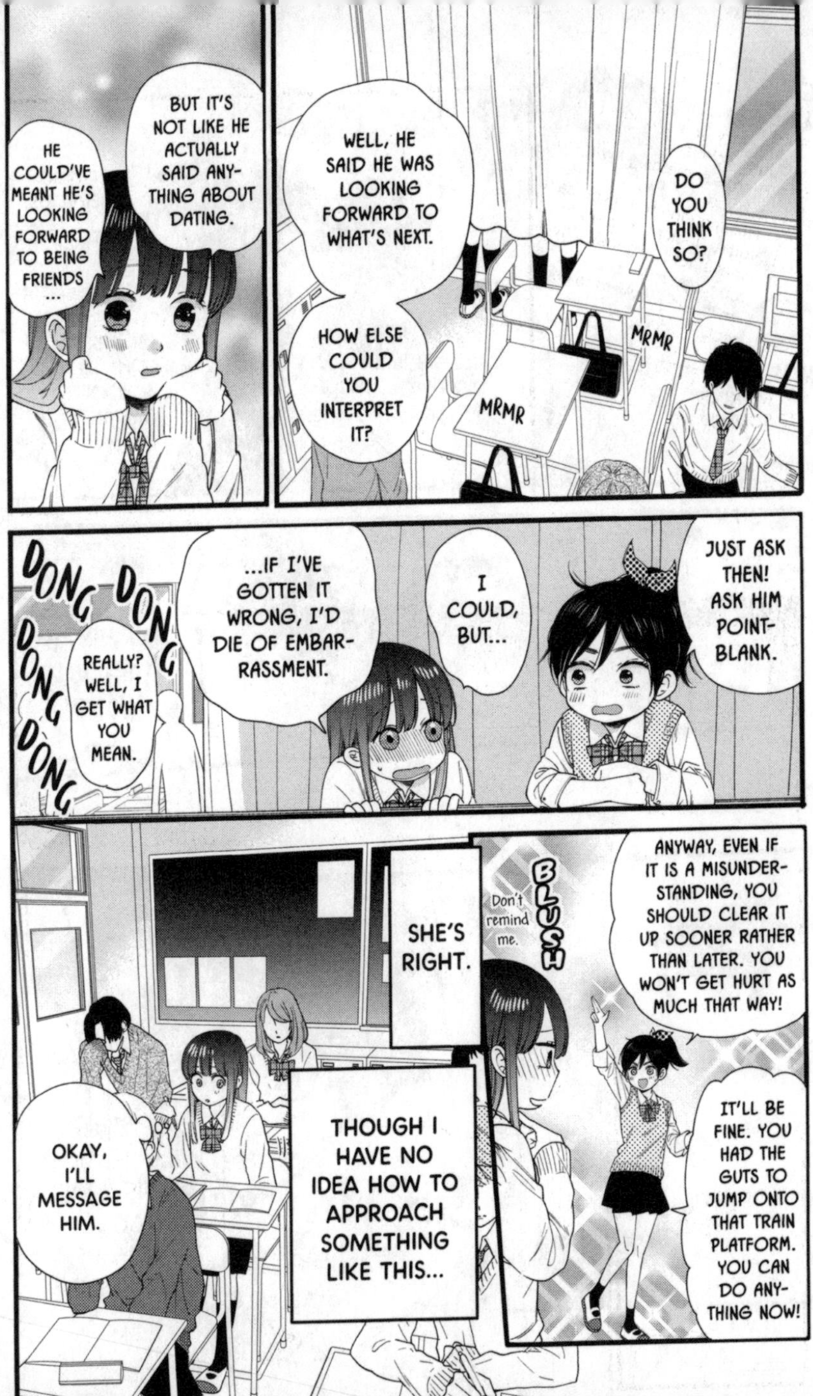
DO YOU THINK SO?
WELL, HE SAID HE WAS LOOKING FORWARD TO WHAT'S NEXT.
HOW ELSE COULD YOU INTERPRET IT?
MRMR
MRMR
BUT IT'S NOT LIKE HE ACTUALLY SAID ANYTHING ABOUT DATING.
HE COULD'VE MEANT HE'S LOOKING FORWARD TO BEING FRIENDS...
JUST ASK THEN! ASK HIM POINT-BLANK.
I COULD, BUT...
...IF I'VE GOTTEN IT WRONG, I'D DIE OF EMBARRASSMENT.
REALLY? WELL, I GET WHAT YOU MEAN.
DONG DONG DONG DONG
ANYWAY, EVEN IF IT IS A MISUNDERSTANDING, YOU SHOULD CLEAR IT UP SOONER RATHER THAN LATER. YOU WON'T GET HURT AS MUCH THAT WAY!
IT'LL BE FINE. YOU HAD THE GUTS TO JUMP ONTO THAT TRAIN PLATFORM. YOU CAN DO ANYTHING NOW!
BLUSH
Don't remind me.
SHE'S RIGHT.
THOUGH I HAVE NO IDEA HOW TO APPROACH SOMETHING LIKE THIS...
OKAY, I'LL MESSAGE HIM.

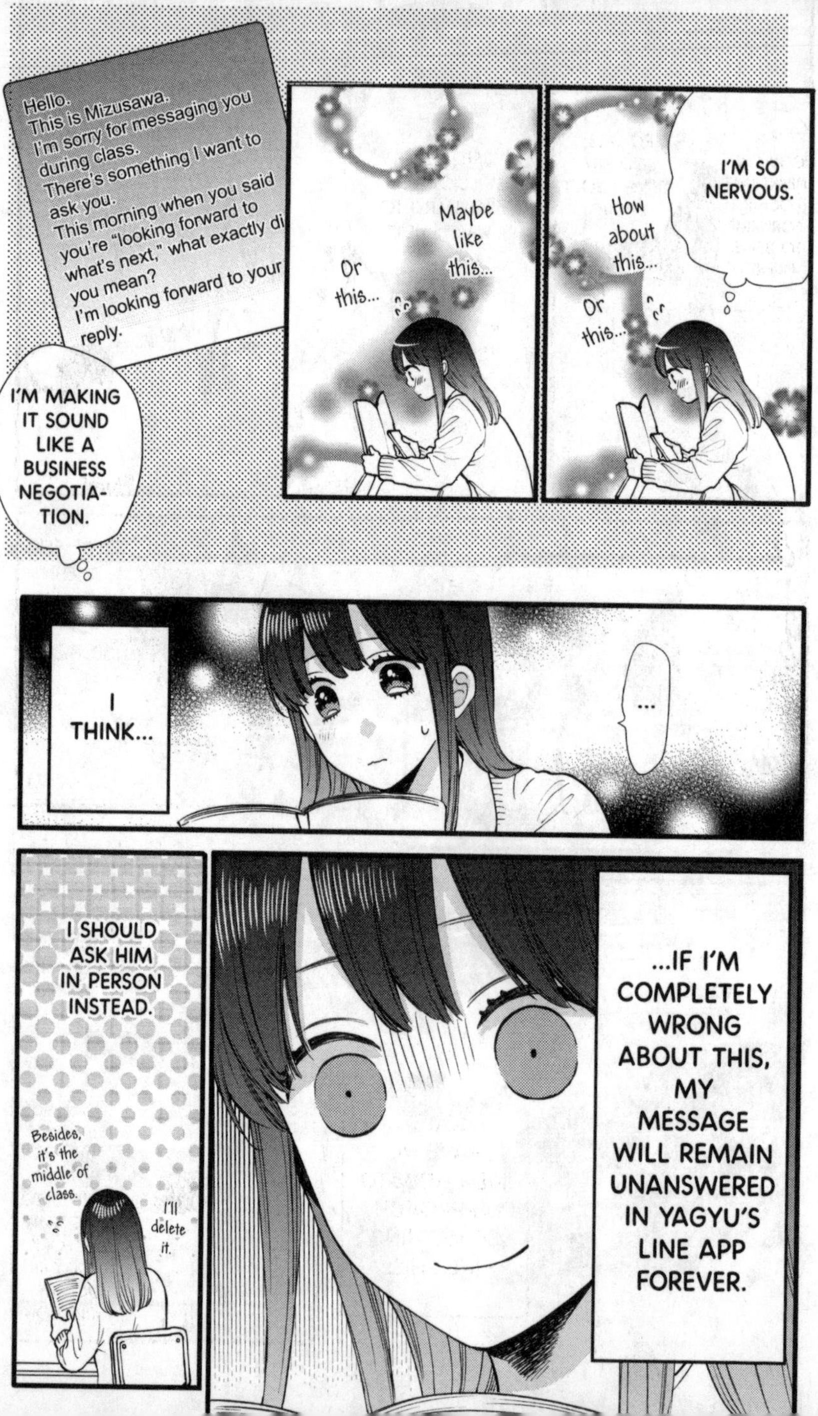
I'M SO NERVOUS.
How about this...
Or this...
Maybe like this...
Or this...
Hello.
This is Mizusawa.
I'm sorry for messaging you during class.
There's something I want to ask you.
This morning when you said you're "looking forward to what's next," what exactly di
you mean?
I'm looking forward to your
reply.
I'M MAKING IT SOUND LIKE A BUSINESS NEGOTIA-TION.
...
I THINK...
...IF I'M COMPLETELY WRONG ABOUT THIS, MY MESSAGE WILL REMAIN UNANSWERED IN YAGYU'S LINE APP FOREVER.
I SHOULD ASK HIM IN PERSON INSTEAD.
Besides, it's the middle of class.
I'll delete it.

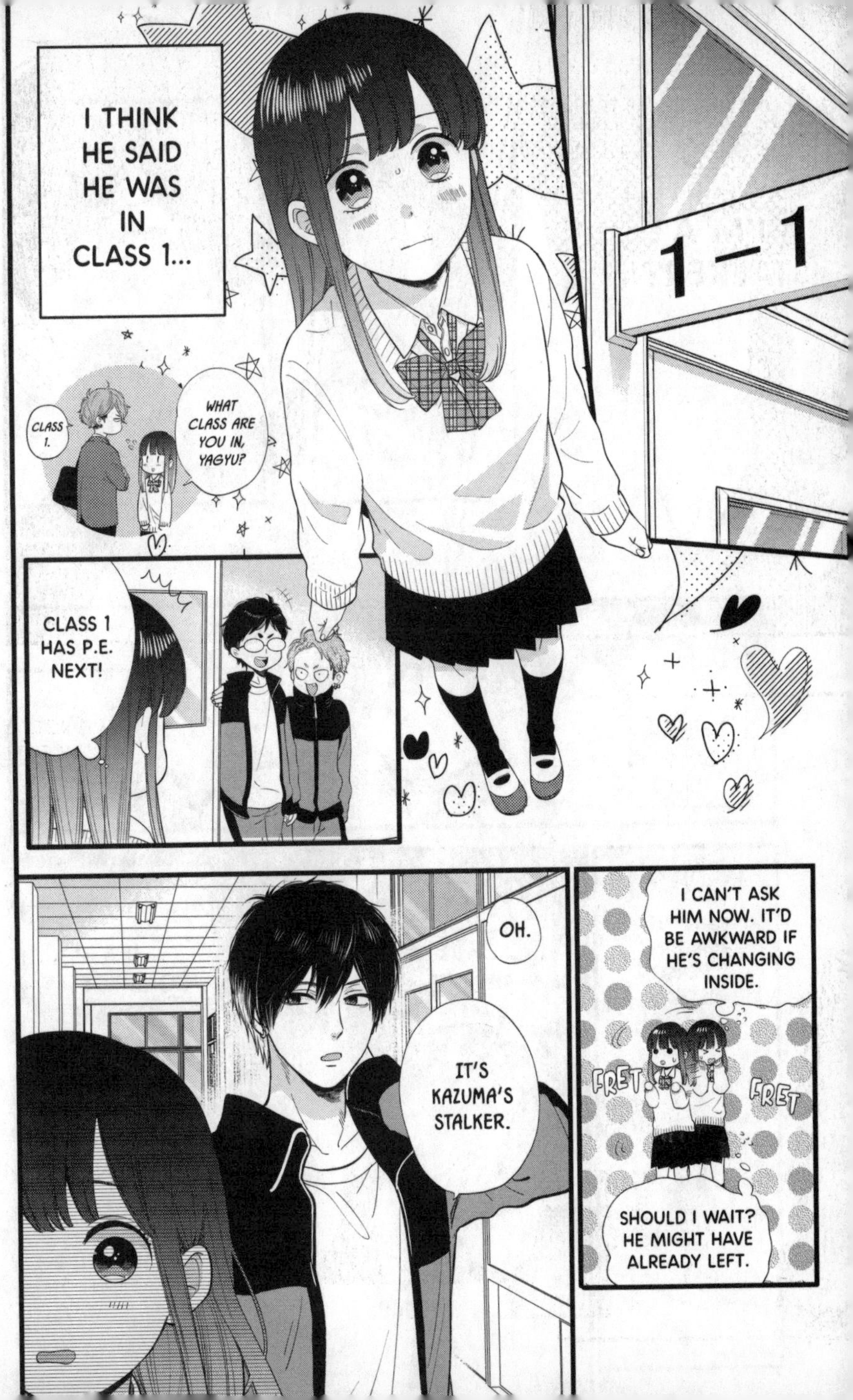
I THINK HE SAID HE WAS IN CLASS 1...
WHAT CLASS ARE YOU IN, YAGYU?
CLASS 1.
1-1
CLASS 1 HAS P.E. NEXT!
I CAN'T ASK HIM NOW. IT'D BE AWKWARD IF HE'S CHANGING INSIDE.
FRET
FRET
SHOULD I WAIT? HE MIGHT HAVE ALREADY LEFT.
OH.
IT'S KAZUMA'S STALKER.

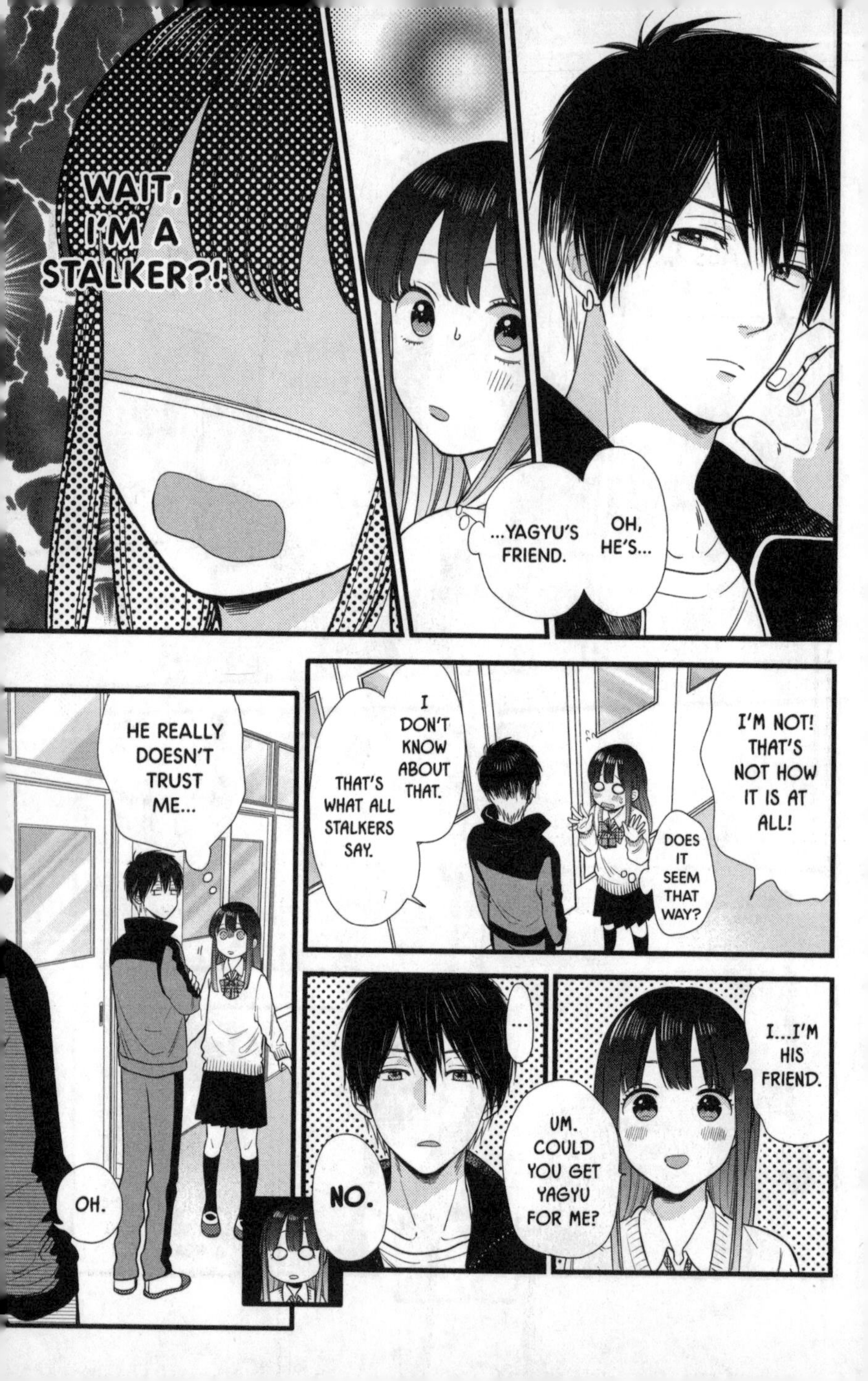
OH, HE'S...
...YAGYU'S FRIEND.
WAIT, I'M A STALKER?!
I'M NOT! THAT'S NOT HOW IT IS AT ALL!
DOES IT SEEM THAT WAY?
I DON'T KNOW ABOUT THAT.
THAT'S WHAT ALL STALKERS SAY.
I...I'M HIS FRIEND.
UM. COULD YOU GET YAGYU FOR ME?
...
NO.
HE REALLY DOESN'T TRUST ME...
OH.

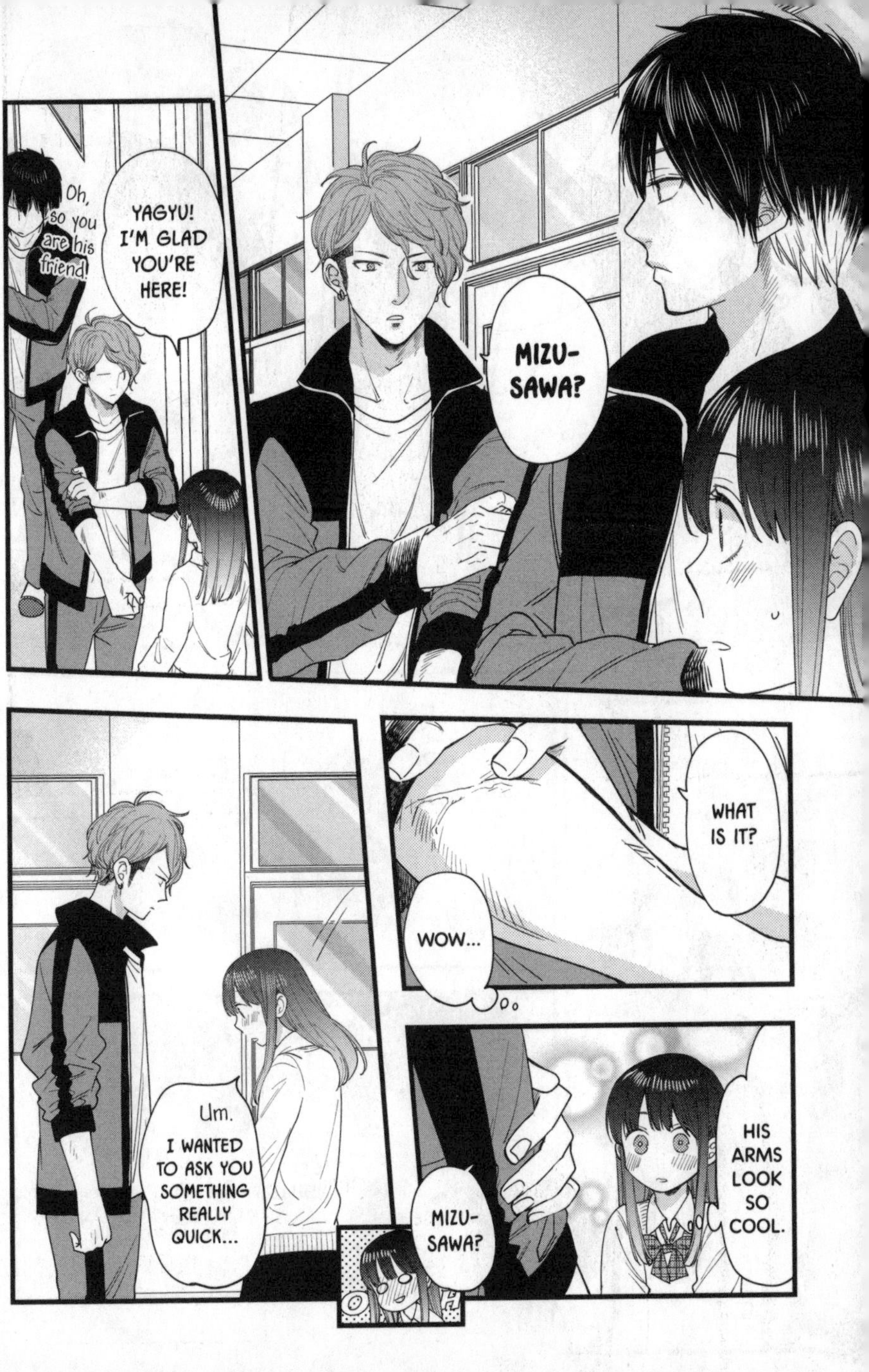
MIZU-SAWA?
YAGYU! I'M GLAD YOU'RE HERE!
Oh, so you are his friend!
WHAT IS IT?
WOW...
HIS ARMS LOOK SO COOL.
MIZU-SAWA?
Um. I WANTED TO ASK YOU SOMETHING REALLY QUICK...

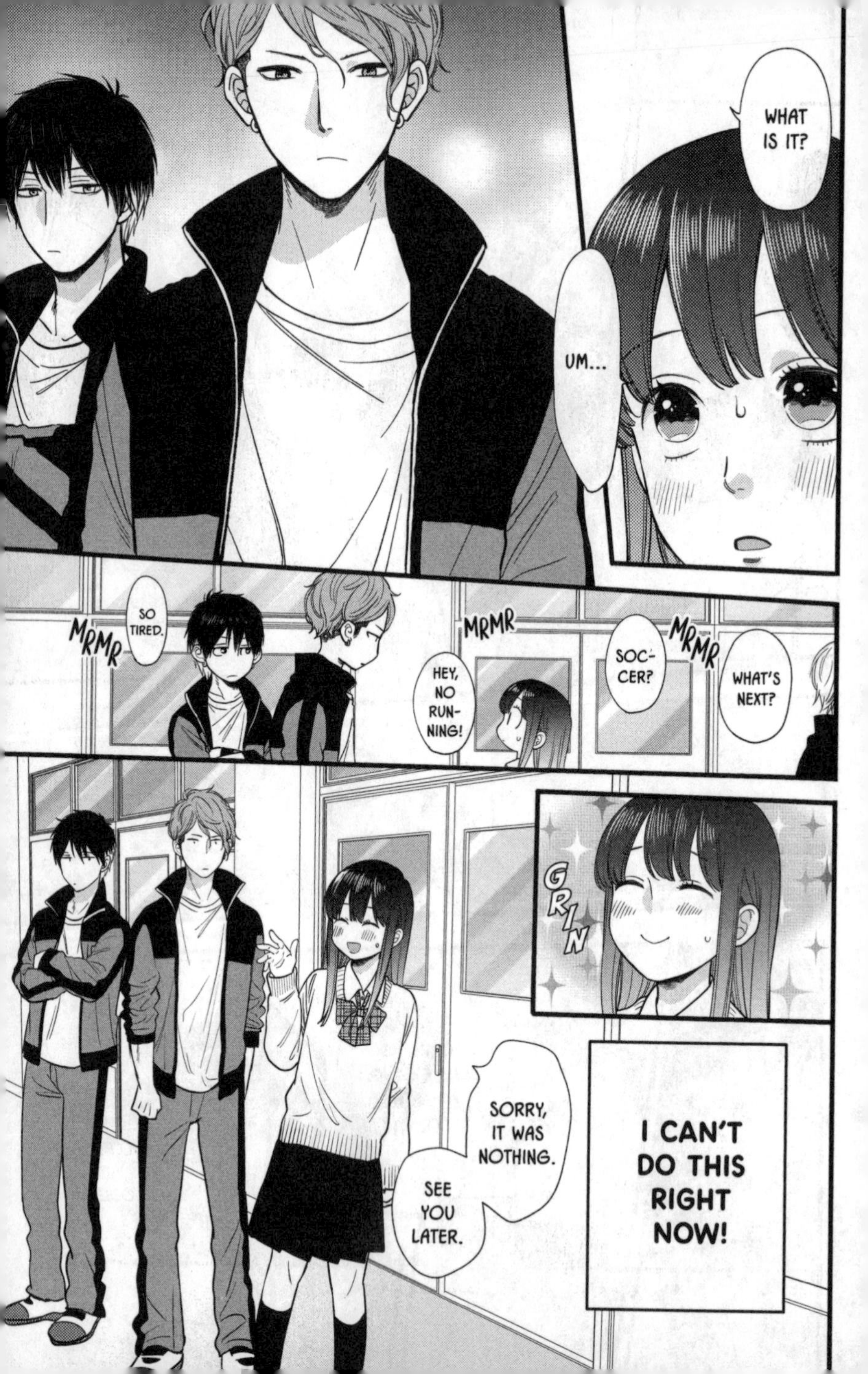
WHAT IS IT?
UM...
WHAT'S NEXT?
MRMR
SOC-CER?
HEY, NO RUN-NING!
MRMR
SO TIRED.
MRMR
GRIN
I CAN'T DO THIS RIGHT NOW!
SORRY, IT WAS NOTHING.
SEE YOU LATER.

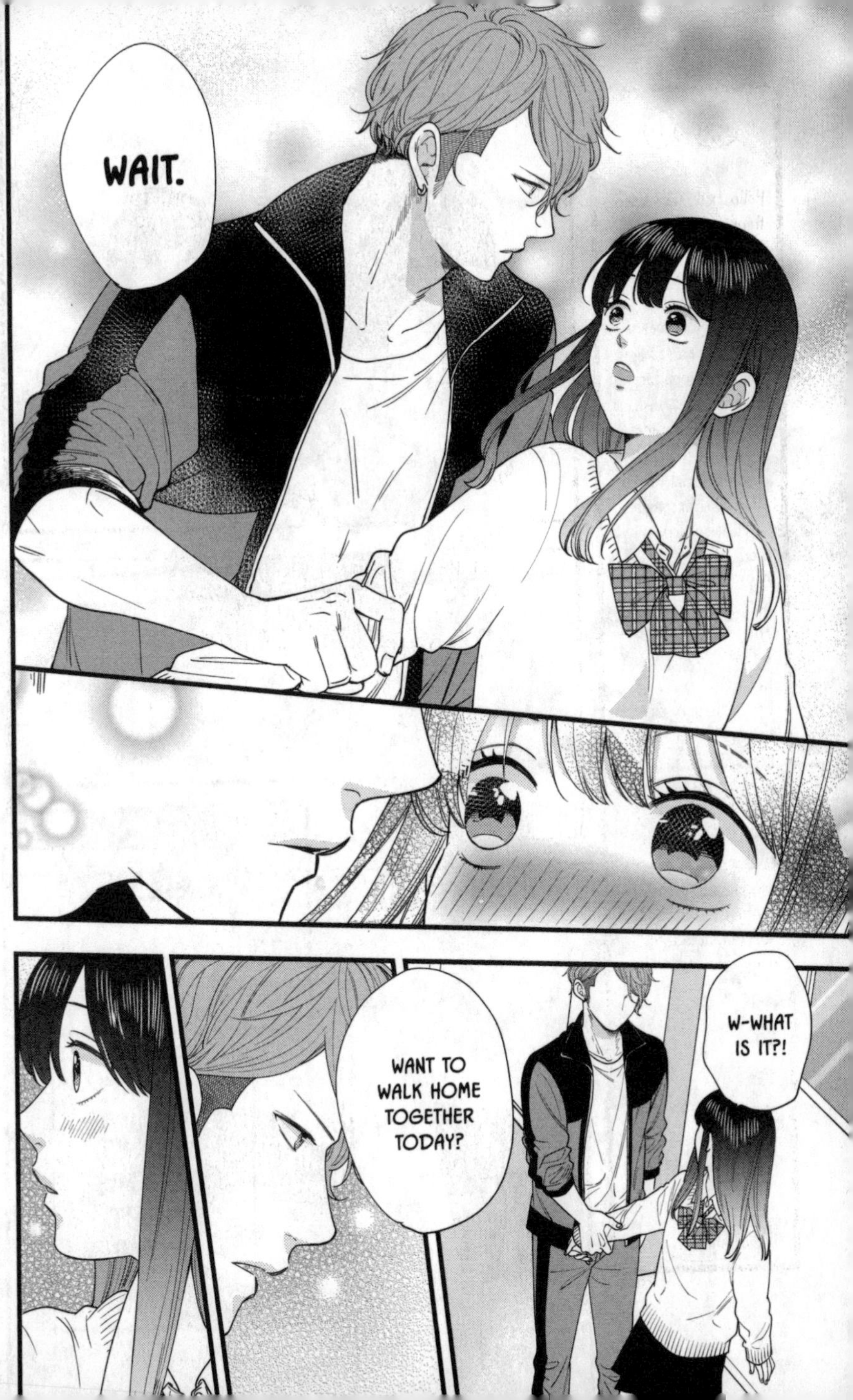
WAIT.
W-WHAT IS IT?!
WANT TO WALK HOME TOGETHER TODAY?

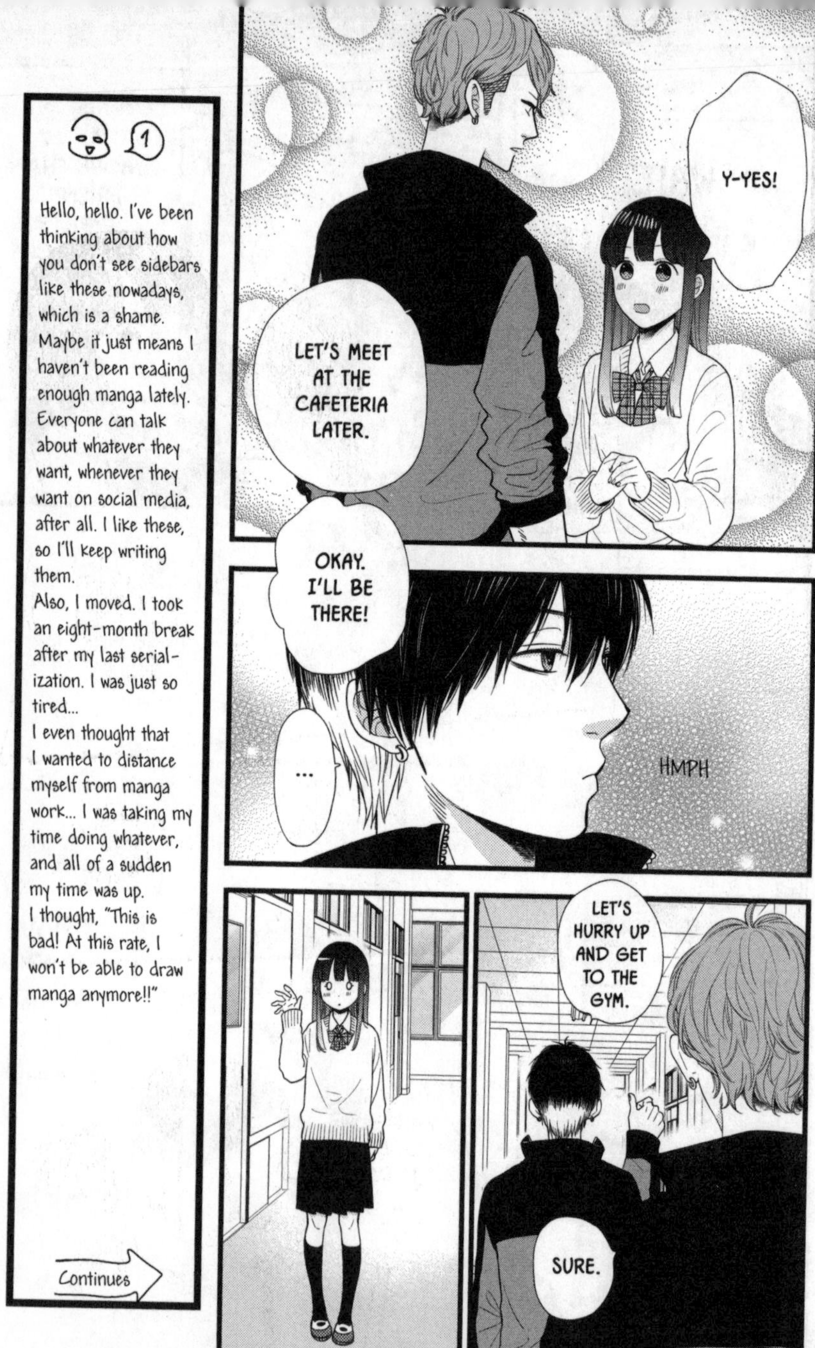
Y-YES!
LET'S MEET AT THE CAFETERIA LATER.
OKAY. I'LL BE THERE!
HMPH
...
LET'S HURRY UP AND GET TO THE GYM.
SURE.

1

Hello, hello. I've been thinking about how you don't see sidebars like these nowadays, which is a shame. Maybe it just means I haven't been reading enough manga lately. Everyone can talk about whatever they want, whenever they want on social media, after all. I like these, so I'll keep writing them.
Also, I moved. I took an eight-month break after my last serialization. I was just so tired...
I even thought that I wanted to distance myself from manga work... I was taking my time doing whatever, and all of a sudden my time was up.
I thought, "This is bad! At this rate, I won't be able to draw manga anymore!!"

Continues

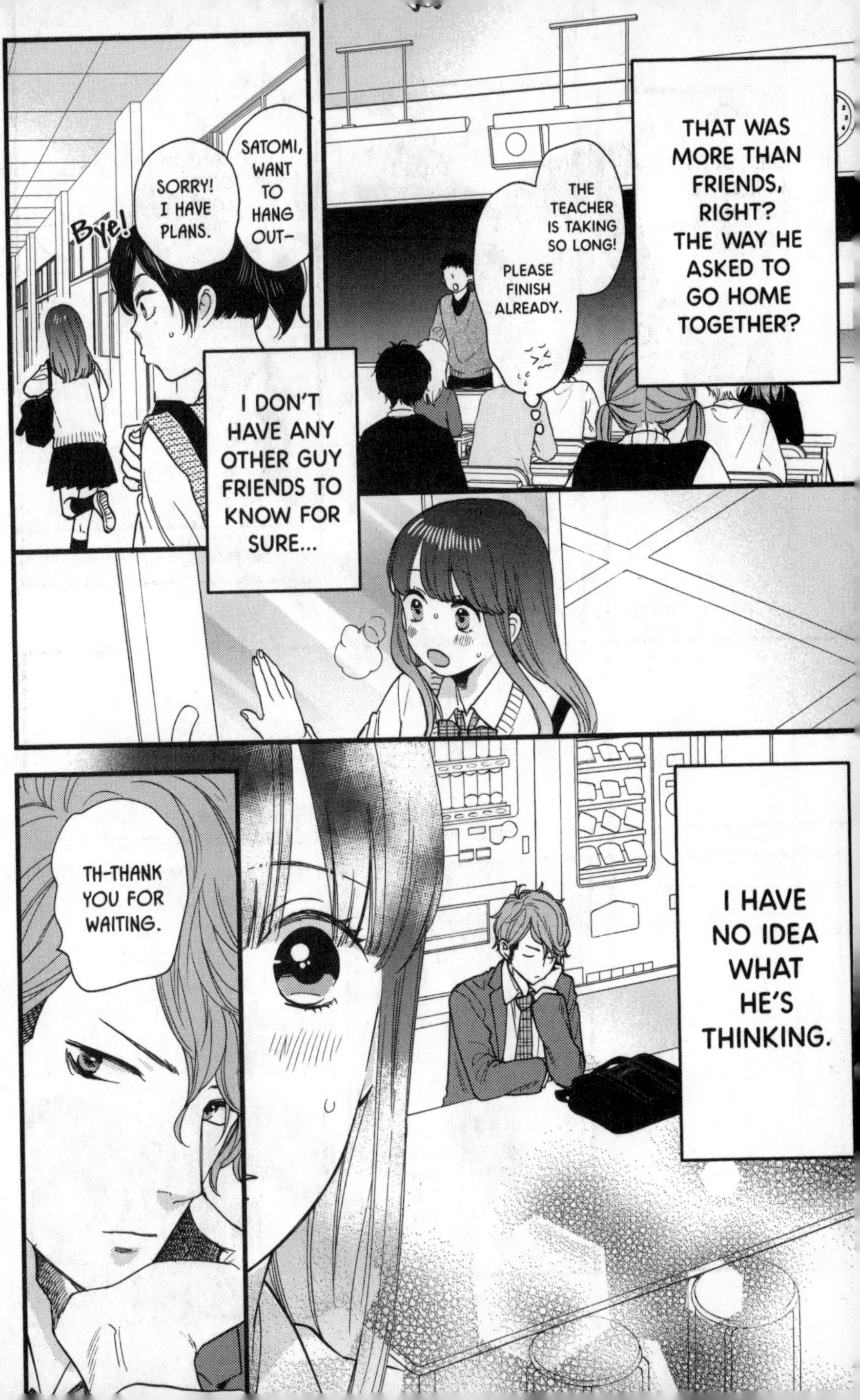

THAT WAS MORE THAN FRIENDS, RIGHT? THE WAY HE ASKED TO GO HOME TOGETHER?
THE TEACHER IS TAKING SO LONG!
PLEASE FINISH ALREADY.
SATOMI, WANT TO HANG OUT—
SORRY! I HAVE PLANS.
Bye!
I DON'T HAVE ANY OTHER GUY FRIENDS TO KNOW FOR SURE...
I HAVE NO IDEA WHAT HE'S THINKING.
TH-THANK YOU FOR WAITING.

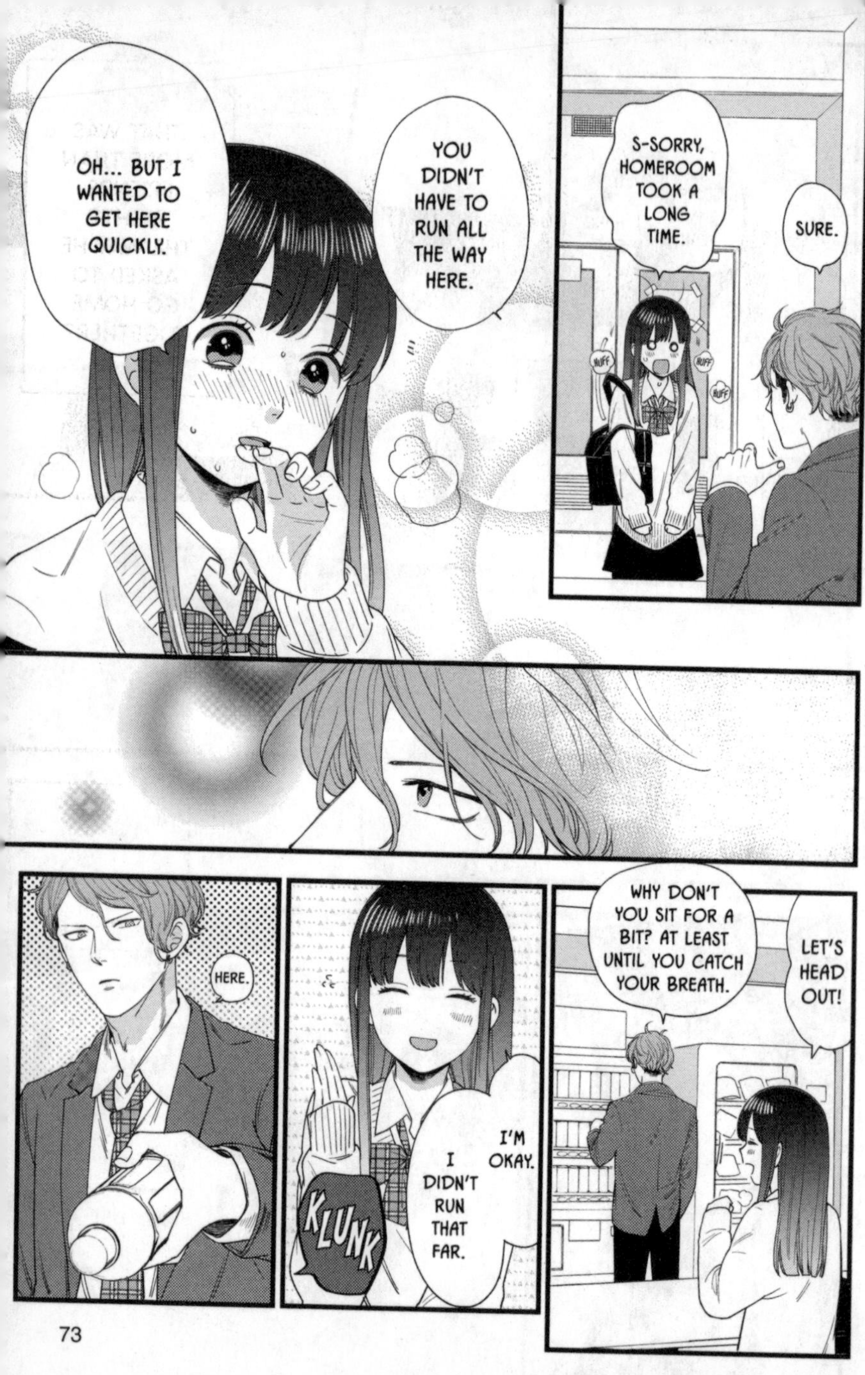
S-SORRY, HOMEROOM TOOK A LONG TIME.
HUFF
HUFF
HUFF
SURE.
YOU DIDN'T HAVE TO RUN ALL THE WAY HERE.
OH... BUT I WANTED TO GET HERE QUICKLY.
LET'S HEAD OUT!
WHY DON'T YOU SIT FOR A BIT? AT LEAST UNTIL YOU CATCH YOUR BREATH.
I'M OKAY.
I DIDN'T RUN THAT FAR.
KLUNK
HERE.

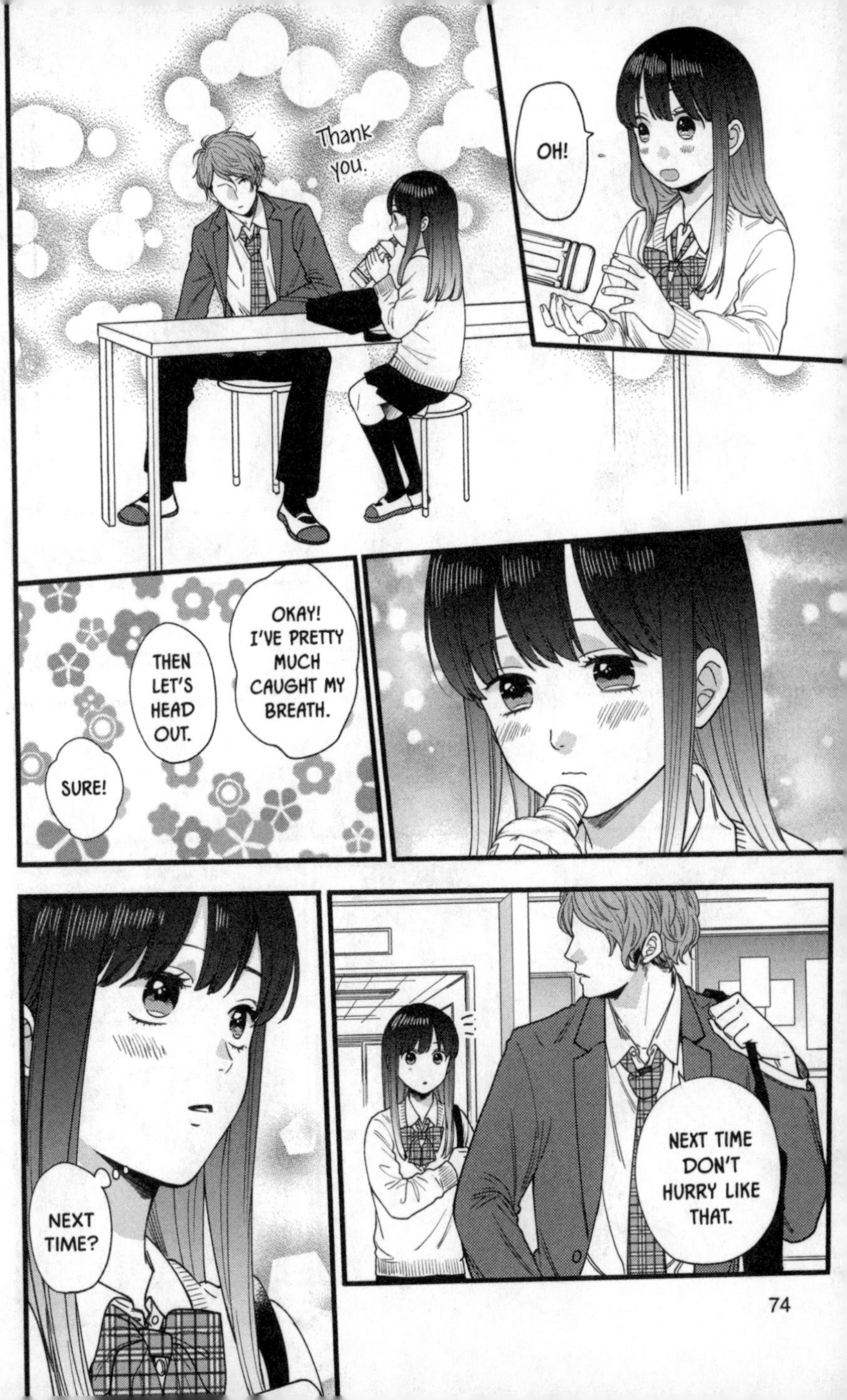
OH!
Thank you.
OKAY! I'VE PRETTY MUCH CAUGHT MY BREATH.
THEN LET'S HEAD OUT.
SURE!
NEXT TIME DON'T HURRY LIKE THAT.
NEXT TIME?

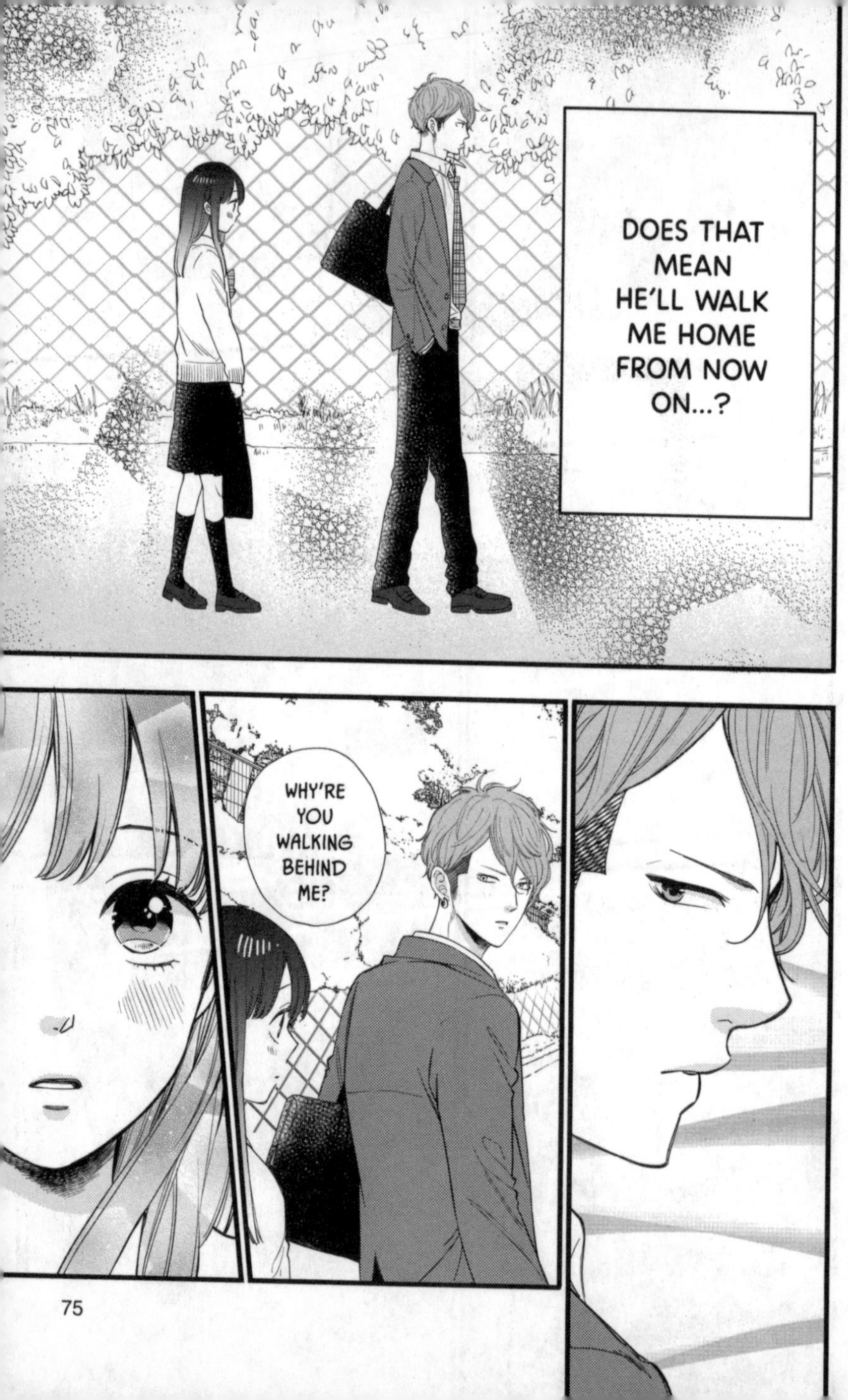
DOES THAT MEAN HE'LL WALK ME HOME FROM NOW ON...?
WHY'RE YOU WALKING BEHIND ME?

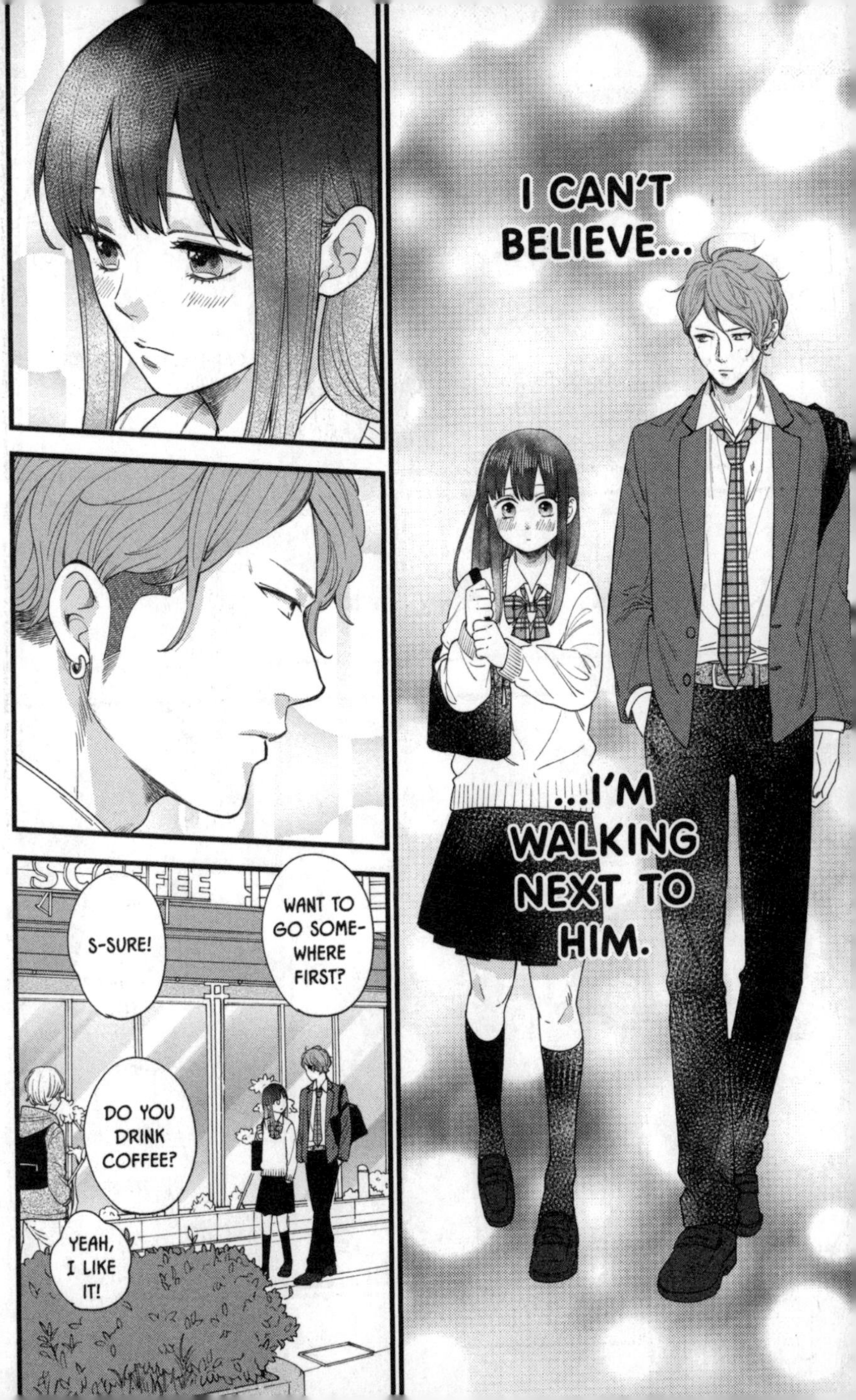
I CAN'T BELIEVE...
...I'M WALKING NEXT TO HIM.
WANT TO GO SOME-WHERE FIRST?
S-SURE!
DO YOU DRINK COFFEE?
YEAH, I LIKE IT!

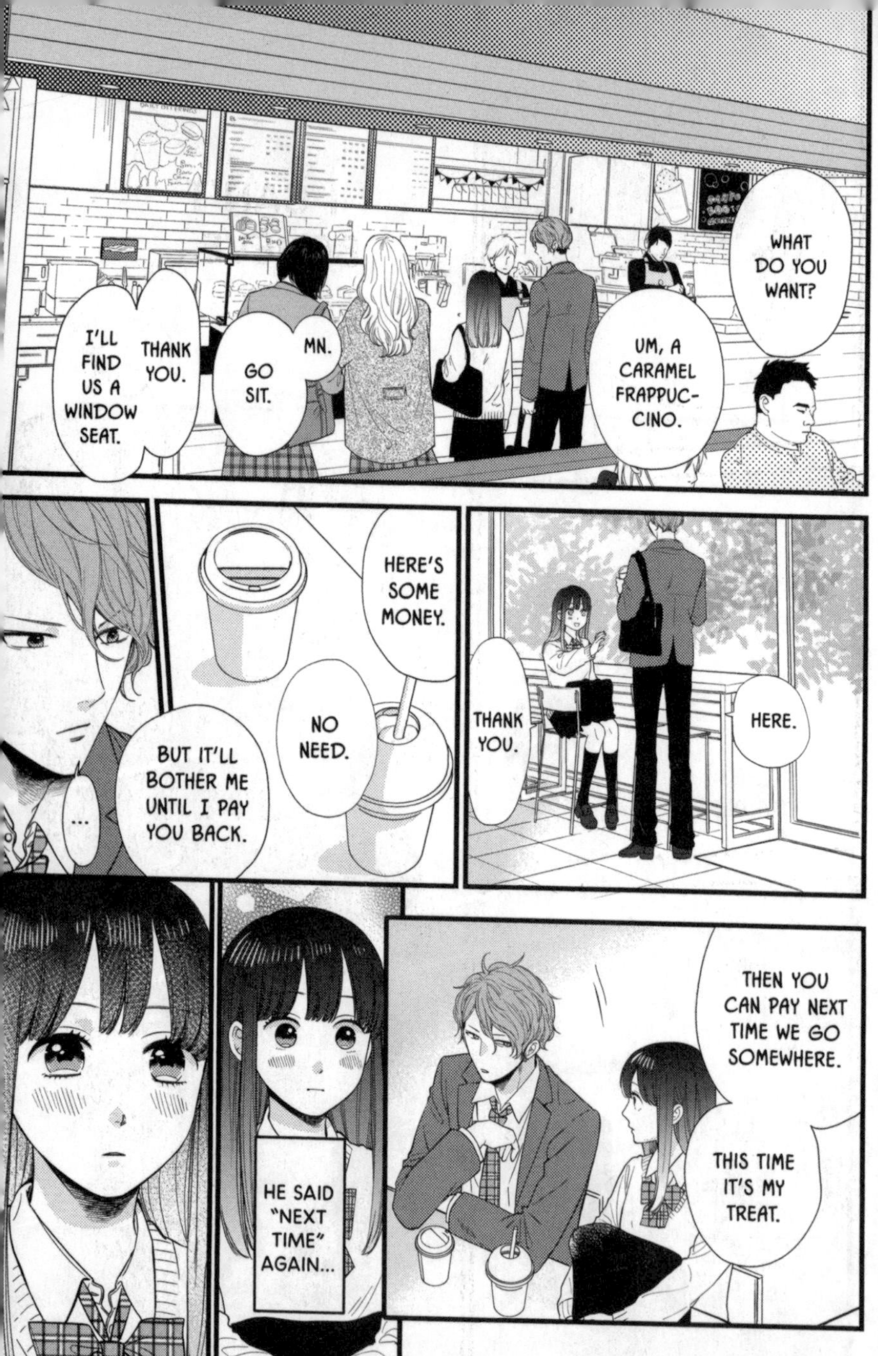
WHAT DO YOU WANT?
UM, A CARAMEL FRAPPUC-CINO.
MN.
GO SIT.
THANK YOU.
I'LL FIND US A WINDOW SEAT.
HERE.
THANK YOU.
HERE'S SOME MONEY.
NO NEED.
BUT IT'LL BOTHER ME UNTIL I PAY YOU BACK.
...
THEN YOU CAN PAY NEXT TIME WE GO SOMEWHERE.
THIS TIME IT'S MY TREAT.
HE SAID "NEXT TIME" AGAIN...

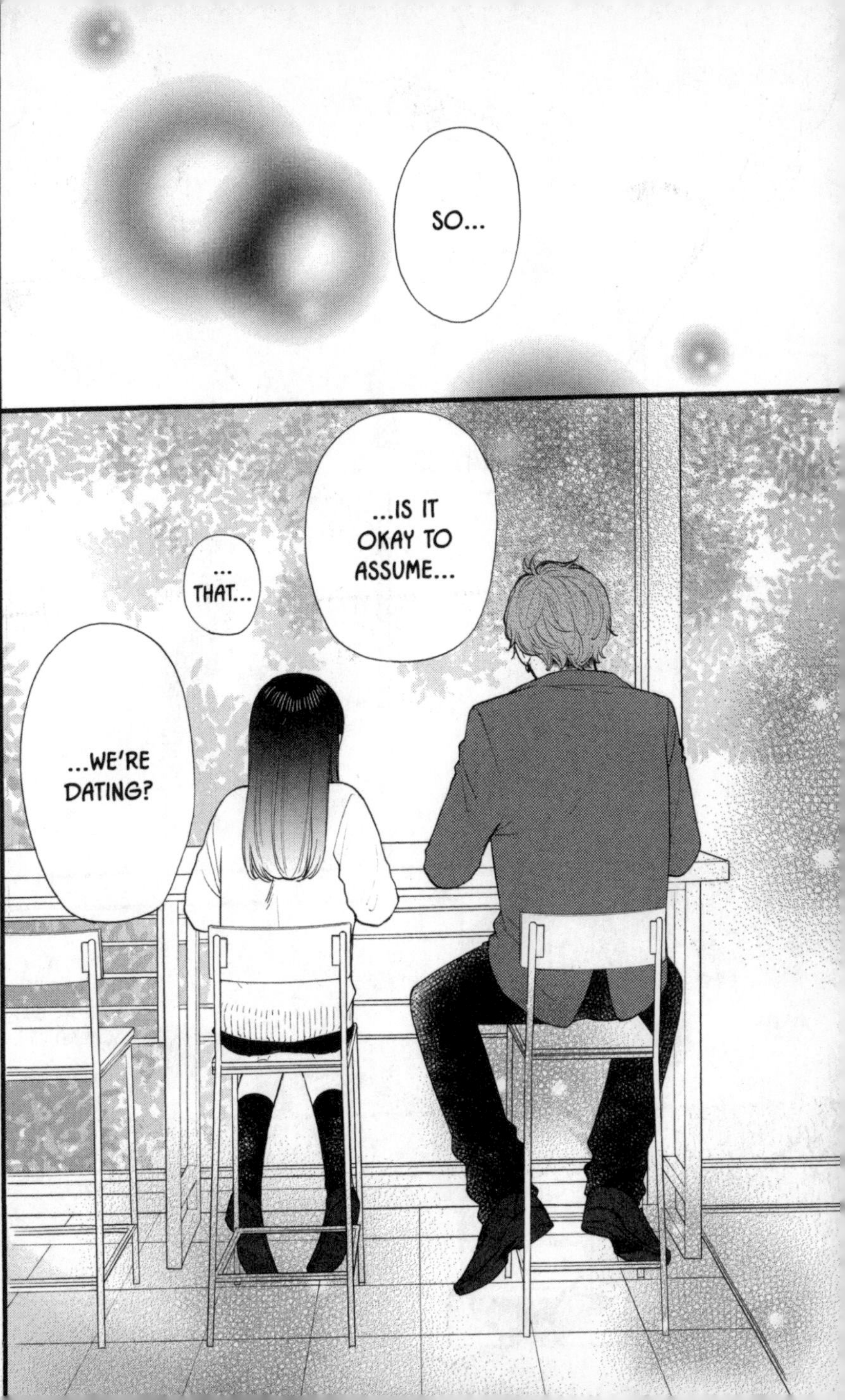
SO...
...IS IT OKAY TO ASSUME...
... THAT...
...WE'RE DATING?

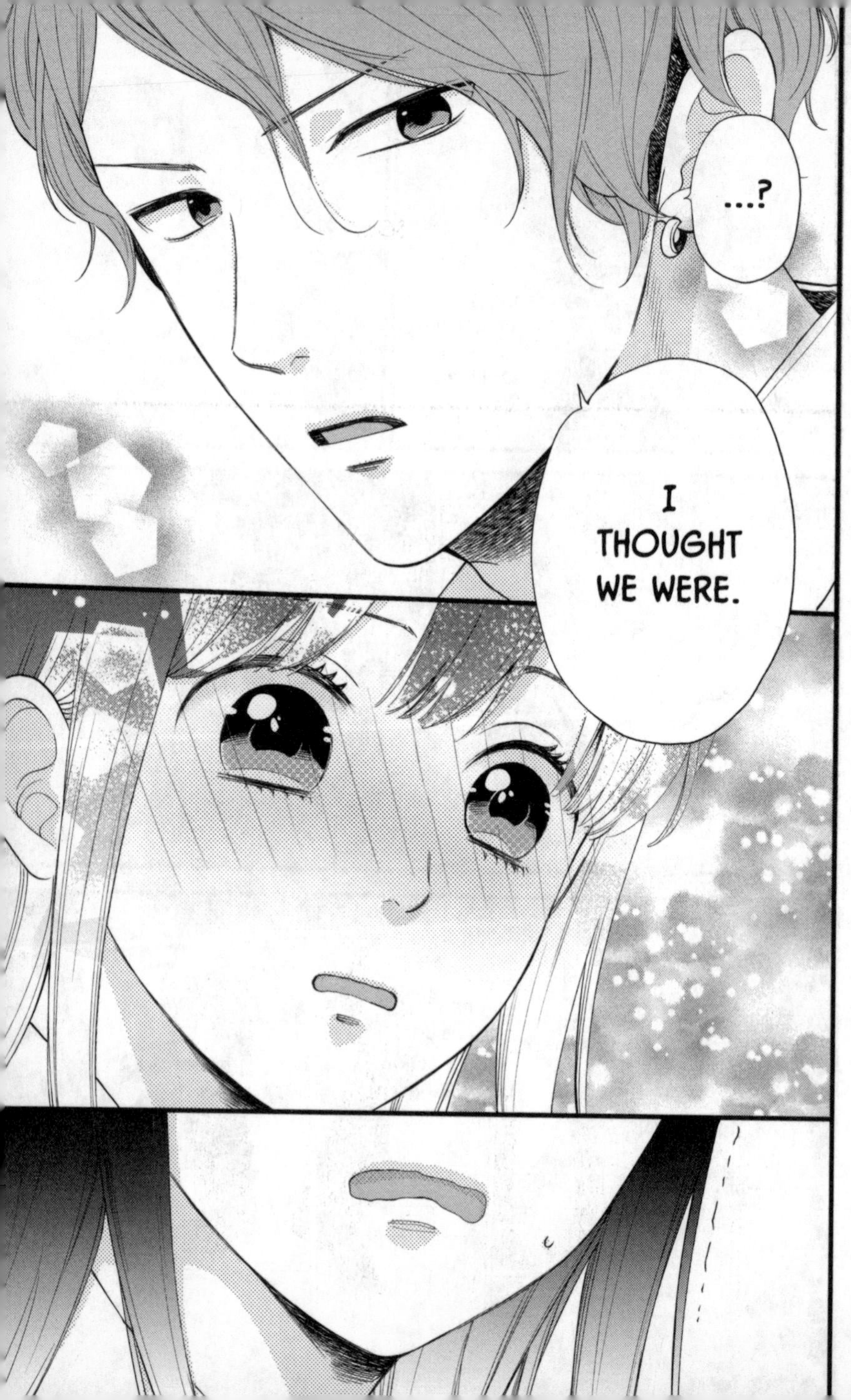
...?
I THOUGHT WE WERE.

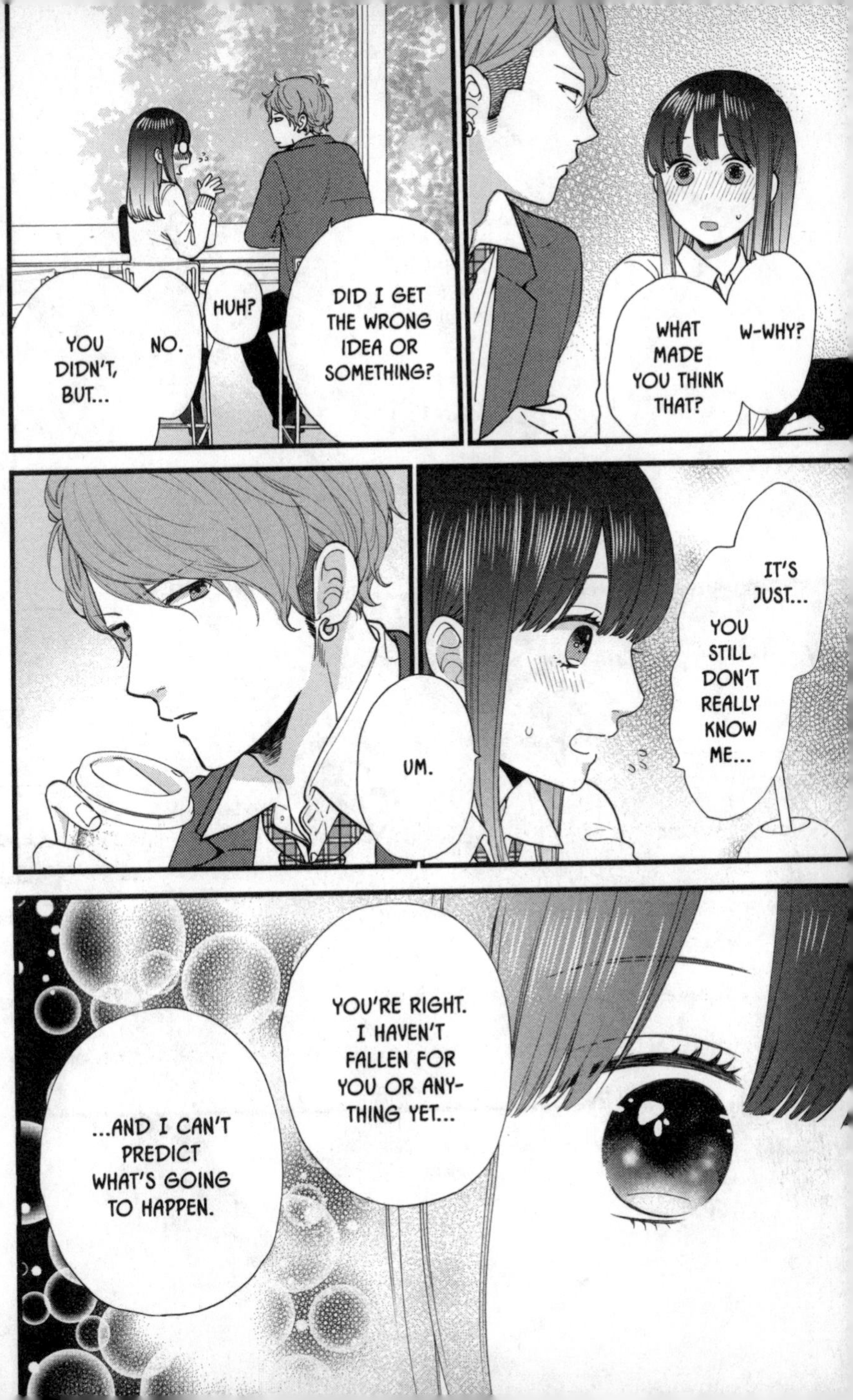
W-WHY?
WHAT MADE YOU THINK THAT?
DID I GET THE WRONG IDEA OR SOMETHING?
HUH?
NO.
YOU DIDN'T, BUT...
IT'S JUST...
YOU STILL DON'T REALLY KNOW ME...
UM.
YOU'RE RIGHT. I HAVEN'T FALLEN FOR YOU OR ANY-THING YET...
...AND I CAN'T PREDICT WHAT'S GOING TO HAPPEN.

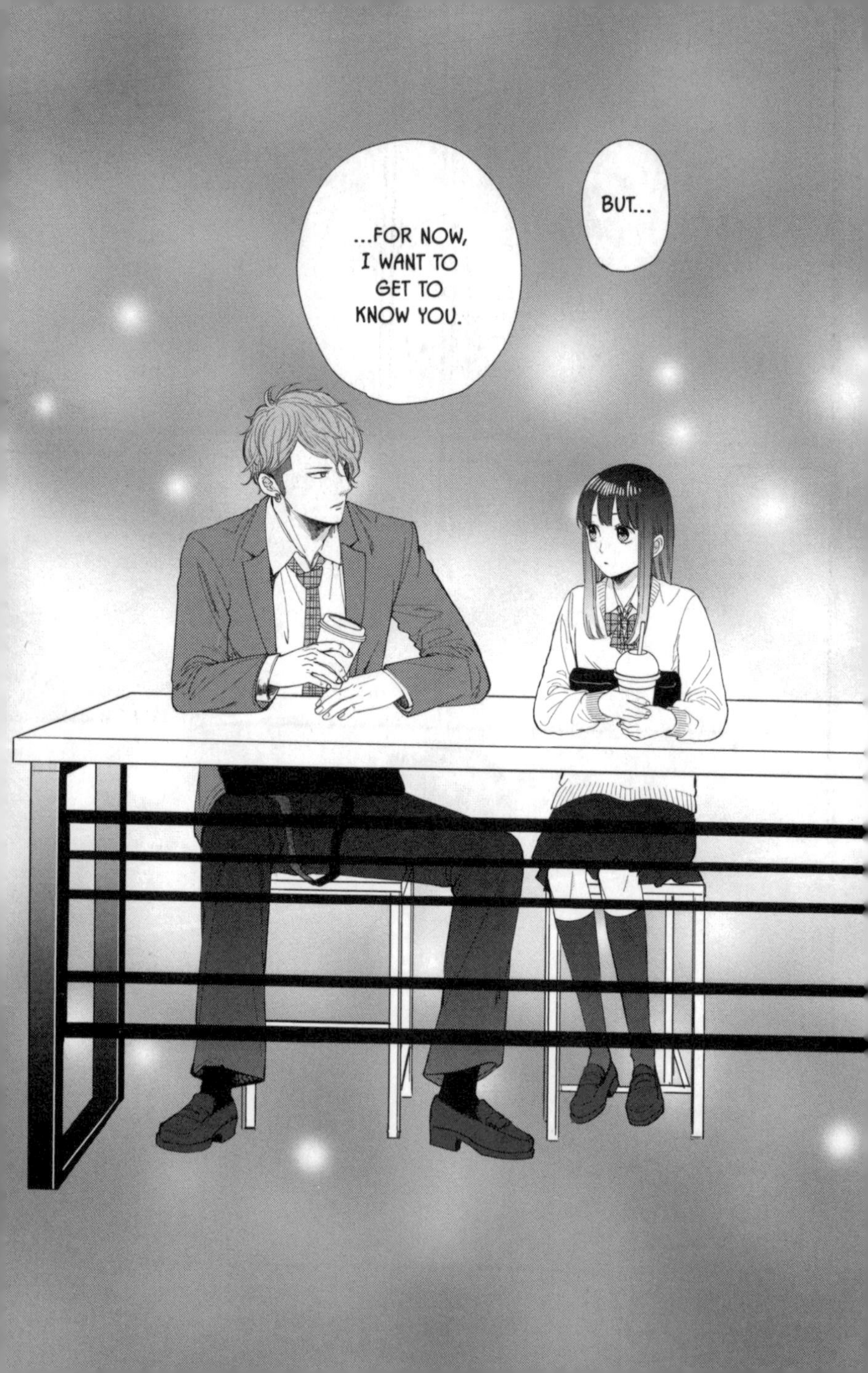
BUT...
...FOR NOW, I WANT TO GET TO KNOW YOU.

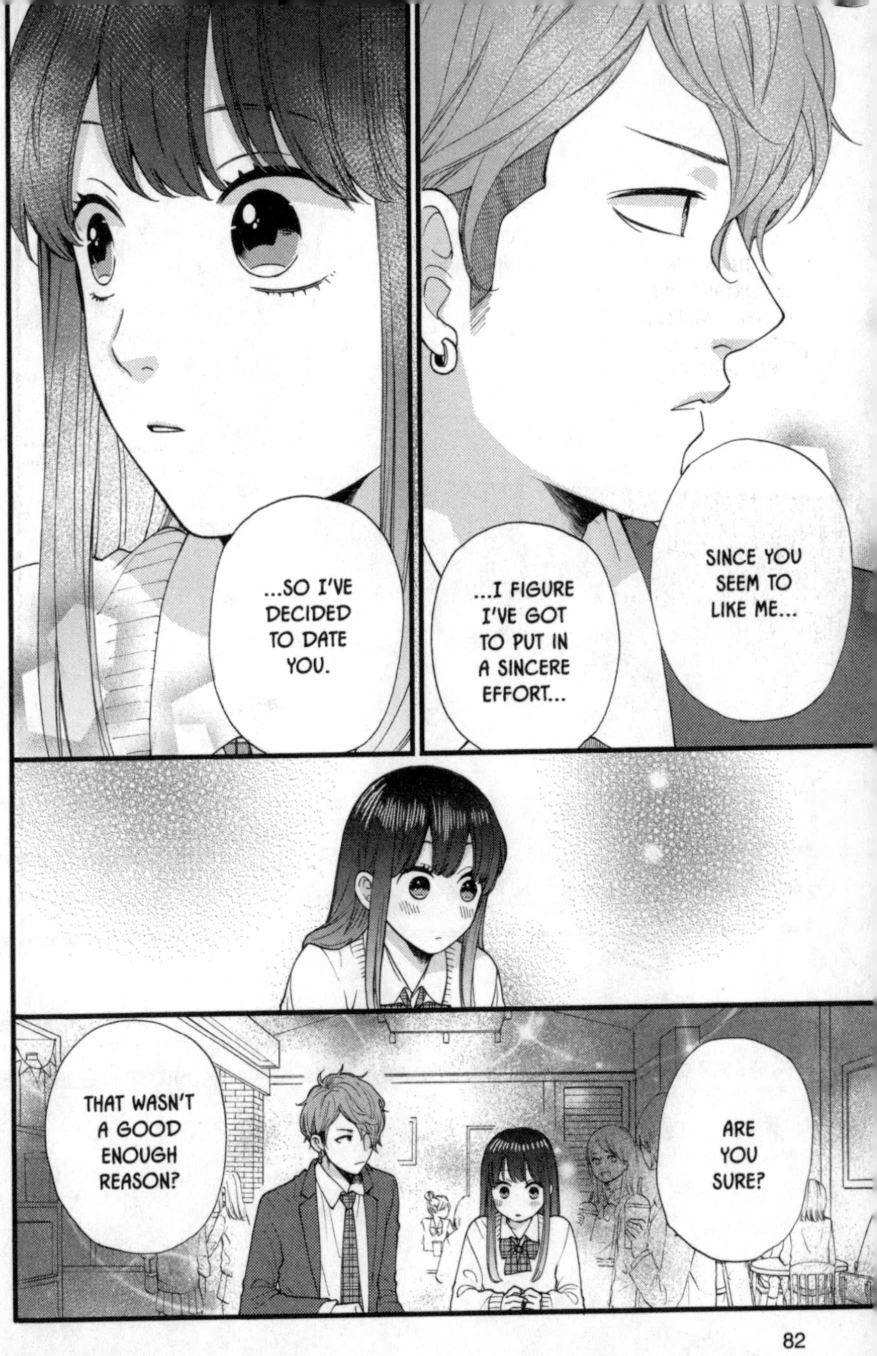
SINCE YOU SEEM TO LIKE ME...
...I FIGURE I'VE GOT TO PUT IN A SINCERE EFFORT...
...SO I'VE DECIDED TO DATE YOU.
ARE YOU SURE?
THAT WASN'T A GOOD ENOUGH REASON?

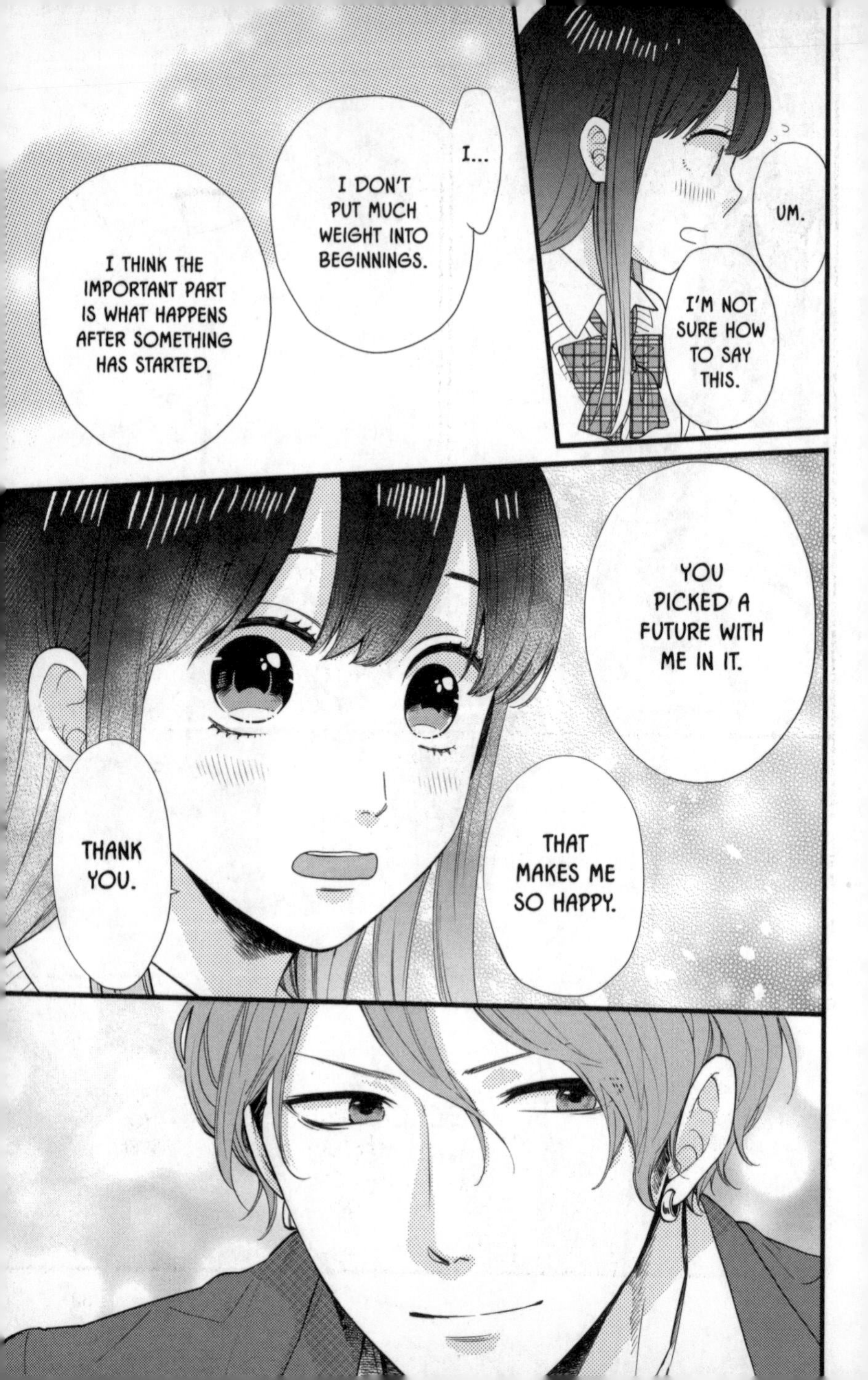
UM.
I'M NOT SURE HOW TO SAY THIS.
I...
I DON'T PUT MUCH WEIGHT INTO BEGINNINGS.
I THINK THE IMPORTANT PART IS WHAT HAPPENS AFTER SOMETHING HAS STARTED.
YOU PICKED A FUTURE WITH ME IN IT.
THAT MAKES ME SO HAPPY.
THANK YOU.

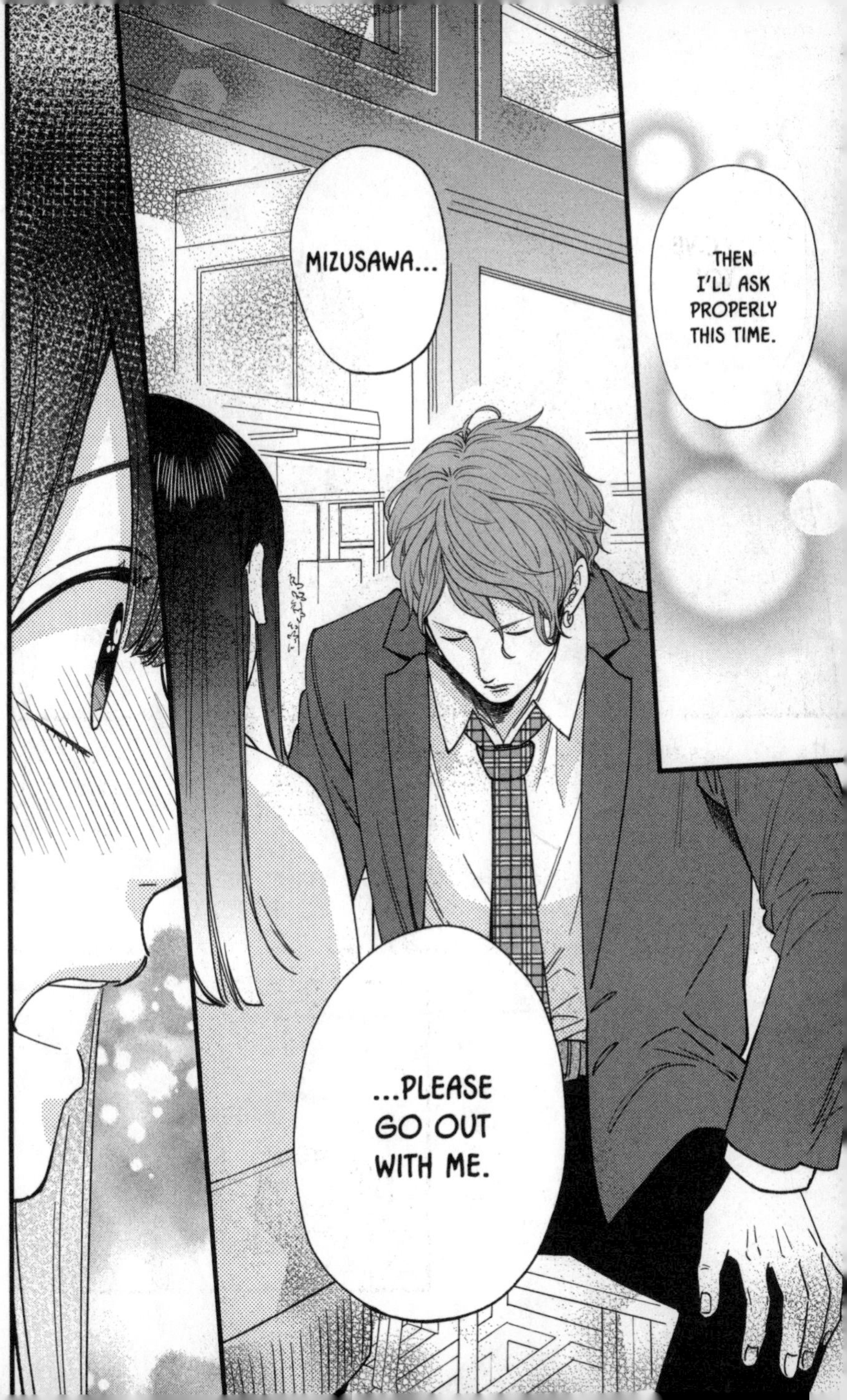
THEN I'LL ASK PROPERLY THIS TIME.
MIZUSAWA...
...PLEASE GO OUT WITH ME.

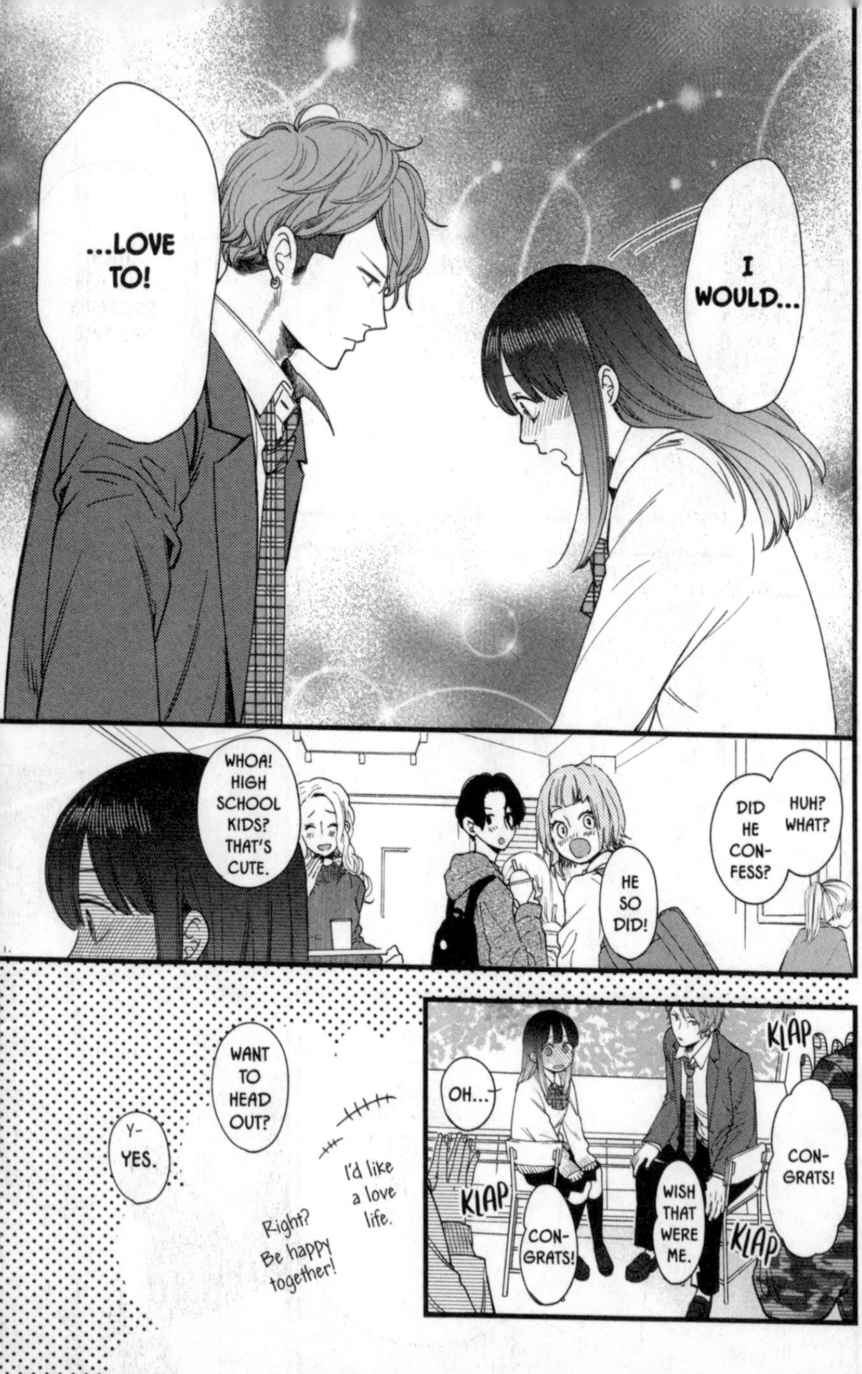
I WOULD...
...LOVE TO!
HUH? WHAT?
DID HE CON-FESS?
HE SO DID!
WHOA! HIGH SCHOOL KIDS? THAT'S CUTE.
KLAP
CON-GRATS!
KLAP
WISH THAT WERE ME.
CON-GRATS!
KLAP
OH...
I'd like a love life.
Right? Be happy together!
WANT TO HEAD OUT?
Y-YES.

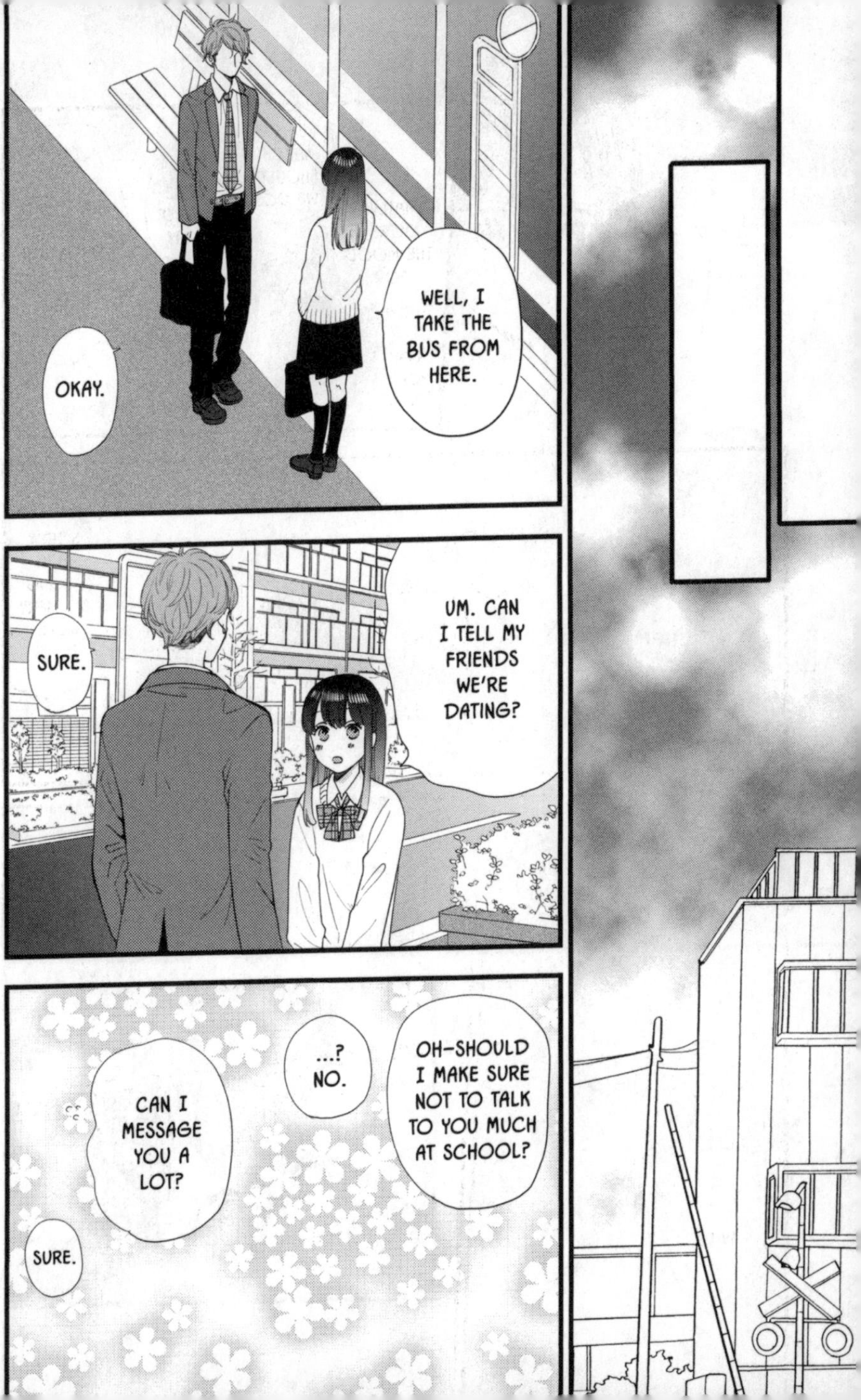
WELL, I TAKE THE BUS FROM HERE.
OKAY.
UM. CAN I TELL MY FRIENDS WE'RE DATING?
SURE.
OH—SHOULD I MAKE SURE NOT TO TALK TO YOU MUCH AT SCHOOL?
...? NO.
CAN I MESSAGE YOU A LOT?
SURE.

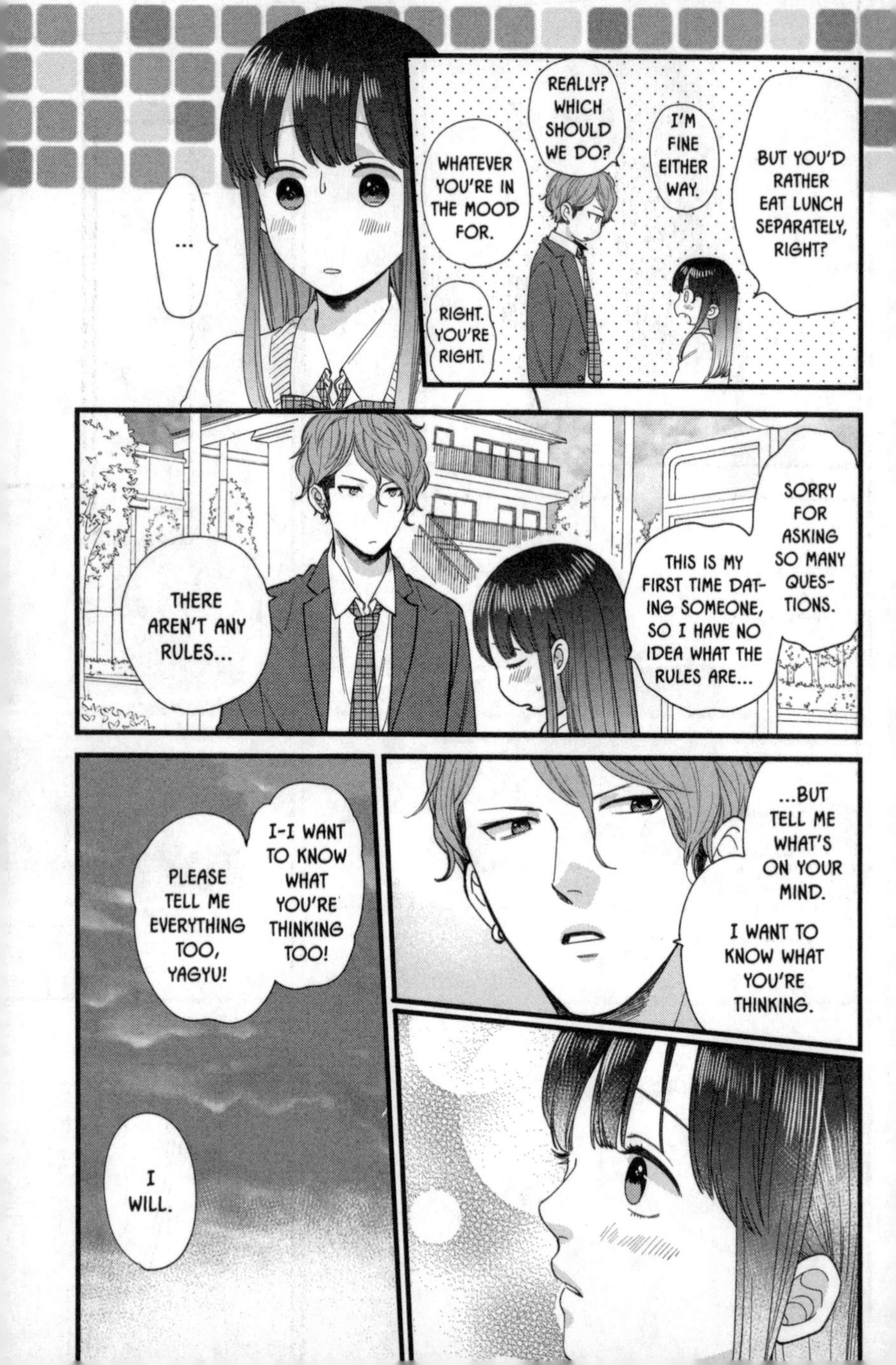
BUT YOU'D RATHER EAT LUNCH SEPARATELY, RIGHT?
I'M FINE EITHER WAY.
REALLY? WHICH SHOULD WE DO?
WHATEVER YOU'RE IN THE MOOD FOR.
RIGHT. YOU'RE RIGHT.
...
SORRY FOR ASKING SO MANY QUES-TIONS.
THIS IS MY FIRST TIME DAT-ING SOMEONE, SO I HAVE NO IDEA WHAT THE RULES ARE...
THERE AREN'T ANY RULES...
...BUT TELL ME WHAT'S ON YOUR MIND.
I WANT TO KNOW WHAT YOU'RE THINKING.
I-I WANT TO KNOW WHAT YOU'RE THINKING TOO!
PLEASE TELL ME EVERYTHING TOO, YAGYU!
I WILL.

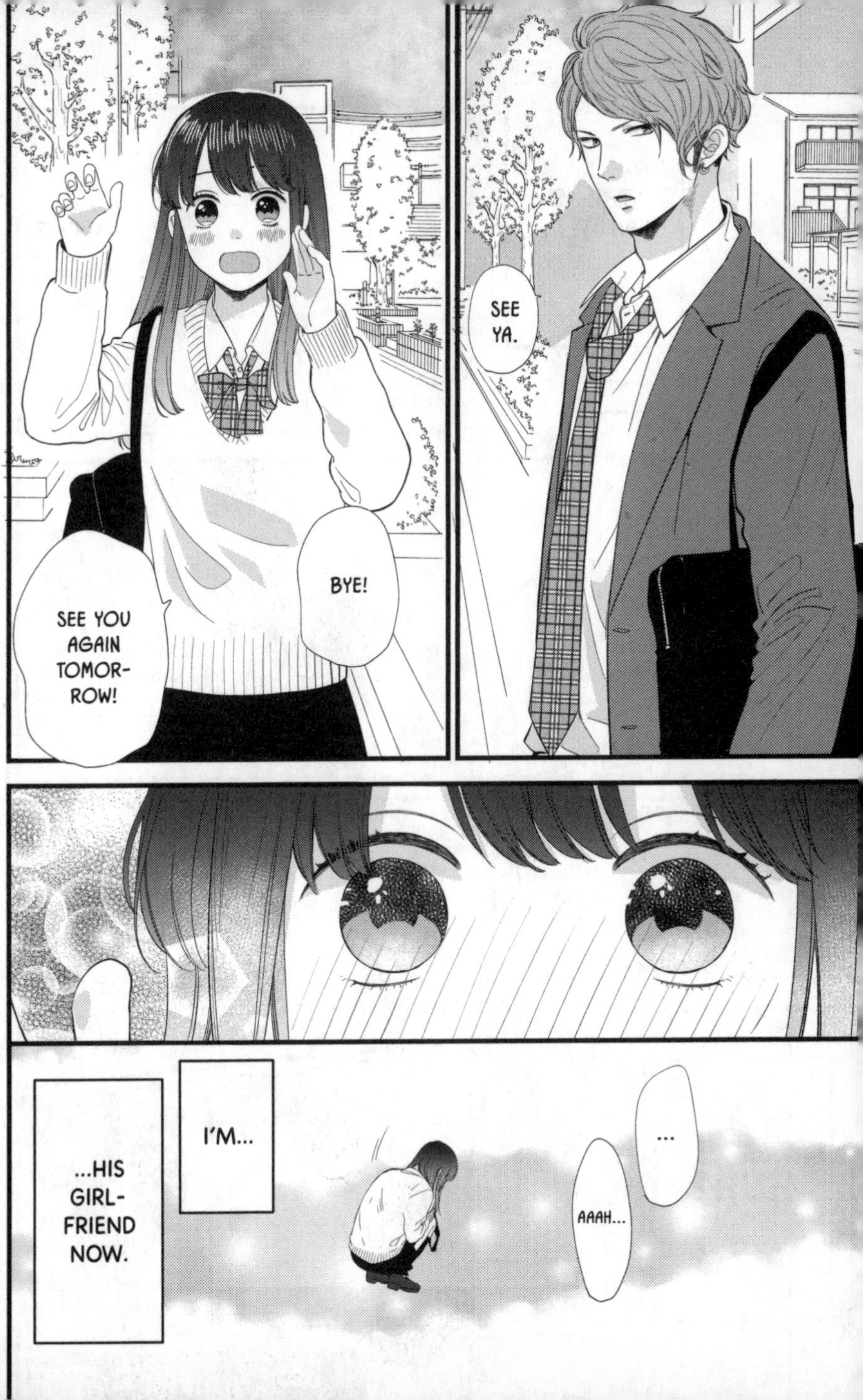
SEE YA.
BYE!
SEE YOU AGAIN TOMORROW!
...
AAAH...
I'M...
...HIS GIRLFRIEND NOW.

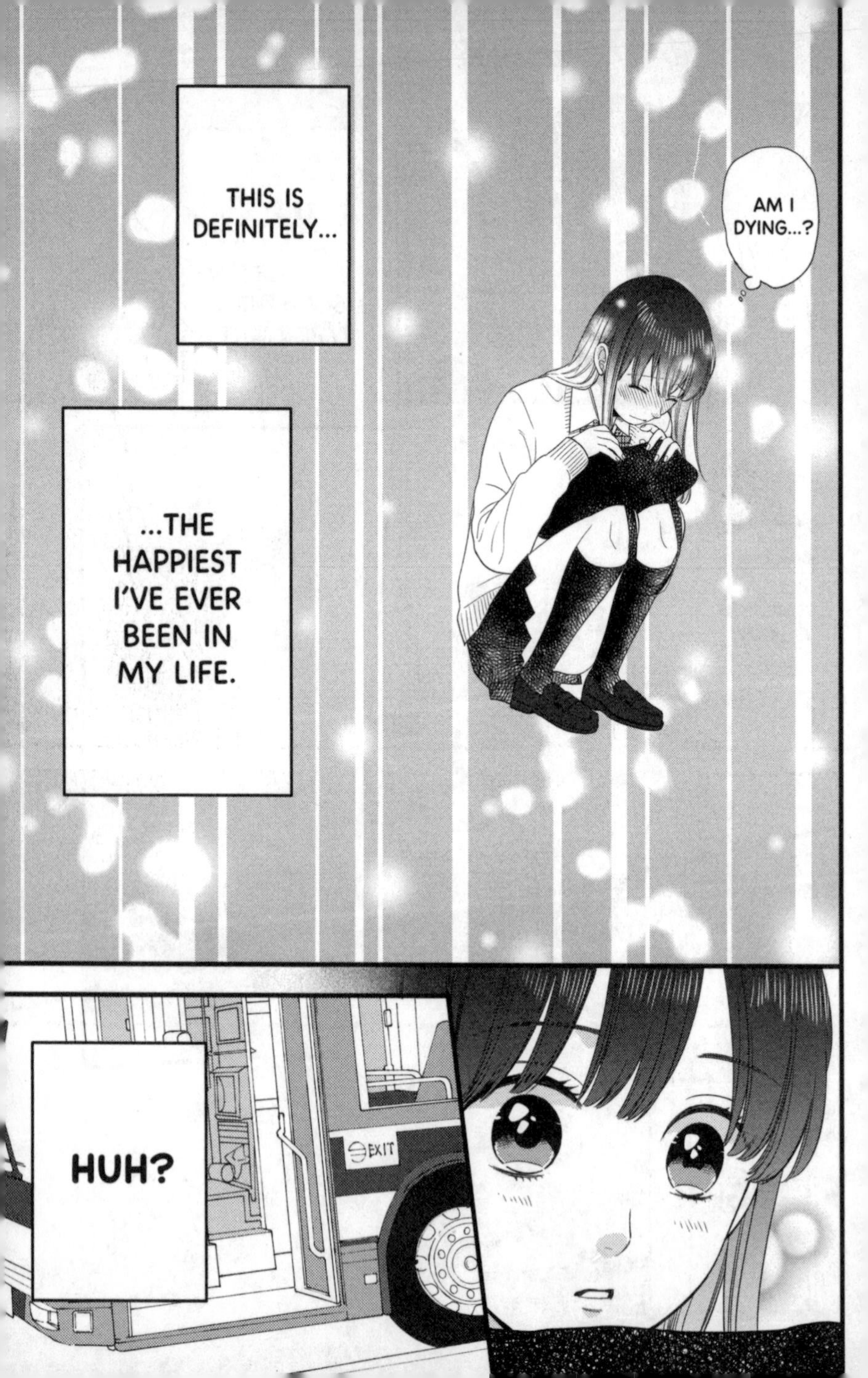
AM I DYING...?
THIS IS DEFINITELY...
...THE HAPPIEST I'VE EVER BEEN IN MY LIFE.
HUH?
EXIT

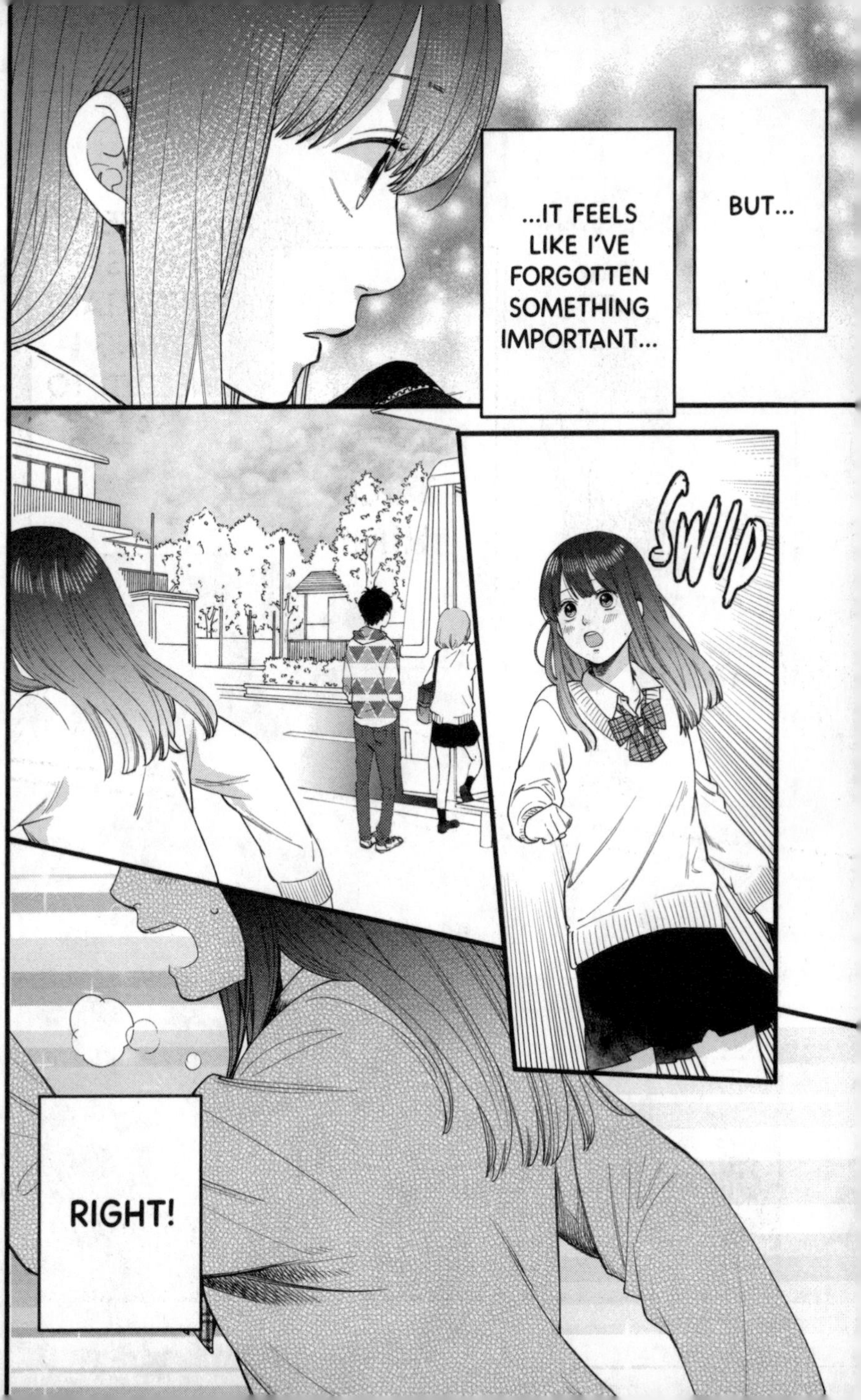
BUT...
...IT FEELS LIKE I'VE FORGOTTEN SOMETHING IMPORTANT...
SWIP
RIGHT!

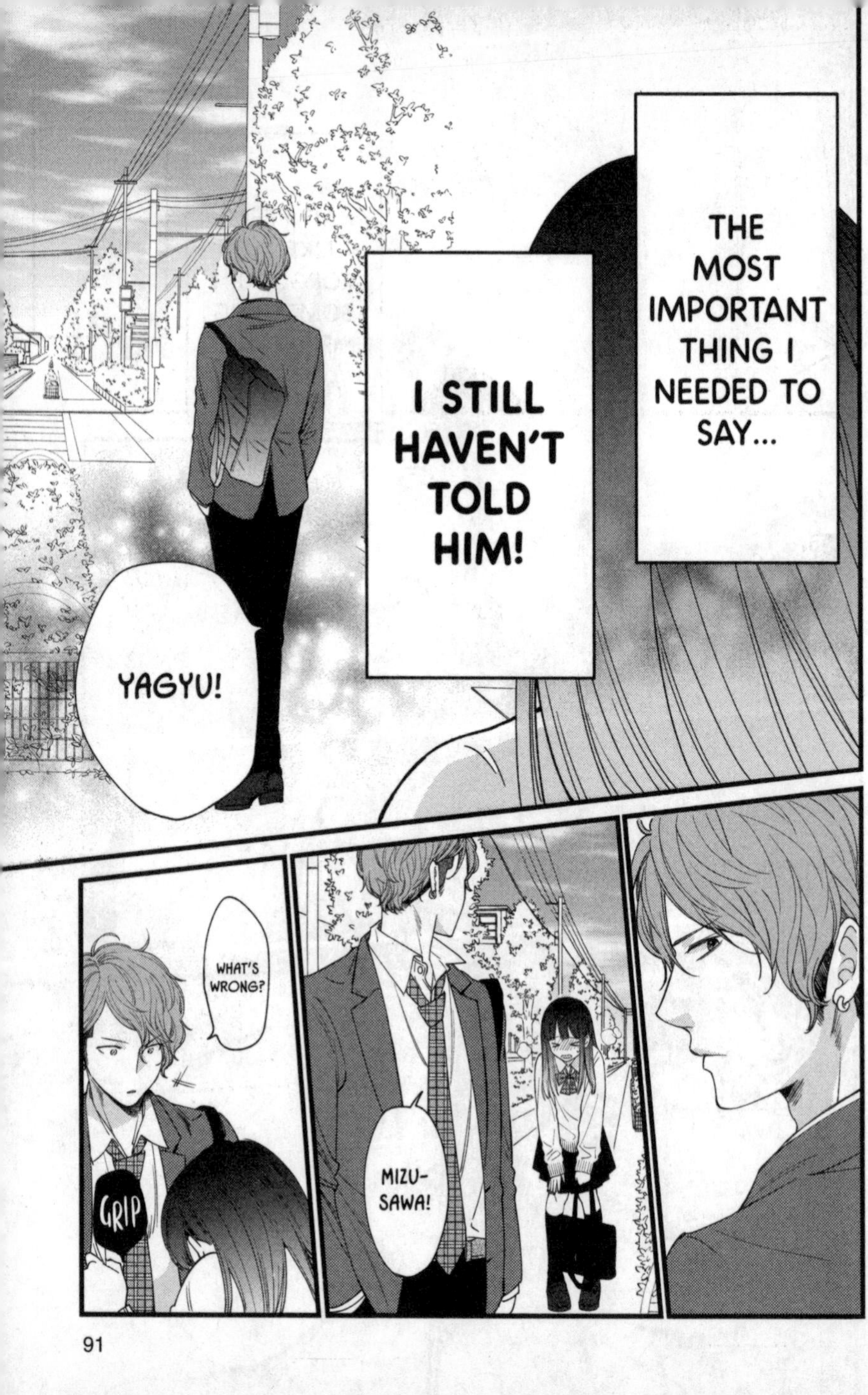
THE MOST IMPORTANT THING I NEEDED TO SAY...
I STILL HAVEN'T TOLD HIM!
YAGYU!
MIZU-SAWA!
WHAT'S WRONG?
GRIP

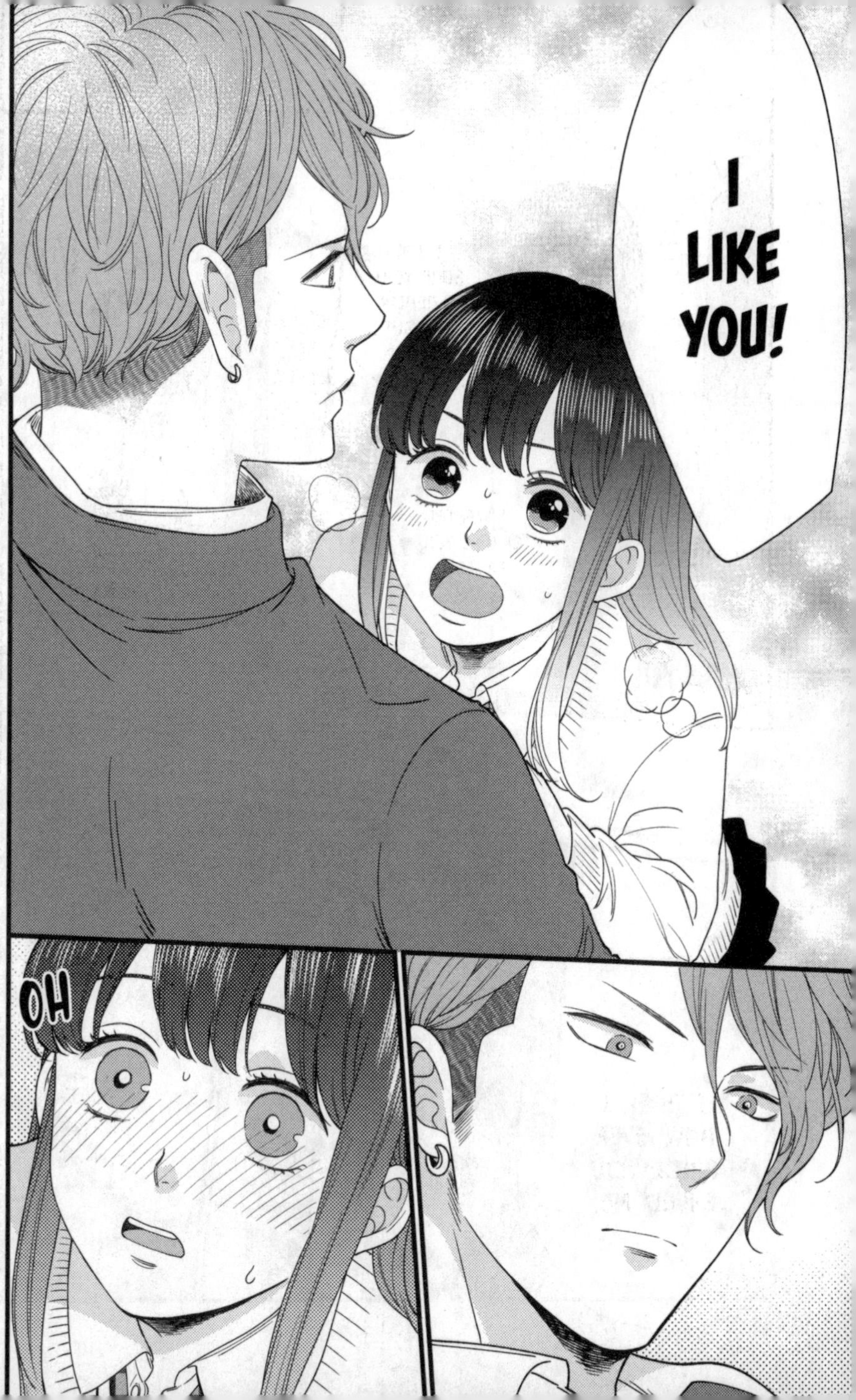
I LIKE YOU!
OH

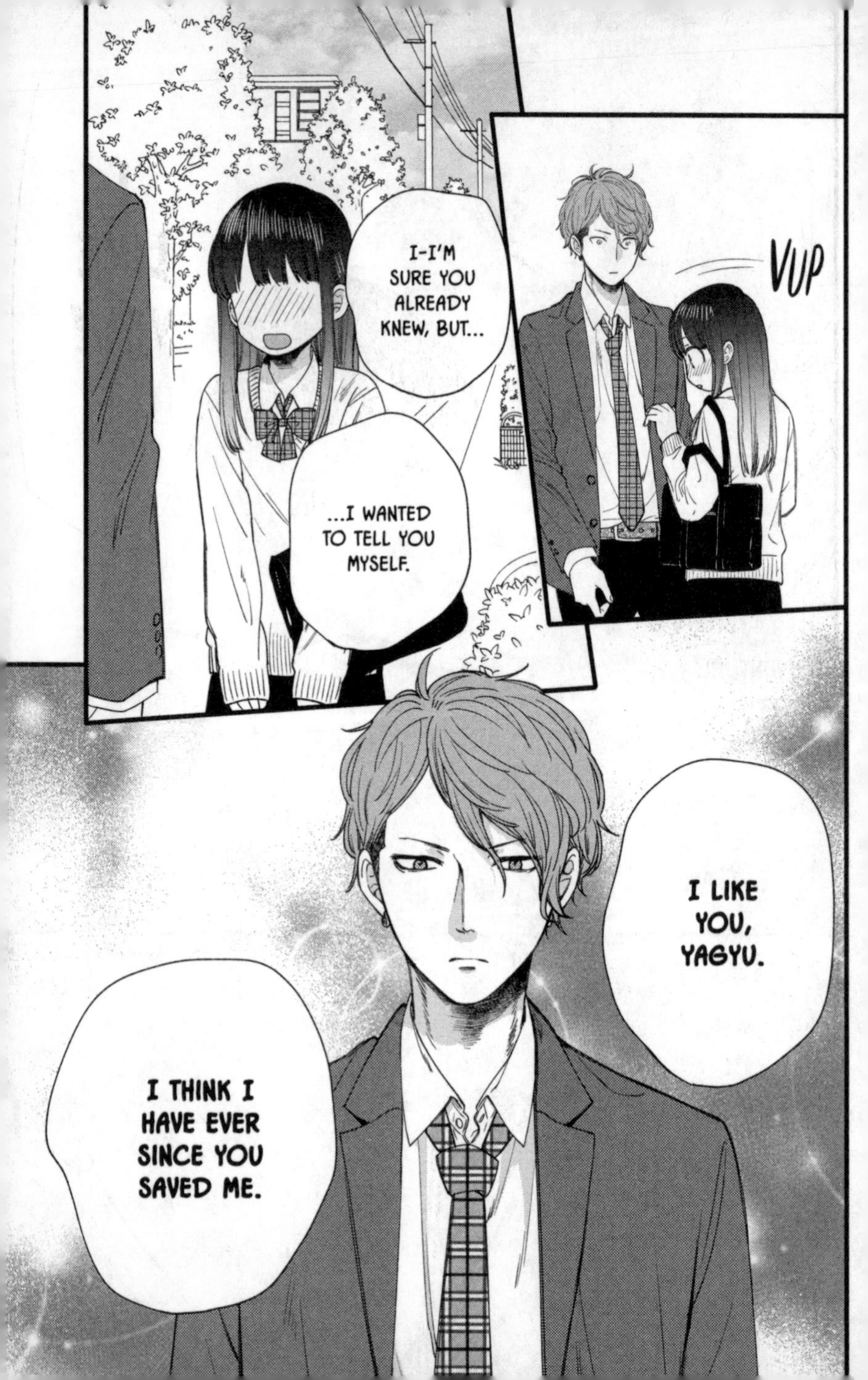
VUP
I-I'M SURE YOU ALREADY KNEW, BUT...
...I WANTED TO TELL YOU MYSELF.
I LIKE YOU, YAGYU.
I THINK I HAVE EVER SINCE YOU SAVED ME.

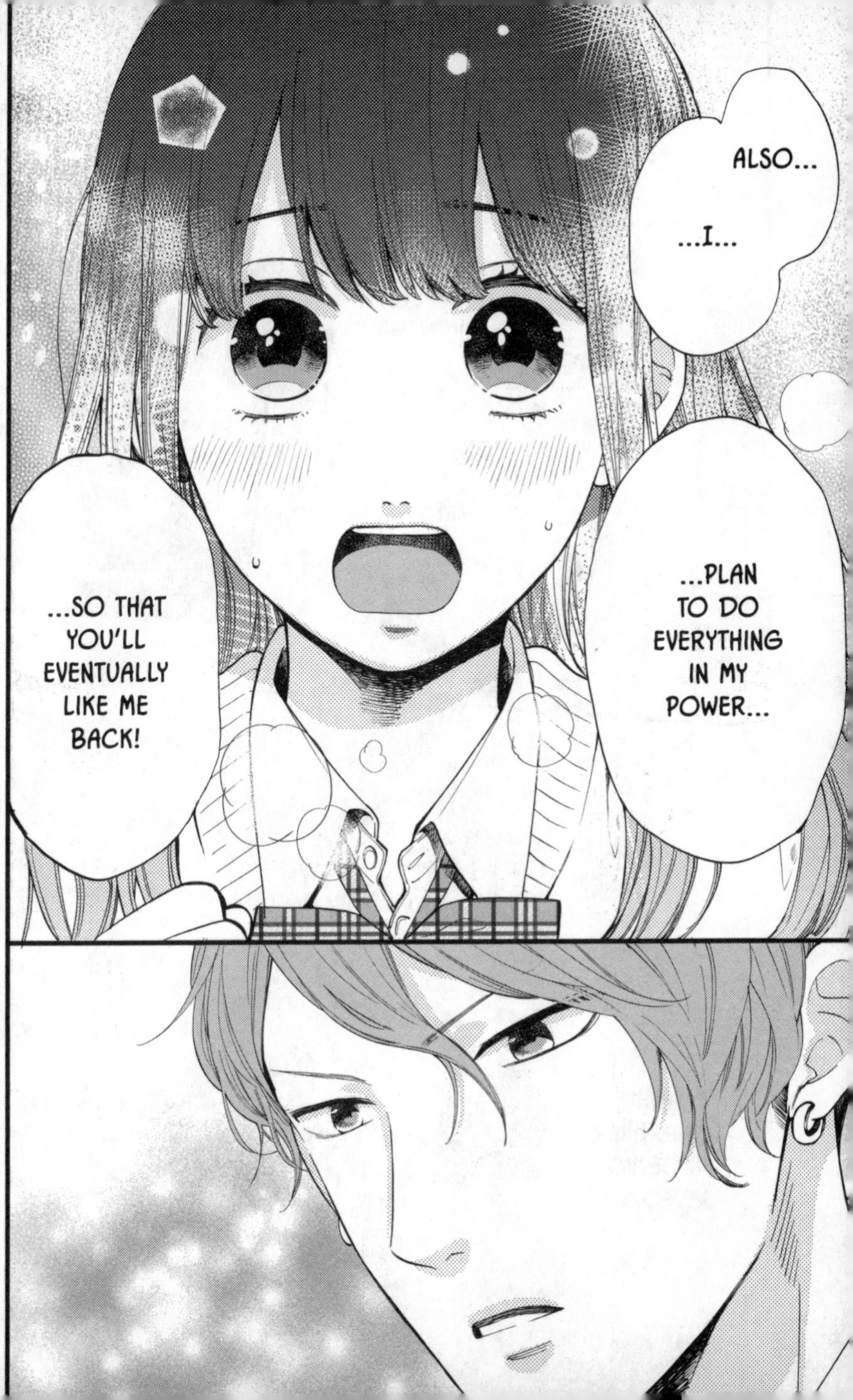
ALSO...
...I...
...PLAN TO DO EVERYTHING IN MY POWER...
...SO THAT YOU'LL EVENTUALLY LIKE ME BACK!

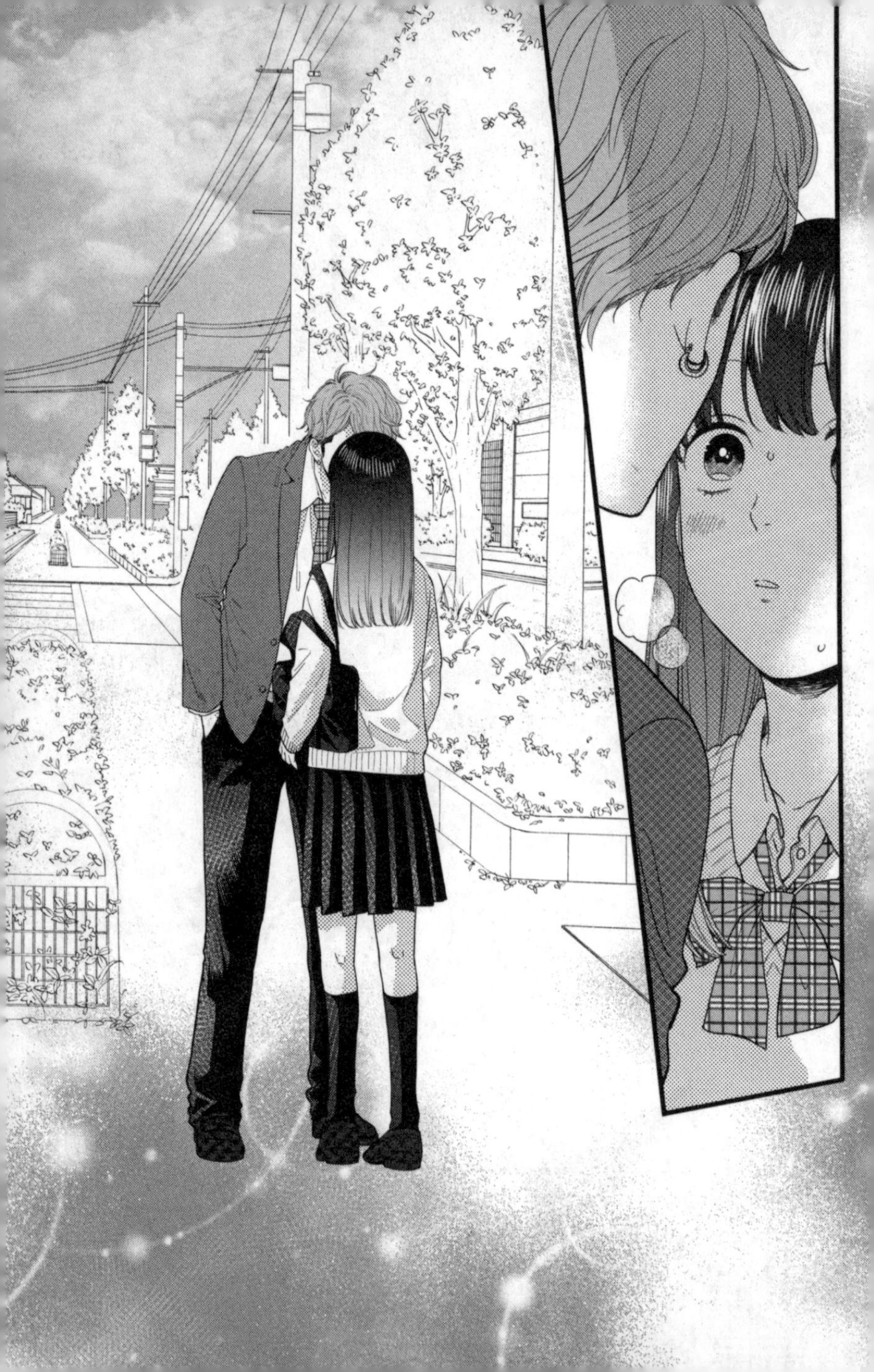

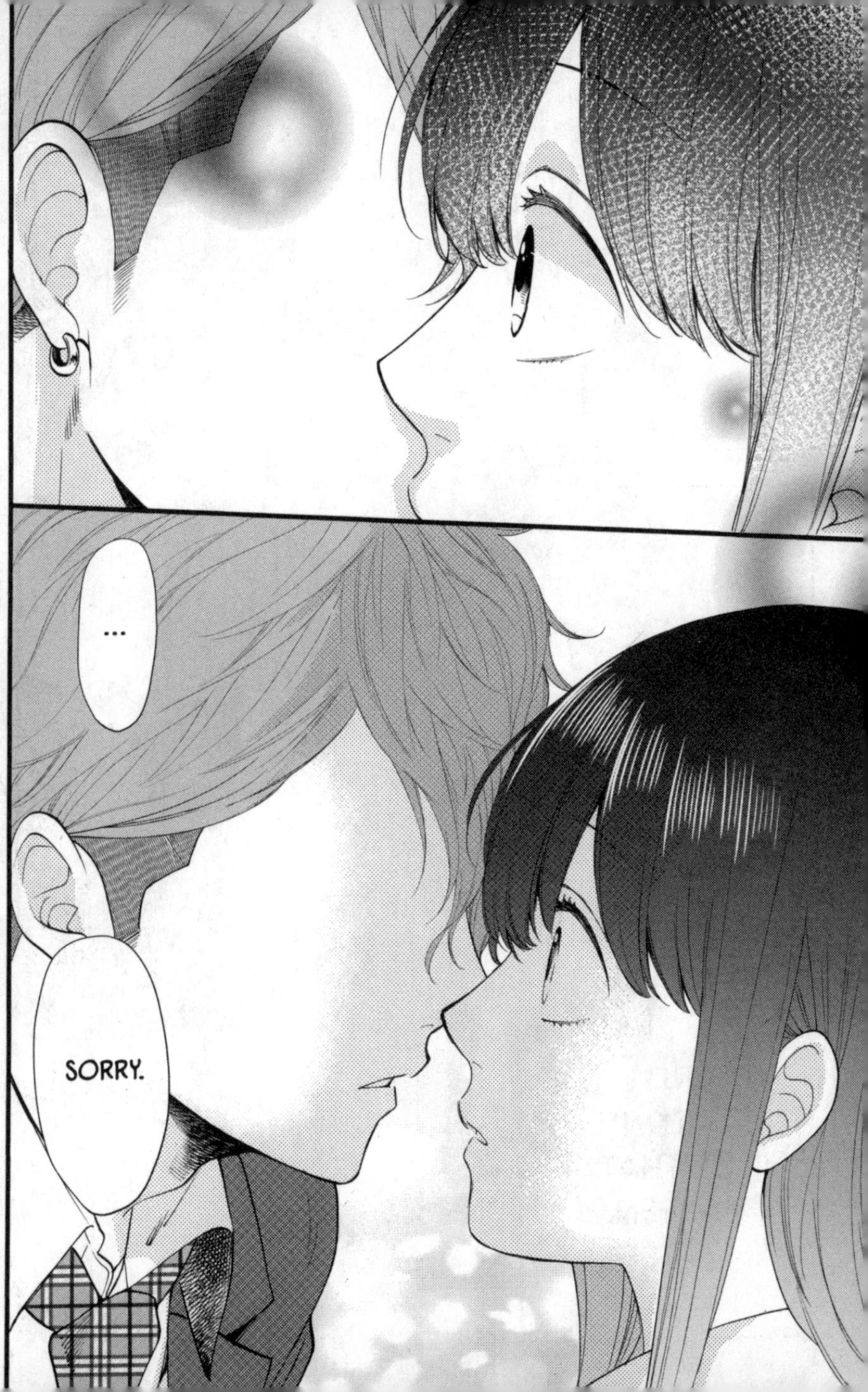
...
SORRY.

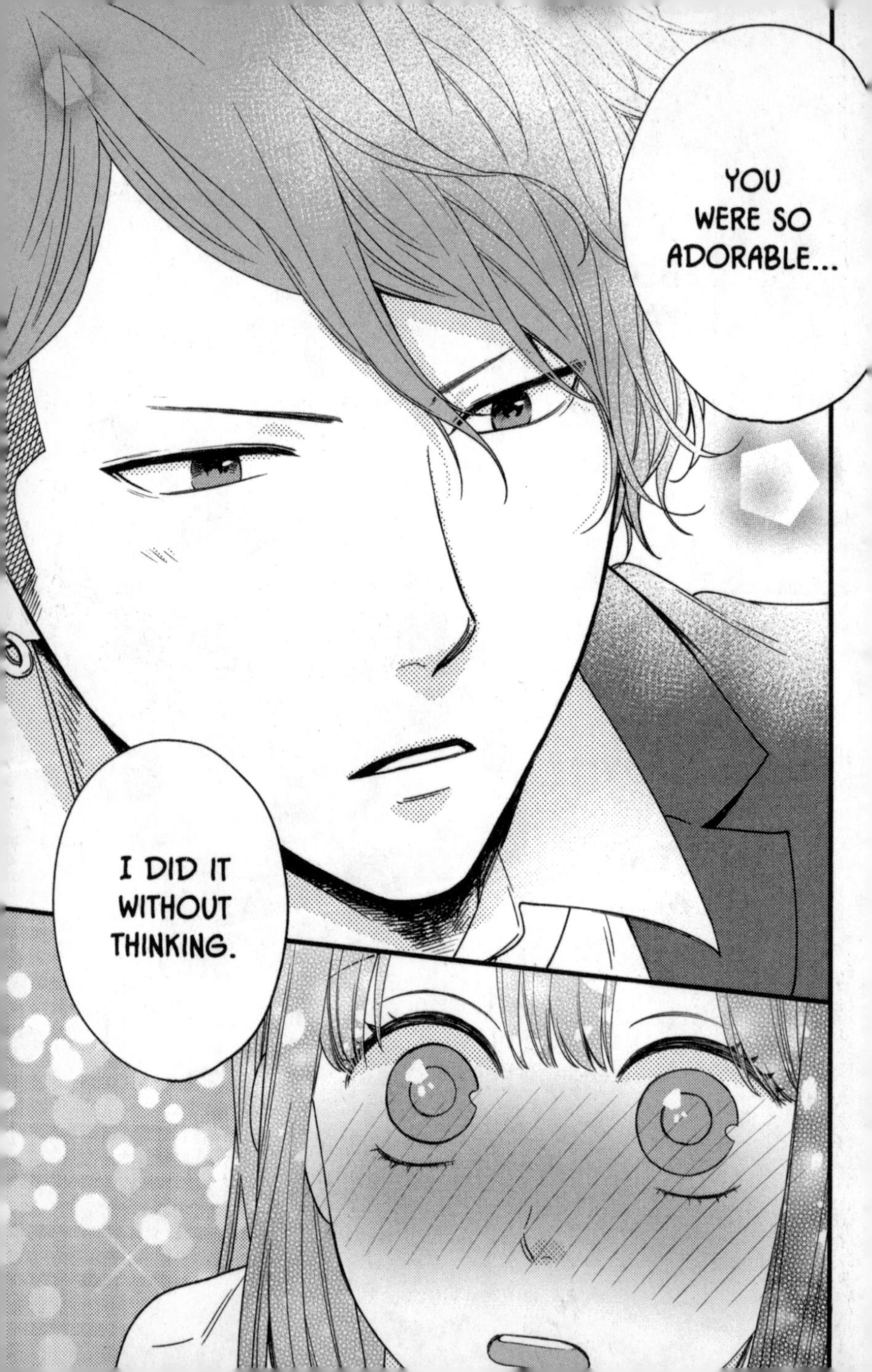
YOU WERE SO ADORABLE...
I DID IT WITHOUT THINKING.

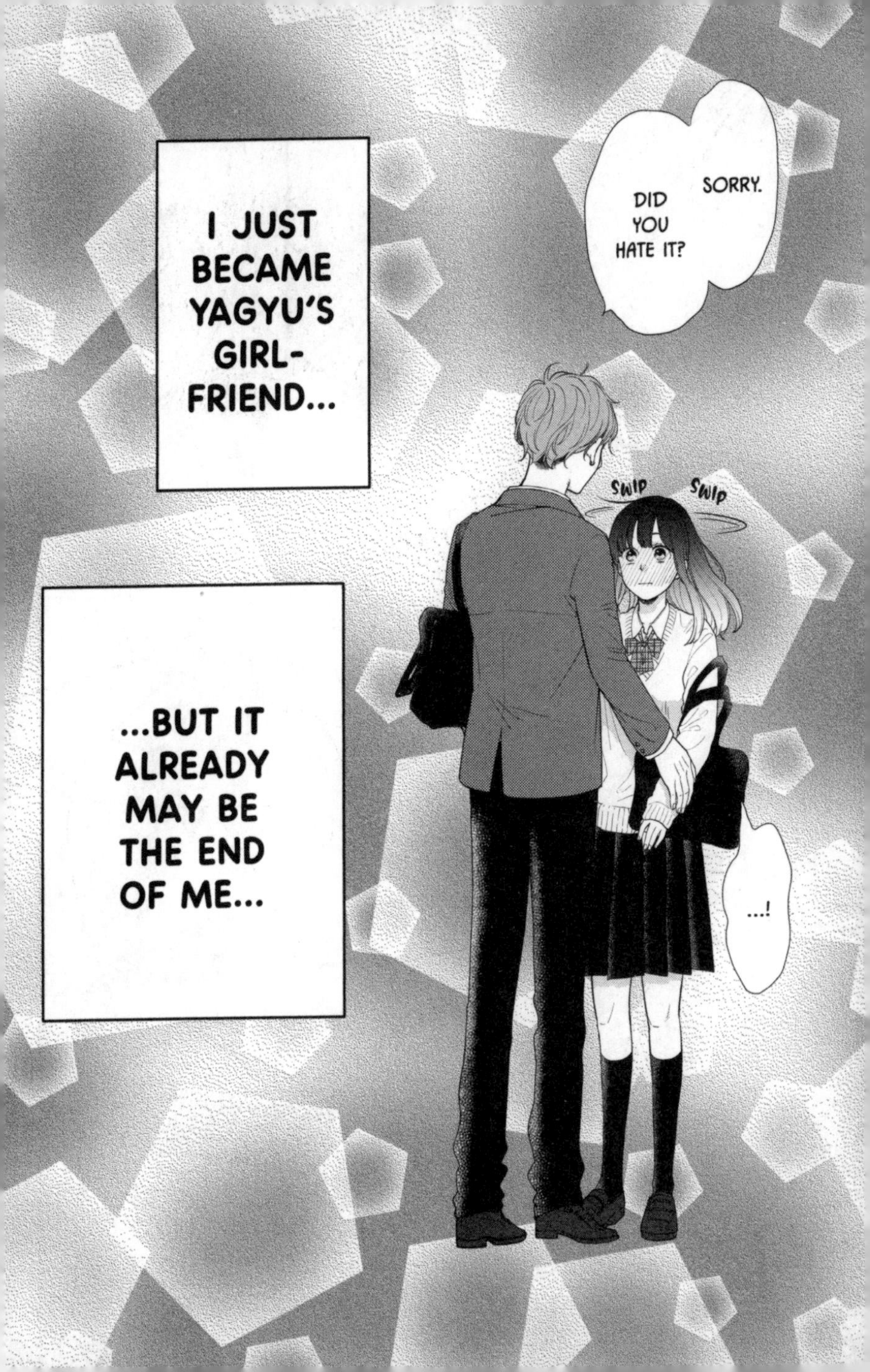
SORRY.
DID YOU HATE IT?
I JUST BECAME YAGYU'S GIRL-FRIEND...
SWIP SWIP
...!
...BUT IT ALREADY MAY BE THE END OF ME...

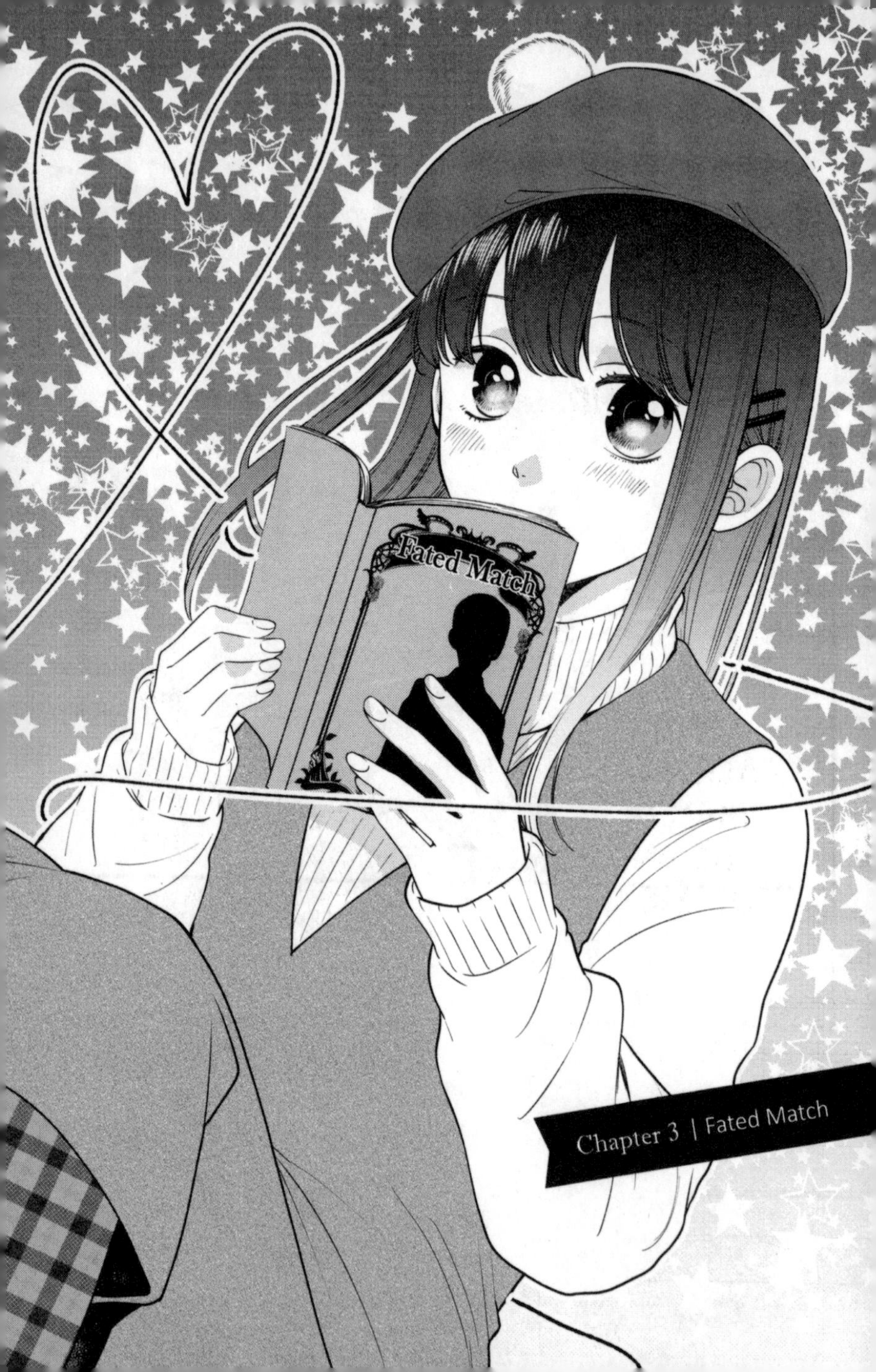
Fated Match
Chapter 3 | Fated Match

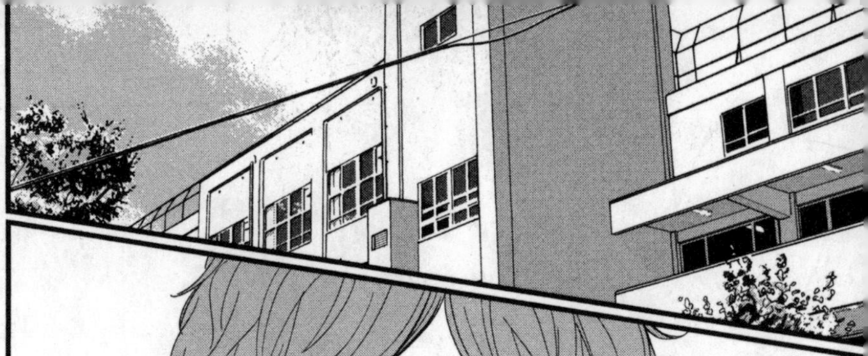
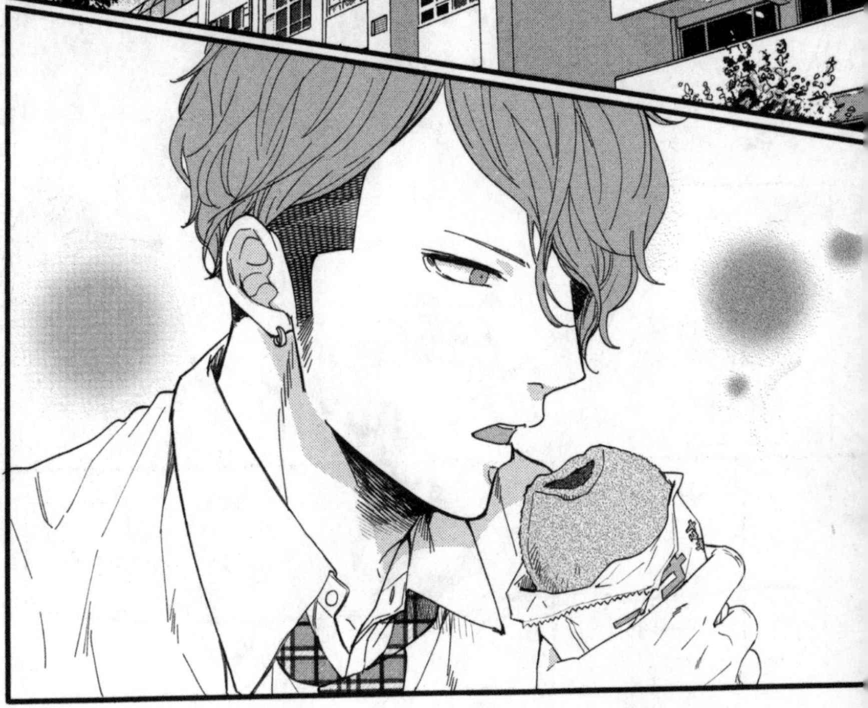
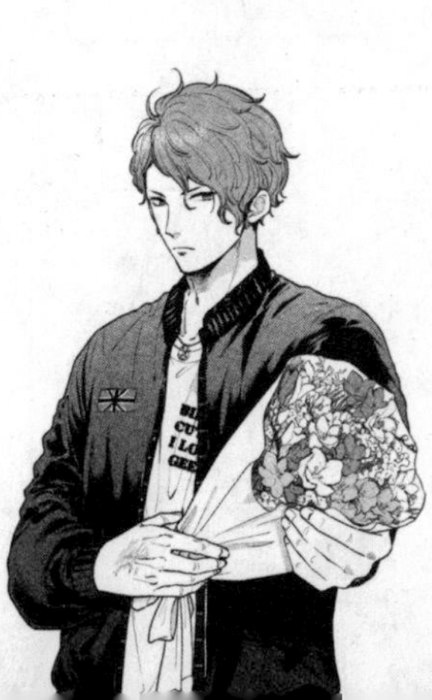

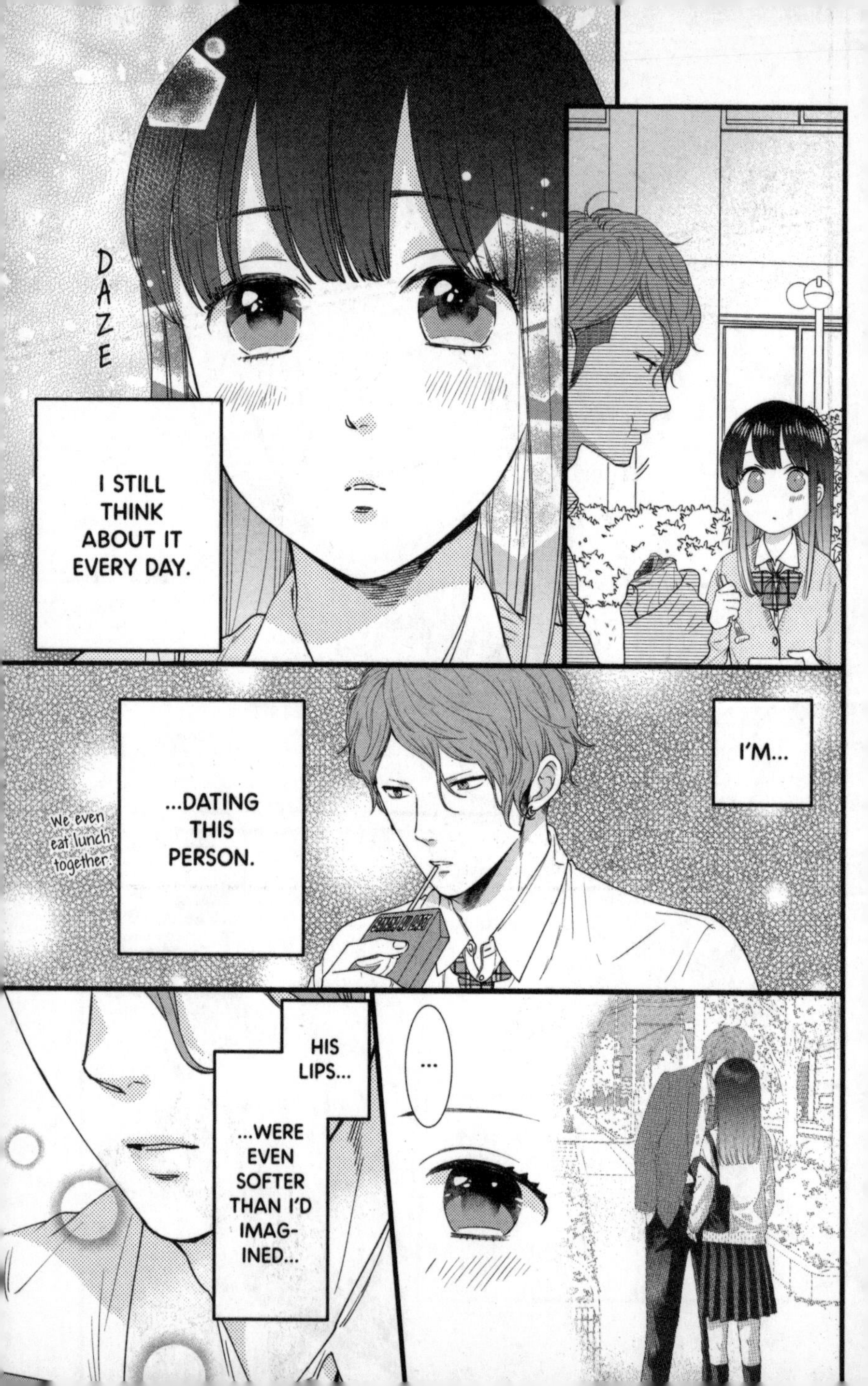
DAZE
I STILL THINK ABOUT IT EVERY DAY.
I'M...
...DATING THIS PERSON.
We even eat lunch together.
...
HIS LIPS...
...WERE EVEN SOFTER THAN I'D IMAG-INED...

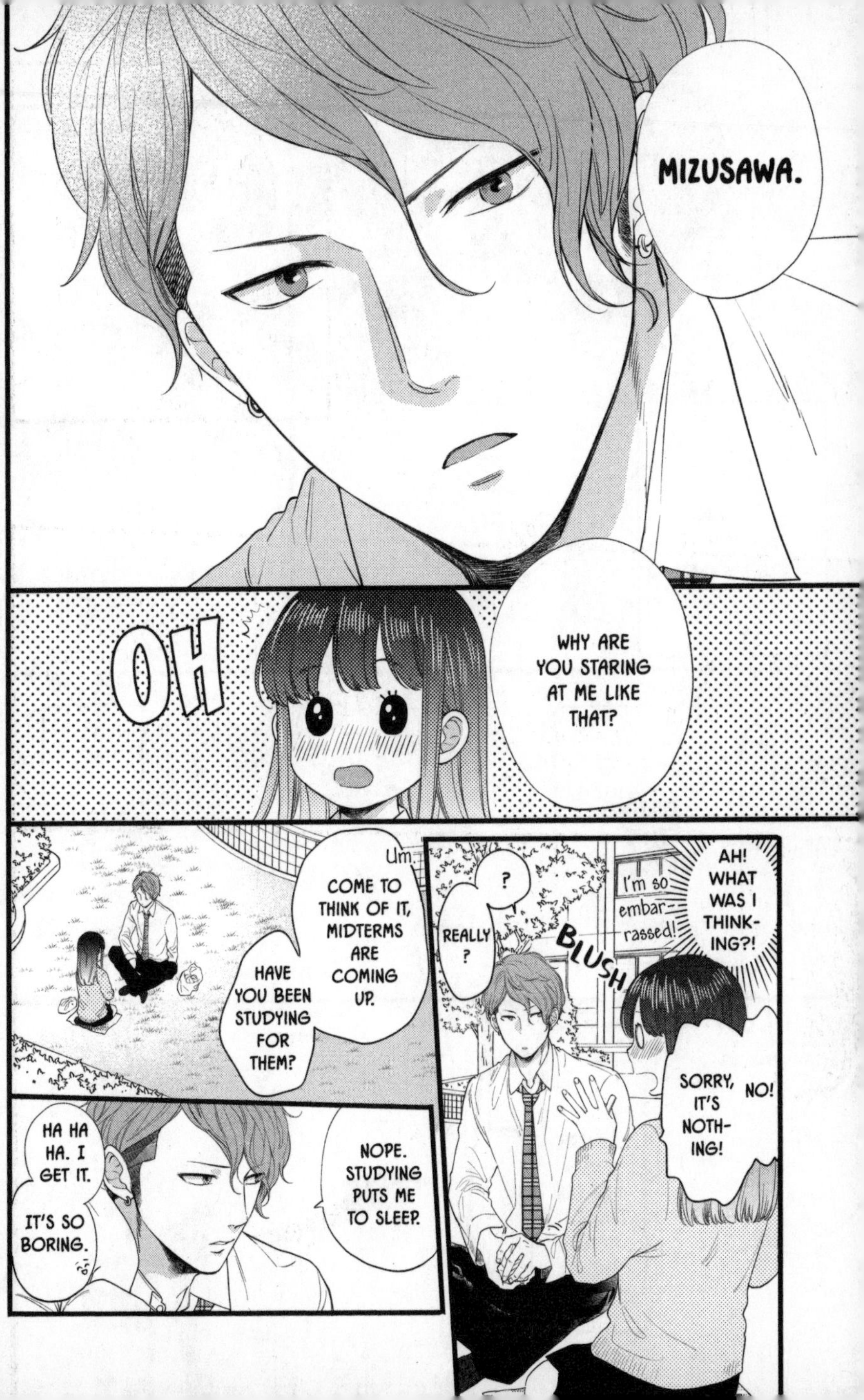
MIZUSAWA.
WHY ARE YOU STARING AT ME LIKE THAT?
OH
AH! WHAT WAS I THINKING?!
I'm so embarrassed!
?
BLUSH
REALLY?
NO!
SORRY, IT'S NOTHING!
Um.
COME TO THINK OF IT, MIDTERMS ARE COMING UP.
HAVE YOU BEEN STUDYING FOR THEM?
NOPE. STUDYING PUTS ME TO SLEEP.
HA HA HA. I GET IT.
IT'S SO BORING.

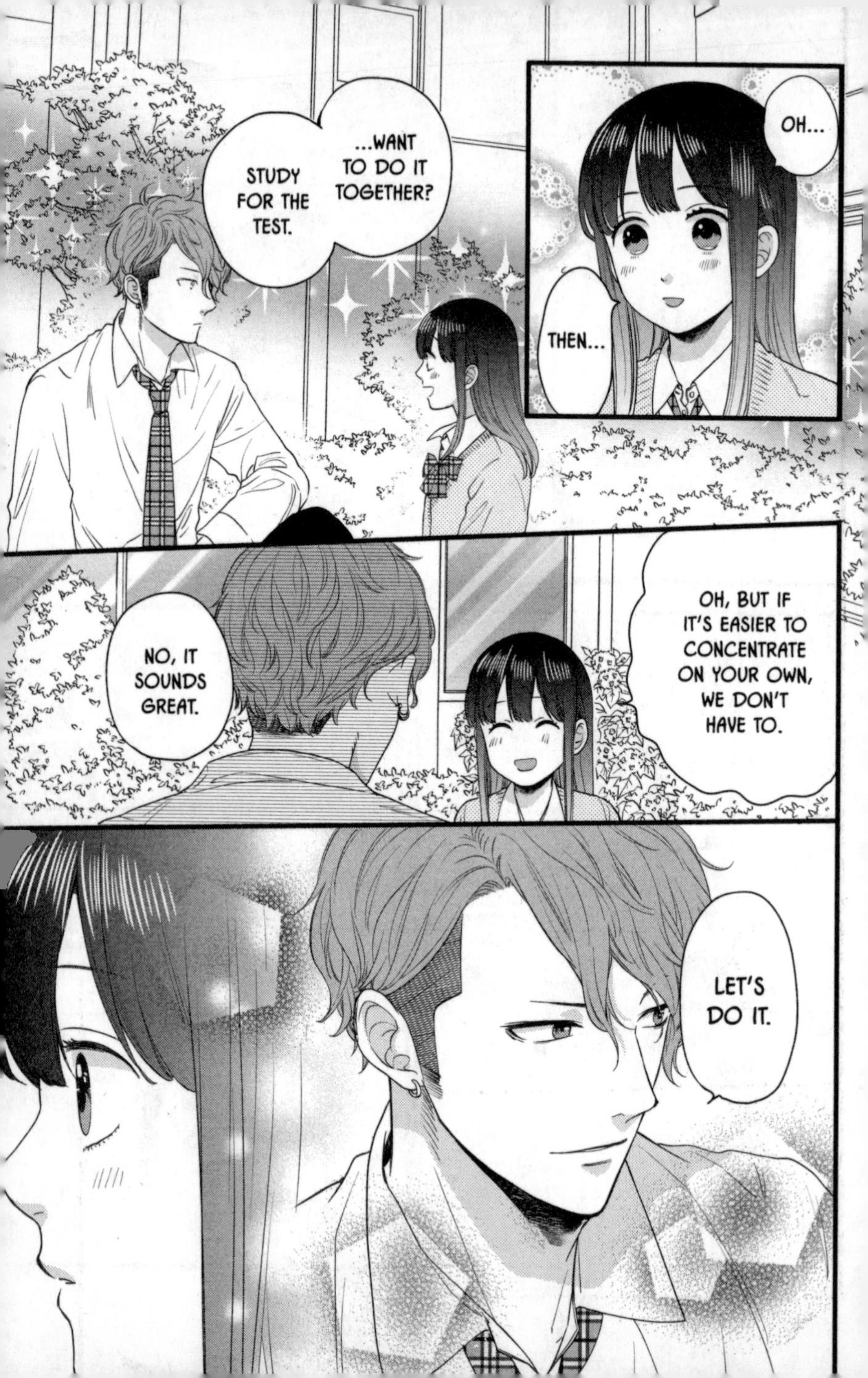
OH...
THEN...
STUDY FOR THE TEST.
...WANT TO DO IT TOGETHER?
OH, BUT IF IT'S EASIER TO CONCENTRATE ON YOUR OWN, WE DON'T HAVE TO.
NO, IT SOUNDS GREAT.
LET'S DO IT.

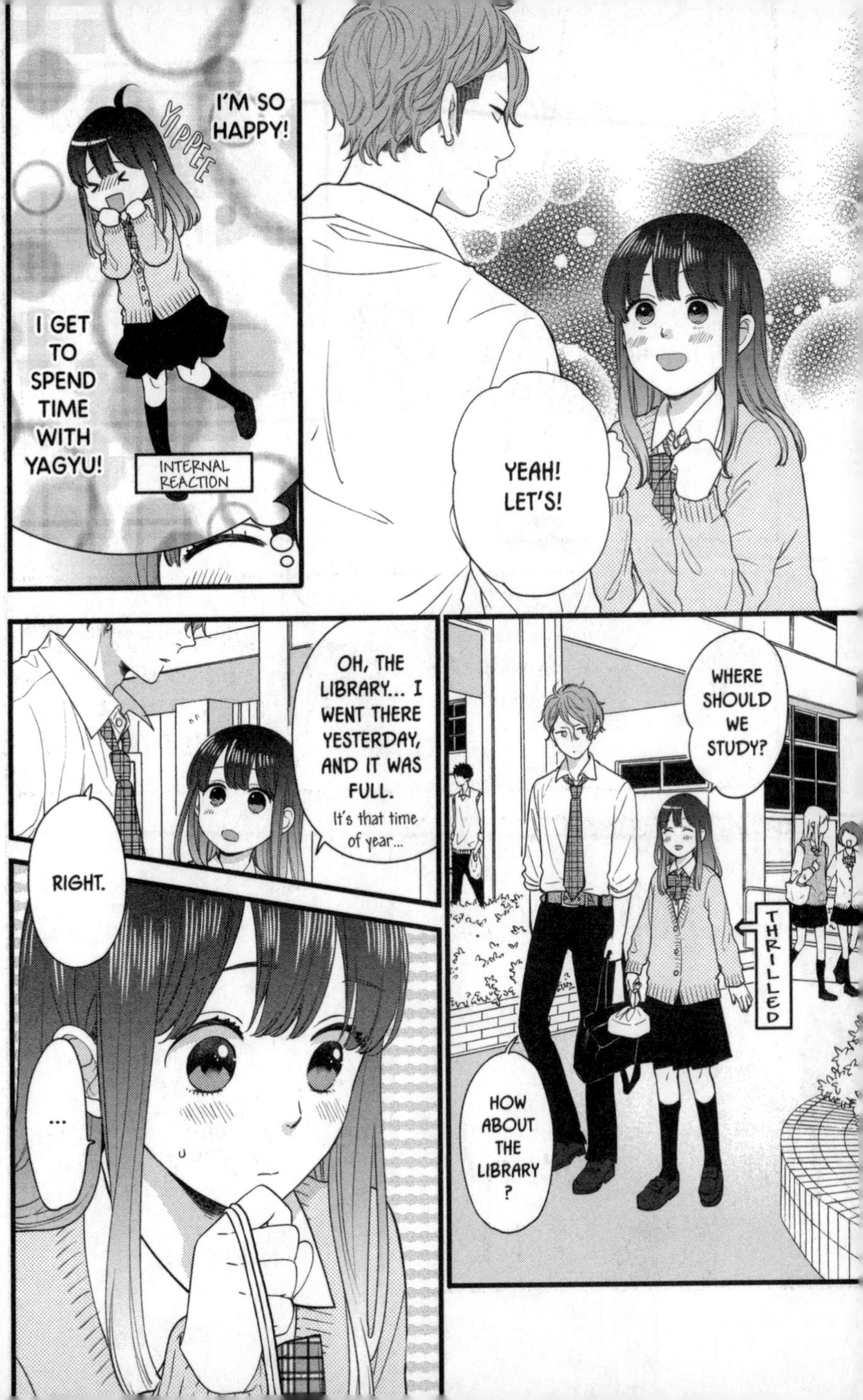
YEAH! LET'S!
I'M SO HAPPY!
YIPPEE
I GET TO SPEND TIME WITH YAGYU!
INTERNAL REACTION
WHERE SHOULD WE STUDY?
THRILLED
HOW ABOUT THE LIBRARY?
OH, THE LIBRARY... I WENT THERE YESTERDAY, AND IT WAS FULL.
It's that time of year...
RIGHT.
...

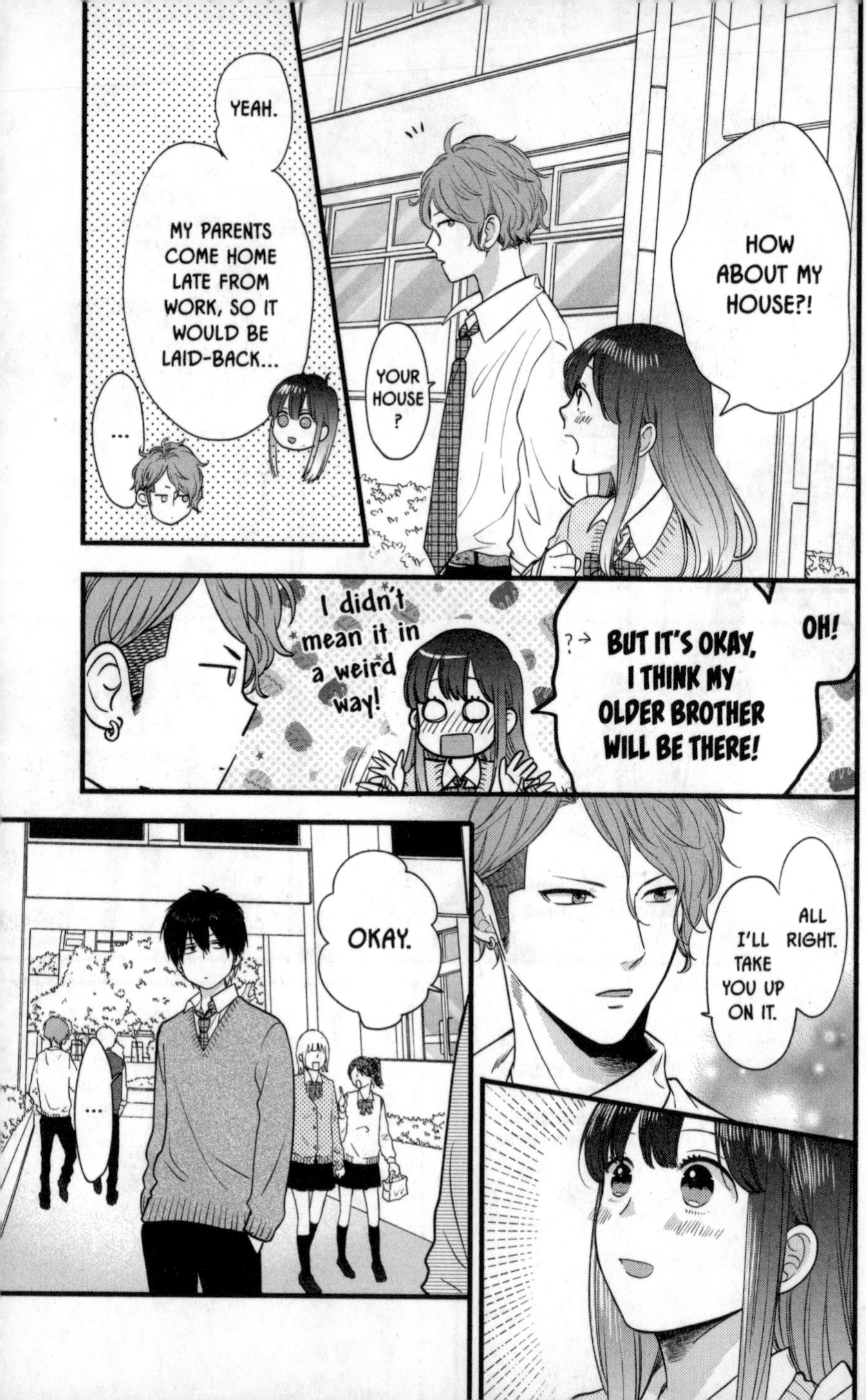
HOW ABOUT MY HOUSE?!
YOUR HOUSE ?
YEAH.
MY PARENTS COME HOME LATE FROM WORK, SO IT WOULD BE LAID-BACK...
...
OH!
BUT IT'S OKAY, I THINK MY OLDER BROTHER WILL BE THERE!
I didn't mean it in a weird way!
ALL RIGHT. I'LL TAKE YOU UP ON IT.
OKAY.
...

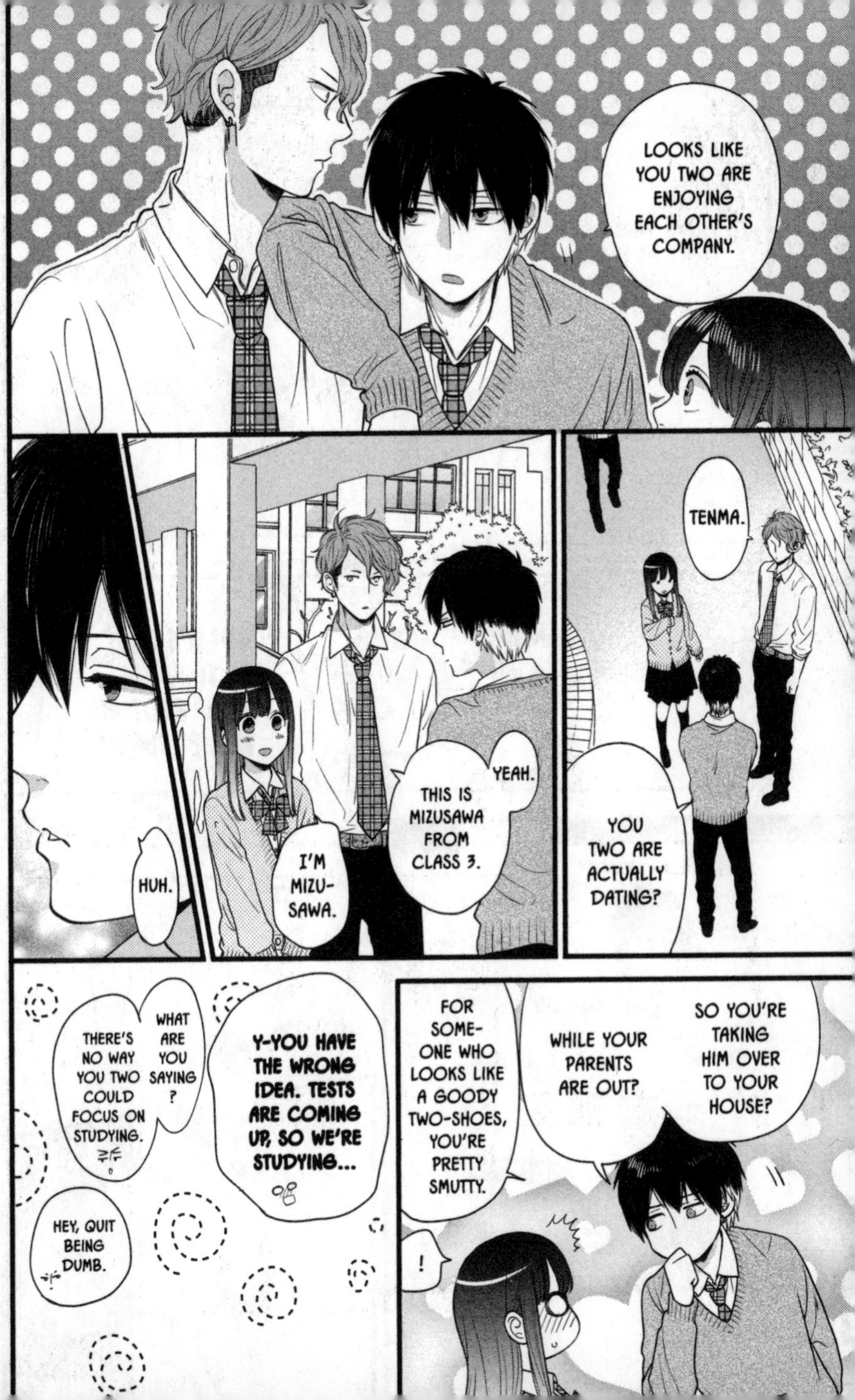
LOOKS LIKE YOU TWO ARE ENJOYING EACH OTHER'S COMPANY.
TENMA.
YOU TWO ARE ACTUALLY DATING?
YEAH.
THIS IS MIZUSAWA FROM CLASS 3.
I'M MIZUSAWA.
HUH.
SO YOU'RE TAKING HIM OVER TO YOUR HOUSE?
WHILE YOUR PARENTS ARE OUT?
FOR SOMEONE WHO LOOKS LIKE A GOODY TWO-SHOES, YOU'RE PRETTY SMUTTY.
!
Y-YOU HAVE THE WRONG IDEA. TESTS ARE COMING UP, SO WE'RE STUDYING...
WHAT ARE YOU SAYING?
THERE'S NO WAY YOU TWO COULD FOCUS ON STUDYING.
HEY, QUIT BEING DUMB.

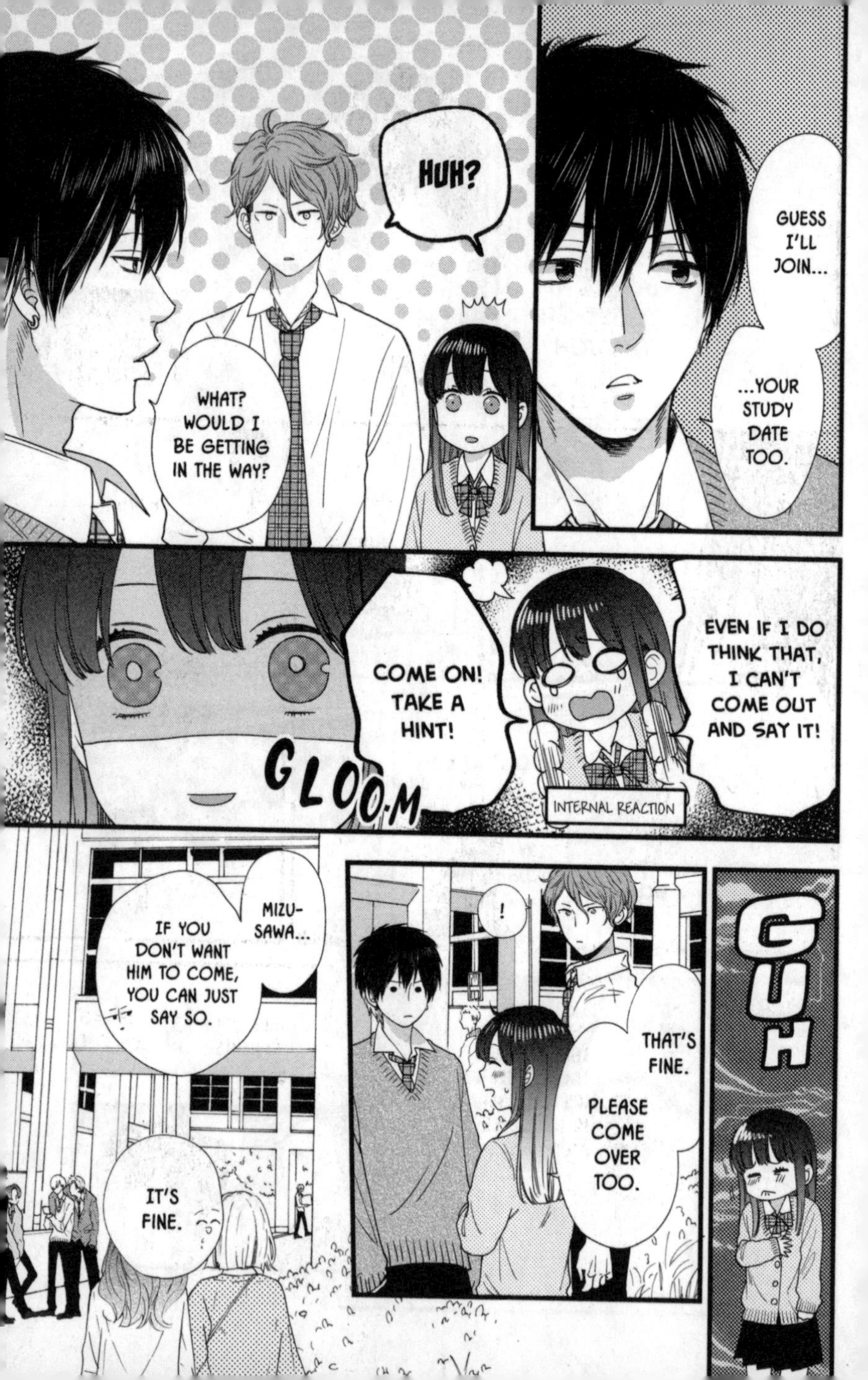
GUESS I'LL JOIN...
...YOUR STUDY DATE TOO.
HUH?
WHAT? WOULD I BE GETTING IN THE WAY?
EVEN IF I DO THINK THAT, I CAN'T COME OUT AND SAY IT!
INTERNAL REACTION
COME ON! TAKE A HINT!
GLOOM
GUH
!
THAT'S FINE.
PLEASE COME OVER TOO.
MIZU-SAWA...
IF YOU DON'T WANT HIM TO COME, YOU CAN JUST SAY SO.
IT'S FINE.

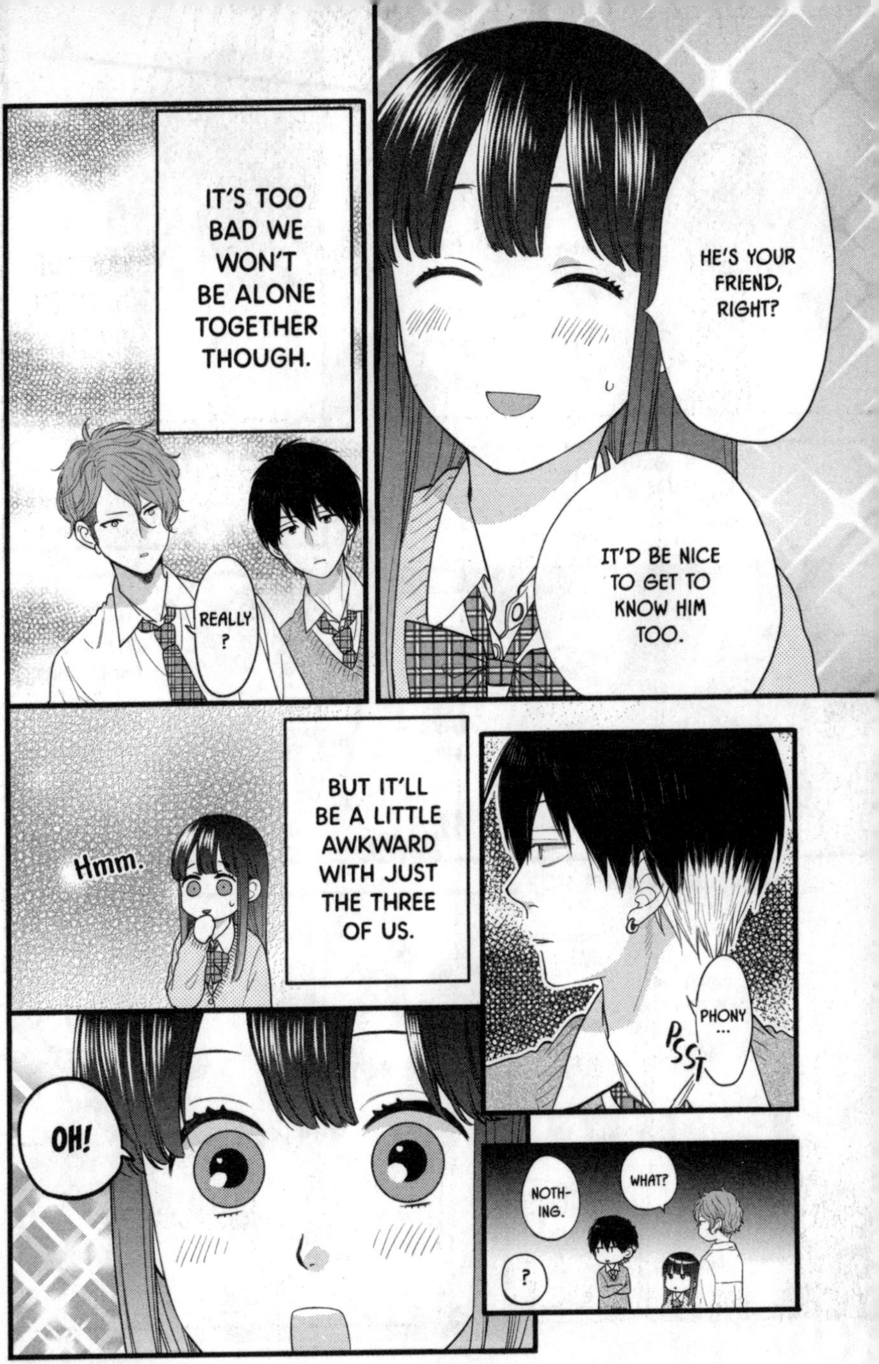
HE'S YOUR FRIEND, RIGHT?
IT'D BE NICE TO GET TO KNOW HIM TOO.
IT'S TOO BAD WE WON'T BE ALONE TOGETHER THOUGH.
REALLY ?
PHONY ...
PSST
WHAT?
NOTH-ING.
?
BUT IT'LL BE A LITTLE AWKWARD WITH JUST THE THREE OF US.
Hmm.
OH!

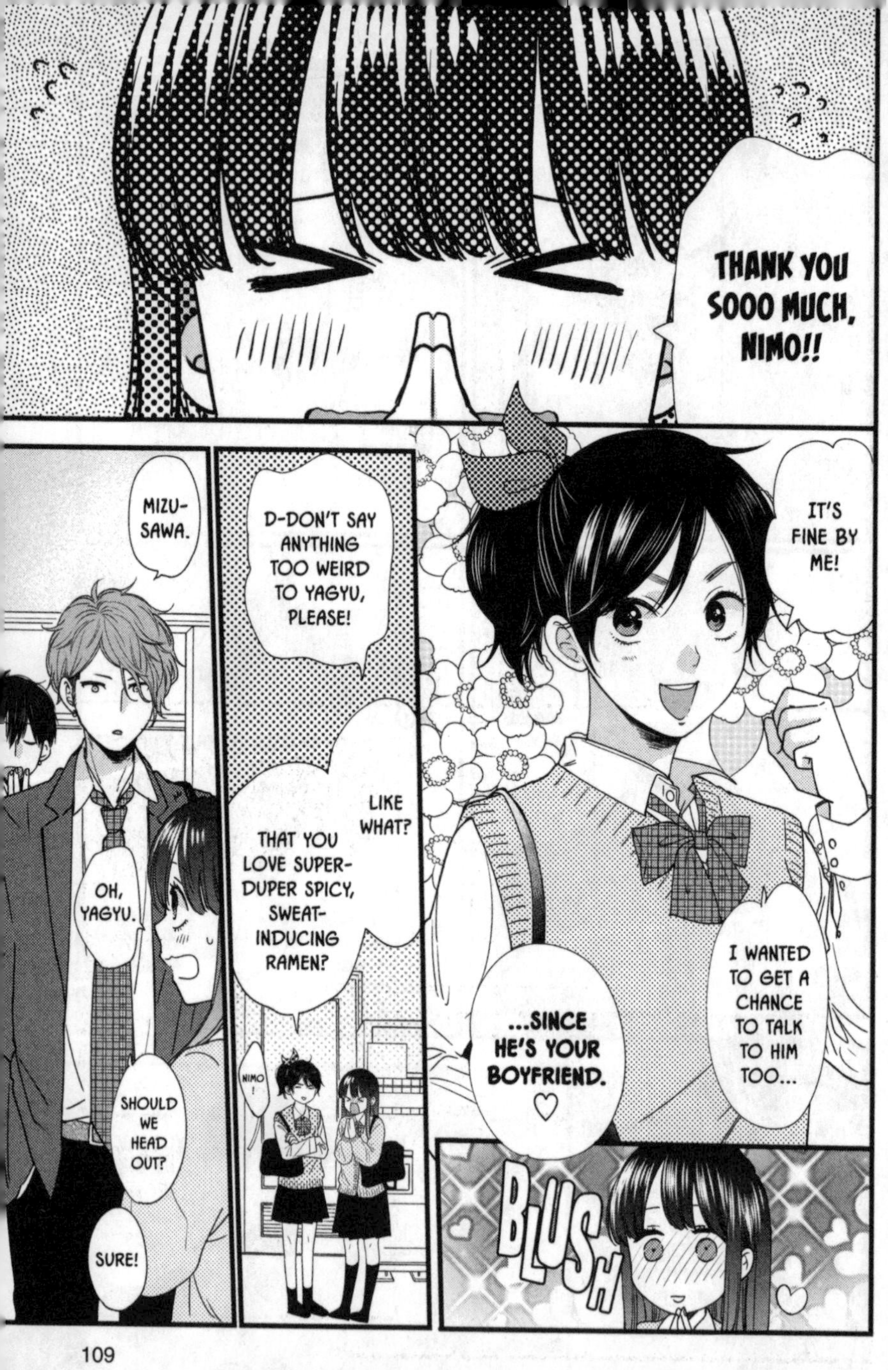
THANK YOU SOOO MUCH, NIMO!!
IT'S FINE BY ME!
I WANTED TO GET A CHANCE TO TALK TO HIM TOO...
...SINCE HE'S YOUR BOYFRIEND. ♡
BLUSH
D-DON'T SAY ANYTHING TOO WEIRD TO YAGYU, PLEASE!
LIKE WHAT?
THAT YOU LOVE SUPER-DUPER SPICY, SWEAT-INDUCING RAMEN?
NIMO!
MIZU-SAWA.
OH, YAGYU.
SHOULD WE HEAD OUT?
SURE!

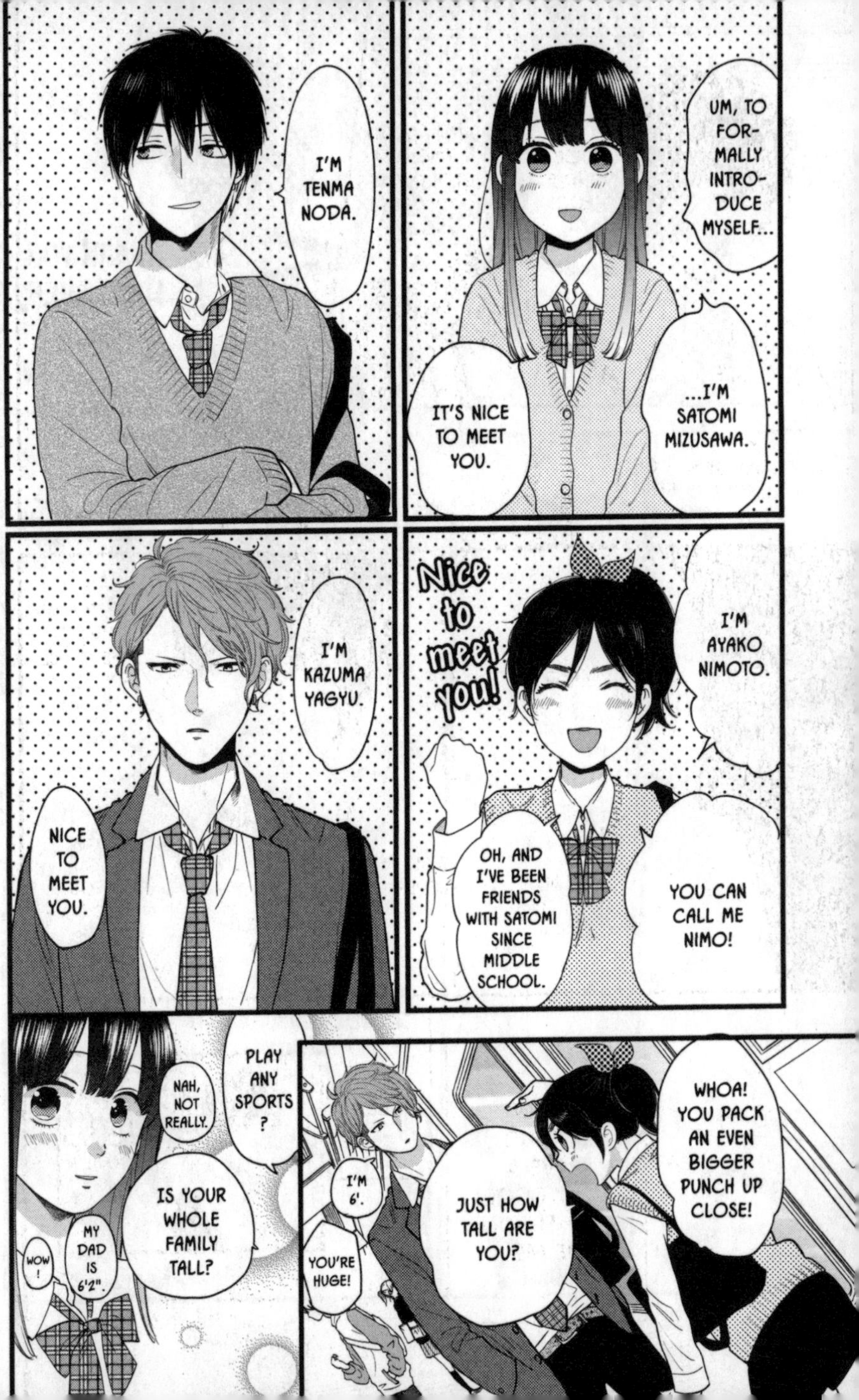
UM, TO FORMALLY INTRODUCE MYSELF...
...I'M SATOMI MIZUSAWA.
IT'S NICE TO MEET YOU.
I'M TENMA NODA.
I'M AYAKO NIMOTO.
Nice to meet you!
YOU CAN CALL ME NIMO!
OH, AND I'VE BEEN FRIENDS WITH SATOMI SINCE MIDDLE SCHOOL.
I'M KAZUMA YAGYU.
NICE TO MEET YOU.
WHOA! YOU PACK AN EVEN BIGGER PUNCH UP CLOSE!
JUST HOW TALL ARE YOU?
I'M 6'.
YOU'RE HUGE!
PLAY ANY SPORTS?
NAH, NOT REALLY.
IS YOUR WHOLE FAMILY TALL?
MY DAD IS 6'2".
WOW!

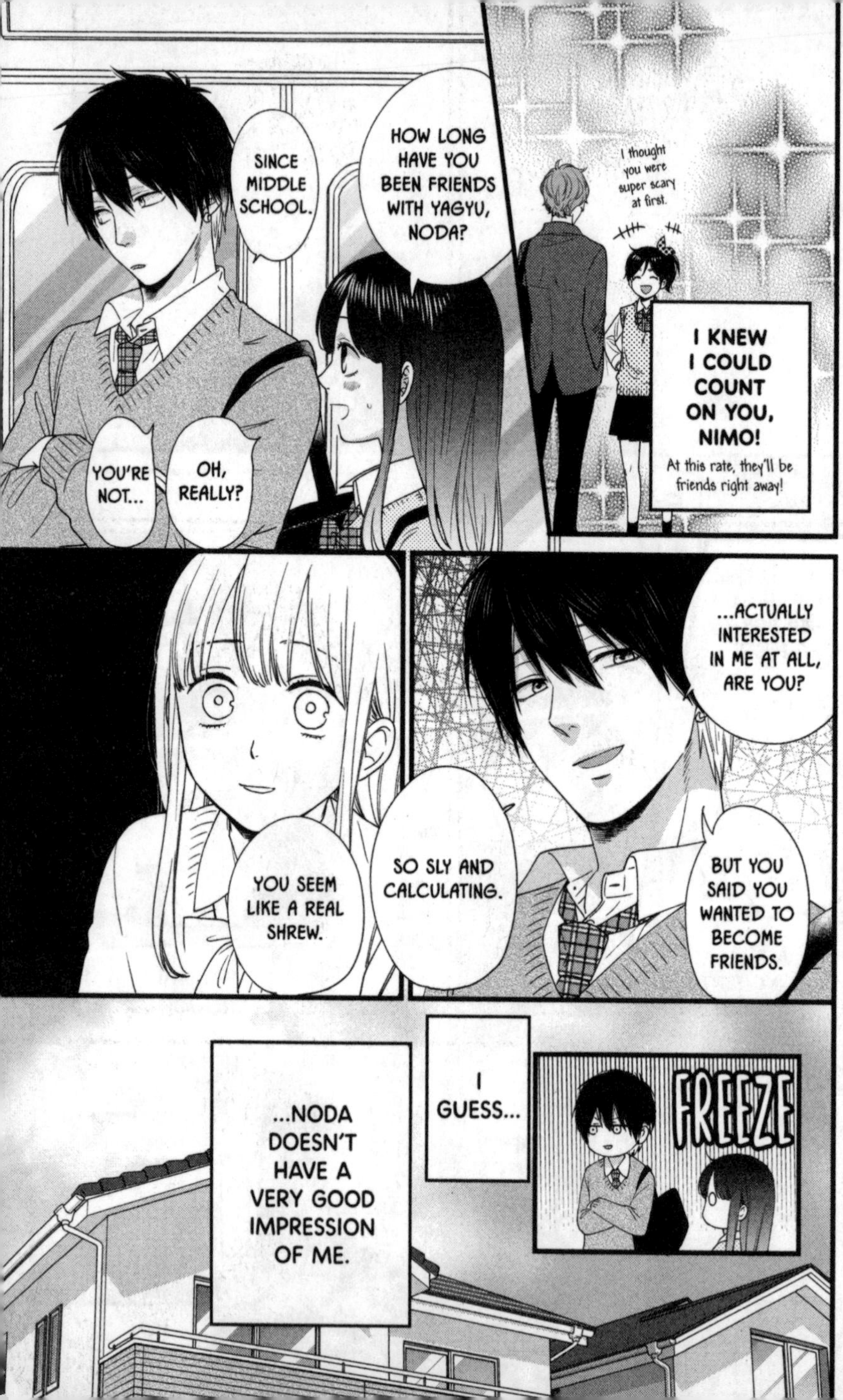
I thought you were super scary at first.
I KNEW I COULD COUNT ON YOU, NIMO!
At this rate, they'll be friends right away!
HOW LONG HAVE YOU BEEN FRIENDS WITH YAGYU, NODA?
SINCE MIDDLE SCHOOL.
OH, REALLY?
YOU'RE NOT...
...ACTUALLY INTERESTED IN ME AT ALL, ARE YOU?
BUT YOU SAID YOU WANTED TO BECOME FRIENDS.
SO SLY AND CALCULATING.
YOU SEEM LIKE A REAL SHREW.
FREEZE
I GUESS...
...NODA DOESN'T HAVE A VERY GOOD IMPRESSION OF ME.

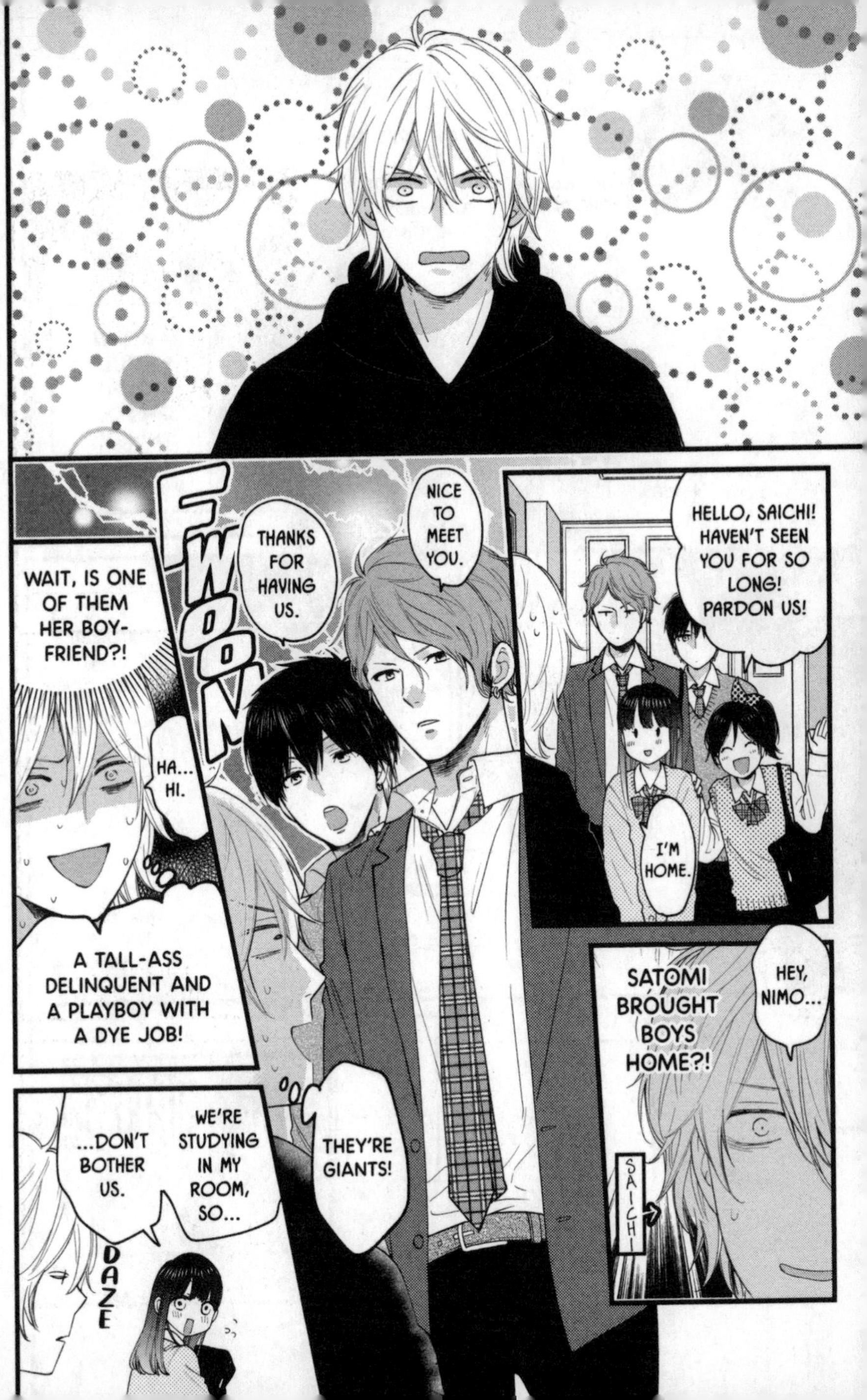
HELLO, SAICHI! HAVEN'T SEEN YOU FOR SO LONG! PARDON US!
I'M HOME.
HEY, NIMO...
SATOMI BROUGHT BOYS HOME?!
SAICHI
NICE TO MEET YOU.
THANKS FOR HAVING US.
FWOOM
WAIT, IS ONE OF THEM HER BOY-FRIEND?!
HA... HI.
A TALL-ASS DELINQUENT AND A PLAYBOY WITH A DYE JOB!
THEY'RE GIANTS!
WE'RE STUDYING IN MY ROOM, SO...
...DON'T BOTHER US.
DAZE

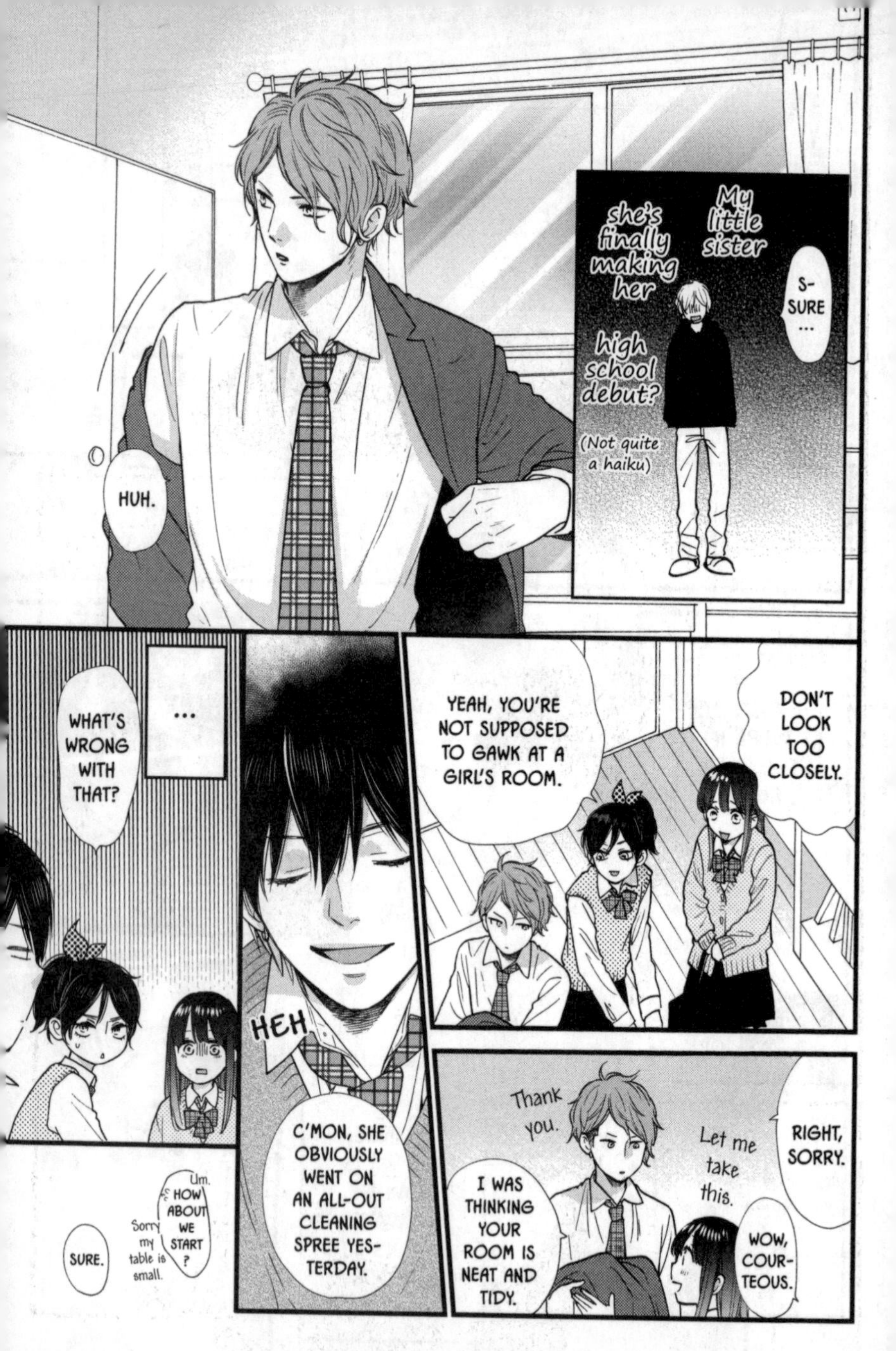
S-SURE...
My little sister
she's finally making her
high school debut?
(Not quite a haiku)
HUH.
DON'T LOOK TOO CLOSELY.
YEAH, YOU'RE NOT SUPPOSED TO GAWK AT A GIRL'S ROOM.
RIGHT, SORRY.
Let me take this.
WOW, COURTEOUS.
Thank you.
I WAS THINKING YOUR ROOM IS NEAT AND TIDY.
HEH
C'MON, SHE OBVIOUSLY WENT ON AN ALL-OUT CLEANING SPREE YES-TERDAY.
...
WHAT'S WRONG WITH THAT?
Um. HOW ABOUT WE START?
Sorry my table is small.
SURE.

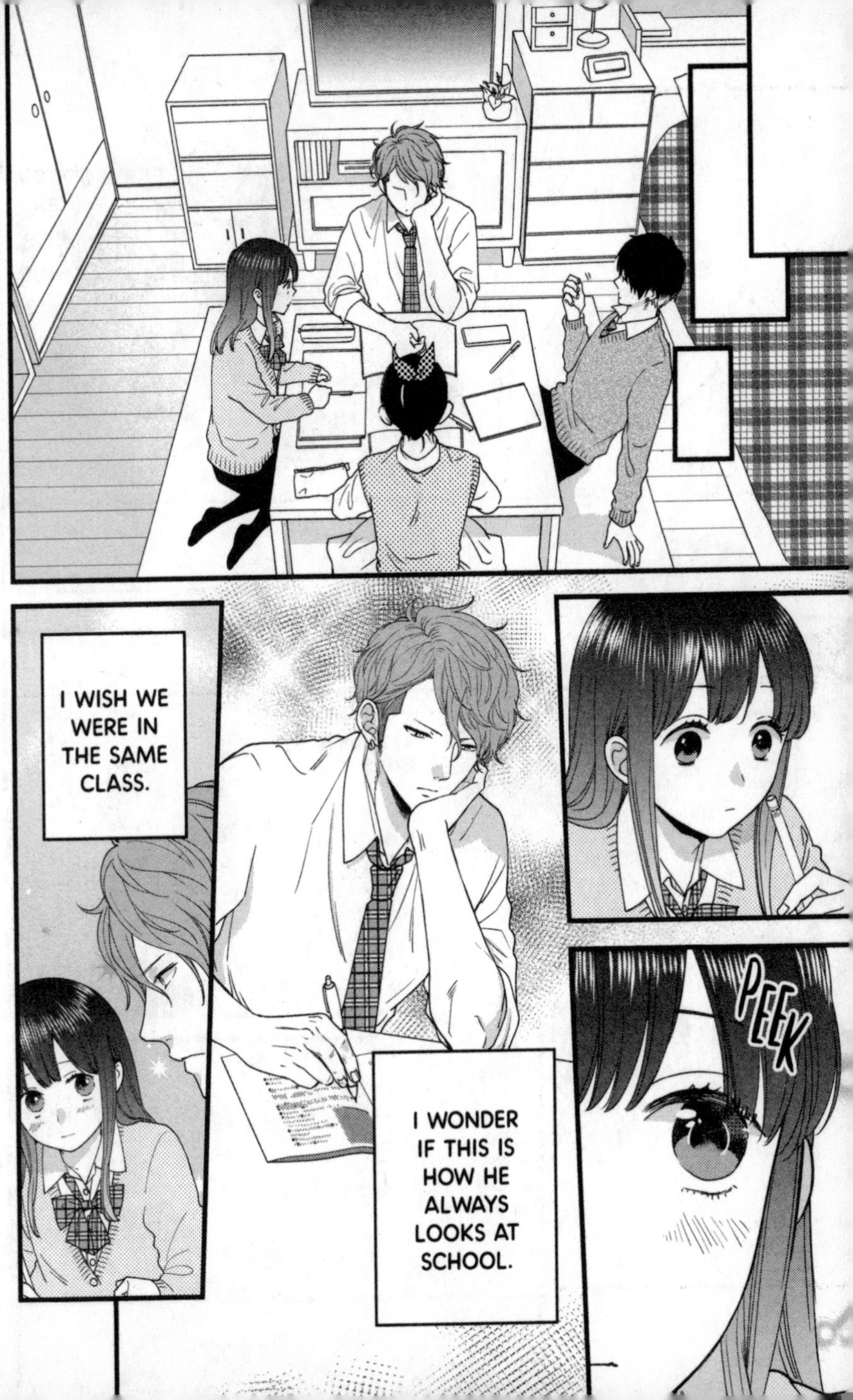
PEEK
I WONDER IF THIS IS HOW HE ALWAYS LOOKS AT SCHOOL.
I WISH WE WERE IN THE SAME CLASS.

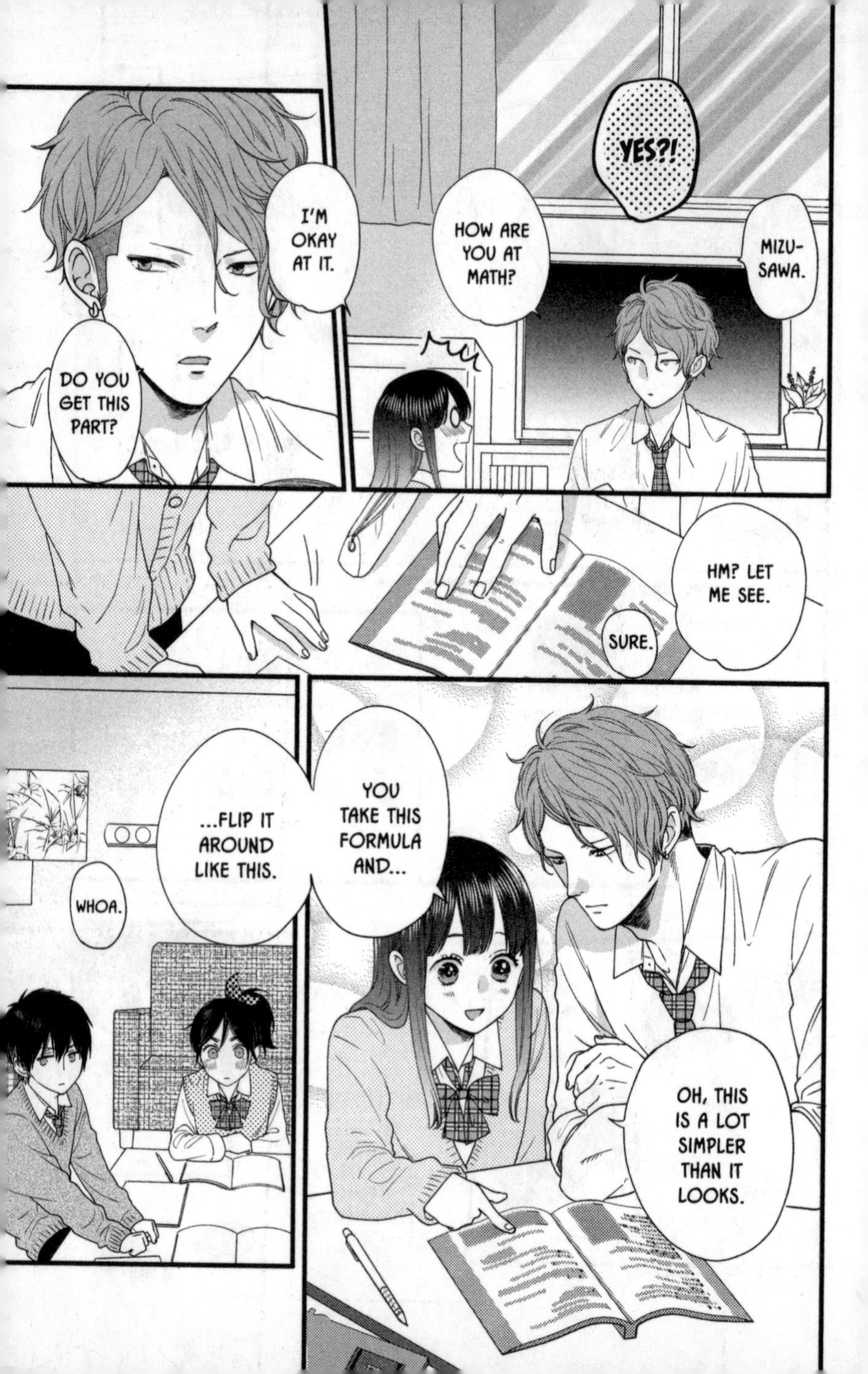
MIZU-SAWA.
YES?!
HOW ARE YOU AT MATH?
I'M OKAY AT IT.
DO YOU GET THIS PART?
HM? LET ME SEE.
SURE.
OH, THIS IS A LOT SIMPLER THAN IT LOOKS.
YOU TAKE THIS FORMULA AND...
...FLIP IT AROUND LIKE THIS.
WHOA.

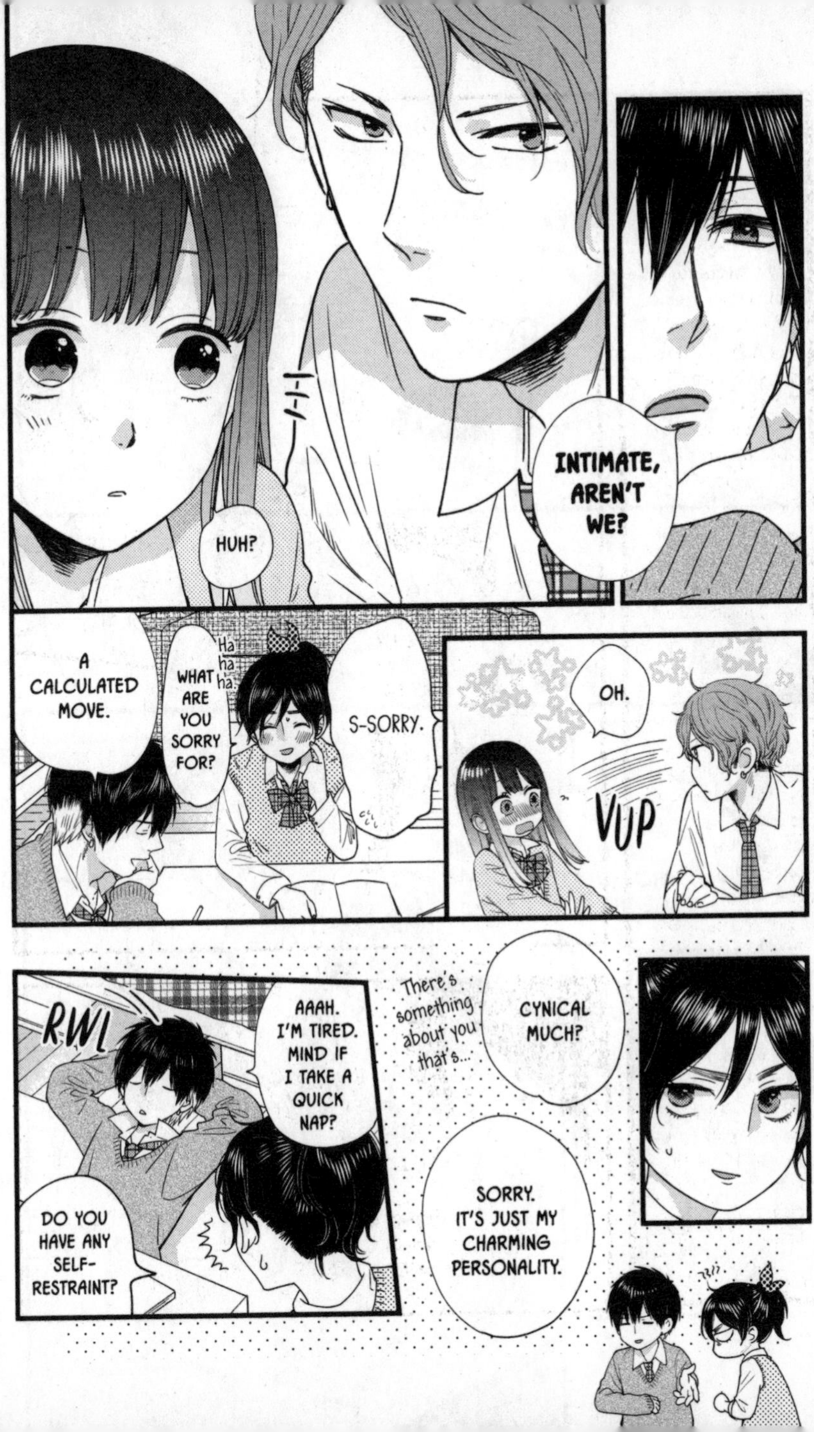
INTIMATE, AREN'T WE?
HUH?
OH.
VUP
S-SORRY.
Ha ha ha.
WHAT ARE YOU SORRY FOR?
A CALCULATED MOVE.
CYNICAL MUCH?
There's something about you that's...
SORRY. IT'S JUST MY CHARMING PERSONALITY.
AAAH. I'M TIRED. MIND IF I TAKE A QUICK NAP?
RWL
DO YOU HAVE ANY SELF-RESTRAINT?

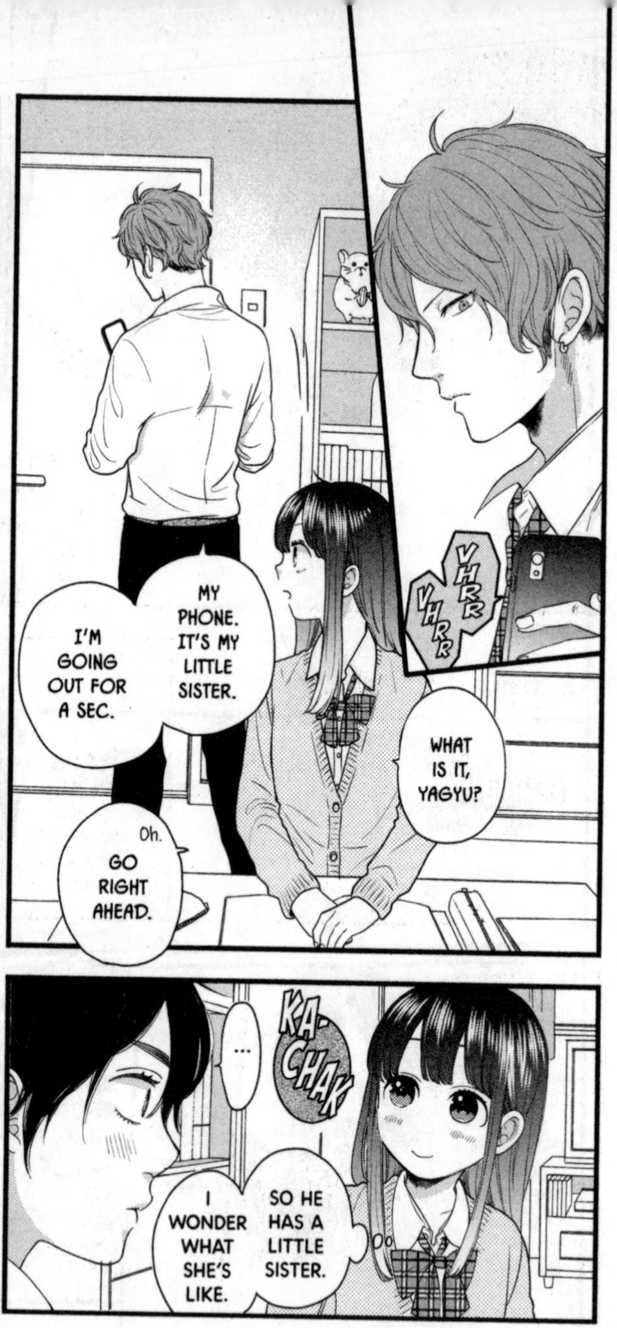
VHRR VHRR
WHAT IS IT, YAGYU?
MY PHONE. IT'S MY LITTLE SISTER.
I'M GOING OUT FOR A SEC.
Oh. GO RIGHT AHEAD.
KA-CHAK
...
SO HE HAS A LITTLE SISTER.
I WONDER WHAT SHE'S LIKE.

2

I think it's pretty dangerous to stop working entirely, so in order to push myself and get a change in environment, I moved. I already mentioned this at the beginning, but, yeah, I moved. The office I have now is separate from my assistants. We used to chat up a storm in the old house when we were in the same room... Well, this is a different environment and it might be good, I thought.
The result: I feel so isolated.
Honestly, I'm lonely... I love to chitchat. I'm already a solitary shut-in... Before I could talk to outside people, but I crushed that opportunity...
Well, we eat meals together though. ♡ Because mealtime is when we can finally talk, we always end up eating for a superlong time. I think we might have gotten more inefficient...? I wonder if this is going to work. It's secretly dawned on me that I might have messed up.

Continues

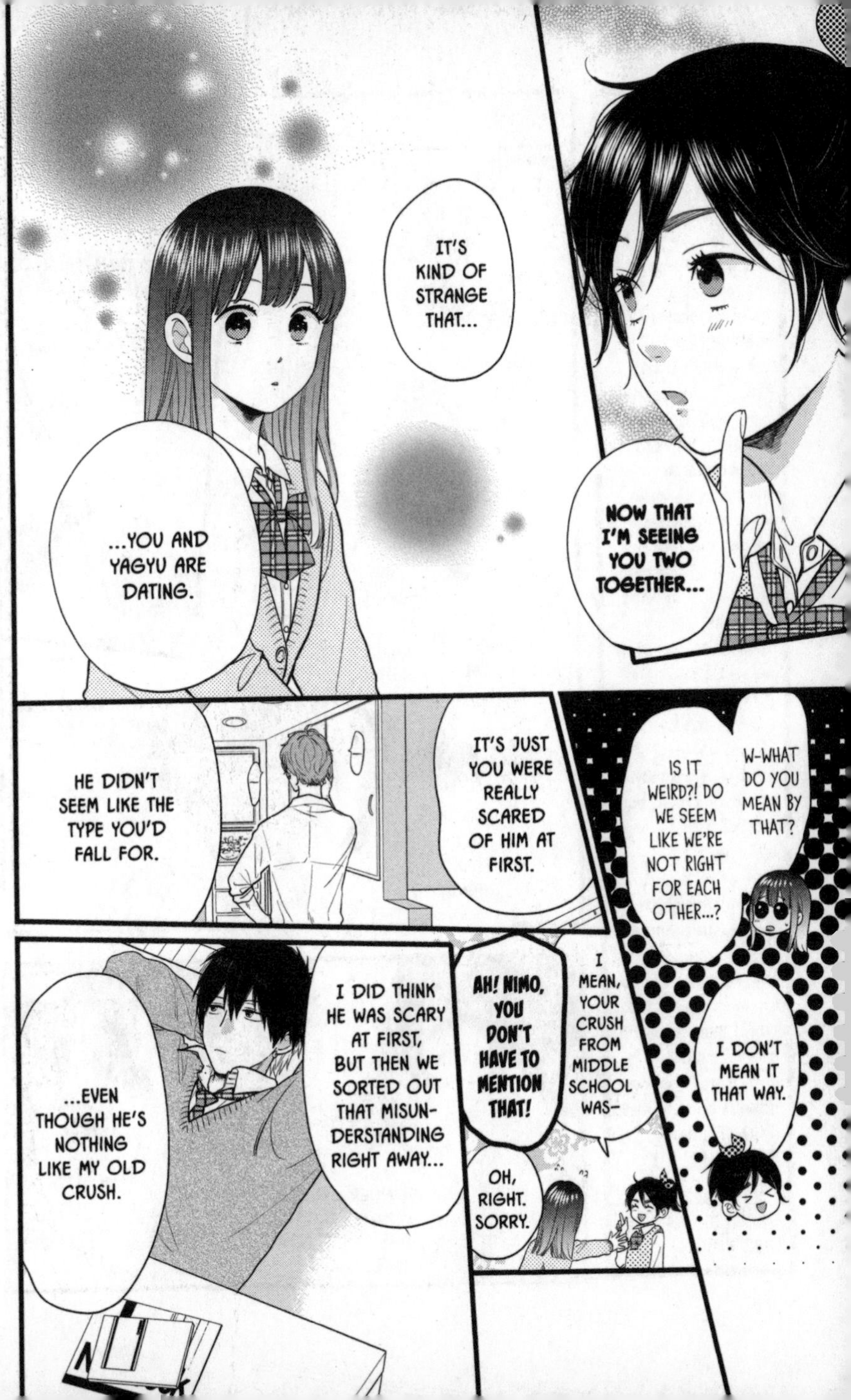
NOW THAT I'M SEEING YOU TWO TOGETHER...
IT'S KIND OF STRANGE THAT...
...YOU AND YAGYU ARE DATING.
W-WHAT DO YOU MEAN BY THAT?
IS IT WEIRD?! DO WE SEEM LIKE WE'RE NOT RIGHT FOR EACH OTHER...?
I DON'T MEAN IT THAT WAY.
IT'S JUST YOU WERE REALLY SCARED OF HIM AT FIRST.
HE DIDN'T SEEM LIKE THE TYPE YOU'D FALL FOR.
I MEAN, YOUR CRUSH FROM MIDDLE SCHOOL WAS-
AH! NIMO, YOU DON'T HAVE TO MENTION THAT!
OH, RIGHT. SORRY.
I DID THINK HE WAS SCARY AT FIRST, BUT THEN WE SORTED OUT THAT MISUNDER-STANDING RIGHT AWAY...
...EVEN THOUGH HE'S NOTHING LIKE MY OLD CRUSH.

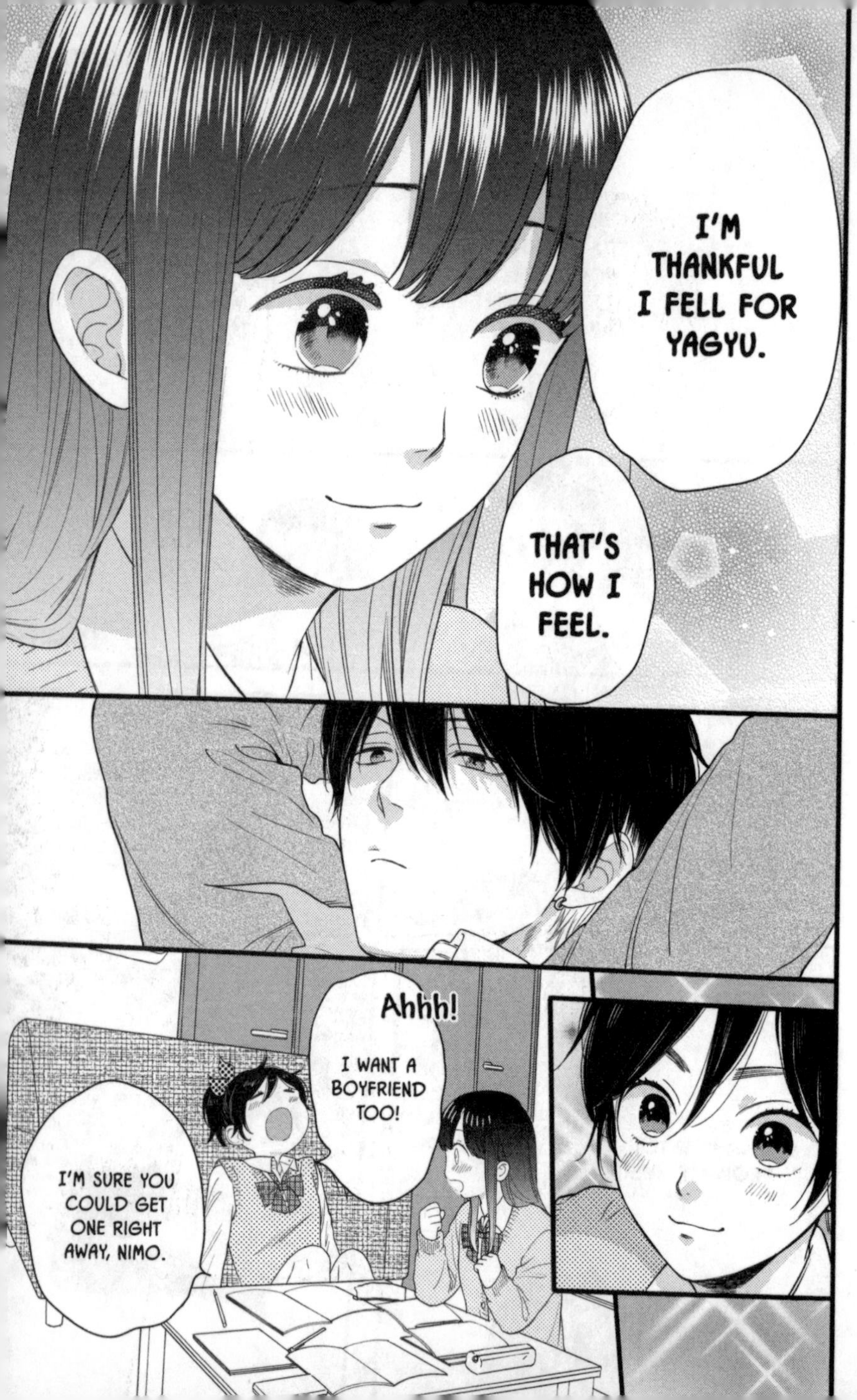
I'M THANKFUL I FELL FOR YAGYU.
THAT'S HOW I FEEL.
Ahhh!
I WANT A BOYFRIEND TOO!
I'M SURE YOU COULD GET ONE RIGHT AWAY, NIMO.

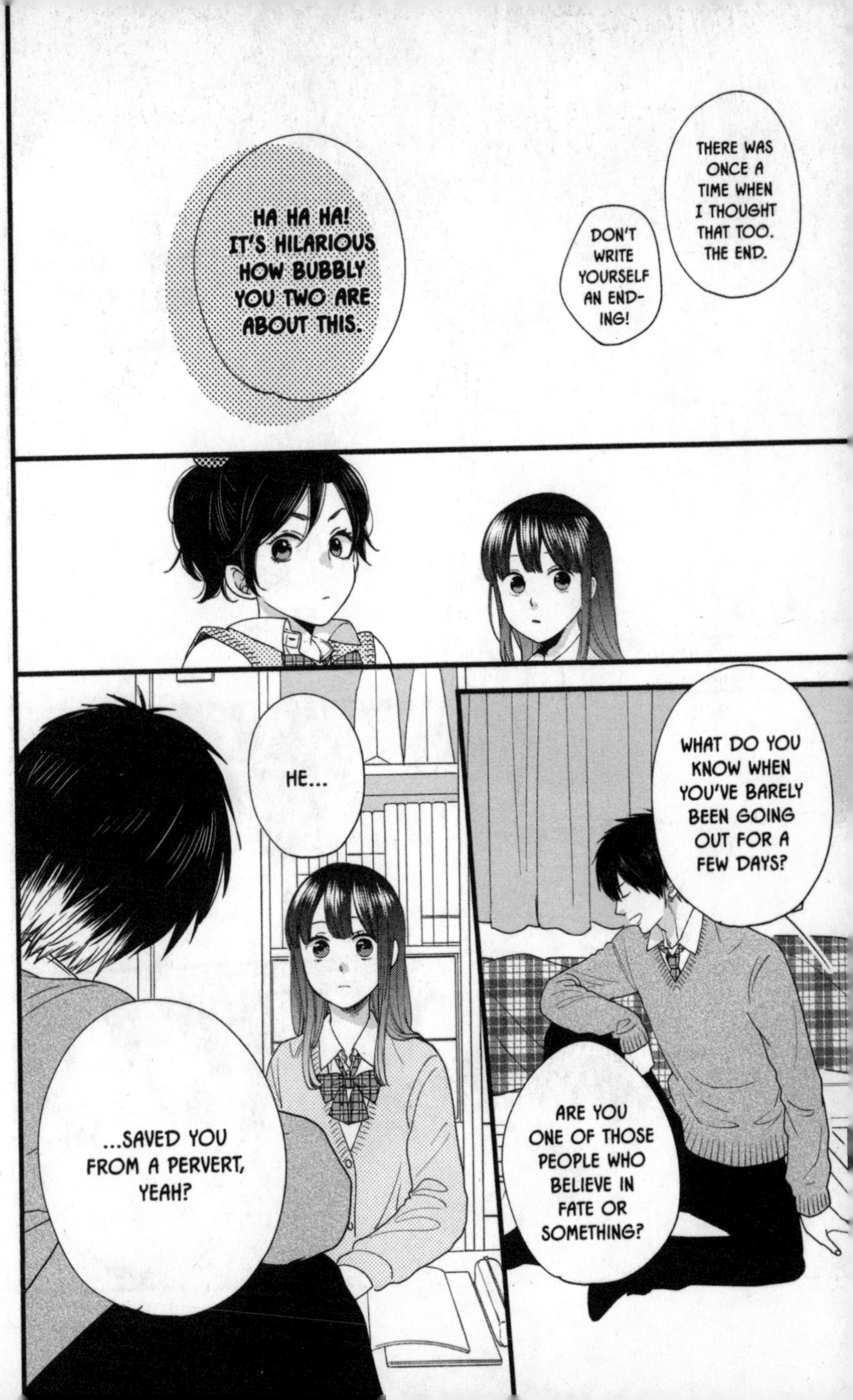
THERE WAS ONCE A TIME WHEN I THOUGHT THAT TOO. THE END.
DON'T WRITE YOURSELF AN END-ING!
HA HA HA! IT'S HILARIOUS HOW BUBBLY YOU TWO ARE ABOUT THIS.
WHAT DO YOU KNOW WHEN YOU'VE BARELY BEEN GOING OUT FOR A FEW DAYS?
ARE YOU ONE OF THOSE PEOPLE WHO BELIEVE IN FATE OR SOMETHING?
HE...
...SAVED YOU FROM A PERVERT, YEAH?

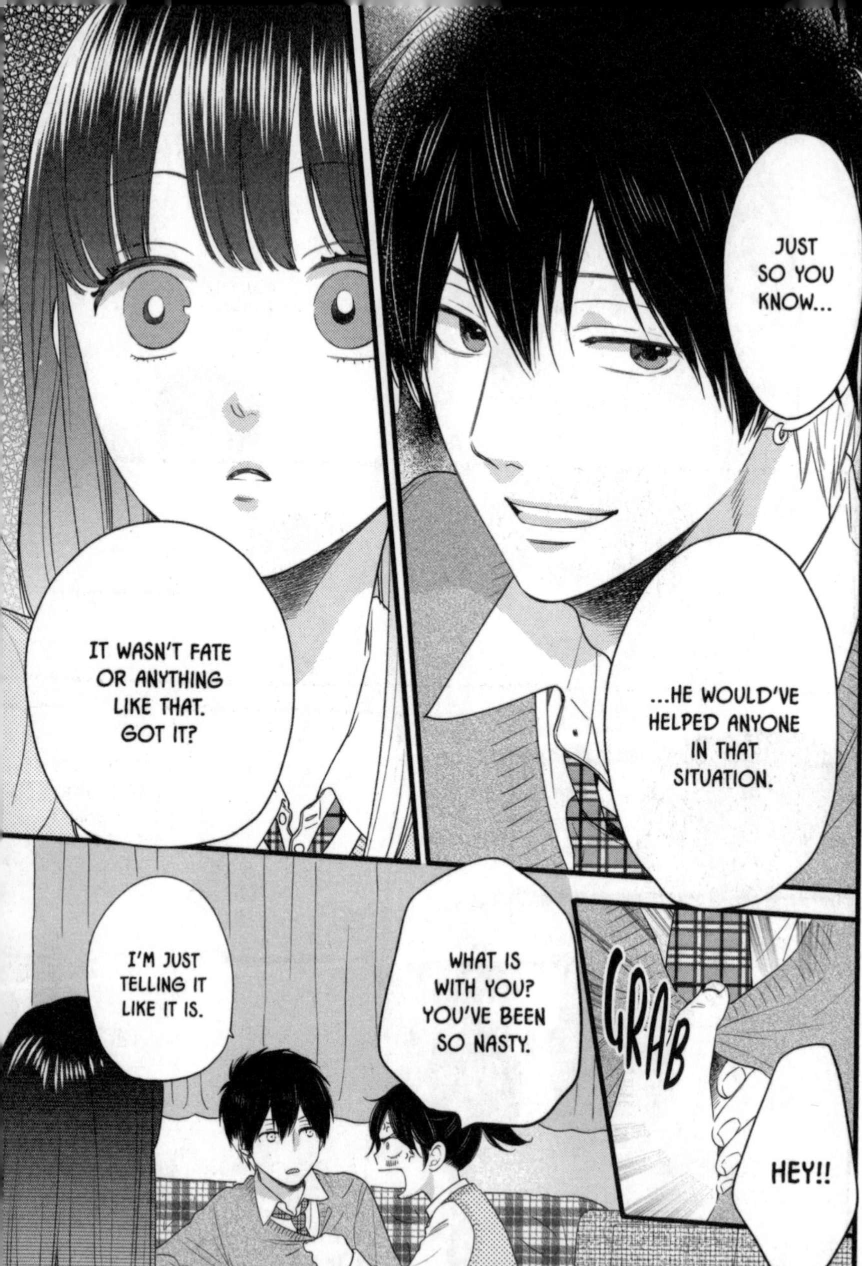
JUST SO YOU KNOW...
...HE WOULD'VE HELPED ANYONE IN THAT SITUATION.
IT WASN'T FATE OR ANYTHING LIKE THAT. GOT IT?
GRAB
HEY!!
WHAT IS WITH YOU? YOU'VE BEEN SO NASTY.
I'M JUST TELLING IT LIKE IT IS.

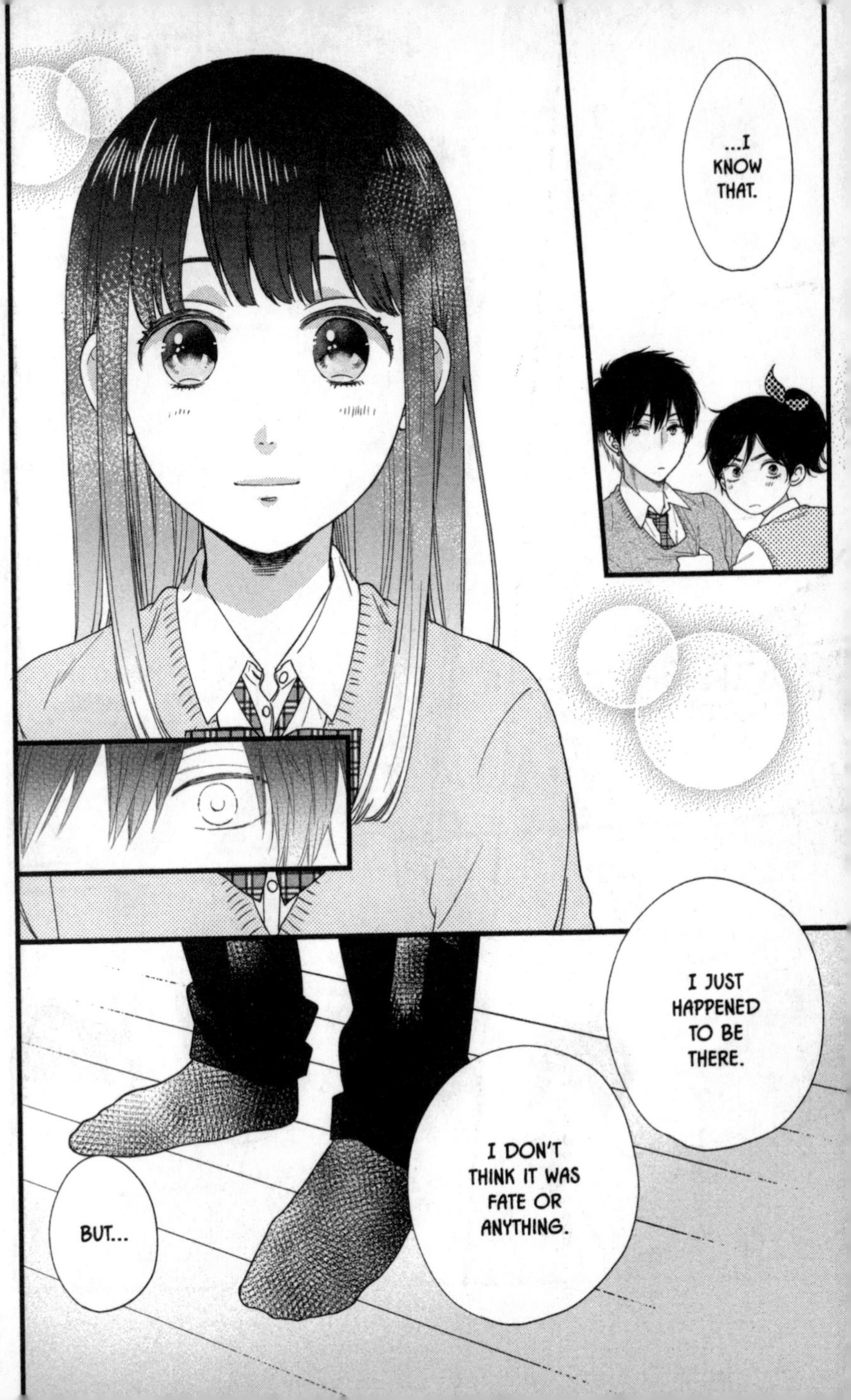
...I KNOW THAT.
I JUST HAPPENED TO BE THERE.
I DON'T THINK IT WAS FATE OR ANYTHING.
BUT...

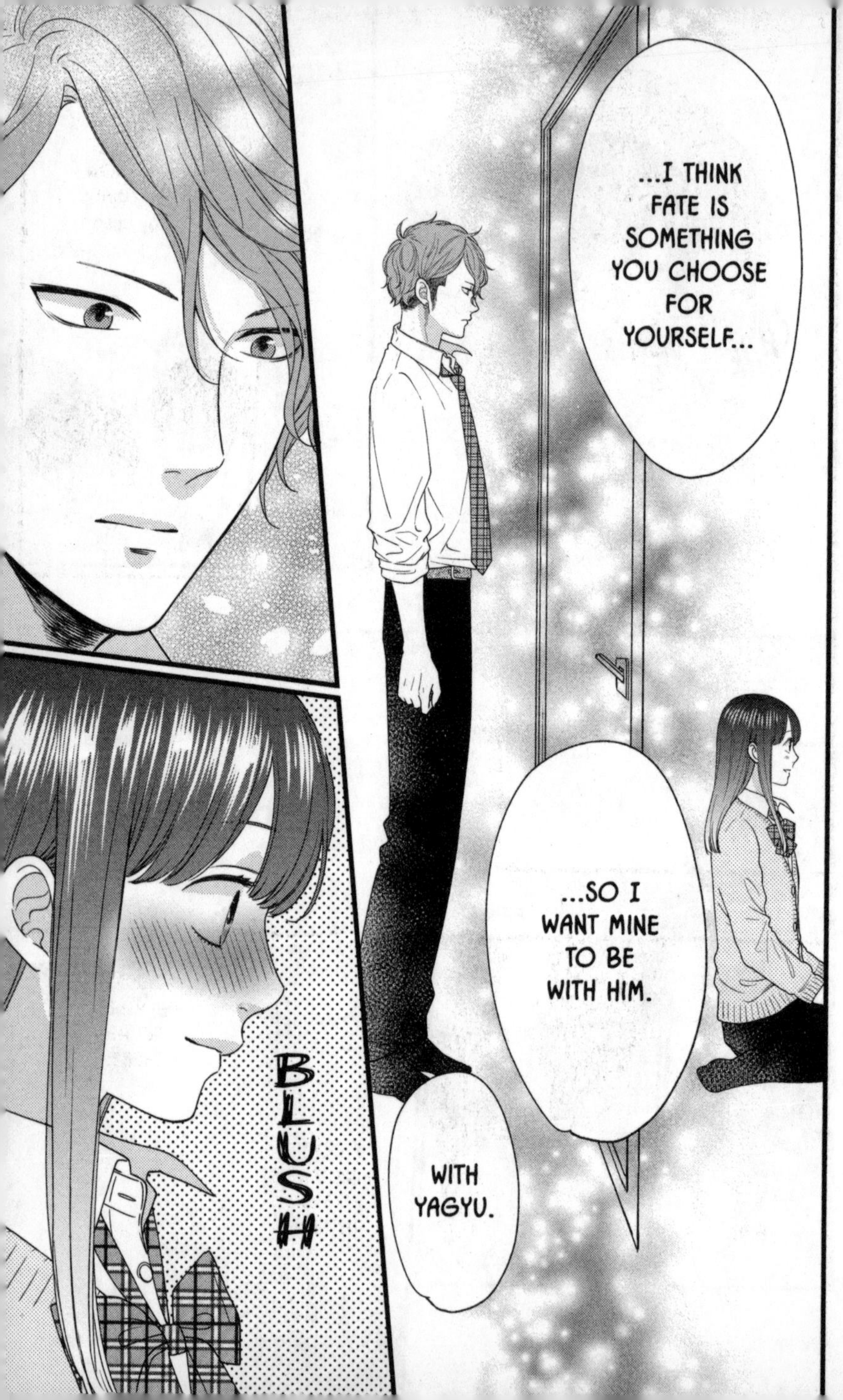
...I THINK FATE IS SOMETHING YOU CHOOSE FOR YOURSELF...
...SO I WANT MINE TO BE WITH HIM.
WITH YAGYU.
BLUSH

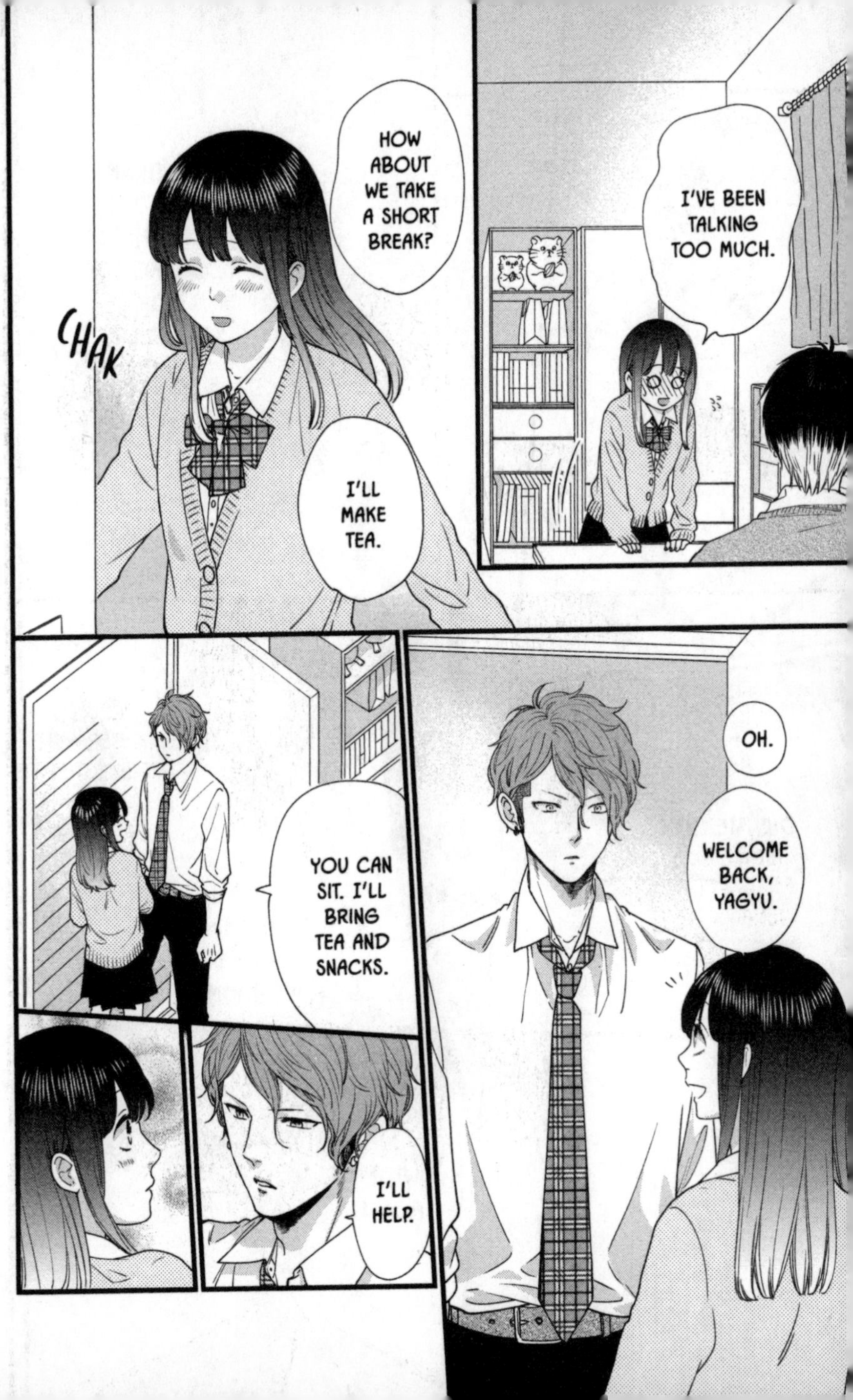
I'VE BEEN TALKING TOO MUCH.
HOW ABOUT WE TAKE A SHORT BREAK?
CHAK
I'LL MAKE TEA.
OH.
WELCOME BACK, YAGYU.
YOU CAN SIT. I'LL BRING TEA AND SNACKS.
I'LL HELP.

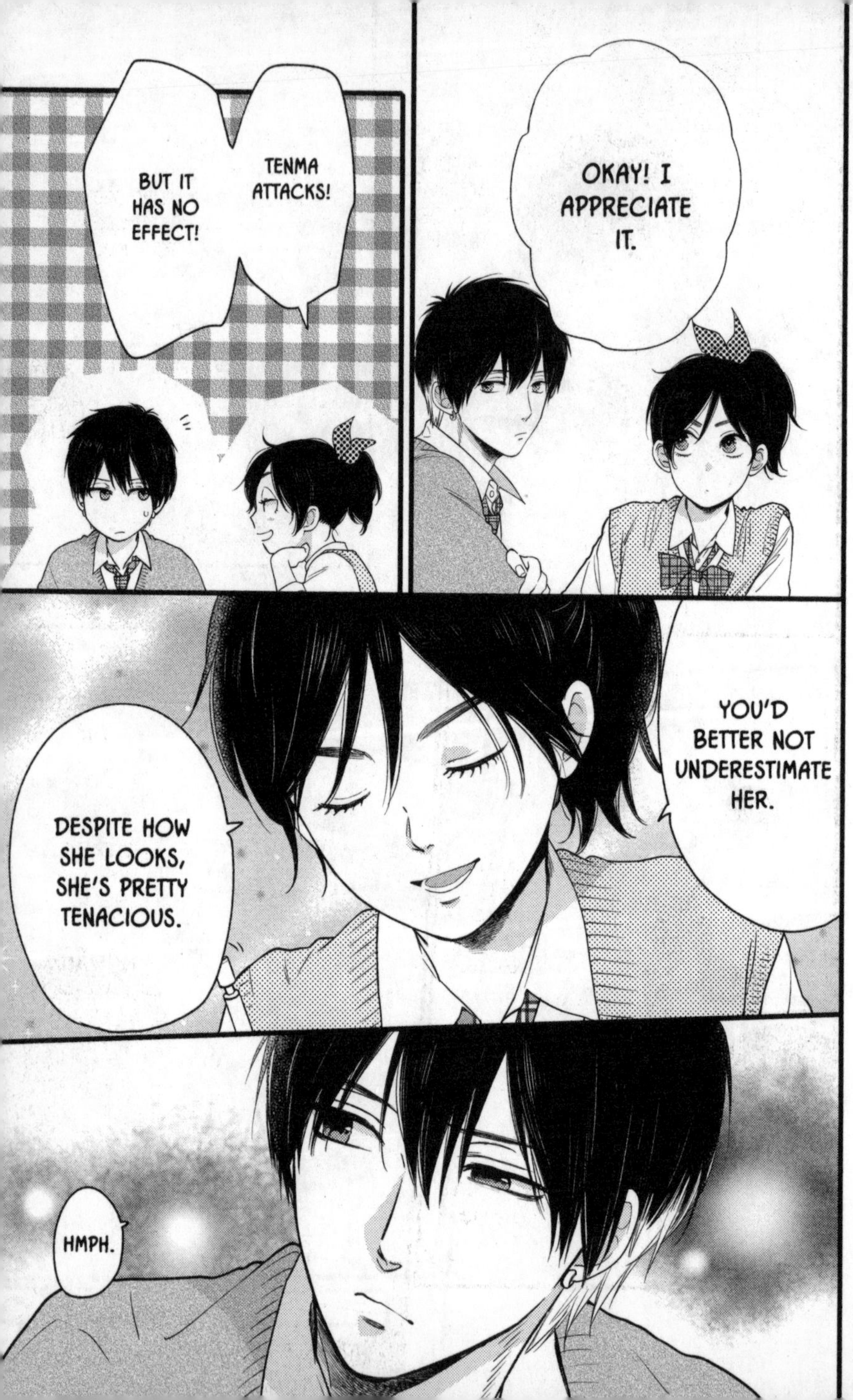
OKAY! I APPRECIATE IT.
TENMA ATTACKS!
BUT IT HAS NO EFFECT!
YOU'D BETTER NOT UNDERESTIMATE HER.
DESPITE HOW SHE LOOKS, SHE'S PRETTY TENACIOUS.
HMPH.

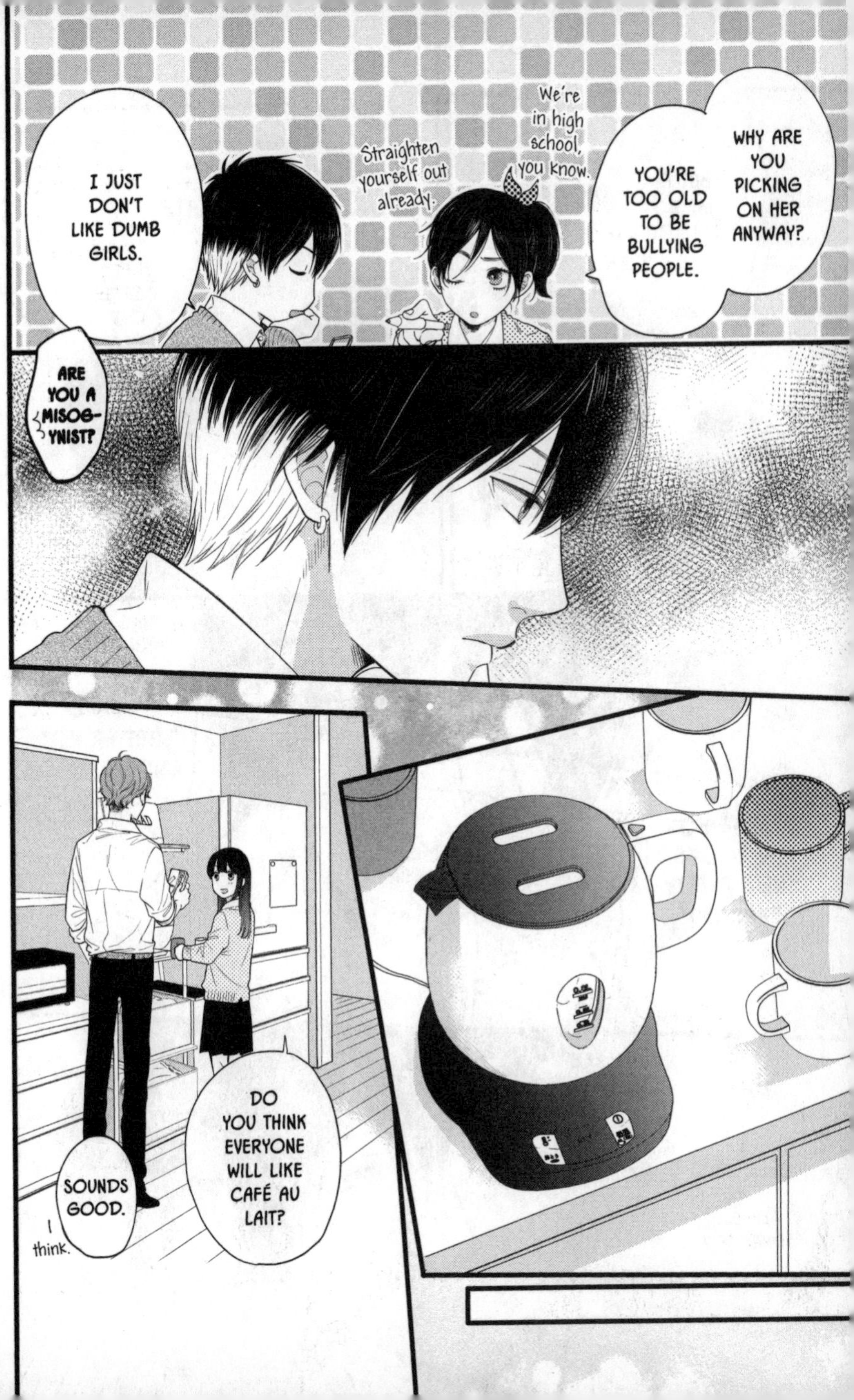
WHY ARE YOU PICKING ON HER ANYWAY?
YOU'RE TOO OLD TO BE BULLYING PEOPLE.
We're in high school, you know.
Straighten yourself out already.
I JUST DON'T LIKE DUMB GIRLS.
ARE YOU A MISOGYNIST?
DO YOU THINK EVERYONE WILL LIKE CAFÉ AU LAIT?
SOUNDS GOOD.
I think.

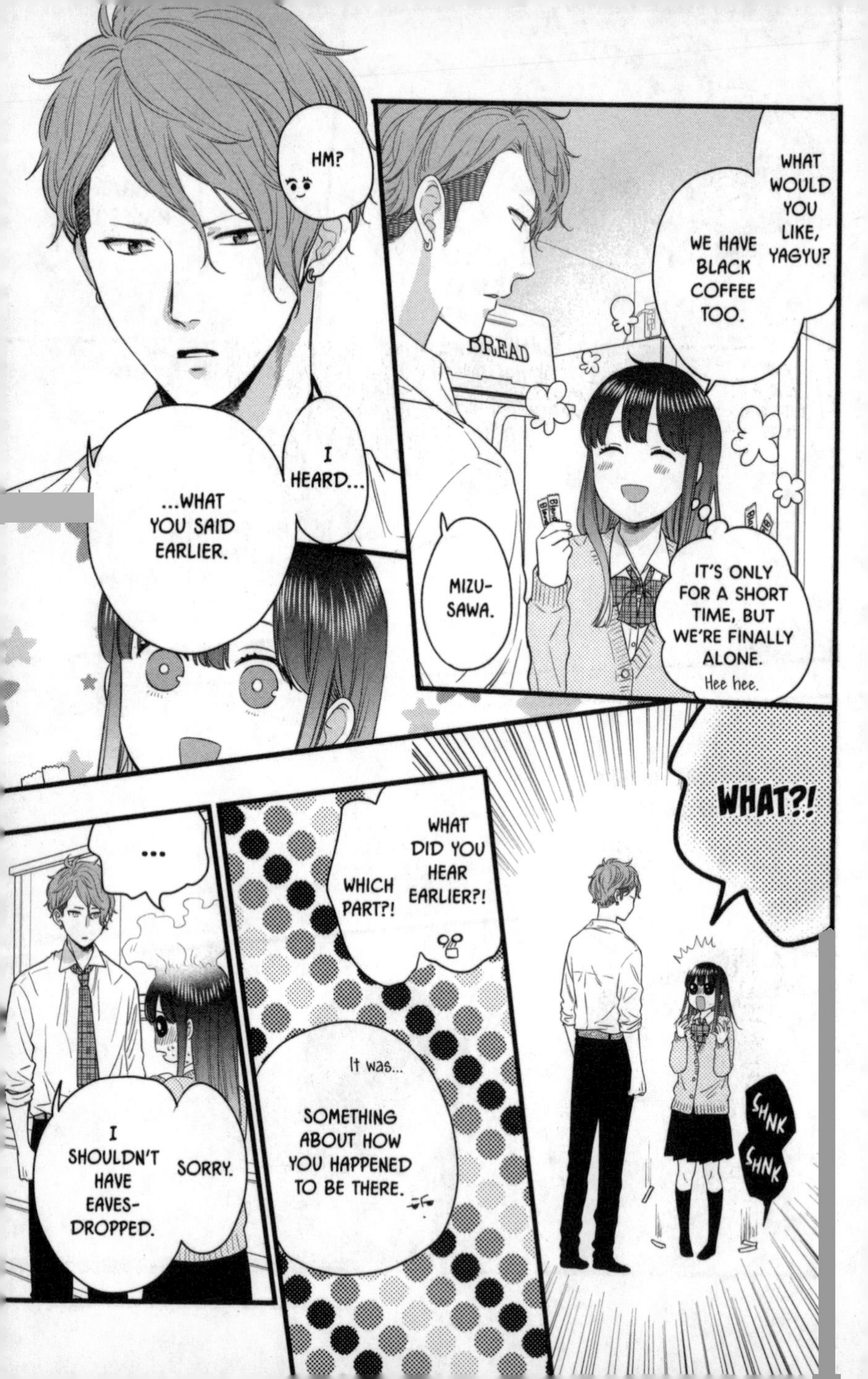
WHAT WOULD YOU LIKE, YAGYU?
WE HAVE BLACK COFFEE TOO.
IT'S ONLY FOR A SHORT TIME, BUT WE'RE FINALLY ALONE.
Hee hee.
MIZU-SAWA.
HM?
I HEARD...
...WHAT YOU SAID EARLIER.
WHAT?!
SHNK
SHNK
WHAT DID YOU HEAR EARLIER?!
WHICH PART?!
It was...
SOMETHING ABOUT HOW YOU HAPPENED TO BE THERE.
...
SORRY.
I SHOULDN'T HAVE EAVES-DROPPED.

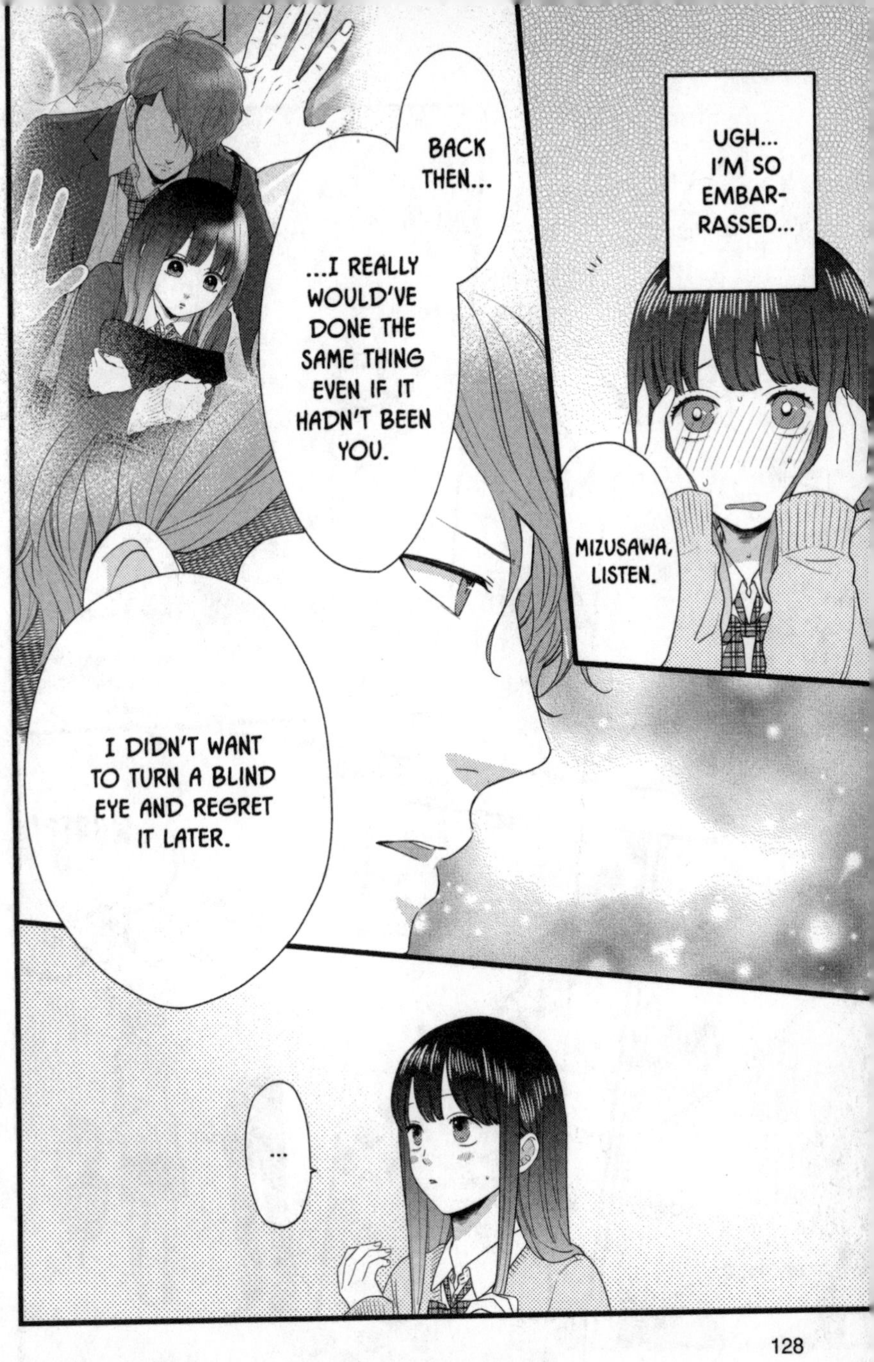
UGH... I'M SO EMBARRASSED...
MIZUSAWA, LISTEN.
BACK THEN...
...I REALLY WOULD'VE DONE THE SAME THING EVEN IF IT HADN'T BEEN YOU.
I DIDN'T WANT TO TURN A BLIND EYE AND REGRET IT LATER.
...

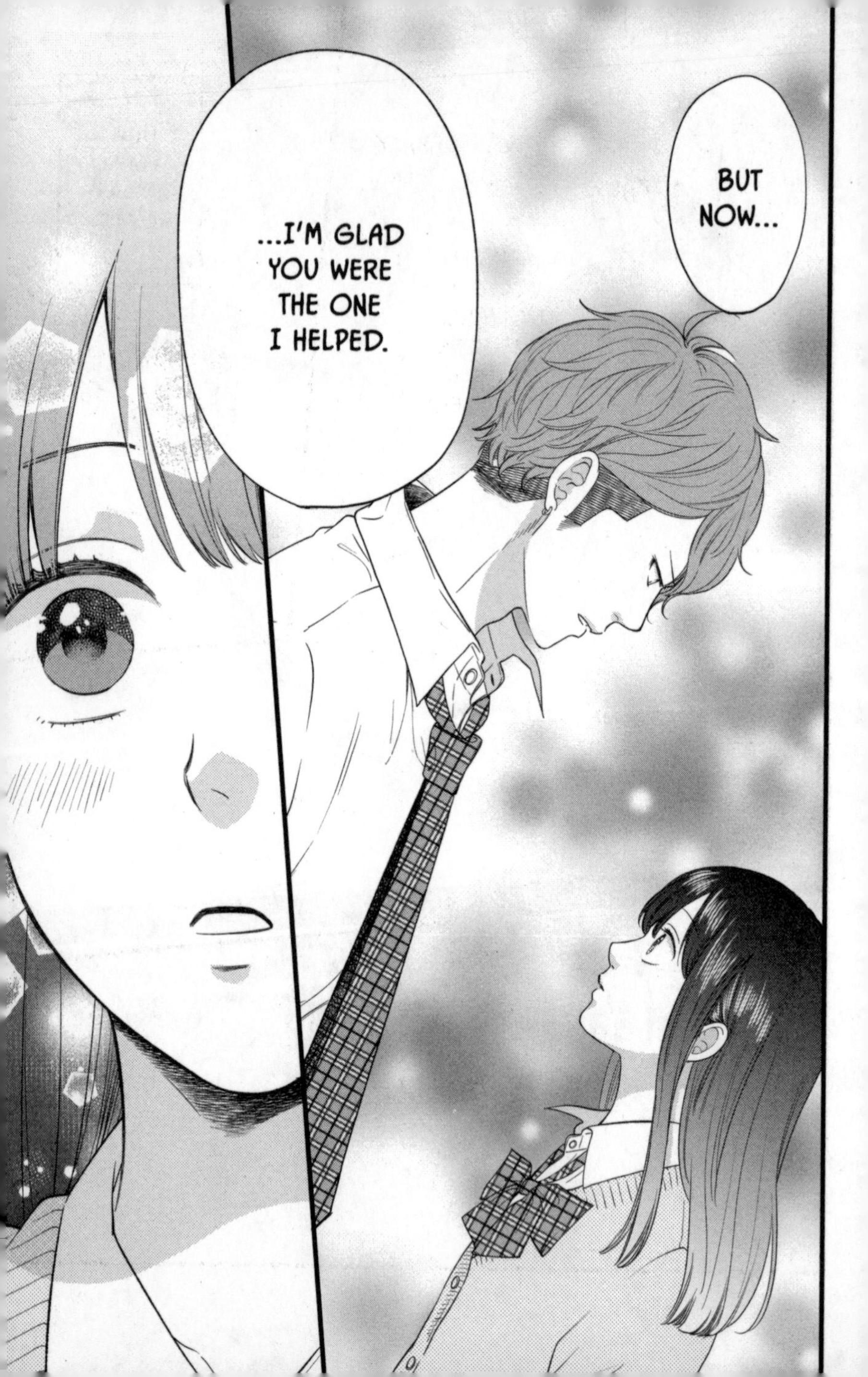
BUT NOW...
...I'M GLAD YOU WERE THE ONE I HELPED.

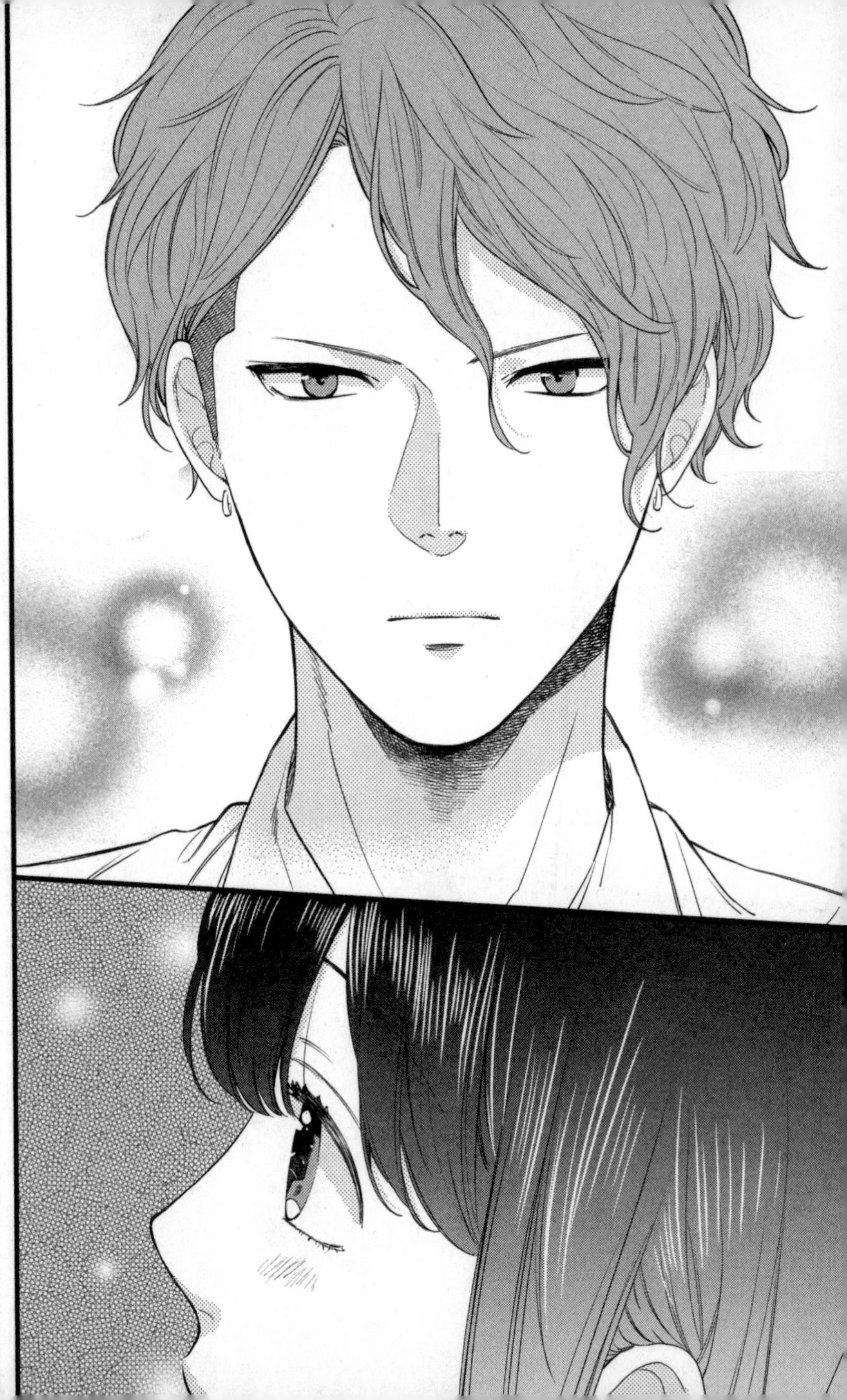

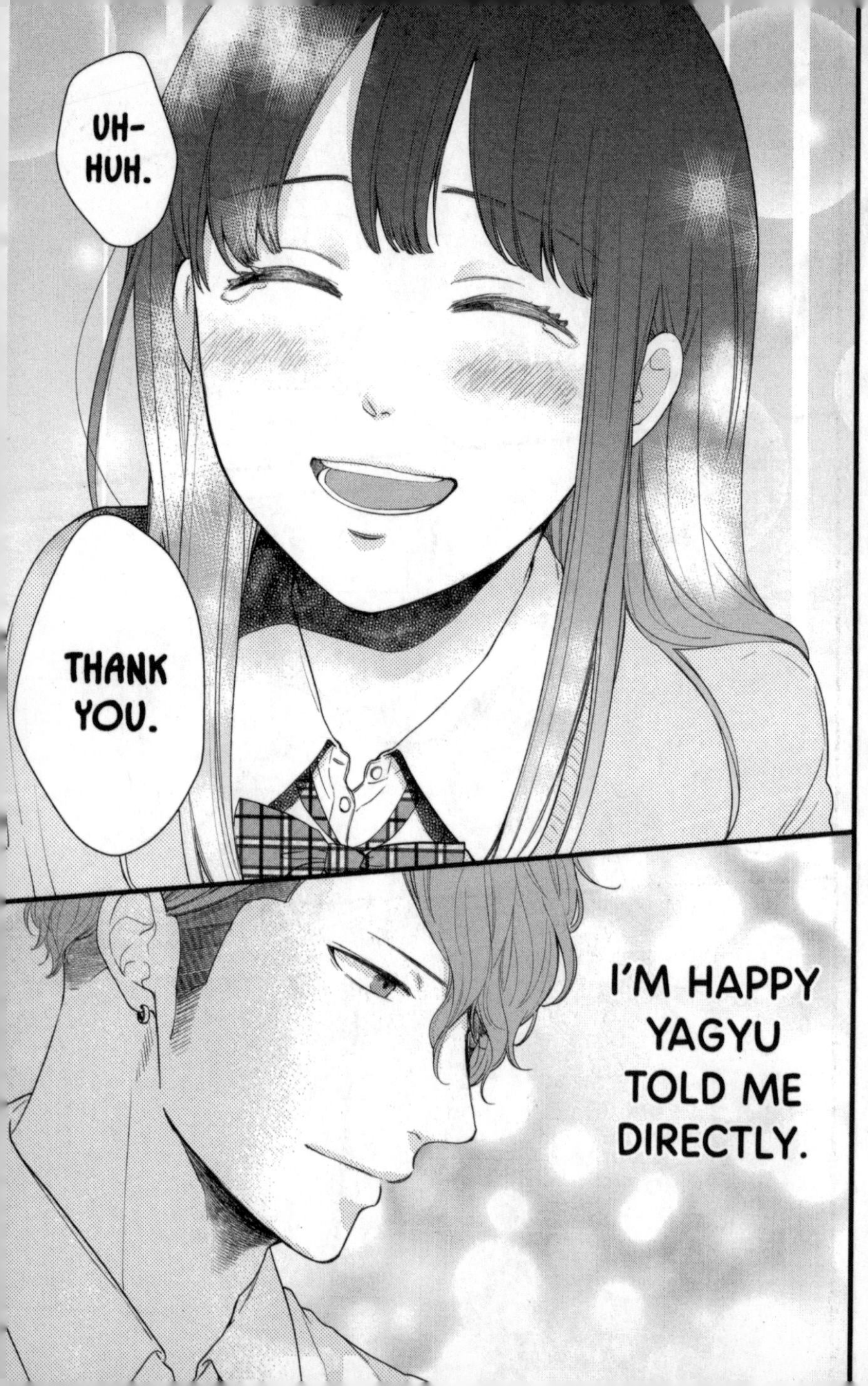
UH-HUH.
THANK YOU.
I'M HAPPY YAGYU TOLD ME DIRECTLY.

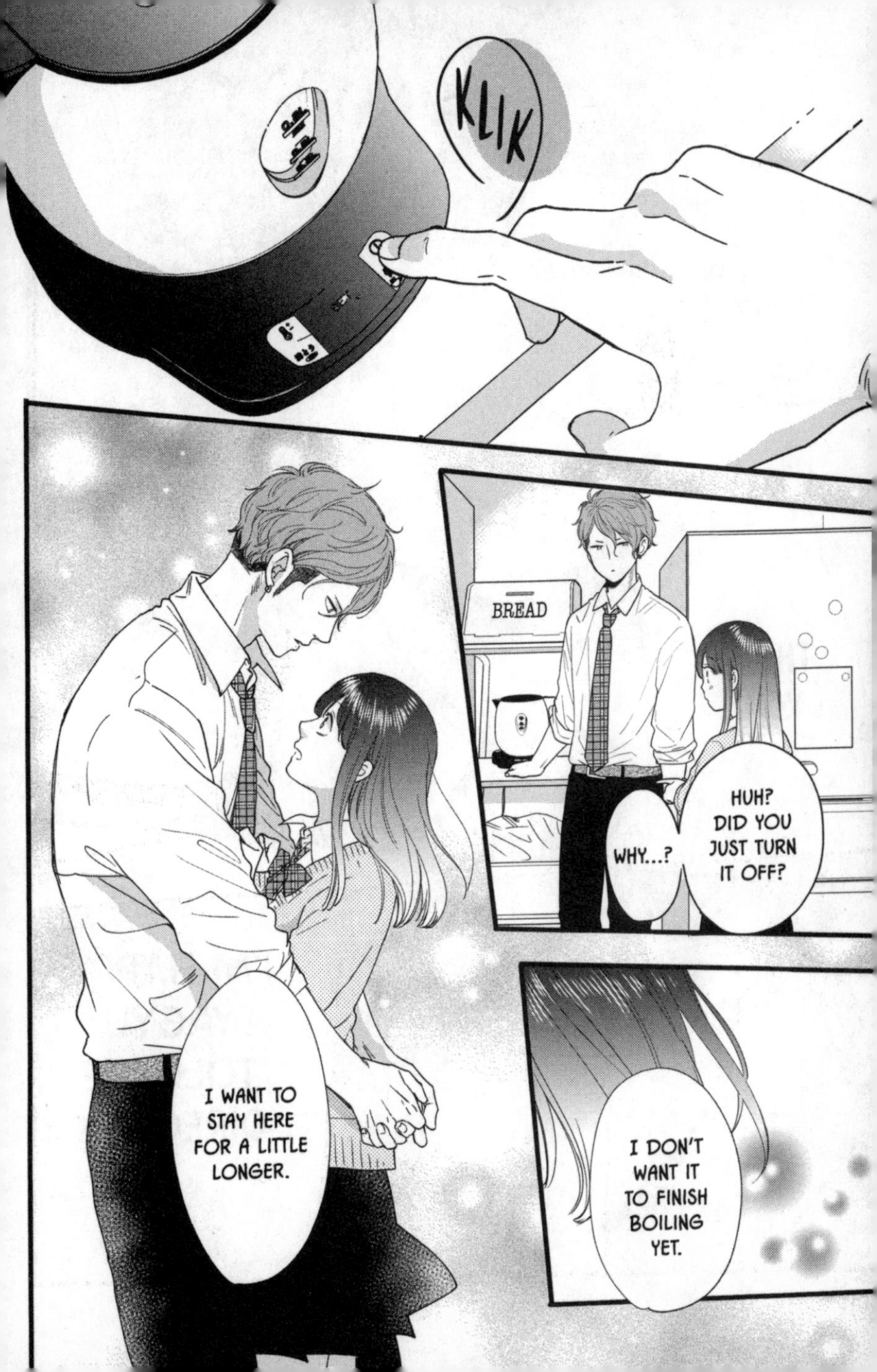
KLIK
HUH? DID YOU JUST TURN IT OFF?
WHY...?
BREAD
I WANT TO STAY HERE FOR A LITTLE LONGER.
I DON'T WANT IT TO FINISH BOILING YET.

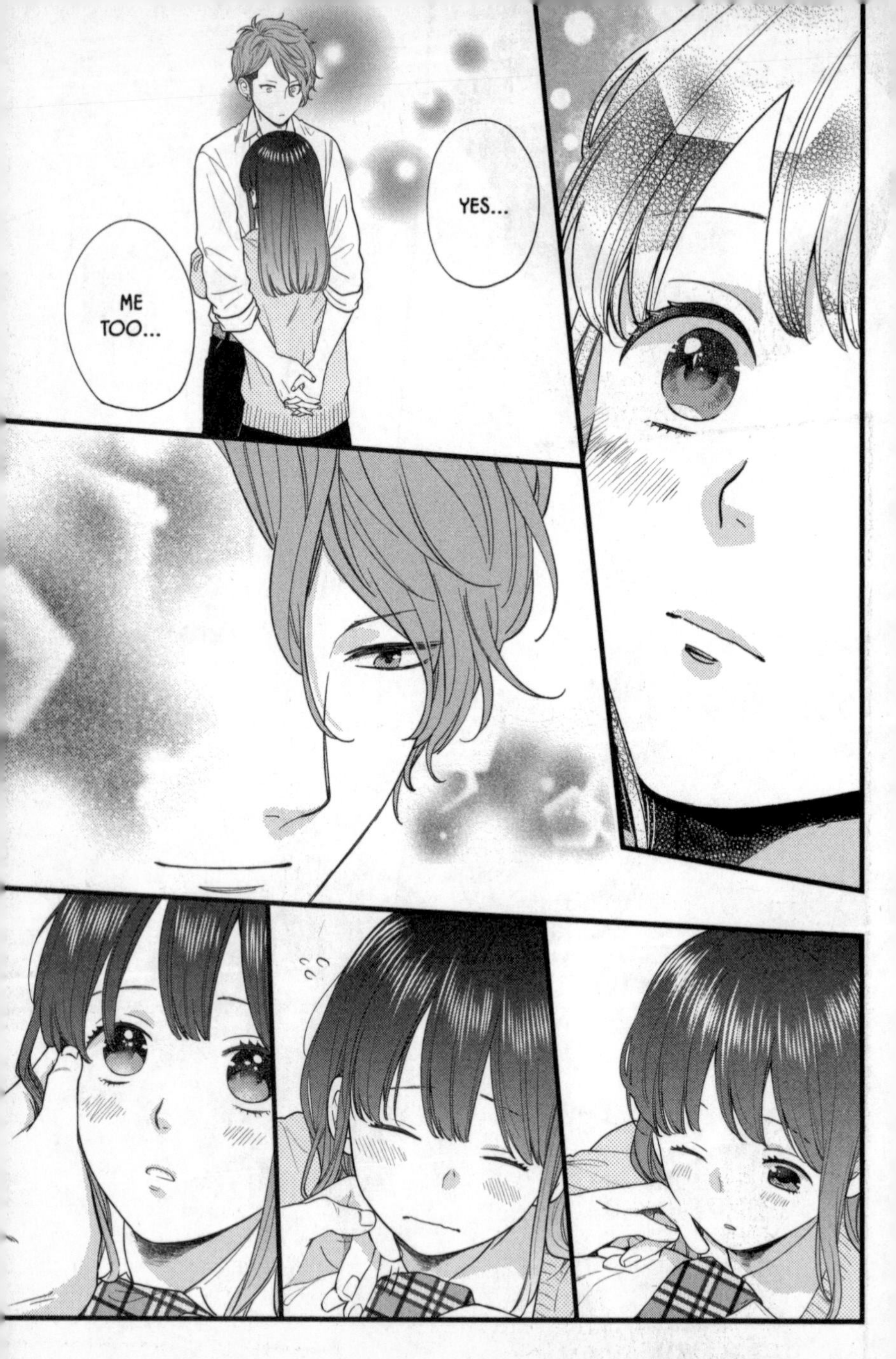
YES...
ME TOO...

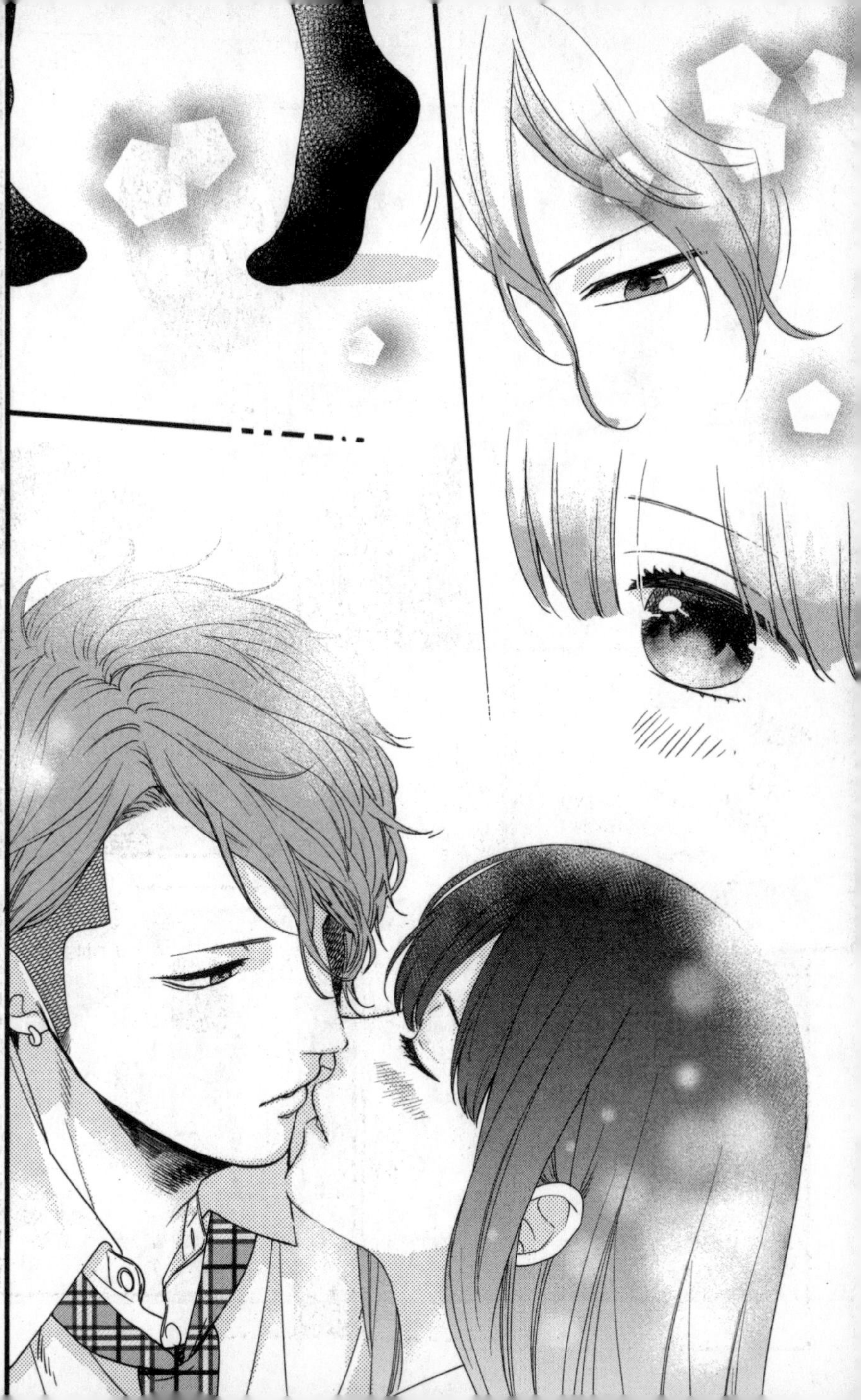

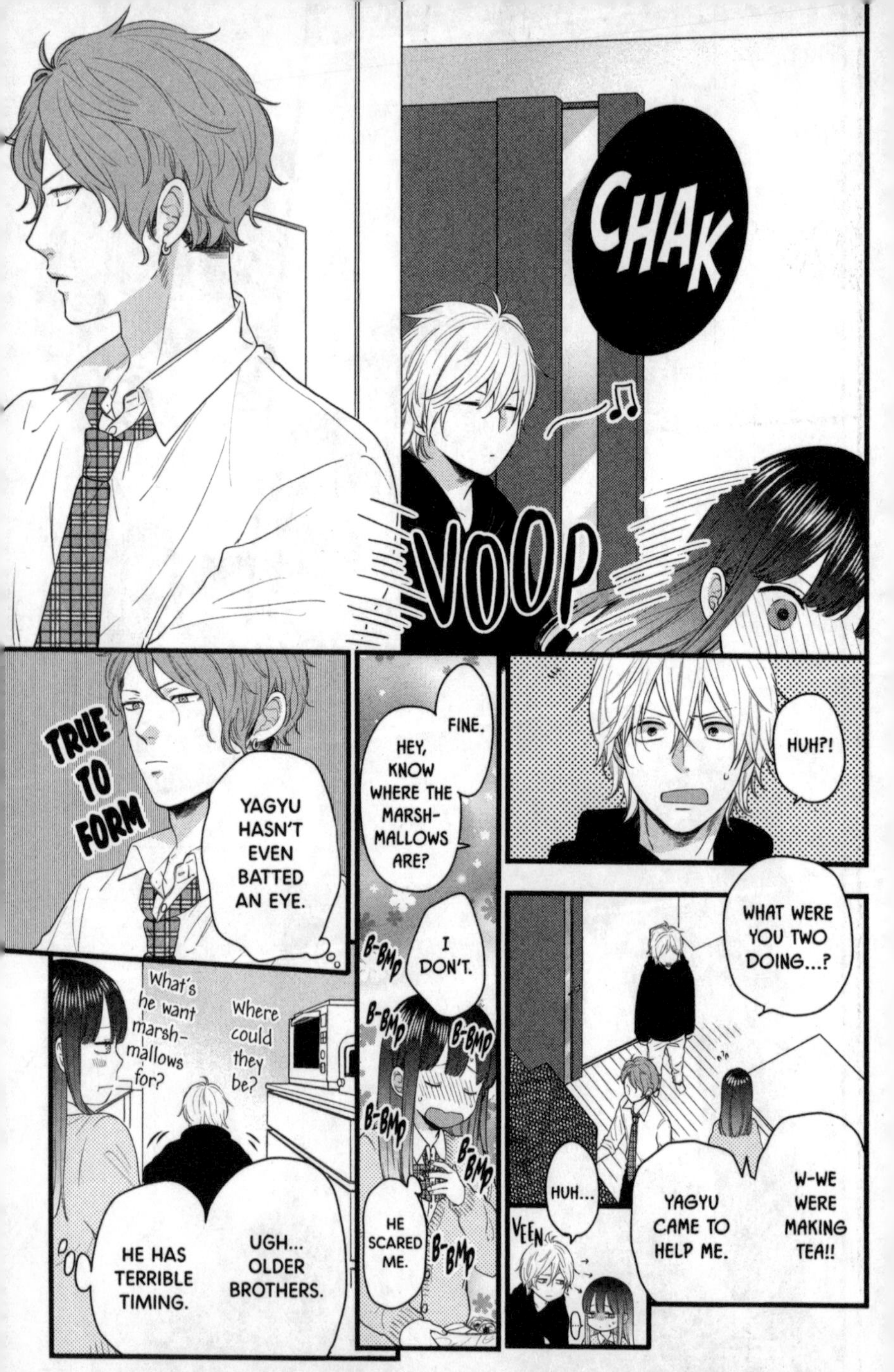
CHAK
VOOP
HUH?!
WHAT WERE YOU TWO DOING...?
W-WE WERE MAKING TEA!!
YAGYU CAME TO HELP ME.
HUH...
VEEN
FINE. HEY, KNOW WHERE THE MARSH-MALLOWS ARE?
I DON'T.
B-BMP
B-BMP
B-BMP
B-BMP
B-BMP
B-BMP
HE SCARED ME.
YAGYU HASN'T EVEN BATTED AN EYE.
TRUE TO FORM
Where could they be?
What's he want marsh-mallows for?
UGH... OLDER BROTHERS.
HE HAS TERRIBLE TIMING.

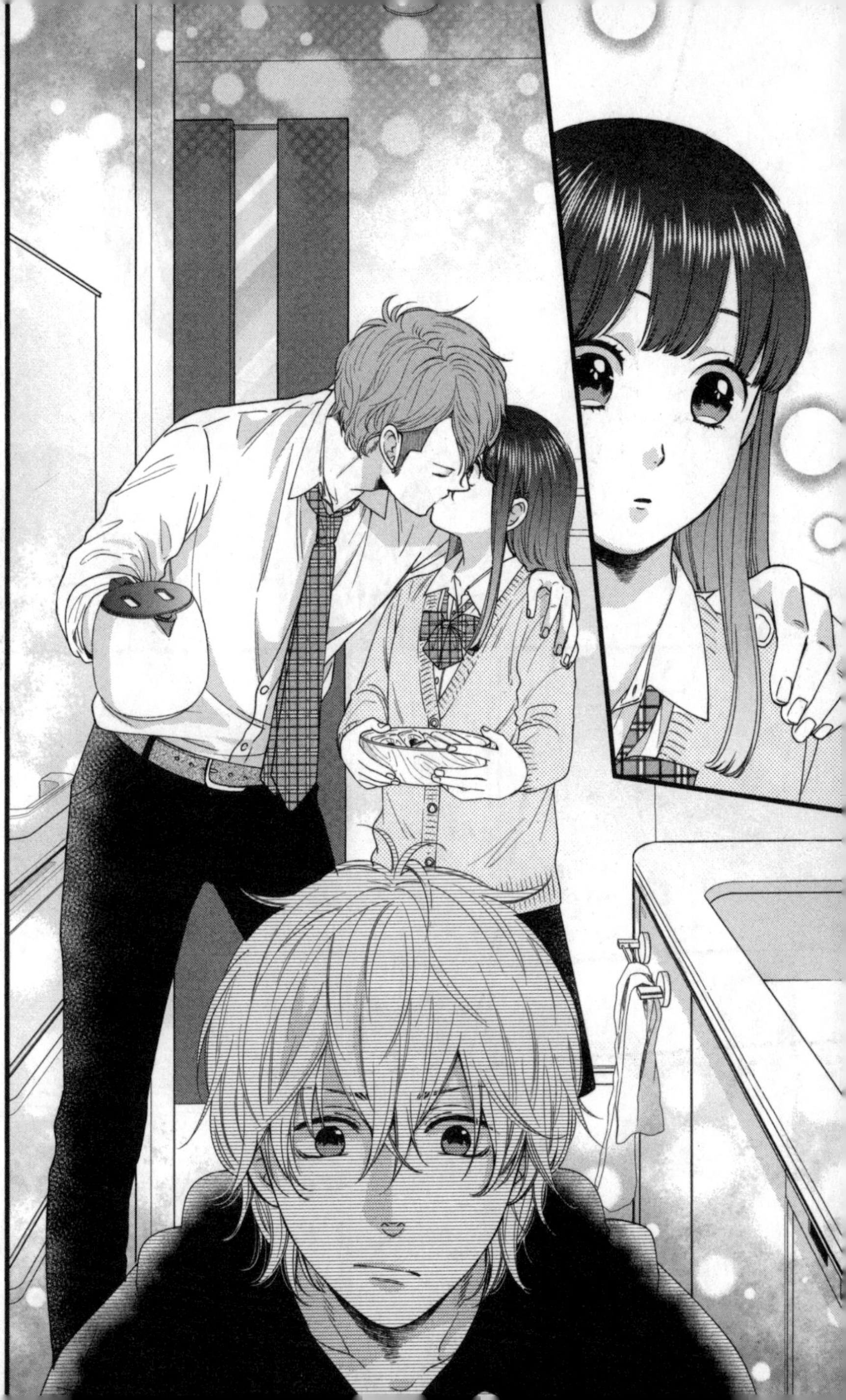

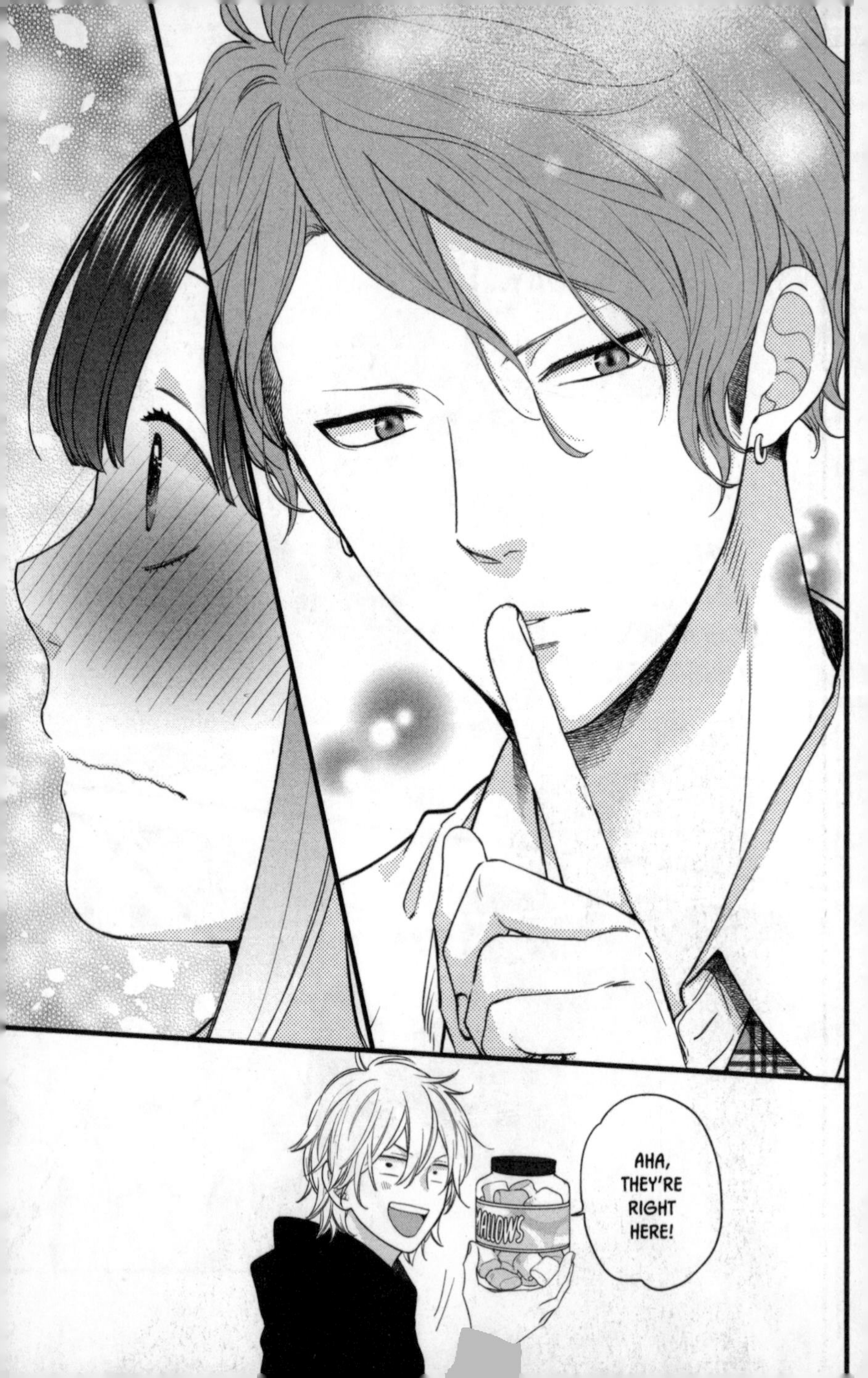
AHA, THEY'RE RIGHT HERE!
MALLOWS

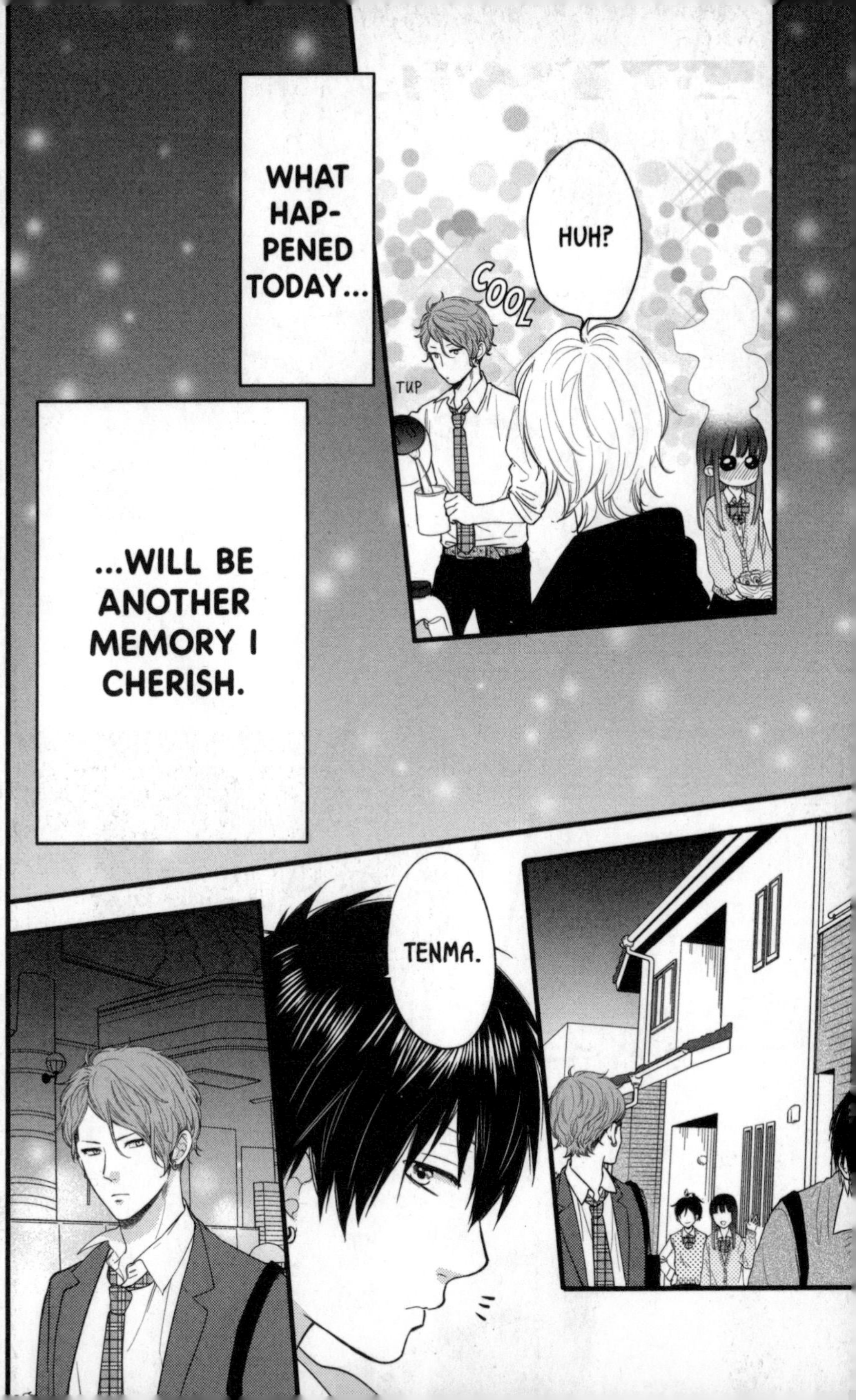
HUH?
COOL
TUP
WHAT HAP-PENED TODAY...
...WILL BE ANOTHER MEMORY I CHERISH.
TENMA.

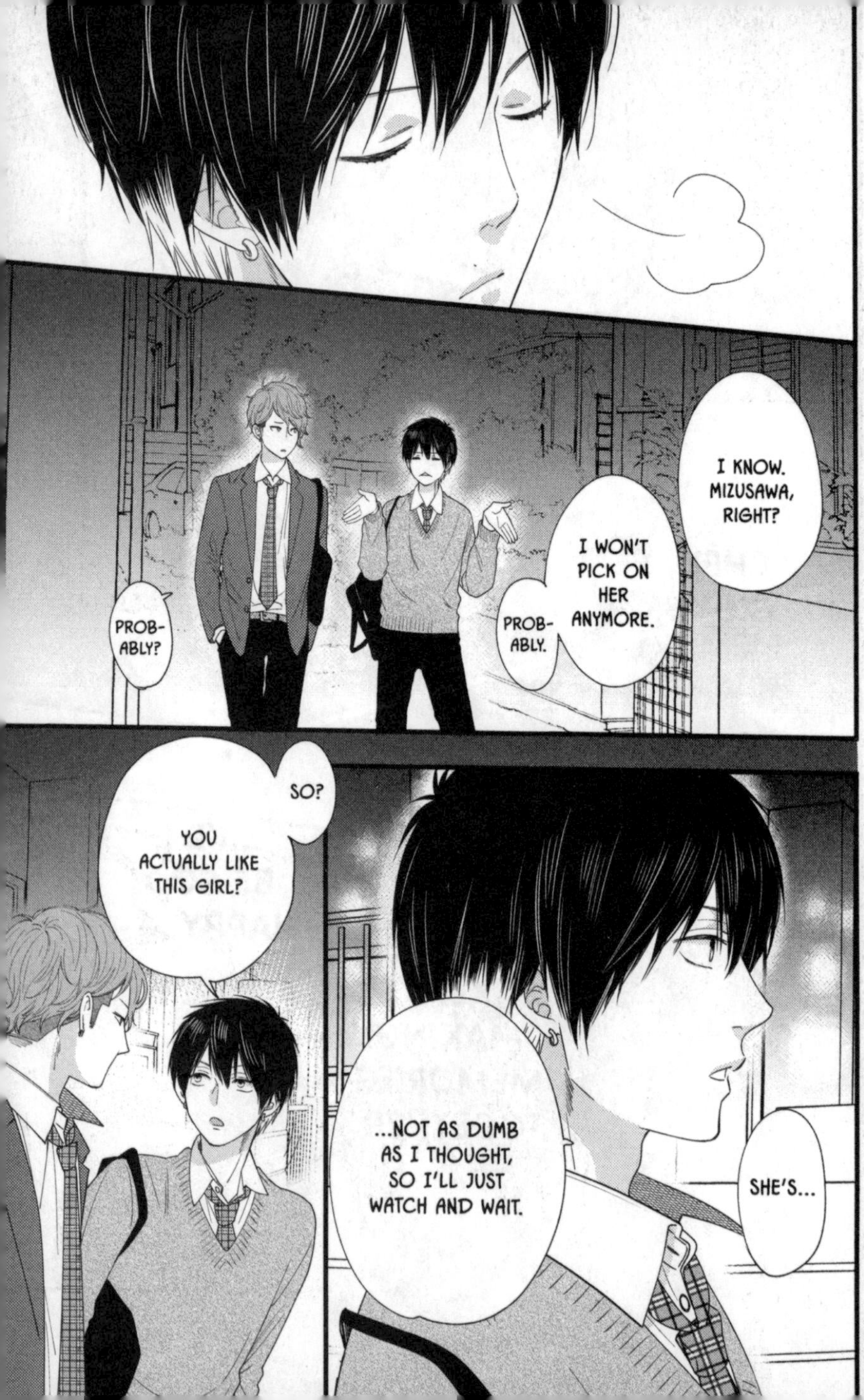
I KNOW. MIZUSAWA, RIGHT?
I WON'T PICK ON HER ANYMORE.
PROB-ABLY.
PROB-ABLY?
SHE'S...
...NOT AS DUMB AS I THOUGHT, SO I'LL JUST WATCH AND WAIT.
SO?
YOU ACTUALLY LIKE THIS GIRL?

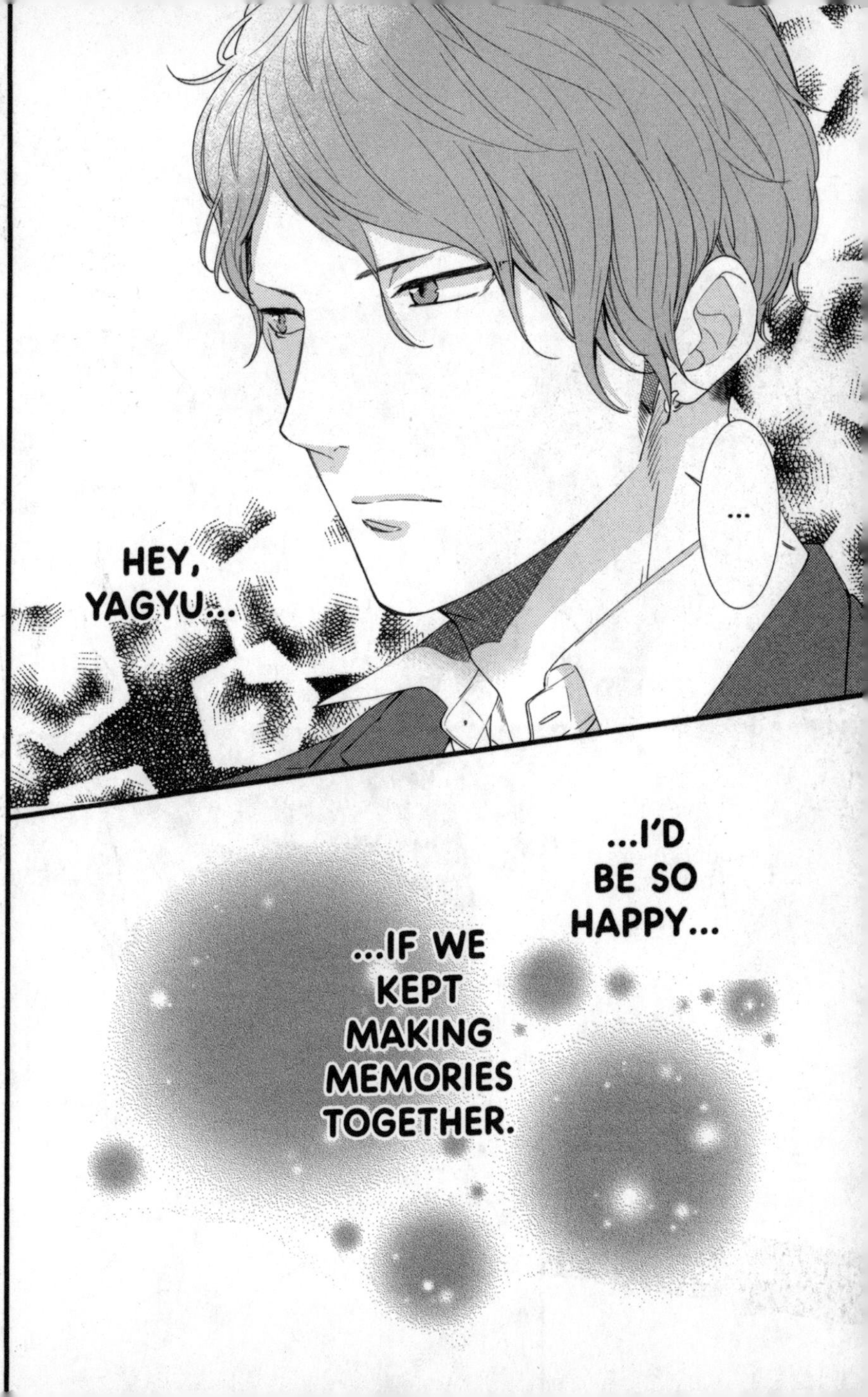
...
HEY, YAGYU...
...I'D BE SO HAPPY...
...IF WE KEPT MAKING MEMORIES TOGETHER.

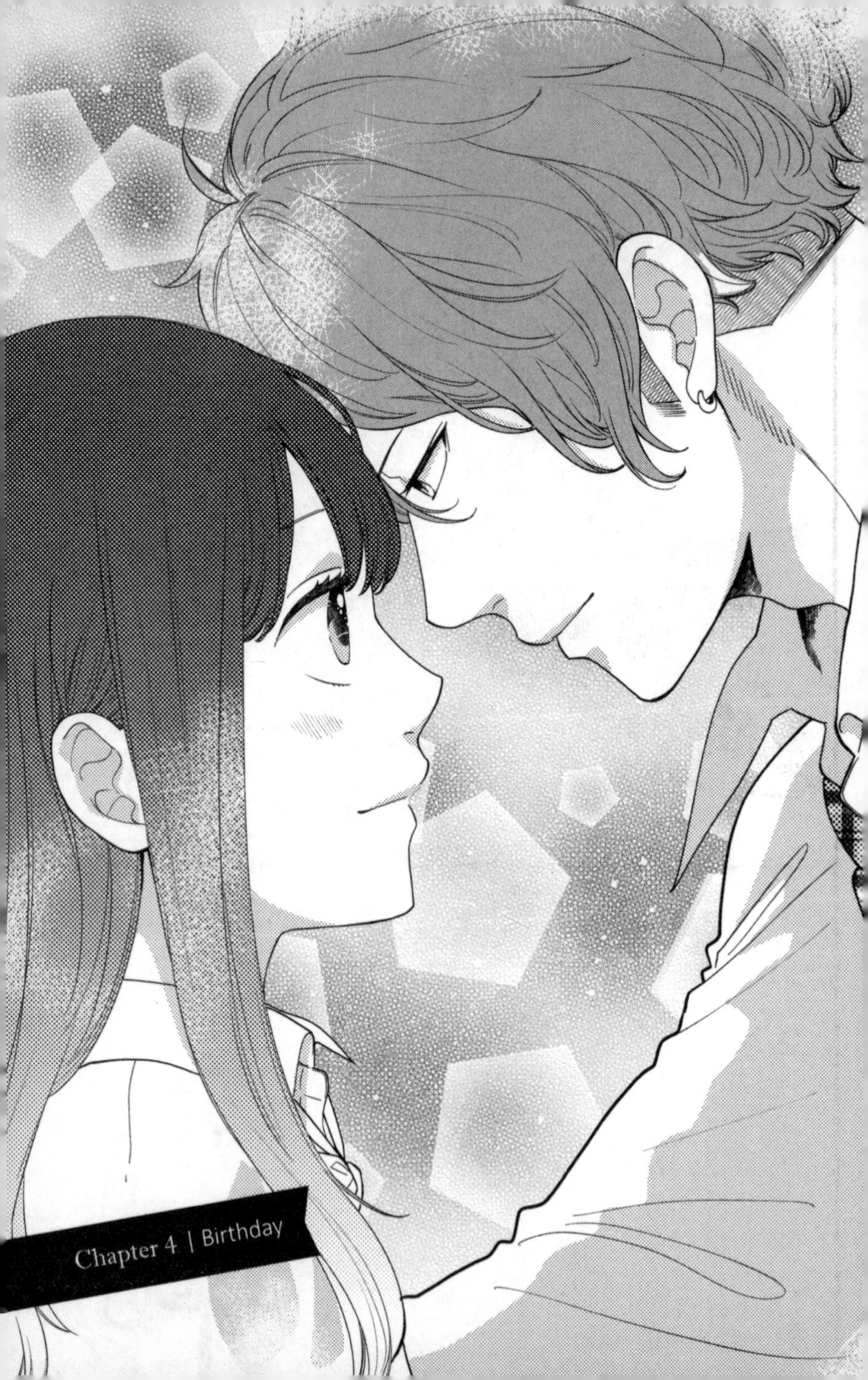
Chapter 4 | Birthday

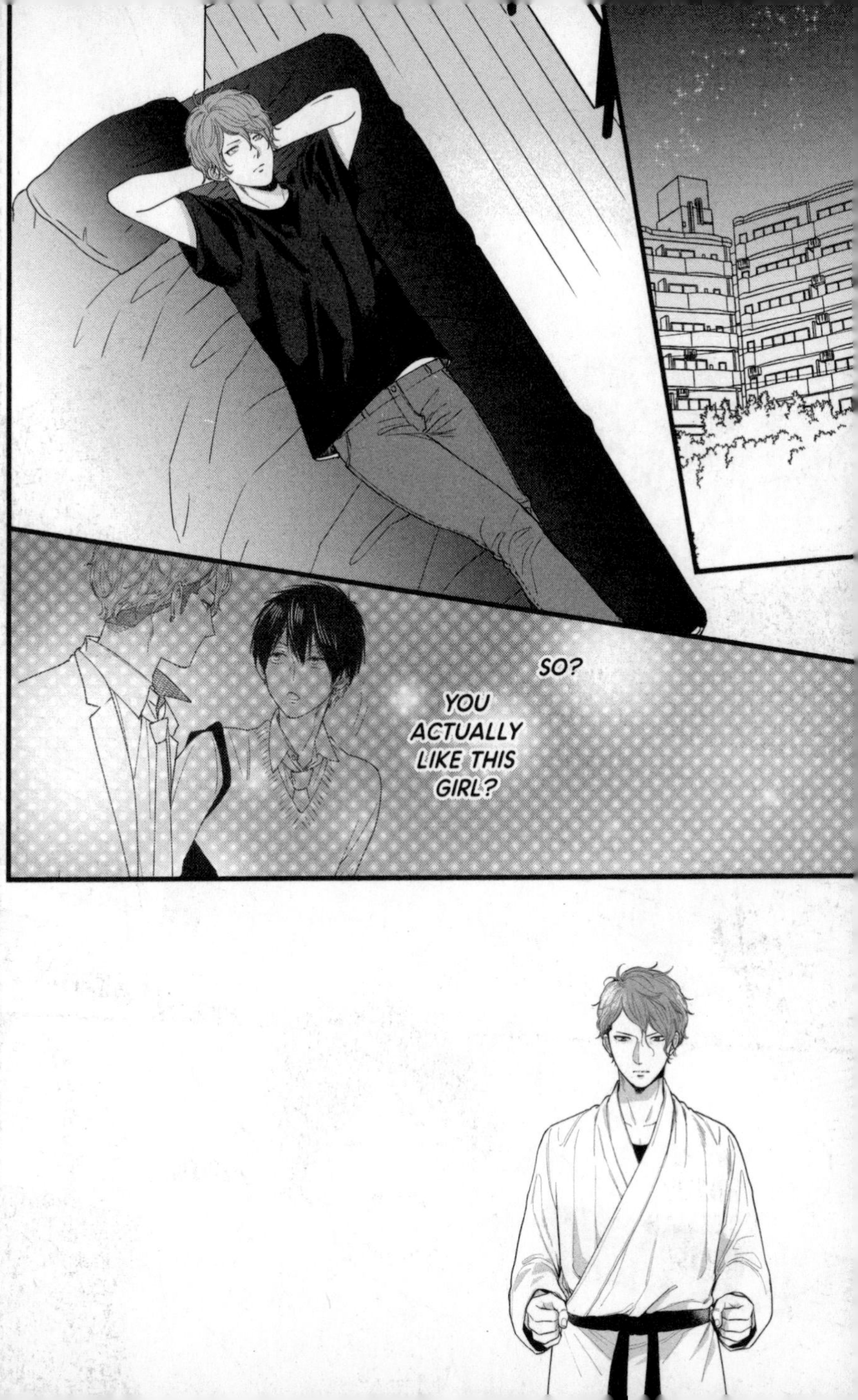
SO?
YOU ACTUALLY LIKE THIS GIRL?

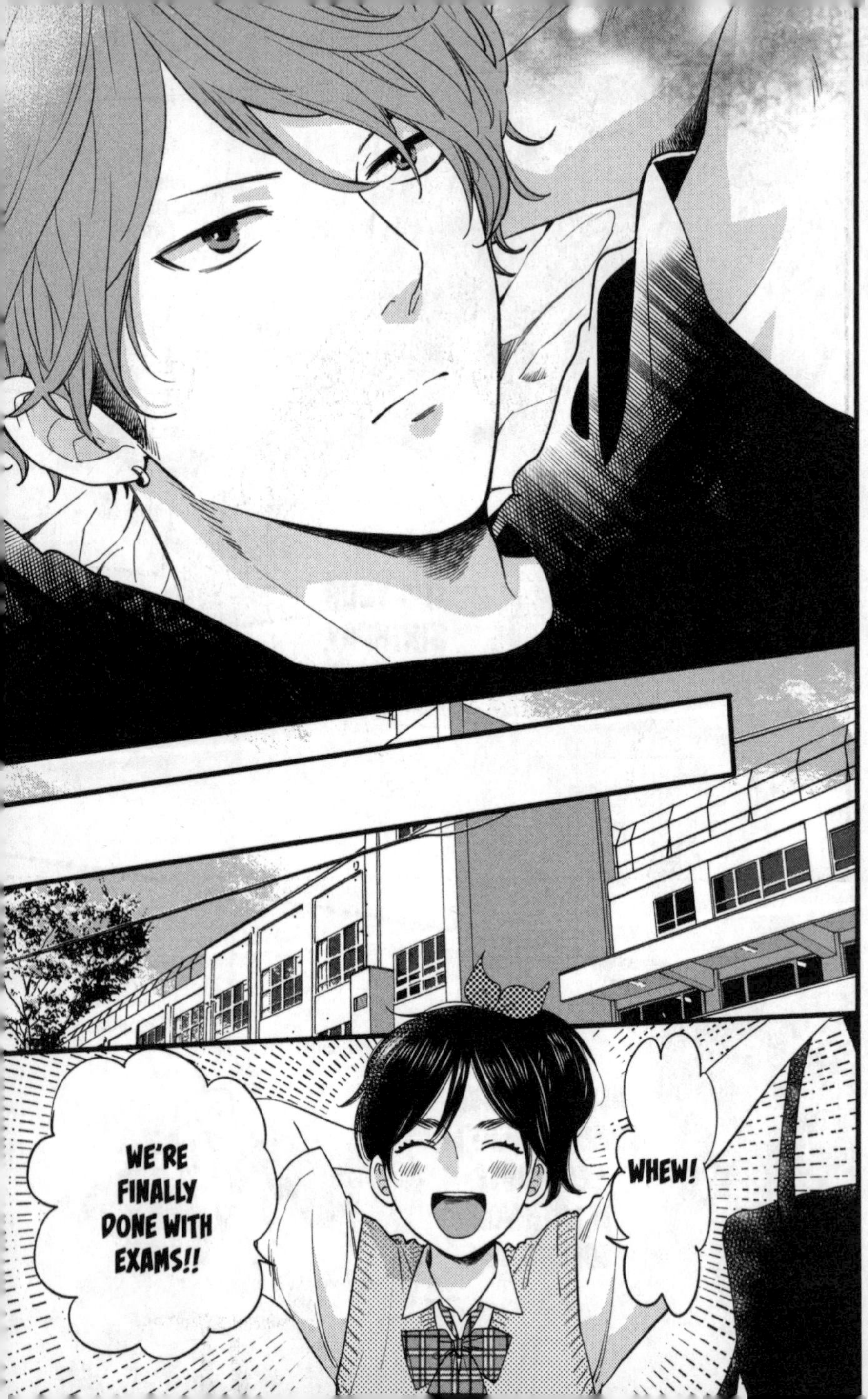
WHEW!
WE'RE FINALLY DONE WITH EXAMS!!

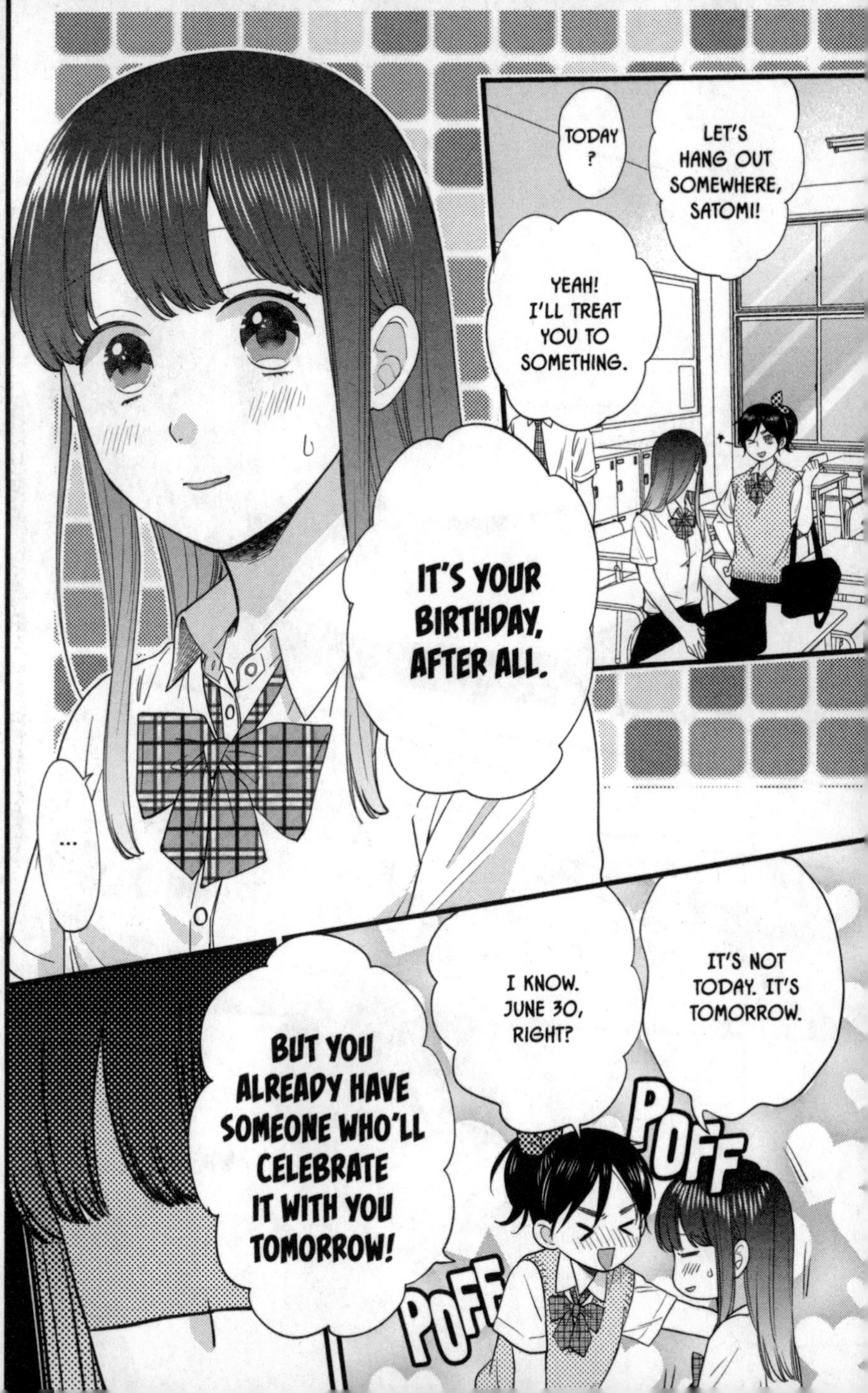
LET'S HANG OUT SOMEWHERE, SATOMI!
TODAY ?
YEAH! I'LL TREAT YOU TO SOMETHING.
IT'S YOUR BIRTHDAY, AFTER ALL.
...
IT'S NOT TODAY. IT'S TOMORROW.
I KNOW. JUNE 30, RIGHT?
BUT YOU ALREADY HAVE SOMEONE WHO'LL CELEBRATE IT WITH YOU TOMORROW!
POFF
POFF

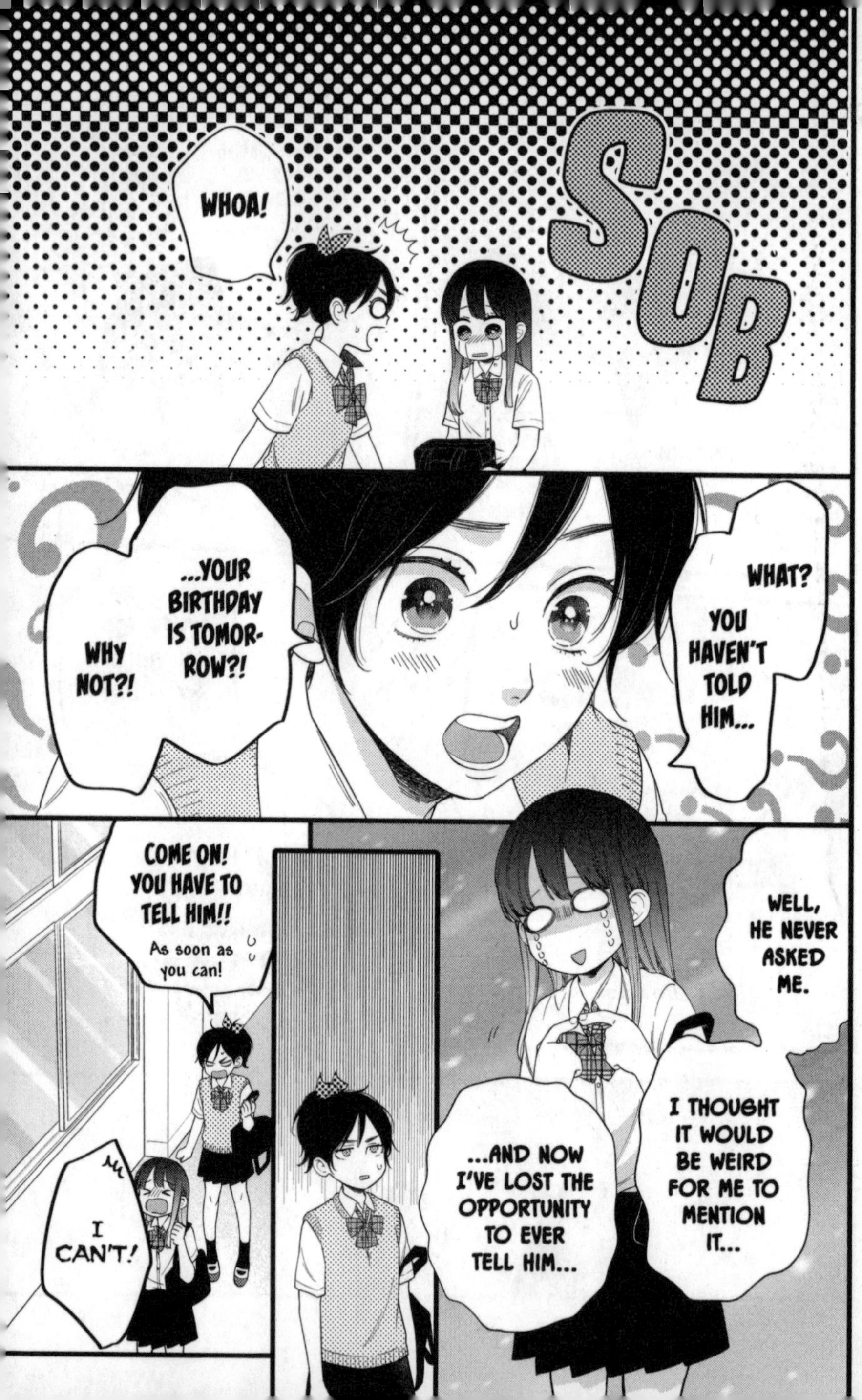
SOB
WHOA!
WHAT? YOU HAVEN'T TOLD HIM...
...YOUR BIRTHDAY IS TOMORROW?! WHY NOT?!
WELL, HE NEVER ASKED ME.
I THOUGHT IT WOULD BE WEIRD FOR ME TO MENTION IT...
...AND NOW I'VE LOST THE OPPORTUNITY TO EVER TELL HIM...
COME ON! YOU HAVE TO TELL HIM!! As soon as you can!
I CAN'T!

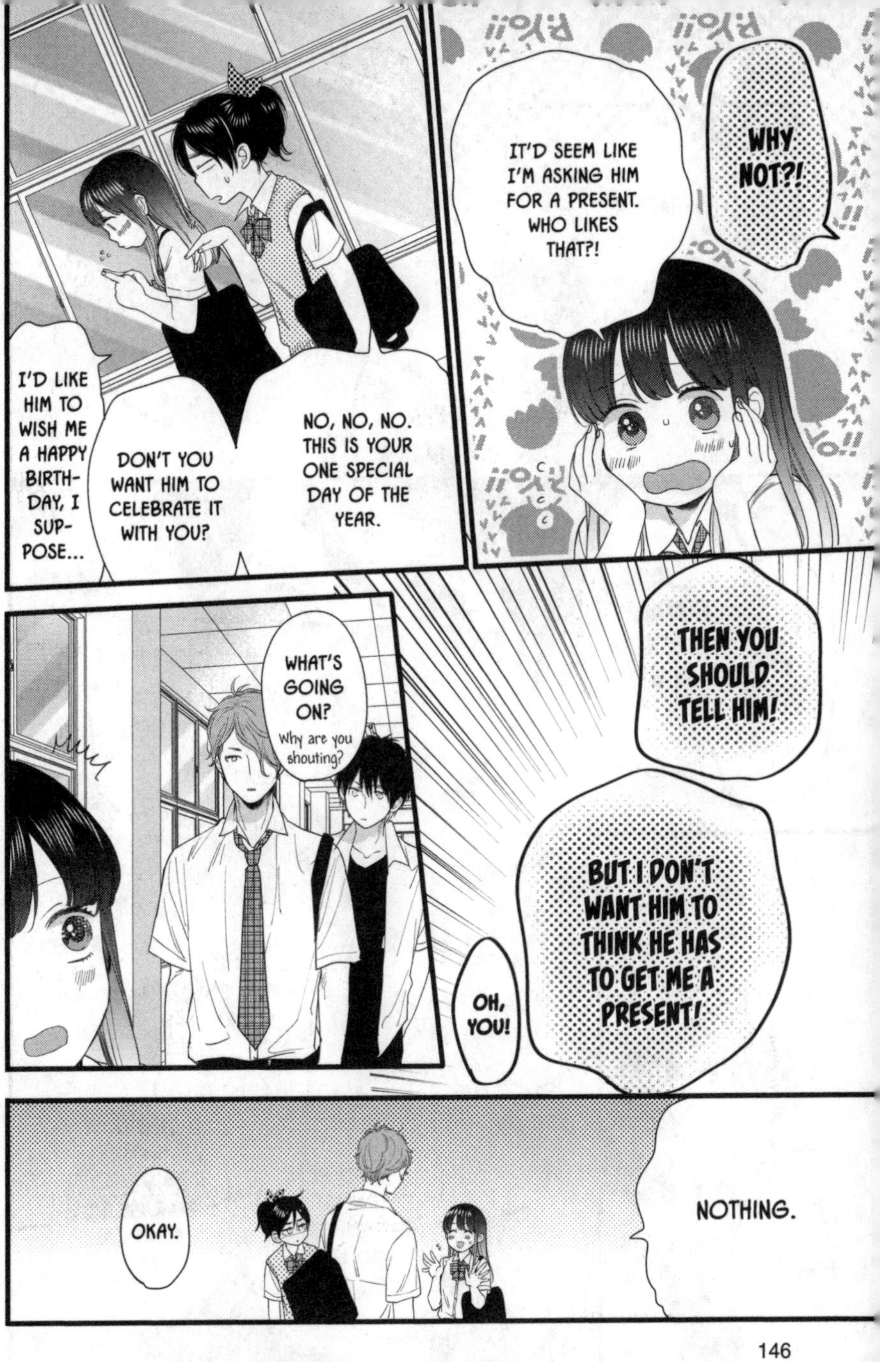
WHY NOT?!
IT'D SEEM LIKE I'M ASKING HIM FOR A PRESENT. WHO LIKES THAT?!
NO, NO, NO. THIS IS YOUR ONE SPECIAL DAY OF THE YEAR.
DON'T YOU WANT HIM TO CELEBRATE IT WITH YOU?
I'D LIKE HIM TO WISH ME A HAPPY BIRTH-DAY, I SUP-POSE...
THEN YOU SHOULD TELL HIM!
BUT I DON'T WANT HIM TO THINK HE HAS TO GET ME A PRESENT!
OH, YOU!
WHAT'S GOING ON?
Why are you shouting?
NOTHING.
OKAY.

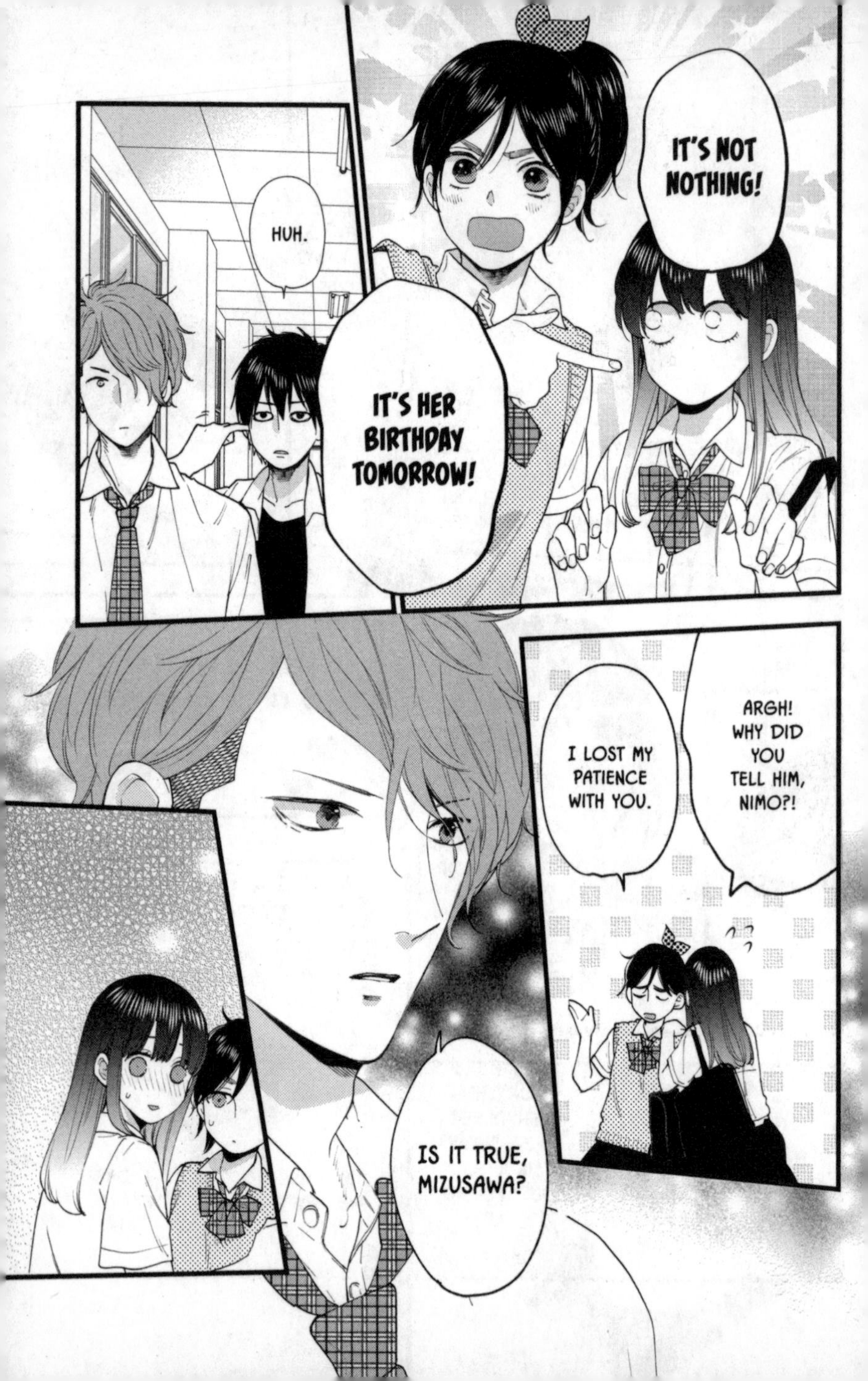
IT'S NOT NOTHING!
IT'S HER BIRTHDAY TOMORROW!
HUH.
ARGH! WHY DID YOU TELL HIM, NIMO?!
I LOST MY PATIENCE WITH YOU.
IS IT TRUE, MIZUSAWA?

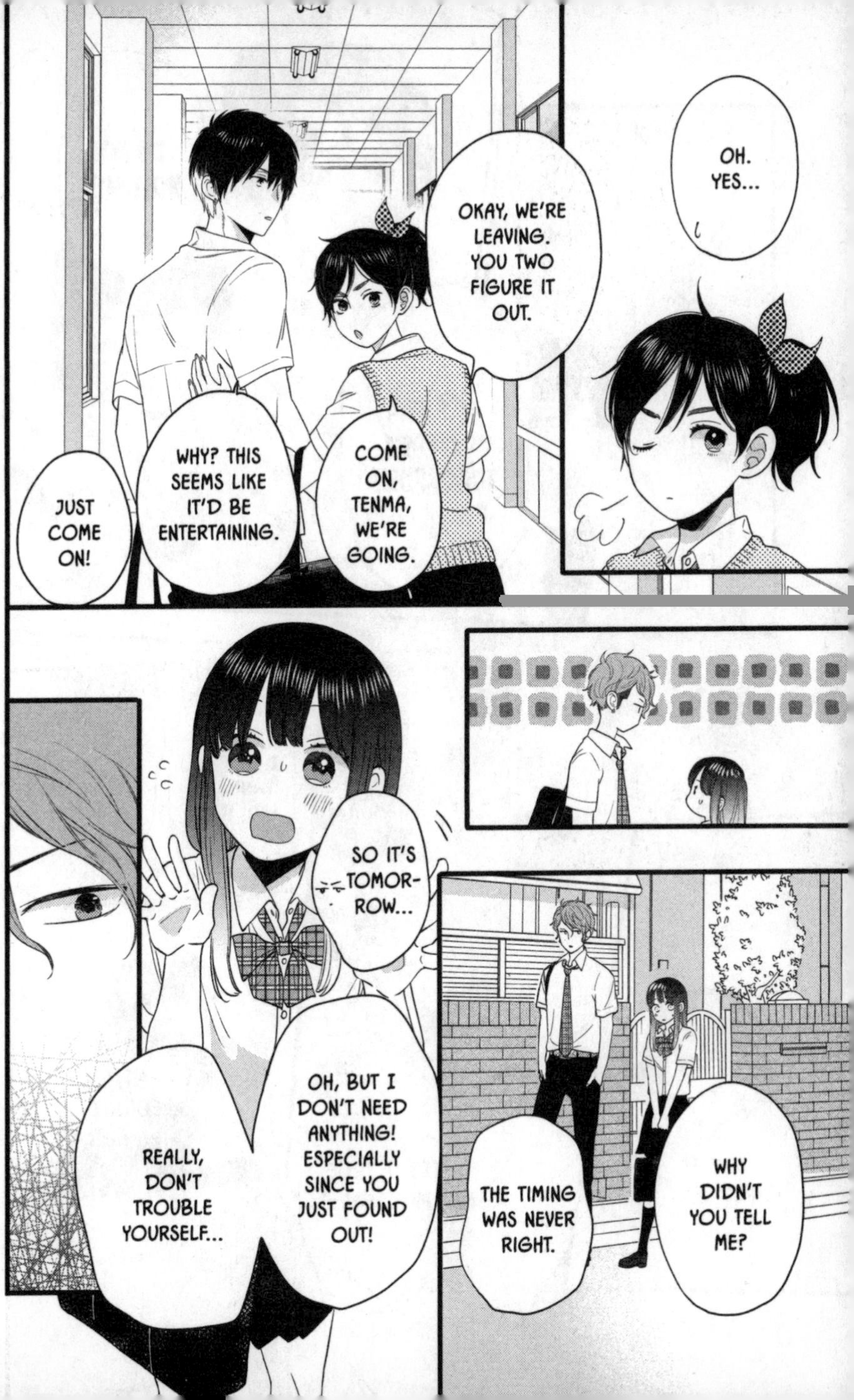
OH. YES...
OKAY, WE'RE LEAVING. YOU TWO FIGURE IT OUT.
COME ON, TENMA, WE'RE GOING.
WHY? THIS SEEMS LIKE IT'D BE ENTERTAINING.
JUST COME ON!
WHY DIDN'T YOU TELL ME?
THE TIMING WAS NEVER RIGHT.
SO IT'S TOMOR-ROW...
OH, BUT I DON'T NEED ANYTHING! ESPECIALLY SINCE YOU JUST FOUND OUT!
REALLY, DON'T TROUBLE YOURSELF...

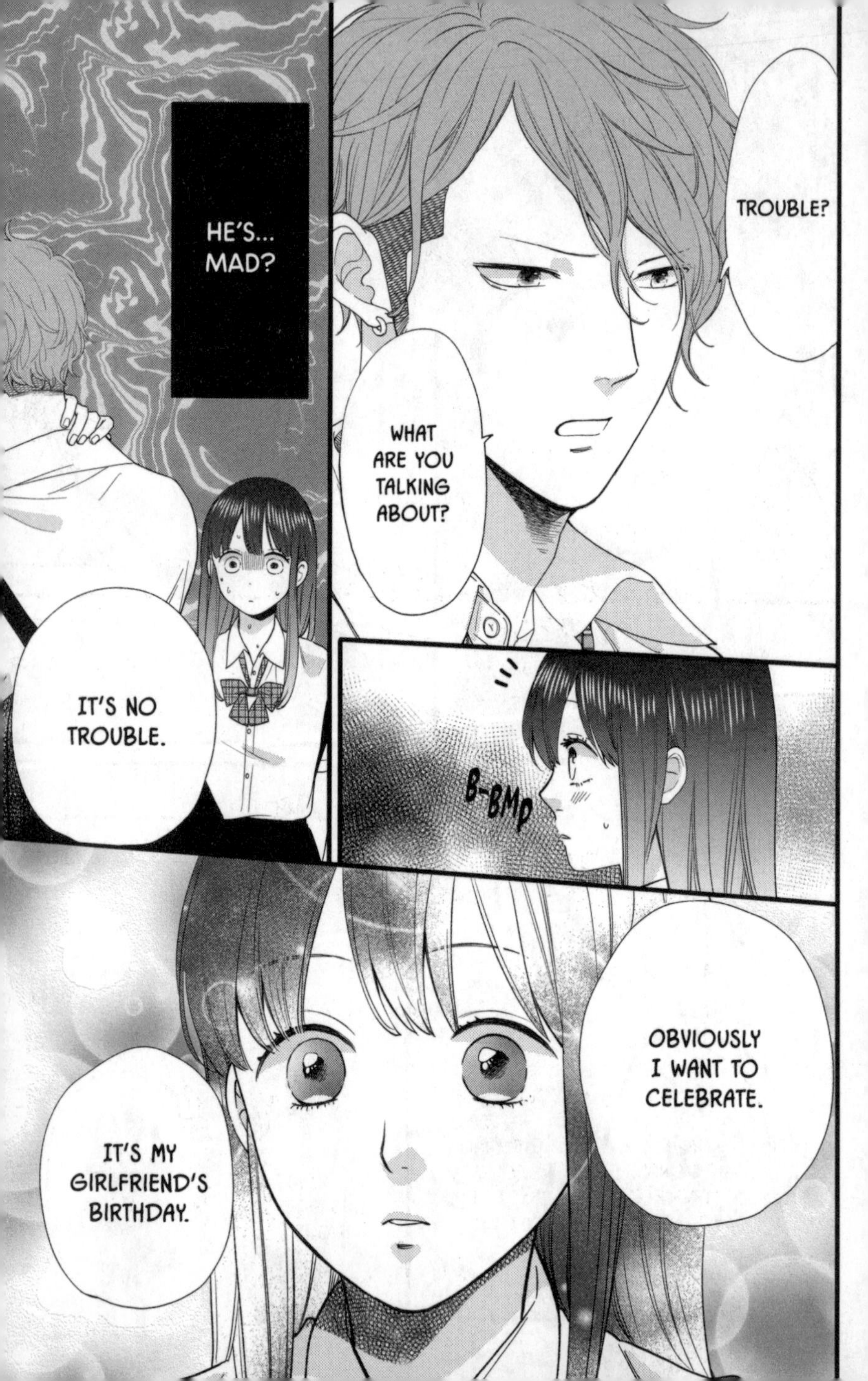
TROUBLE?
WHAT ARE YOU TALKING ABOUT?
B-BMP
HE'S... MAD?
IT'S NO TROUBLE.
OBVIOUSLY I WANT TO CELEBRATE.
IT'S MY GIRLFRIEND'S BIRTHDAY.

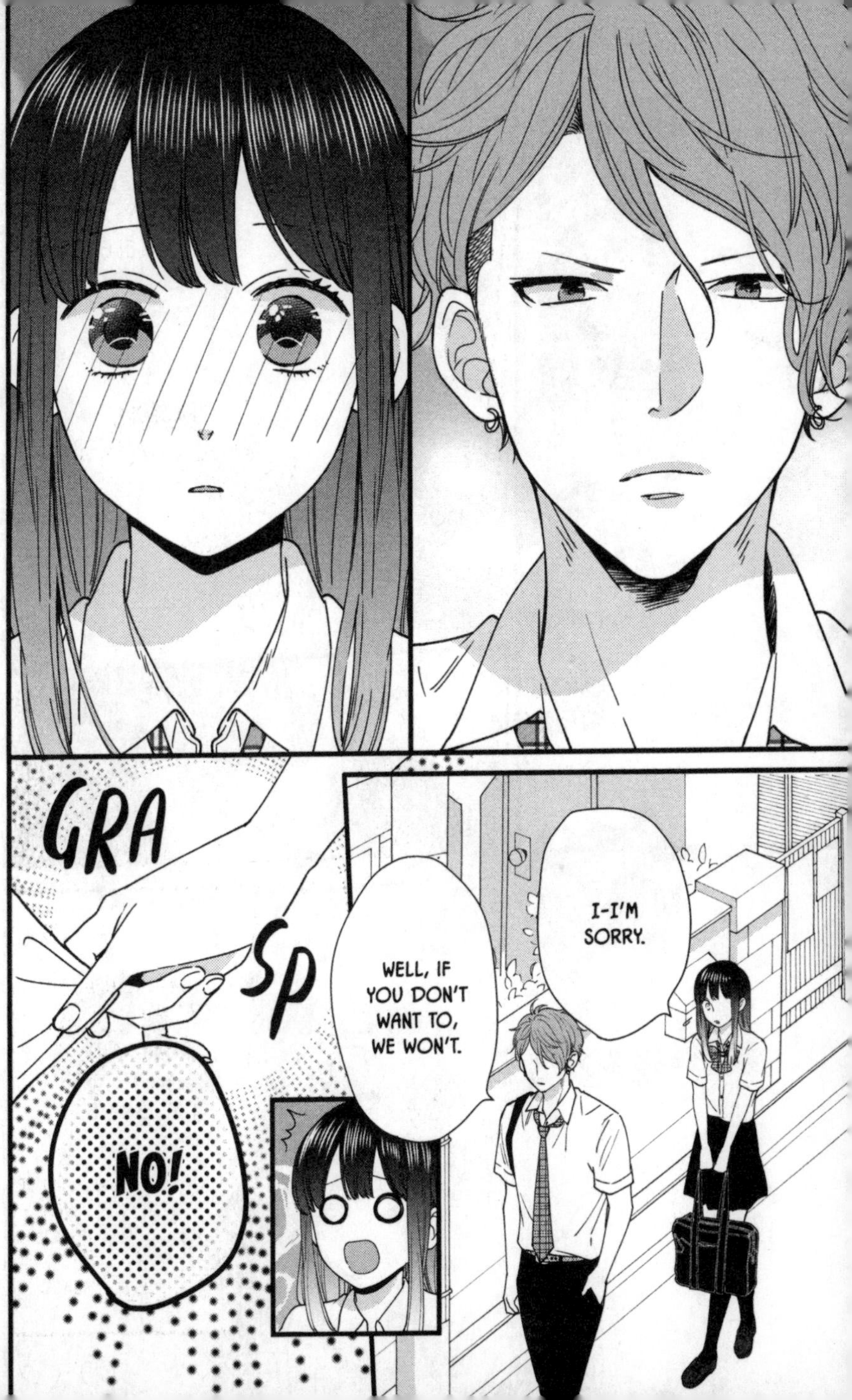
I-I'M SORRY.
WELL, IF YOU DON'T WANT TO, WE WON'T.
GRA
SP
NO!

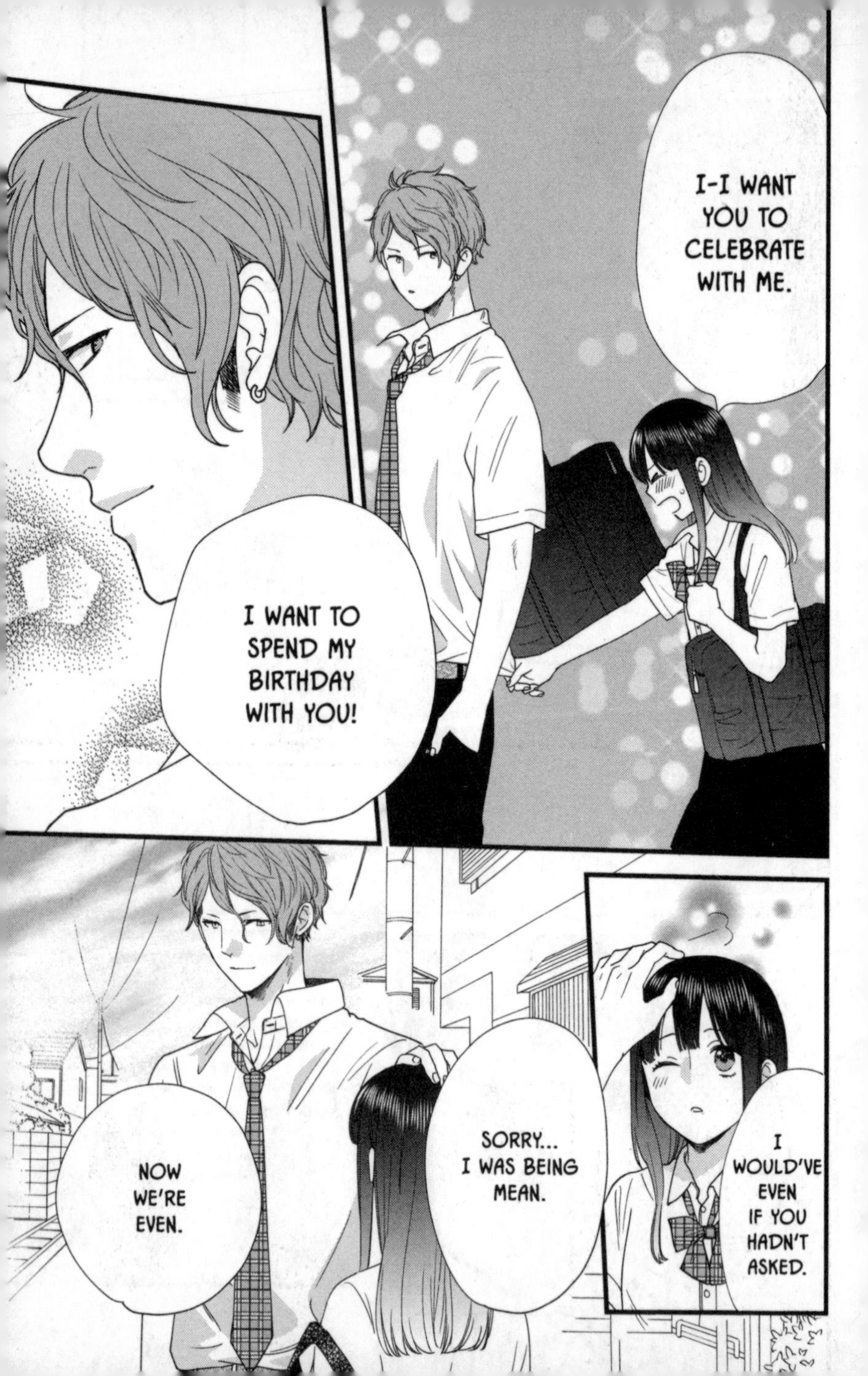
I-I WANT YOU TO CELEBRATE WITH ME.
I WANT TO SPEND MY BIRTHDAY WITH YOU!
I WOULD'VE EVEN IF YOU HADN'T ASKED.
SORRY... I WAS BEING MEAN.
NOW WE'RE EVEN.

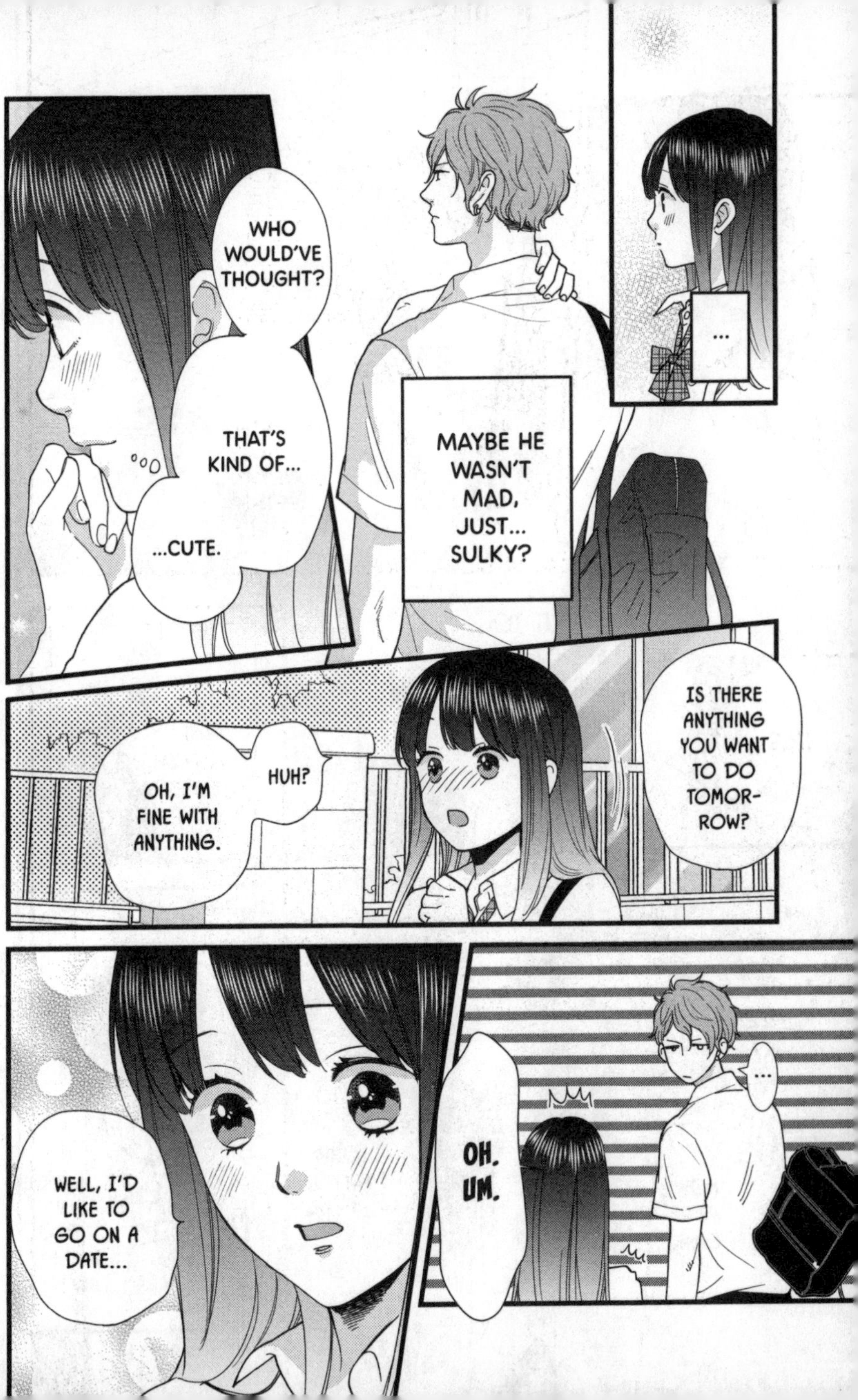
...
MAYBE HE WASN'T MAD, JUST... SULKY?
WHO WOULD'VE THOUGHT?
THAT'S KIND OF...
...CUTE.
IS THERE ANYTHING YOU WANT TO DO TOMORROW?
HUH?
OH, I'M FINE WITH ANYTHING.
...
OH. UM.
WELL, I'D LIKE TO GO ON A DATE...

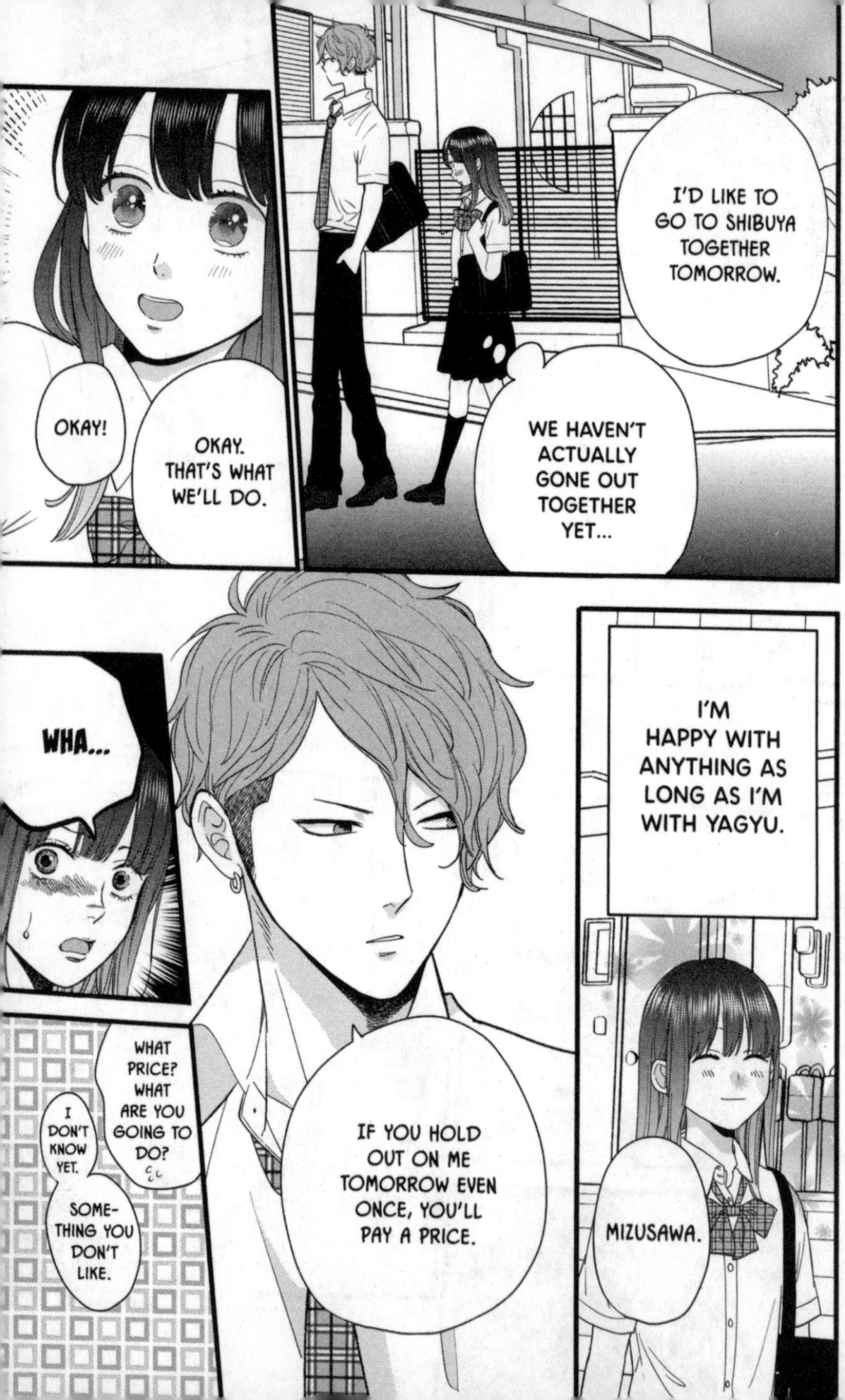
I'D LIKE TO GO TO SHIBUYA TOGETHER TOMORROW.
WE HAVEN'T ACTUALLY GONE OUT TOGETHER YET...
OKAY. THAT'S WHAT WE'LL DO.
OKAY!
I'M HAPPY WITH ANYTHING AS LONG AS I'M WITH YAGYU.
MIZUSAWA.
IF YOU HOLD OUT ON ME TOMORROW EVEN ONCE, YOU'LL PAY A PRICE.
WHA...
WHAT PRICE? WHAT ARE YOU GOING TO DO?
I DON'T KNOW YET.
SOME-THING YOU DON'T LIKE.

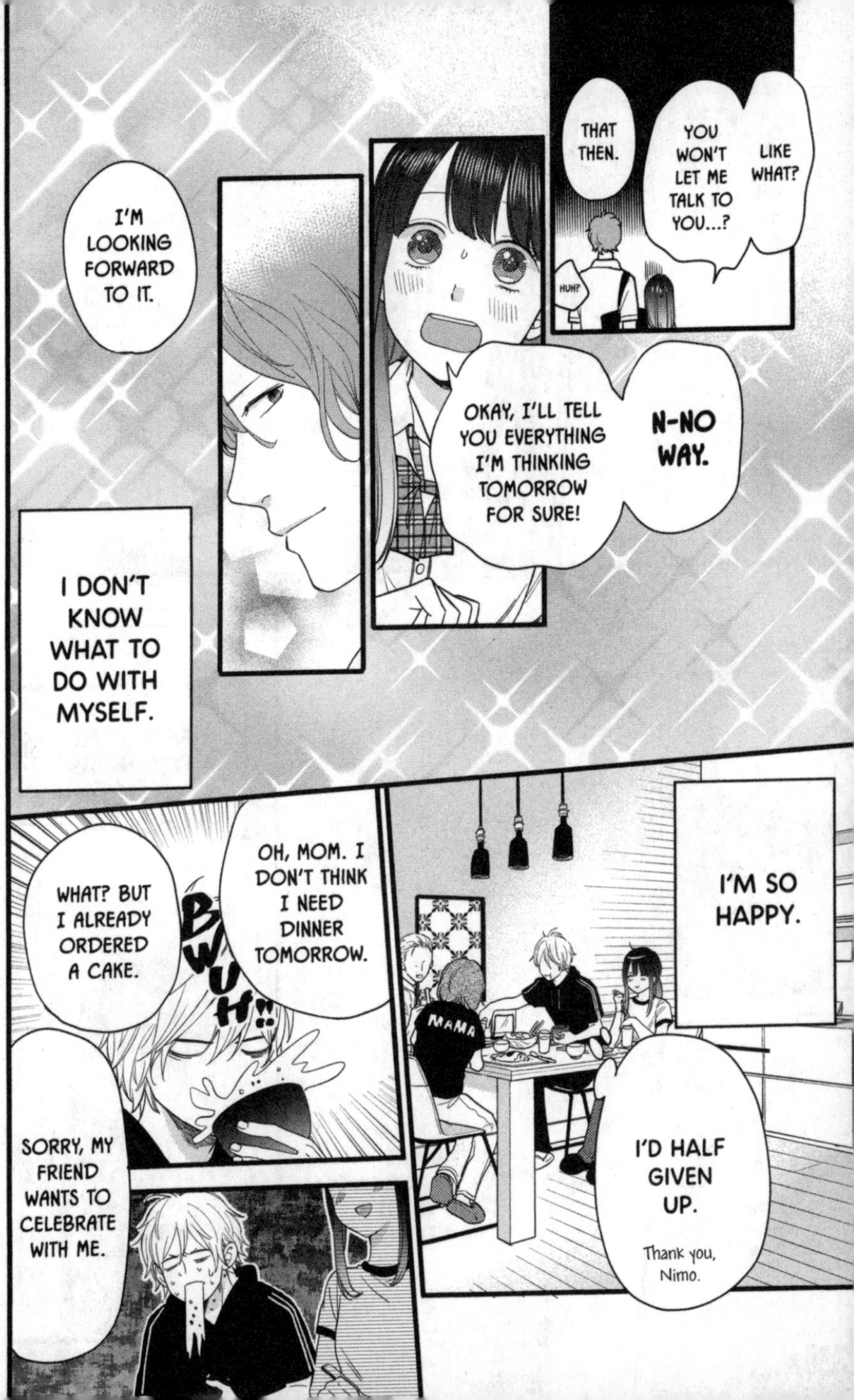
LIKE WHAT?
YOU WON'T LET ME TALK TO YOU...?
HUH?
THAT THEN.
N-NO WAY.
OKAY, I'LL TELL YOU EVERYTHING I'M THINKING TOMORROW FOR SURE!
I'M LOOKING FORWARD TO IT.
I DON'T KNOW WHAT TO DO WITH MYSELF.
I'M SO HAPPY.
MAMA
I'D HALF GIVEN UP.
Thank you, Nimo.
OH, MOM. I DON'T THINK I NEED DINNER TOMORROW.
WHAT? BUT I ALREADY ORDERED A CAKE.
BWUH!!
SORRY, MY FRIEND WANTS TO CELEBRATE WITH ME.

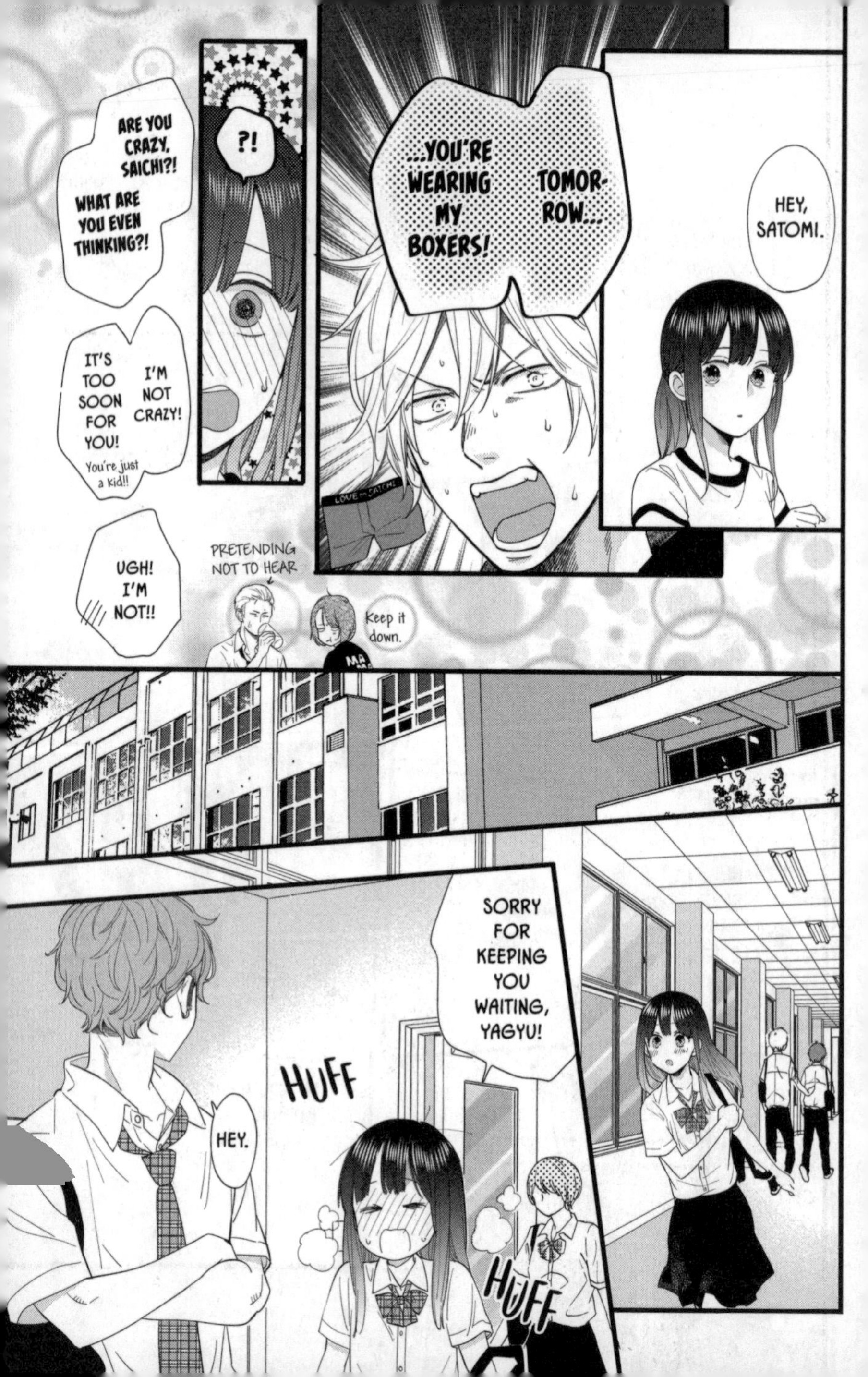
HEY, SATOMI.
TOMORROW...
...YOU'RE WEARING MY BOXERS!
?!
ARE YOU CRAZY, SAICHI?!
WHAT ARE YOU EVEN THINKING?!
I'M NOT CRAZY!
IT'S TOO SOON FOR YOU!
You're just a kid!!
Keep it down.
PRETENDING NOT TO HEAR
UGH! I'M NOT!!
SORRY FOR KEEPING YOU WAITING, YAGYU!
HUFF
HUFF
HEY.

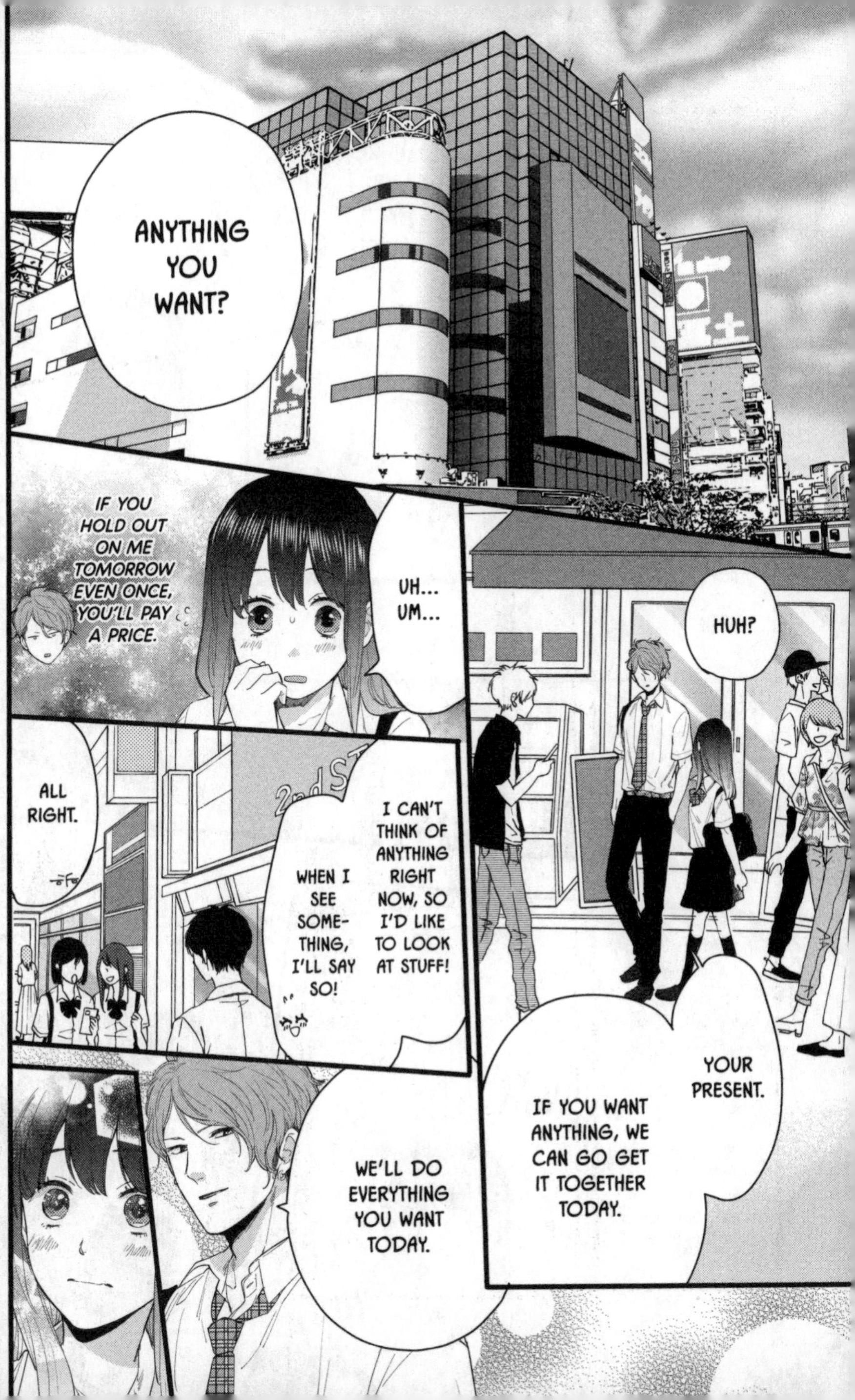
ANYTHING YOU WANT?
HUH?
YOUR PRESENT.
IF YOU WANT ANYTHING, WE CAN GO GET IT TOGETHER TODAY.
WE'LL DO EVERYTHING YOU WANT TODAY.
IF YOU HOLD OUT ON ME TOMORROW EVEN ONCE, YOU'LL PAY A PRICE.
UH... UM...
I CAN'T THINK OF ANYTHING RIGHT NOW, SO I'D LIKE TO LOOK AT STUFF!
WHEN I SEE SOME-THING, I'LL SAY SO!
ALL RIGHT.

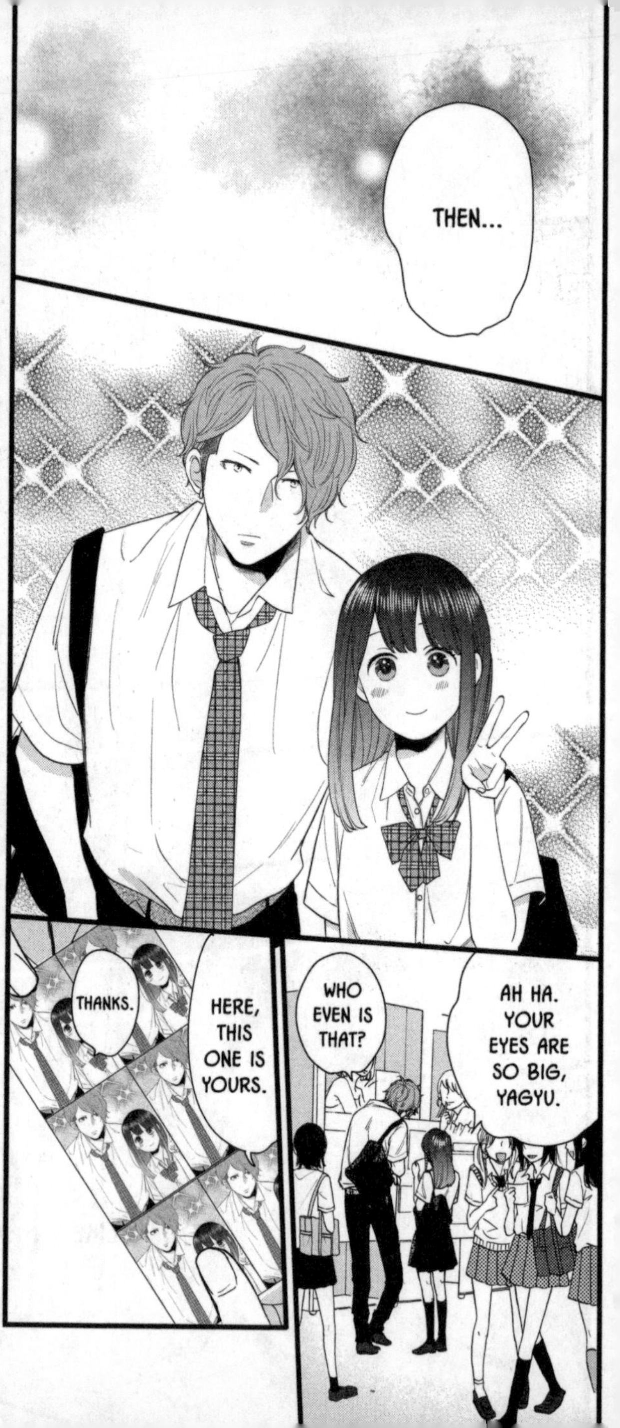
THEN...
AH HA. YOUR EYES ARE SO BIG, YAGYU.
WHO EVEN IS THAT?
HERE, THIS ONE IS YOURS.
THANKS.

③

Oh, right. I had an assistant, Kiko Nankata, who had worked for me since about 2005. She moved on after the final chapter of my last serialization. It was a bitter decision. She was my partner for nearly 15 years, and even though she didn't talk much, she knew the job and me really well. Most importantly, she made my deadlines a breeze...
After she left, I didn't know what to do.
She held a pretty important role in the company she worked for when she wasn't with me. Because she'd worked as my background assistant for so long, I never called in other artists, which was also an issue.
Well, we worked it out so she would move on when I was going to have my long break. When I remember the days we used to work together, I get so emotional. Well, we're friends, so we meet up regularly anyway. Ha ha. It's just different from when we worked together! It felt like we were comrades in arms! It was nice. But now I have Kawori Sakai, who joined me during *Haibara,* and also Akane, who recently came aboard. They're both so fun and nice!! (They're so nice, I could cry...)
I'm not alone!! I'm looking forward to working with the both of them.
Oh, I fully moved to digital for this series as well. How is it?

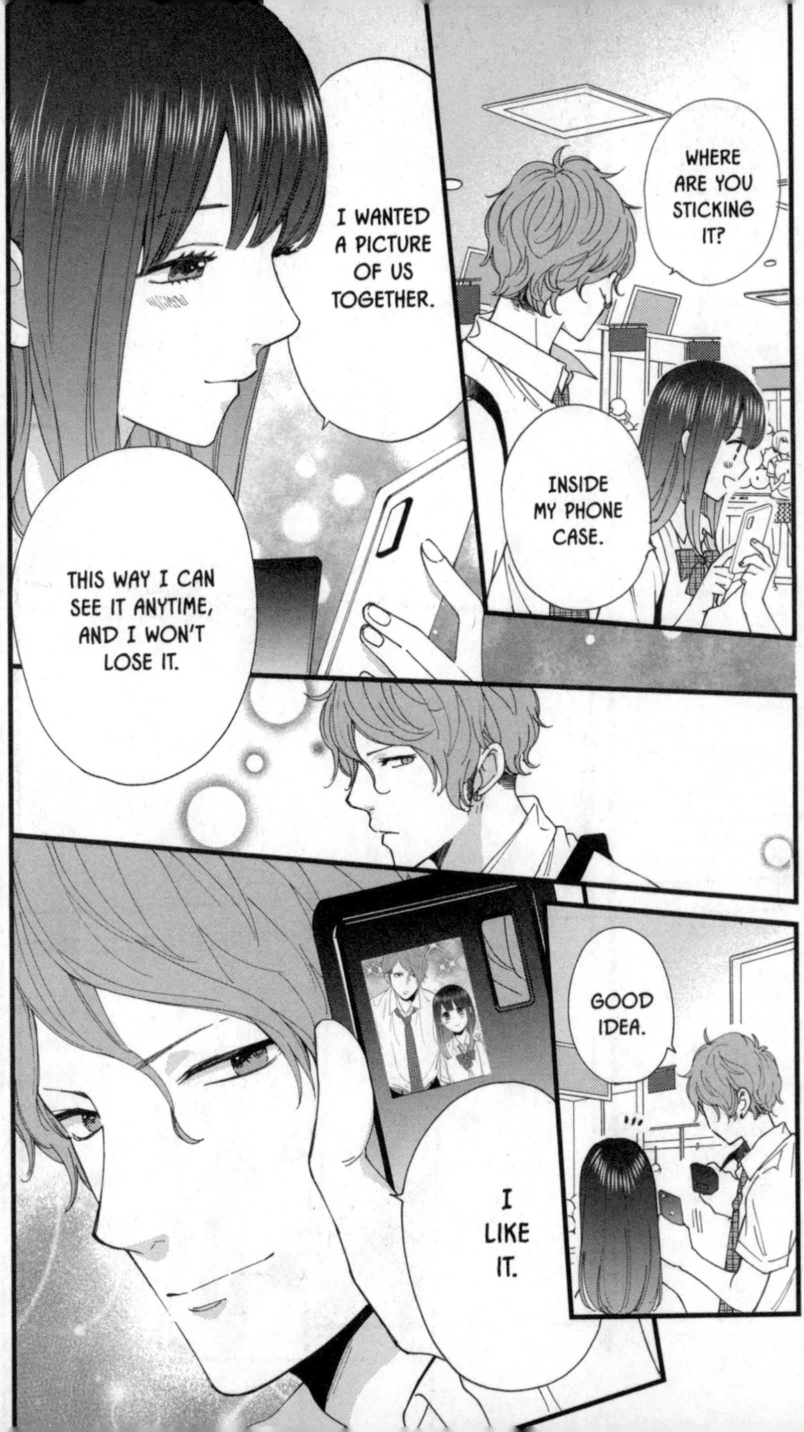
WHERE ARE YOU STICKING IT?
INSIDE MY PHONE CASE.
I WANTED A PICTURE OF US TOGETHER.
THIS WAY I CAN SEE IT ANYTIME, AND I WON'T LOSE IT.
GOOD IDEA.
I LIKE IT.

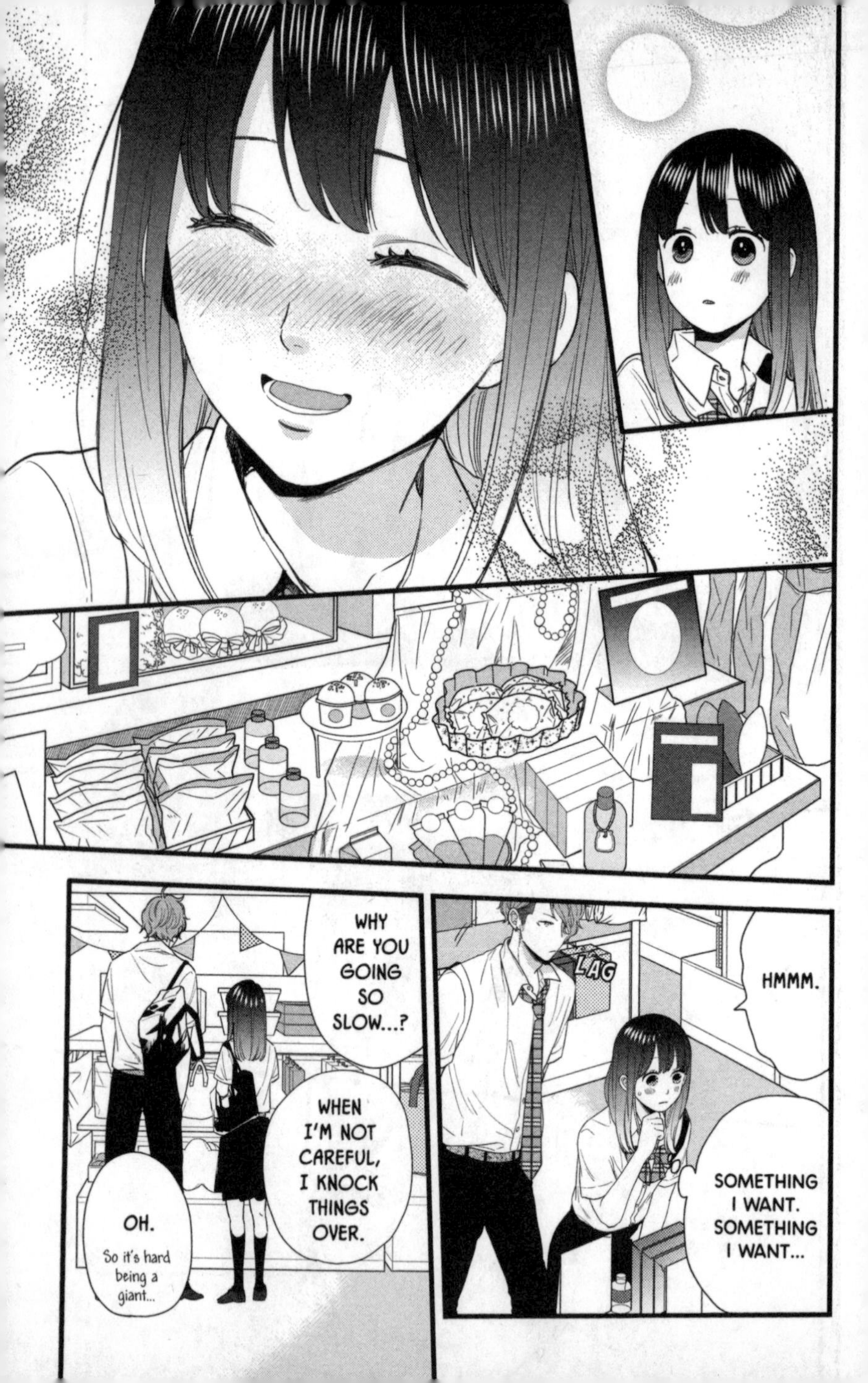
HMMM.
LAG
SOMETHING I WANT. SOMETHING I WANT...
WHY ARE YOU GOING SO SLOW...?
WHEN I'M NOT CAREFUL, I KNOCK THINGS OVER.
OH.
So it's hard being a giant...

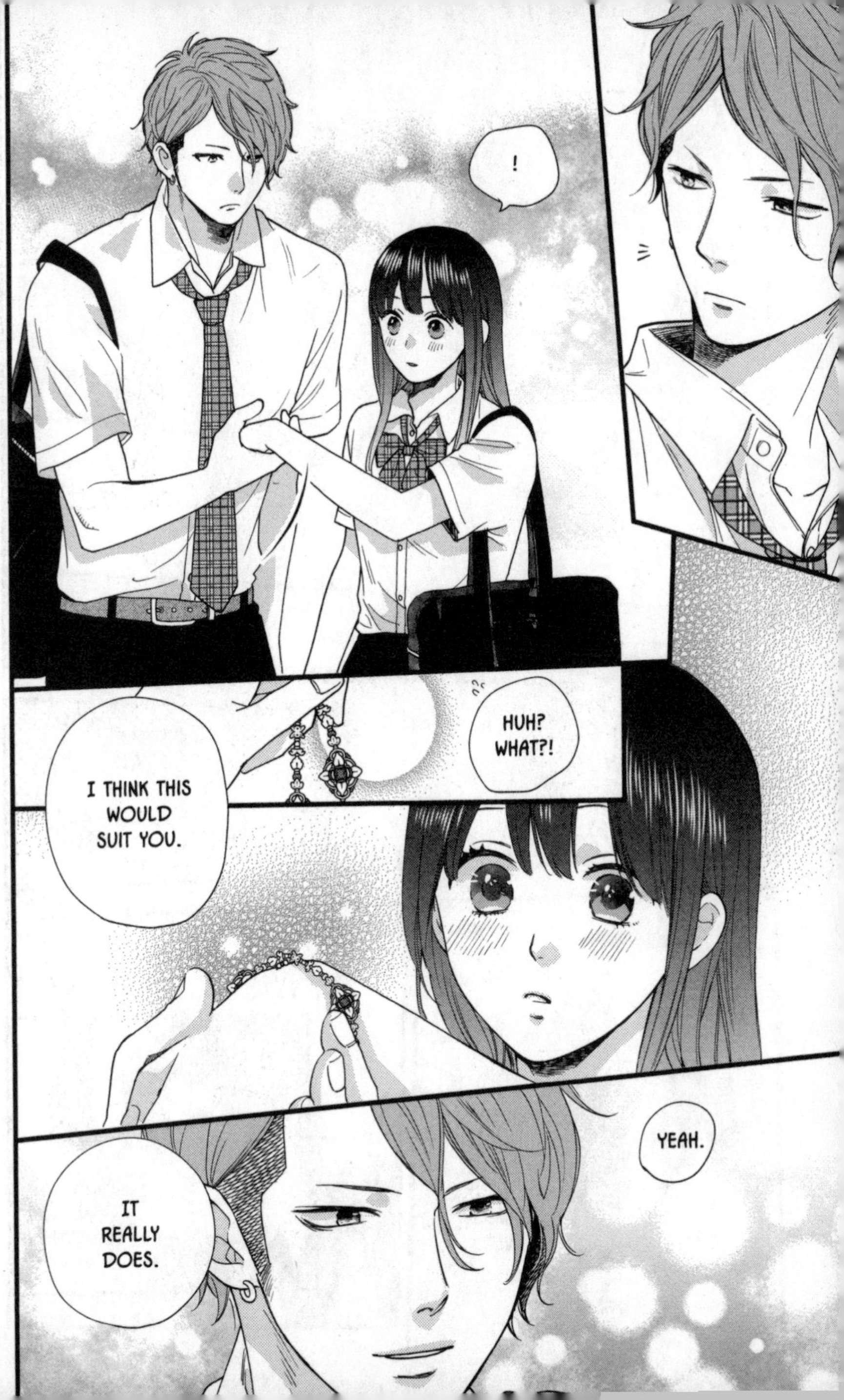
!
HUH? WHAT?!
I THINK THIS WOULD SUIT YOU.
YEAH.
IT REALLY DOES.

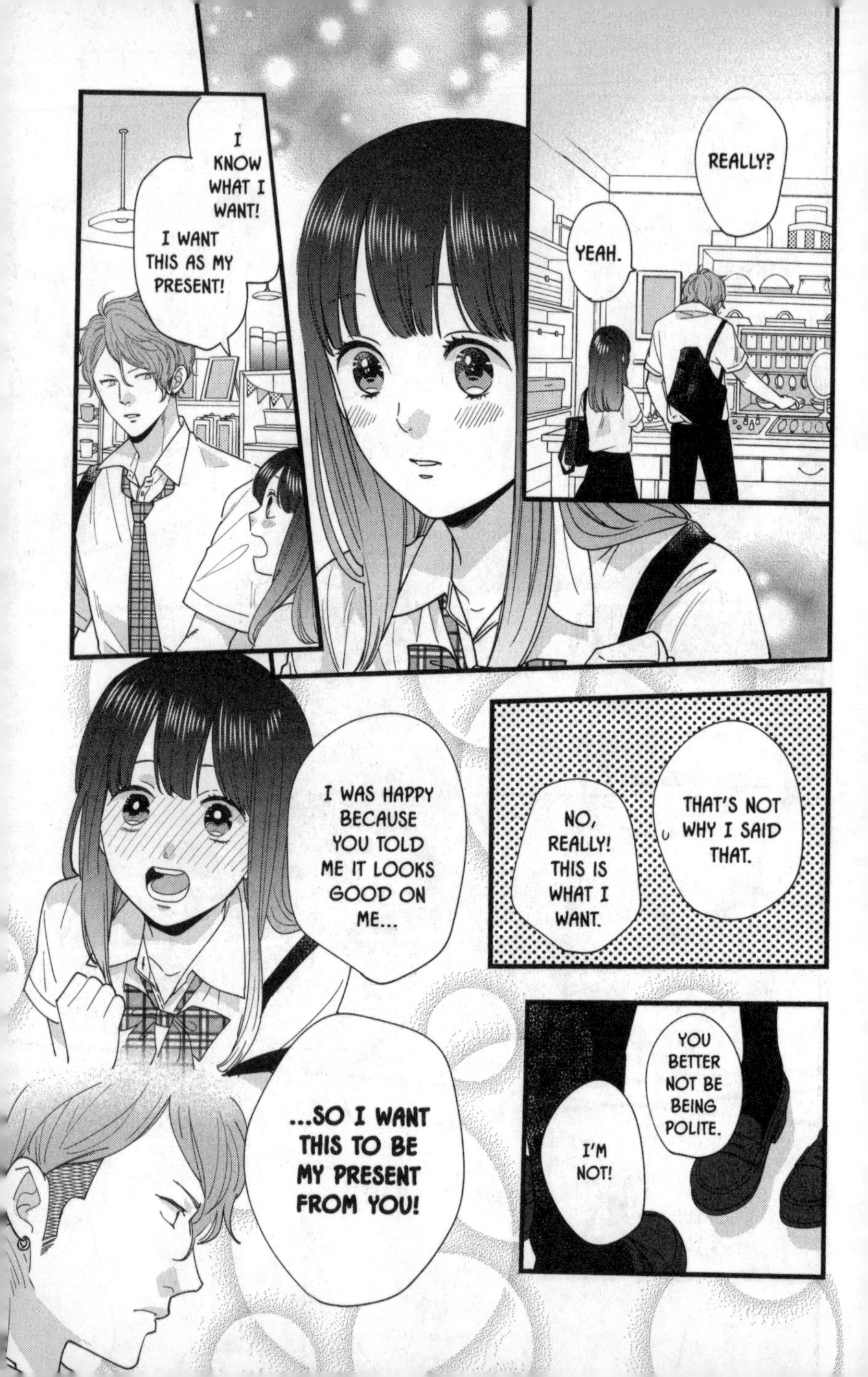
REALLY?
YEAH.
I KNOW WHAT I WANT!
I WANT THIS AS MY PRESENT!
THAT'S NOT WHY I SAID THAT.
NO, REALLY! THIS IS WHAT I WANT.
YOU BETTER NOT BE BEING POLITE.
I'M NOT!
I WAS HAPPY BECAUSE YOU TOLD ME IT LOOKS GOOD ON ME...
...SO I WANT THIS TO BE MY PRESENT FROM YOU!

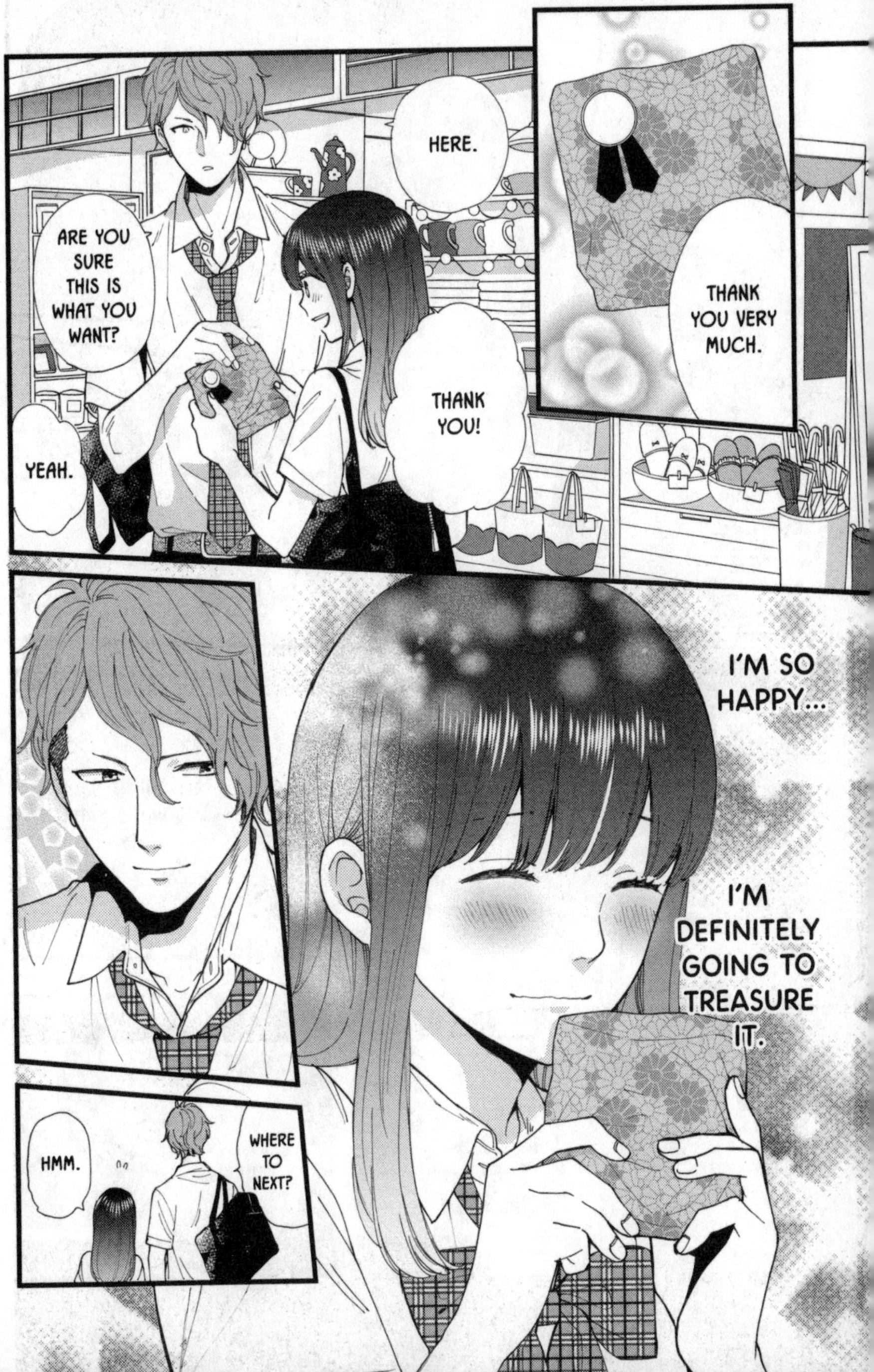
THANK YOU VERY MUCH.
HERE.
THANK YOU!
ARE YOU SURE THIS IS WHAT YOU WANT?
YEAH.
I'M SO HAPPY...
I'M DEFINITELY GOING TO TREASURE IT.
WHERE TO NEXT?
HMM.

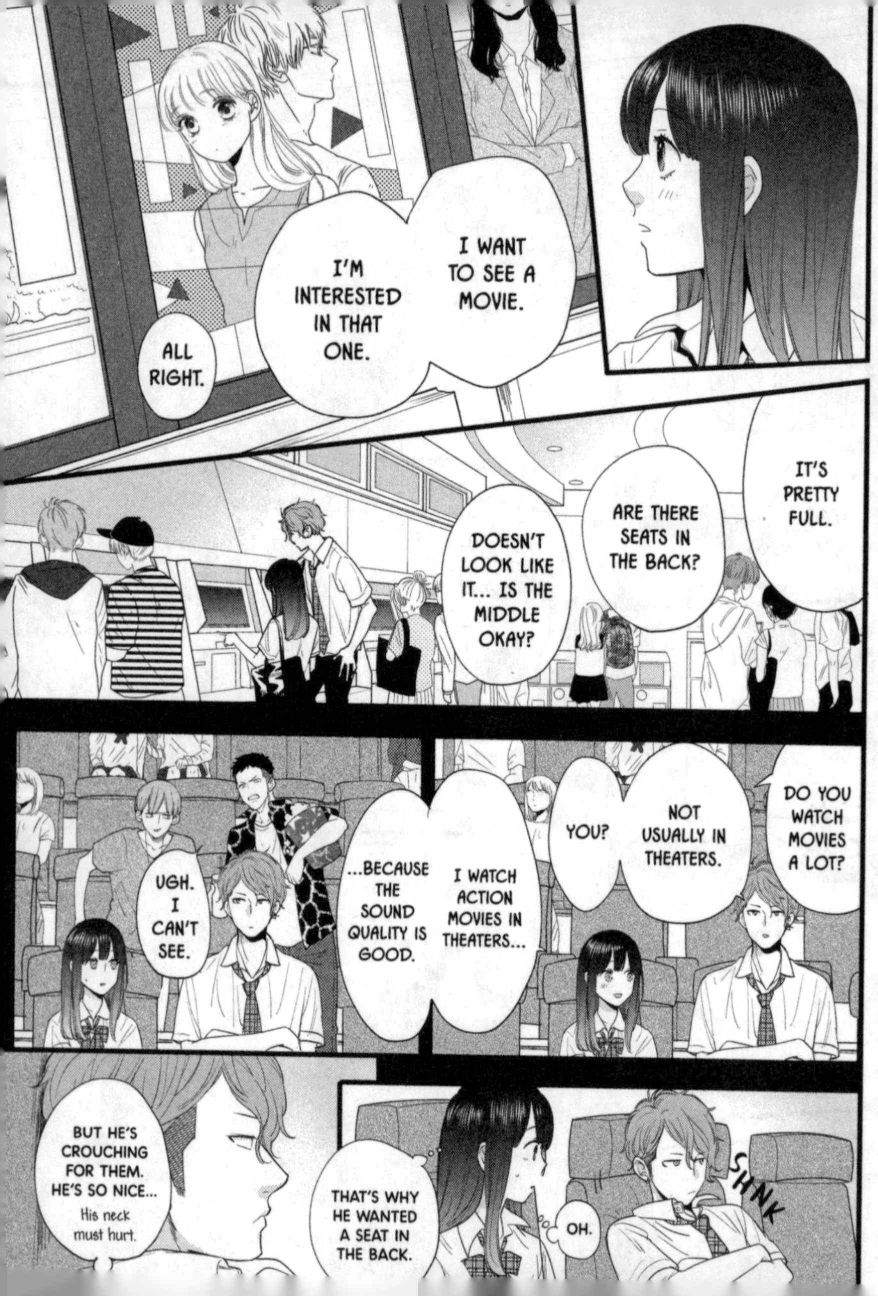
I WANT TO SEE A MOVIE.
I'M INTERESTED IN THAT ONE.
ALL RIGHT.
IT'S PRETTY FULL.
ARE THERE SEATS IN THE BACK?
DOESN'T LOOK LIKE IT... IS THE MIDDLE OKAY?
DO YOU WATCH MOVIES A LOT?
NOT USUALLY IN THEATERS.
YOU?
I WATCH ACTION MOVIES IN THEATERS...
...BECAUSE THE SOUND QUALITY IS GOOD.
UGH. I CAN'T SEE.
SHNK
OH.
THAT'S WHY HE WANTED A SEAT IN THE BACK.
BUT HE'S CROUCHING FOR THEM. HE'S SO NICE...
His neck must hurt.

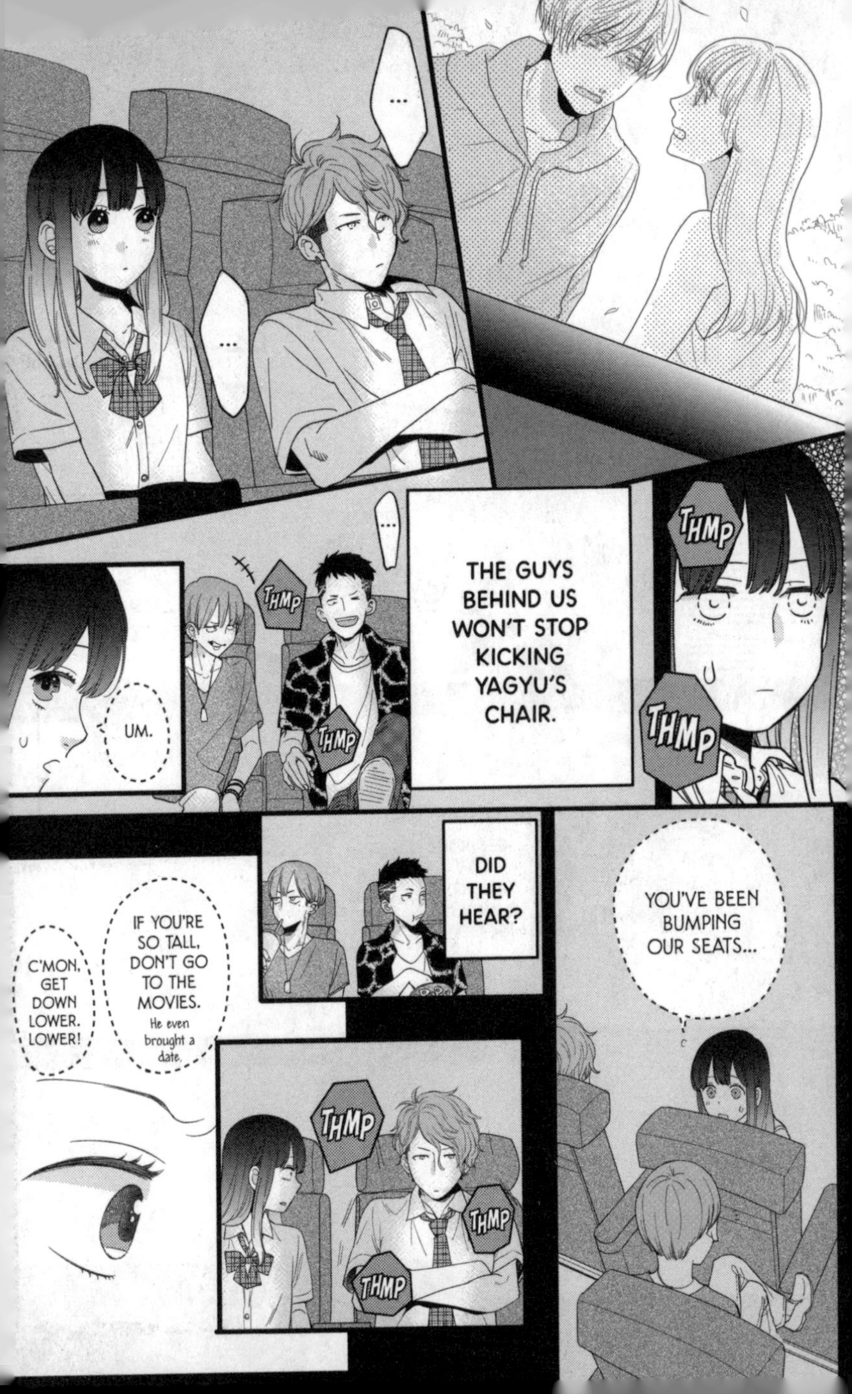
...
...
THMP
THMP
...
THE GUYS BEHIND US WON'T STOP KICKING YAGYU'S CHAIR.
THMP
THMP
UM.
YOU'VE BEEN BUMPING OUR SEATS...
DID THEY HEAR?
IF YOU'RE SO TALL, DON'T GO TO THE MOVIES.
He even brought a date.
C'MON, GET DOWN LOWER. LOWER!
THMP
THMP
THMP

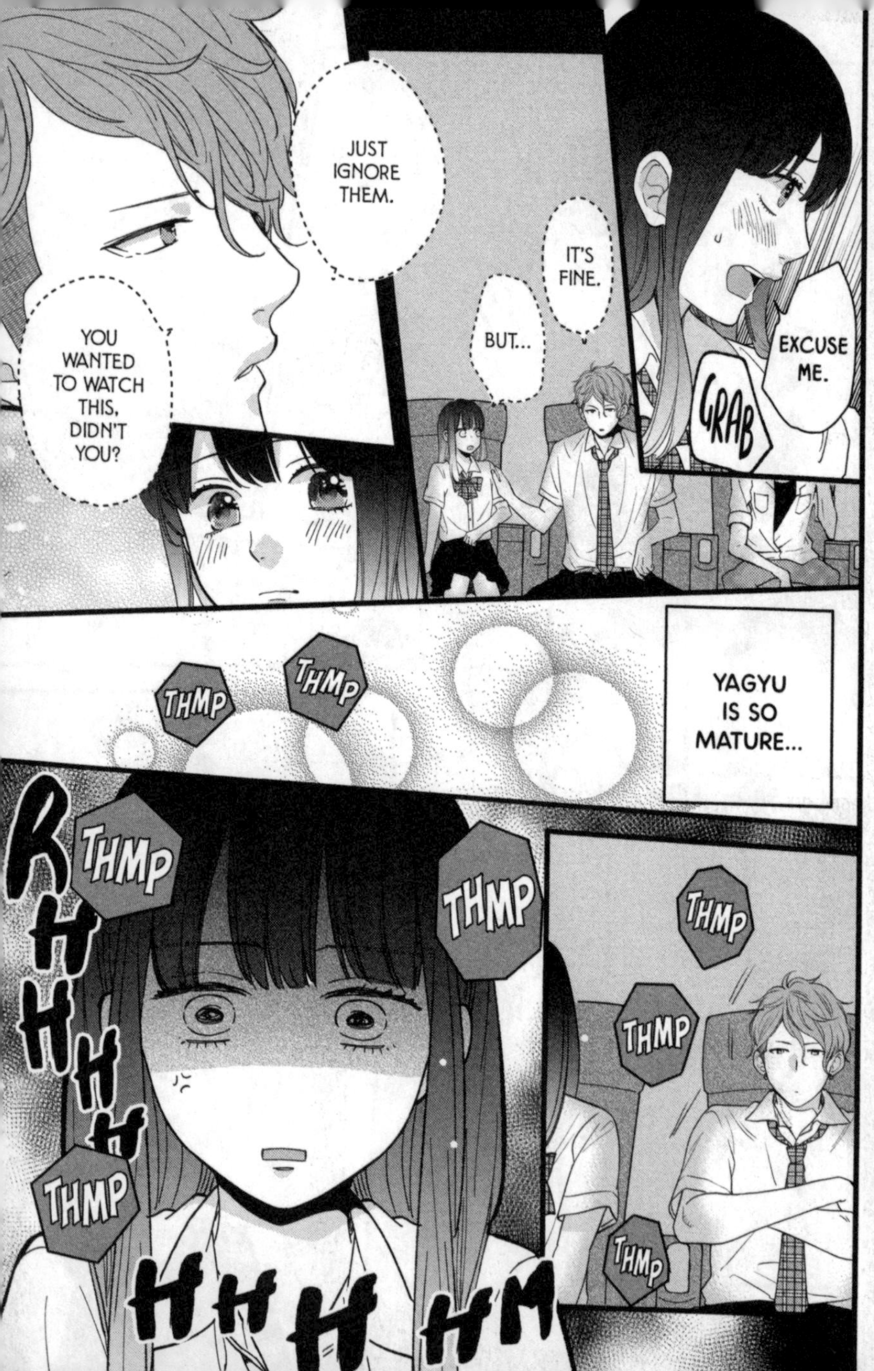
EXCUSE ME.
GRAB
IT'S FINE.
BUT...
JUST IGNORE THEM.
YOU WANTED TO WATCH THIS, DIDN'T YOU?
YAGYU IS SO MATURE...
THMP
THMP
THMP
THMP
THMP
THMP
THMP
THMP
RHHHH
HHHHM

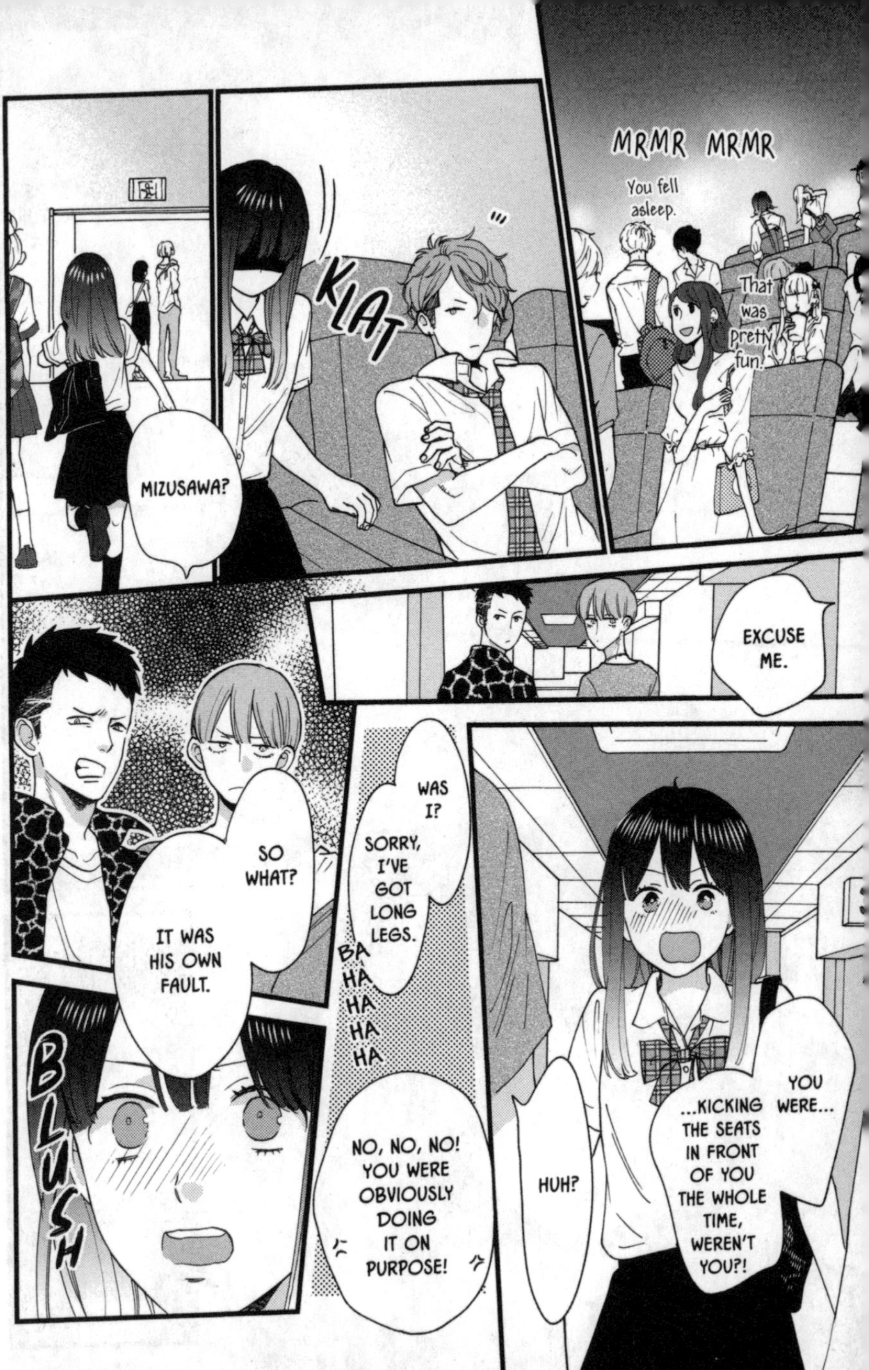
MRMR MRMR
You fell asleep.
That was pretty fun!
"
KLAT
MIZUSAWA?
EXCUSE ME.
YOU WERE...
...KICKING THE SEATS IN FRONT OF YOU THE WHOLE TIME, WEREN'T YOU?!
HUH?
WAS I?
SORRY, I'VE GOT LONG LEGS.
BAHAHAHAHA
NO, NO, NO! YOU WERE OBVIOUSLY DOING IT ON PURPOSE!
SO WHAT?
IT WAS HIS OWN FAULT.
BLUSH

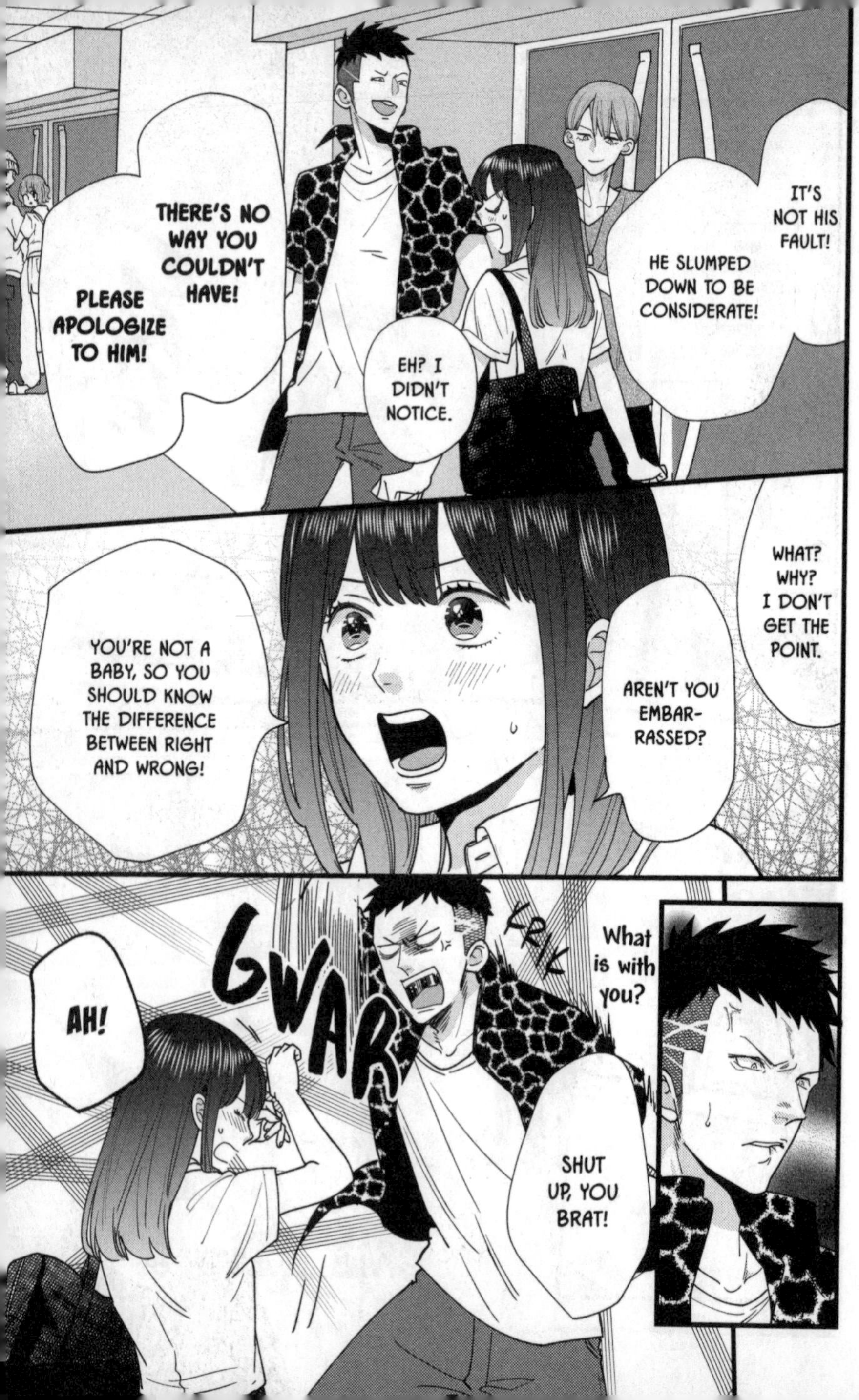
IT'S NOT HIS FAULT!
HE SLUMPED DOWN TO BE CONSIDERATE!
EH? I DIDN'T NOTICE.
THERE'S NO WAY YOU COULDN'T HAVE!
PLEASE APOLOGIZE TO HIM!
WHAT? WHY? I DON'T GET THE POINT.
AREN'T YOU EMBAR-RASSED?
YOU'RE NOT A BABY, SO YOU SHOULD KNOW THE DIFFERENCE BETWEEN RIGHT AND WRONG!
What is with you?
KRIK
GWAR
SHUT UP, YOU BRAT!
AH!

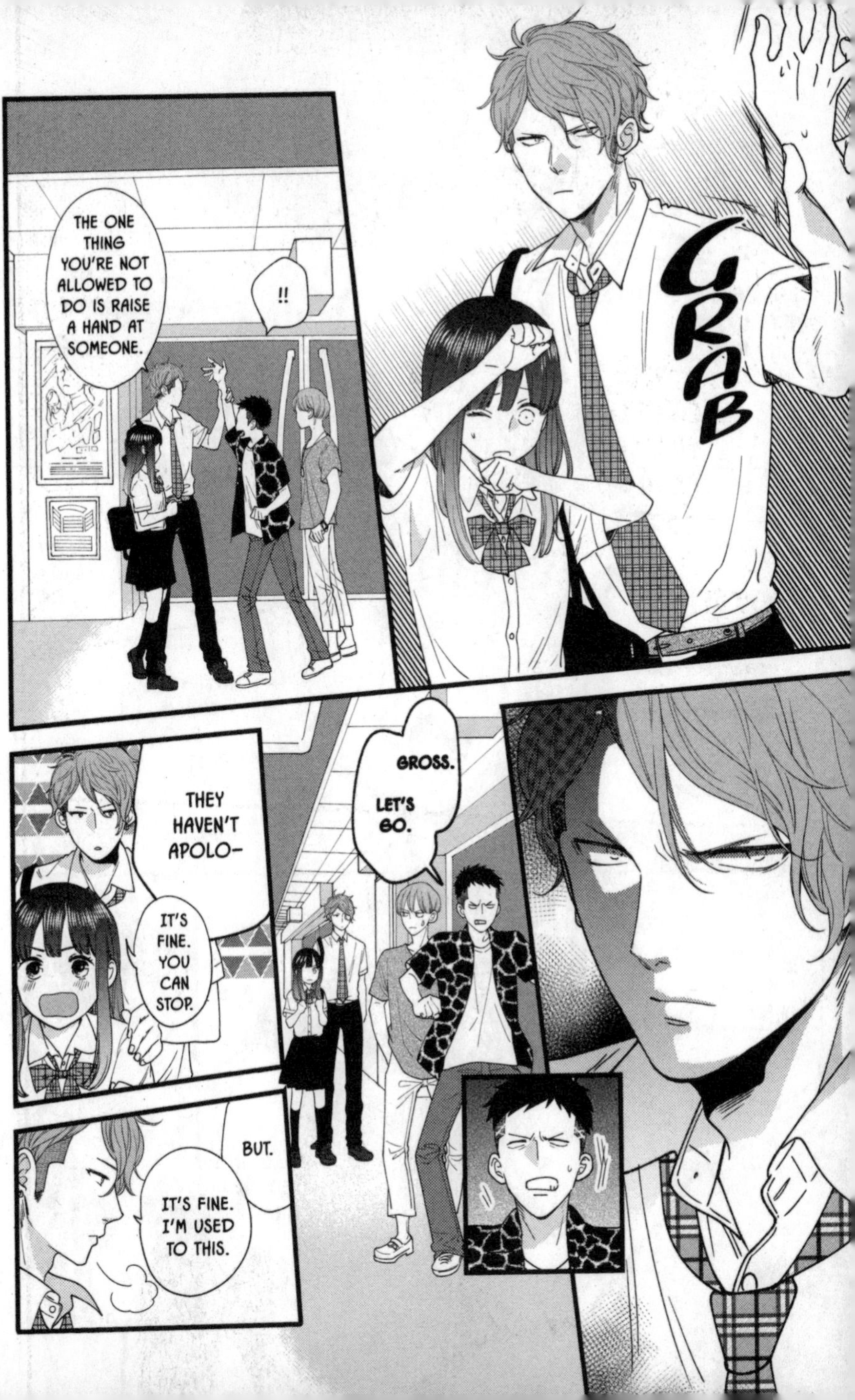
GRAB
THE ONE THING YOU'RE NOT ALLOWED TO DO IS RAISE A HAND AT SOMEONE.
!!
GROSS.
LET'S GO.
THEY HAVEN'T APOLO-
IT'S FINE. YOU CAN STOP.
BUT.
IT'S FINE. I'M USED TO THIS.

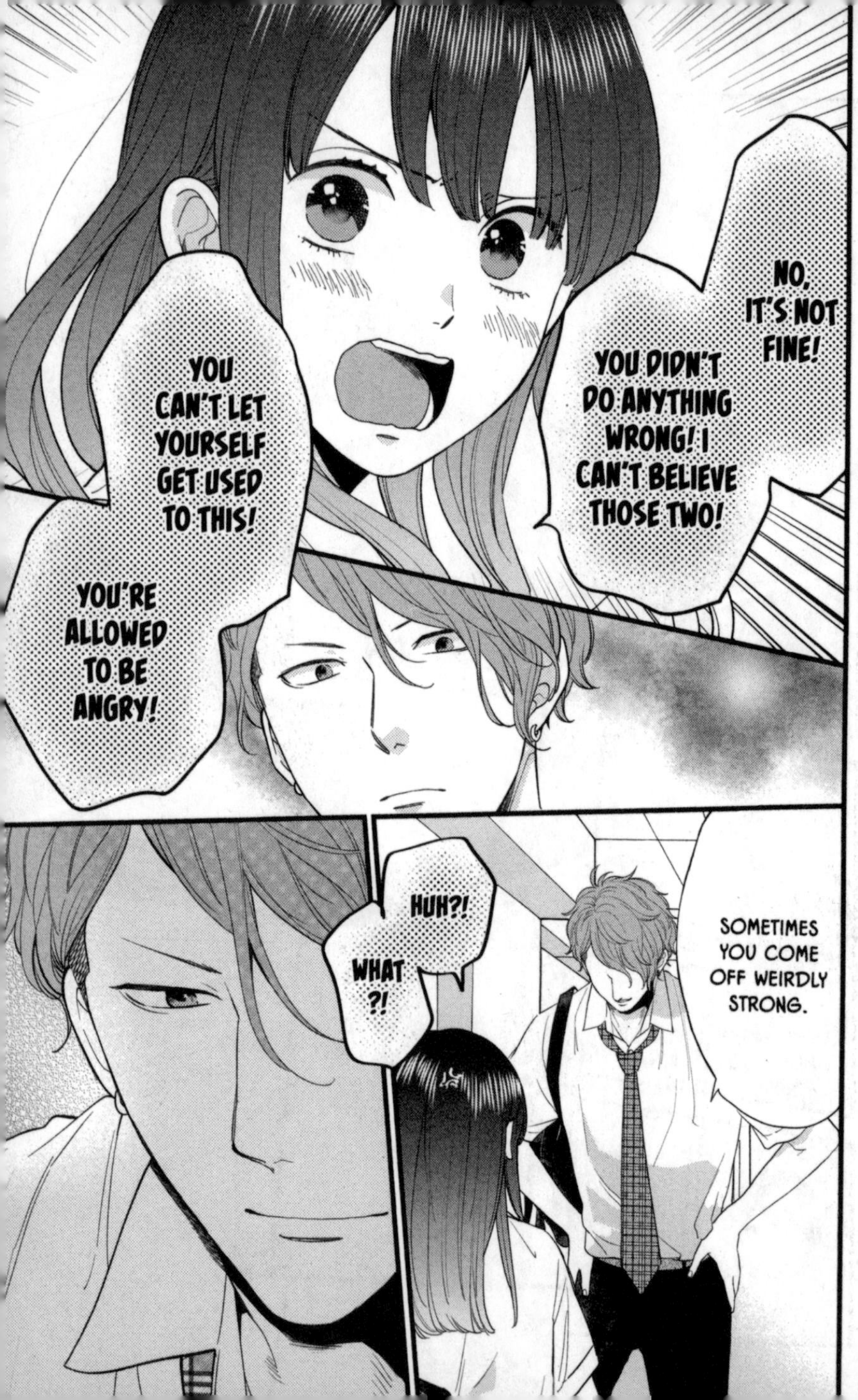
NO, IT'S NOT FINE!
YOU DIDN'T DO ANYTHING WRONG! I CAN'T BELIEVE THOSE TWO!
YOU CAN'T LET YOURSELF GET USED TO THIS!
YOU'RE ALLOWED TO BE ANGRY!
SOMETIMES YOU COME OFF WEIRDLY STRONG.
HUH?!
WHAT ?!

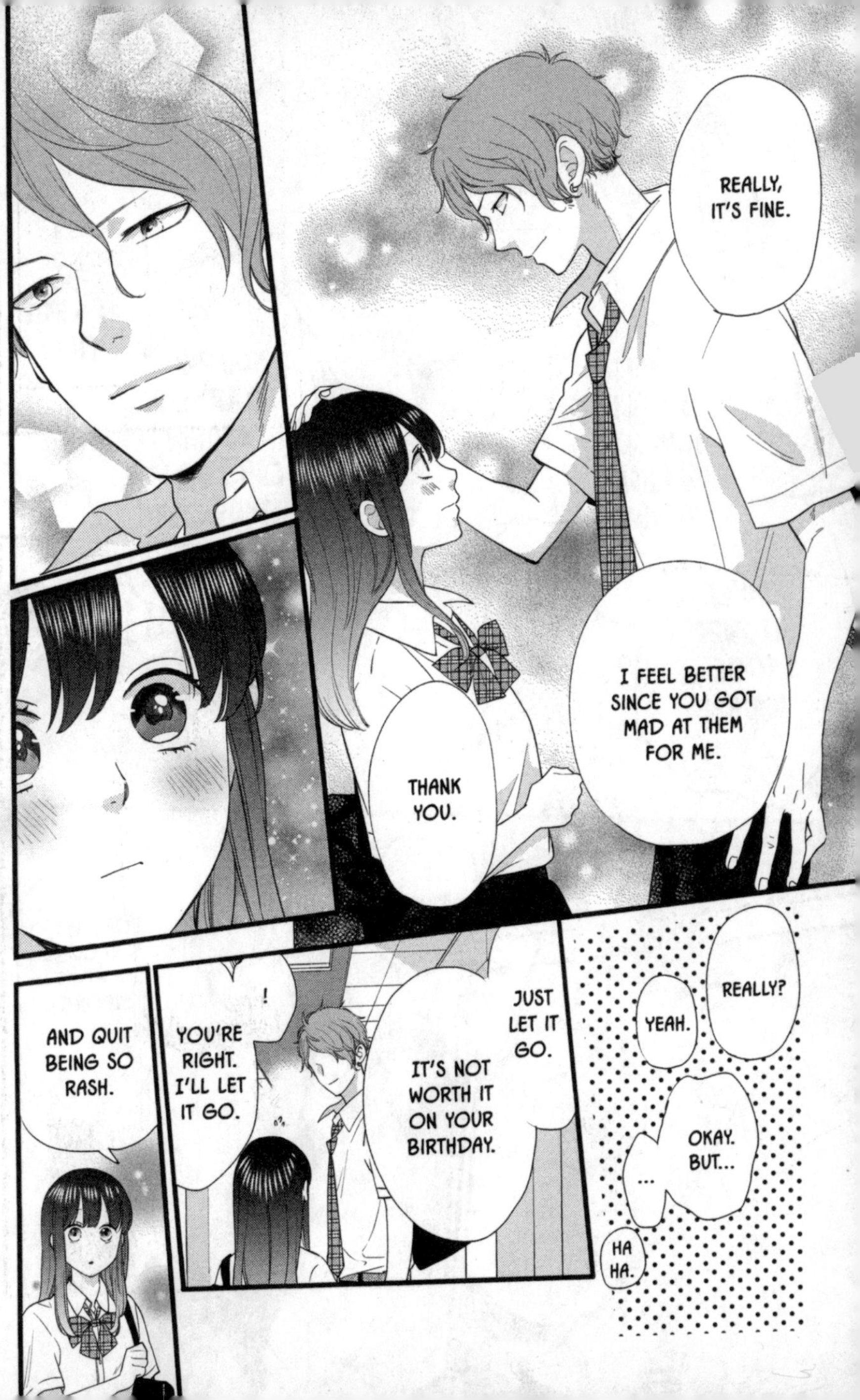
REALLY, IT'S FINE.
I FEEL BETTER SINCE YOU GOT MAD AT THEM FOR ME.
THANK YOU.
REALLY?
YEAH.
OKAY. BUT...
...
HA HA.
JUST LET IT GO.
IT'S NOT WORTH IT ON YOUR BIRTHDAY.
!
YOU'RE RIGHT. I'LL LET IT GO.
AND QUIT BEING SO RASH.

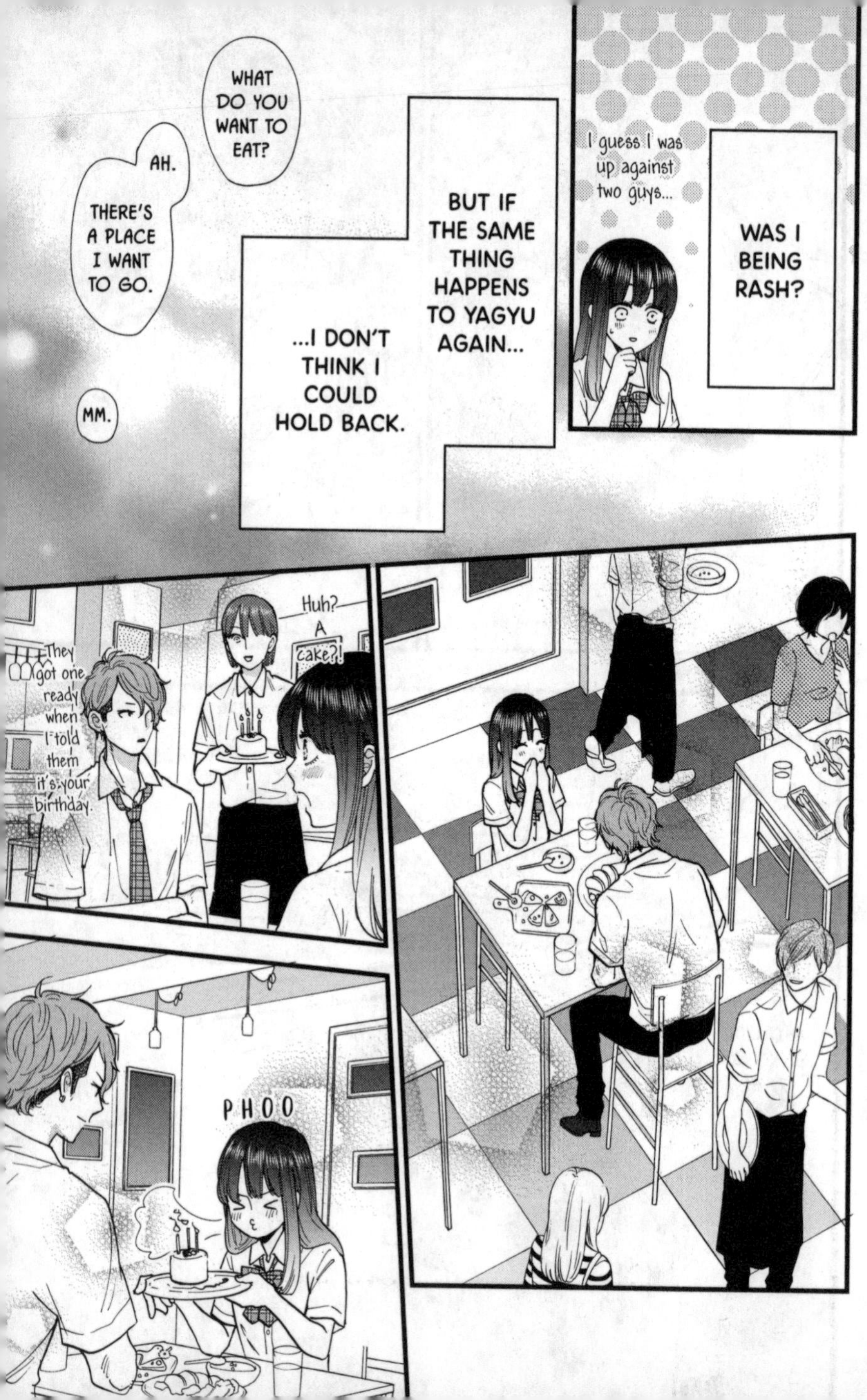
I guess I was up against two guys...
WAS I BEING RASH?
BUT IF THE SAME THING HAPPENS TO YAGYU AGAIN...
...I DON'T THINK I COULD HOLD BACK.
WHAT DO YOU WANT TO EAT?
AH.
THERE'S A PLACE I WANT TO GO.
MM.
Huh? A cake?!
They got one ready when I told them it's your birthday.
PHOO

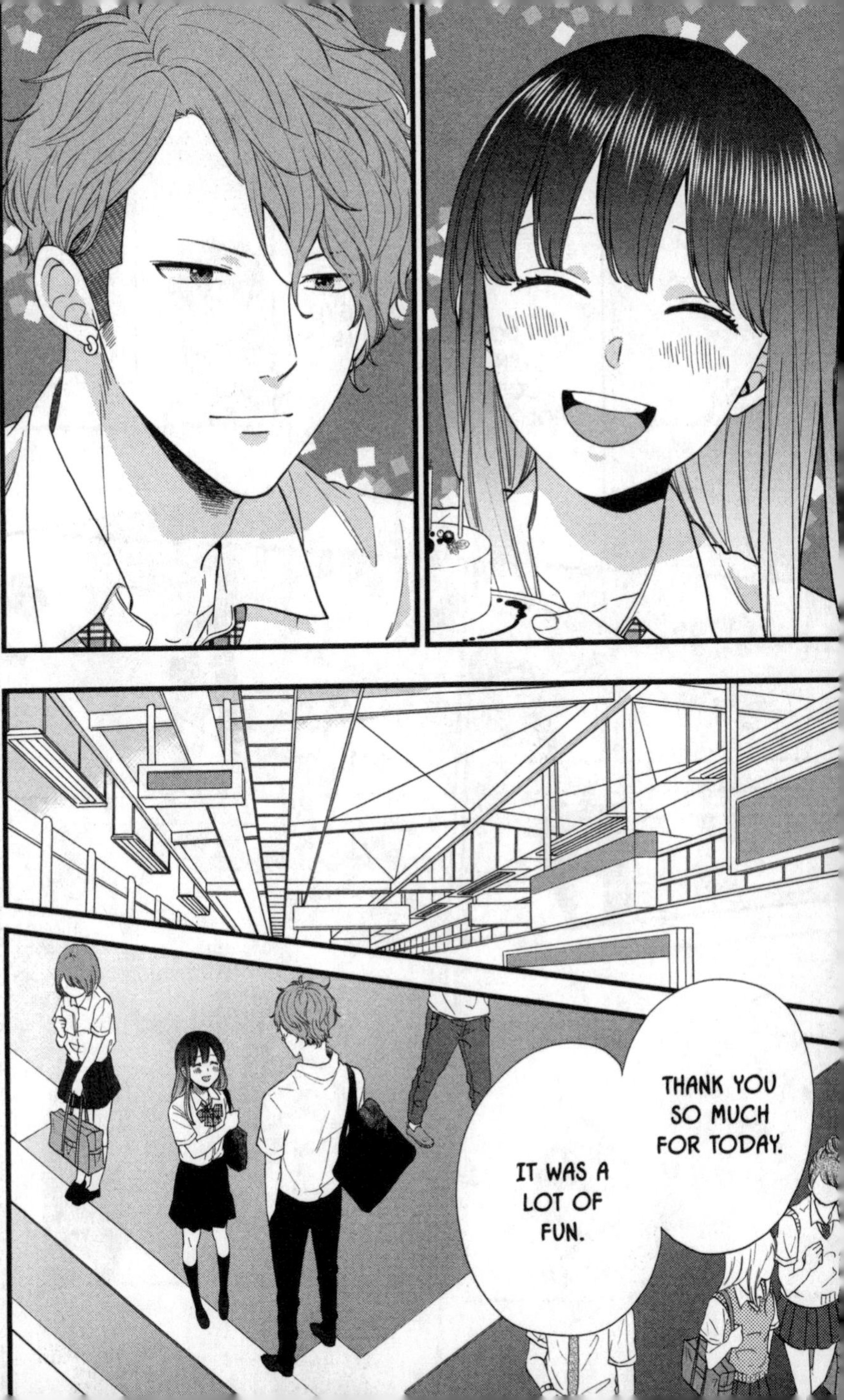
THANK YOU SO MUCH FOR TODAY.
IT WAS A LOT OF FUN.

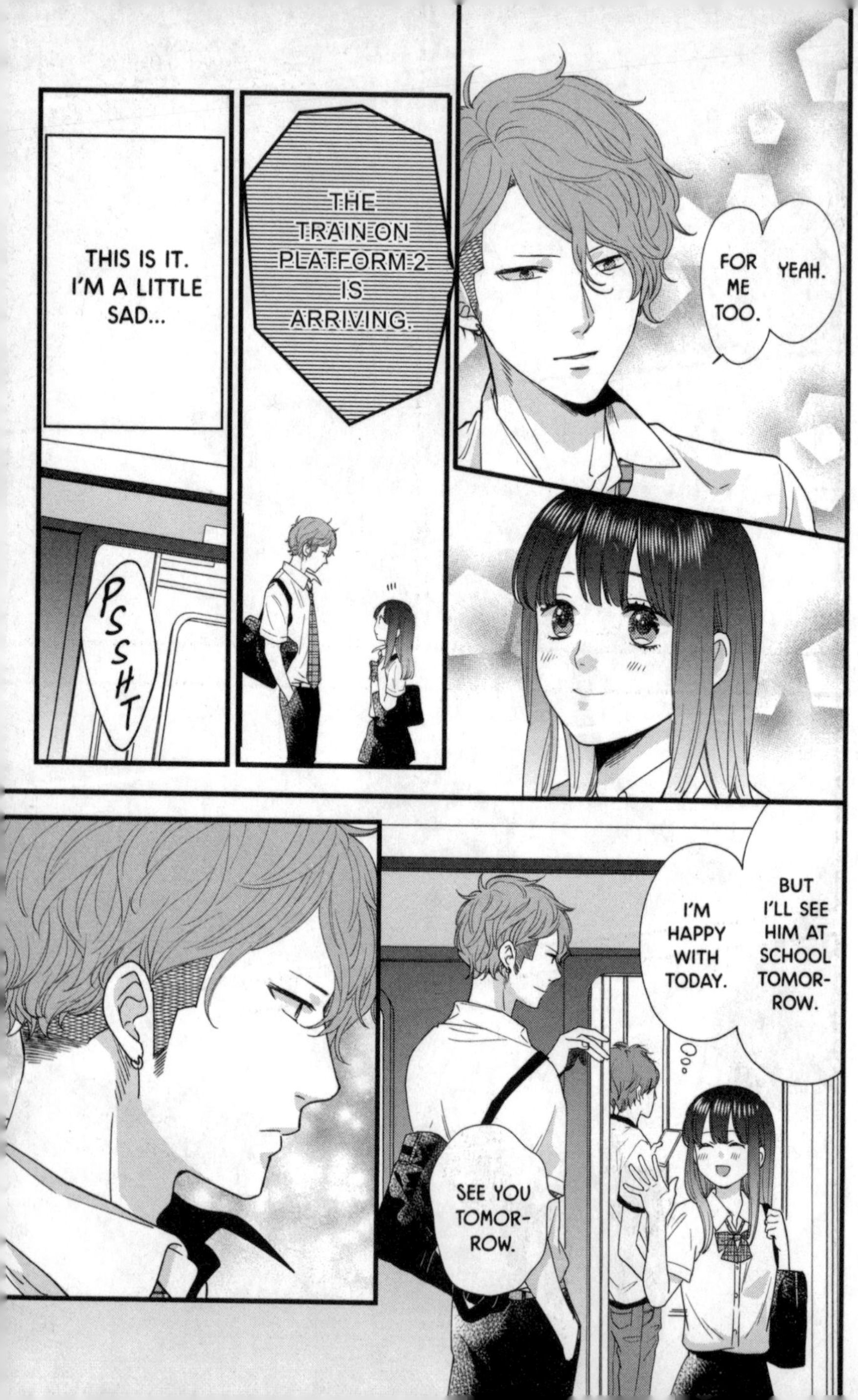
YEAH.
FOR ME TOO.
THE TRAIN ON PLATFORM 2 IS ARRIVING.
THIS IS IT. I'M A LITTLE SAD...
PSSHT
BUT I'LL SEE HIM AT SCHOOL TOMORROW.
I'M HAPPY WITH TODAY.
SEE YOU TOMORROW.

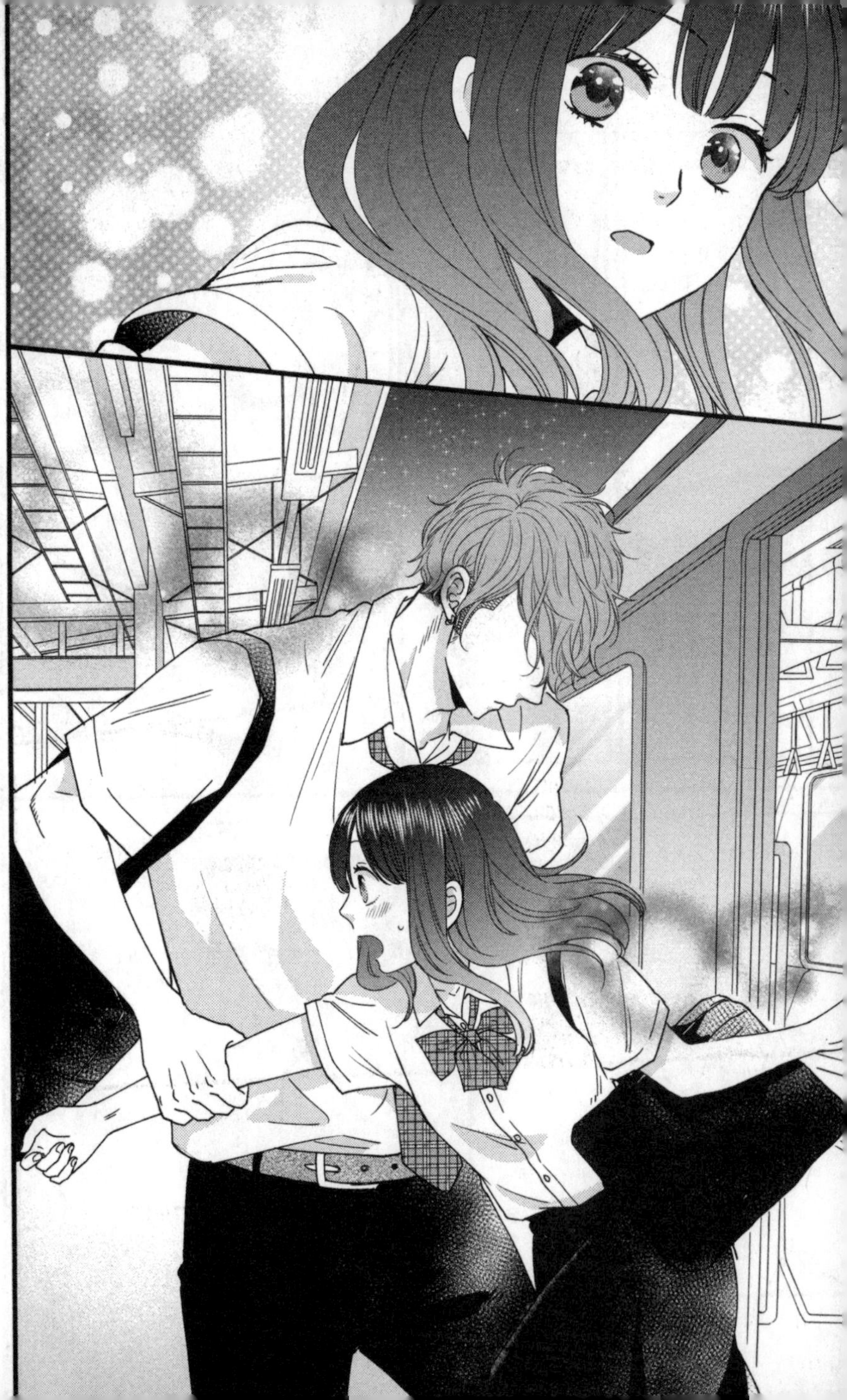

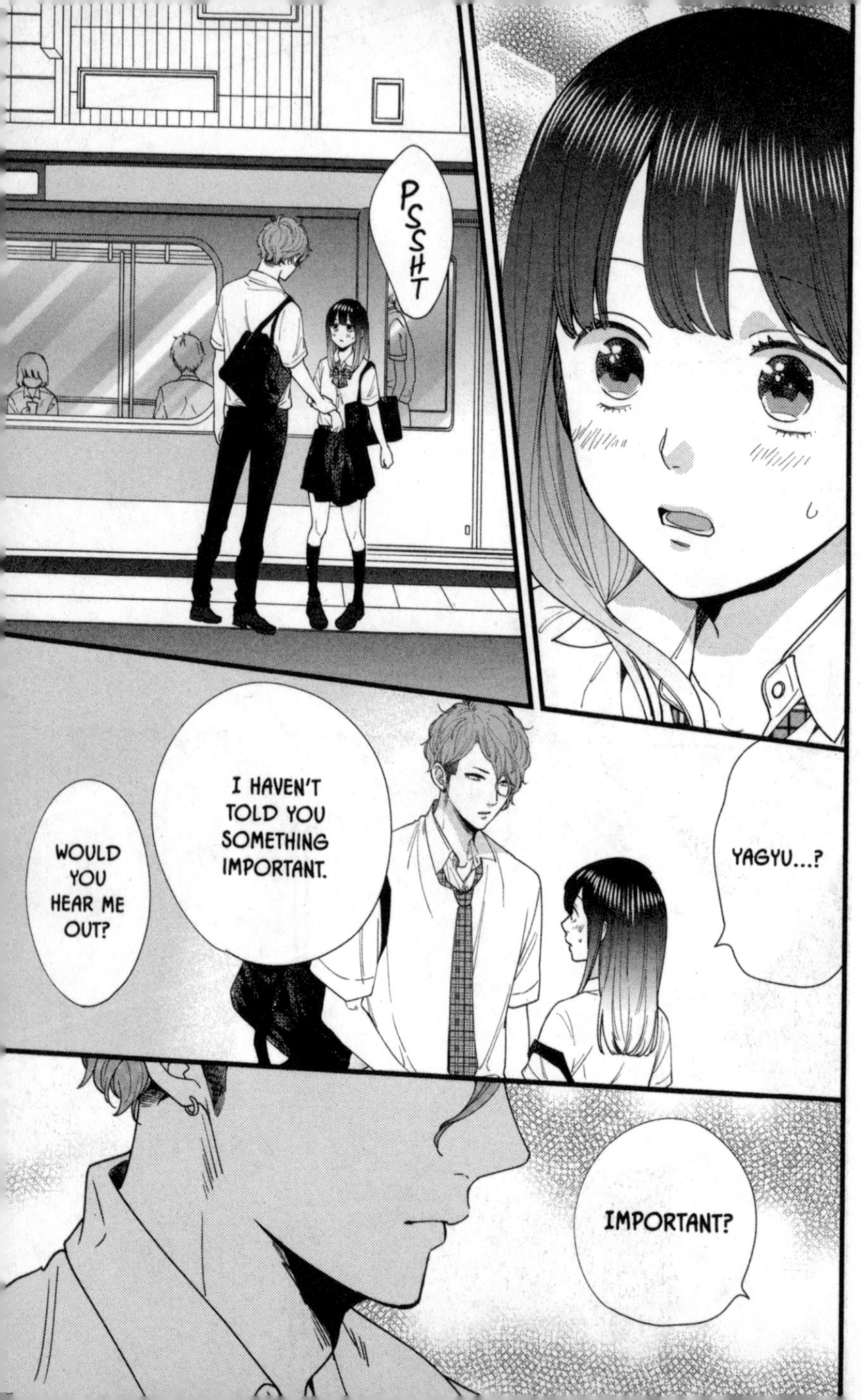
PSSHT
YAGYU...?
I HAVEN'T TOLD YOU SOMETHING IMPORTANT.
WOULD YOU HEAR ME OUT?
IMPORTANT?

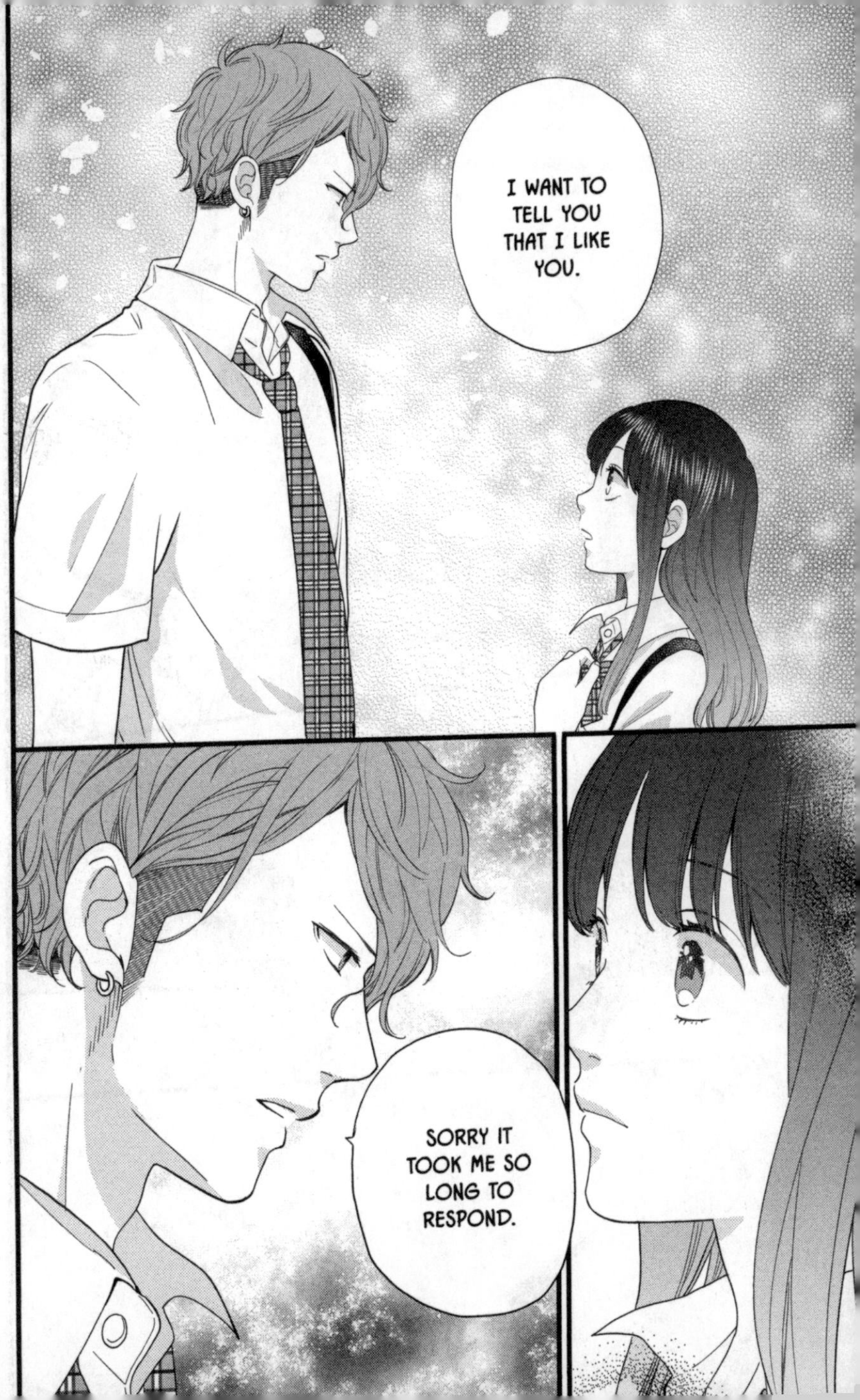
I WANT TO TELL YOU THAT I LIKE YOU.
SORRY IT TOOK ME SO LONG TO RESPOND.

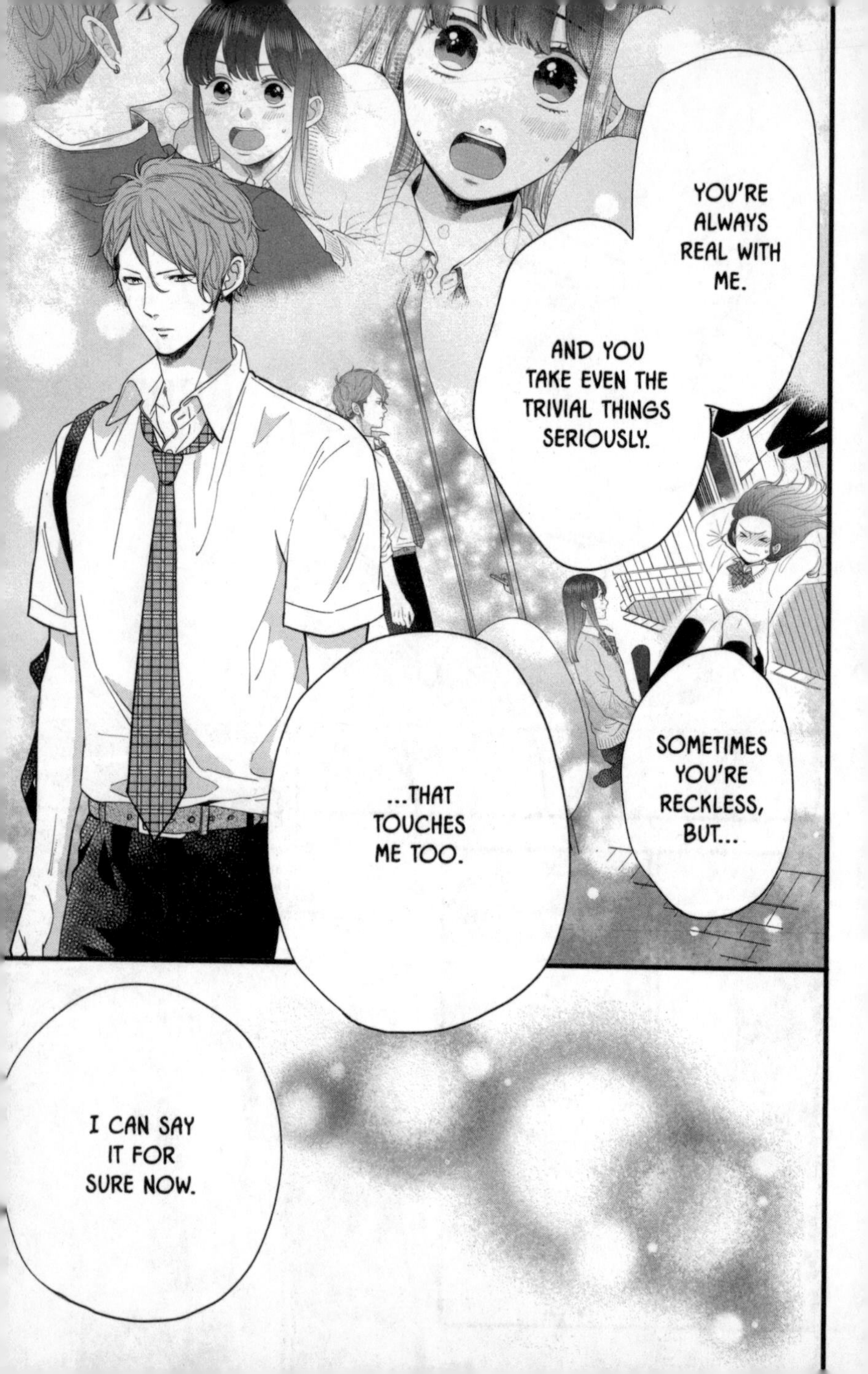
YOU'RE ALWAYS REAL WITH ME.
AND YOU TAKE EVEN THE TRIVIAL THINGS SERIOUSLY.
SOMETIMES YOU'RE RECKLESS, BUT...
...THAT TOUCHES ME TOO.
I CAN SAY IT FOR SURE NOW.

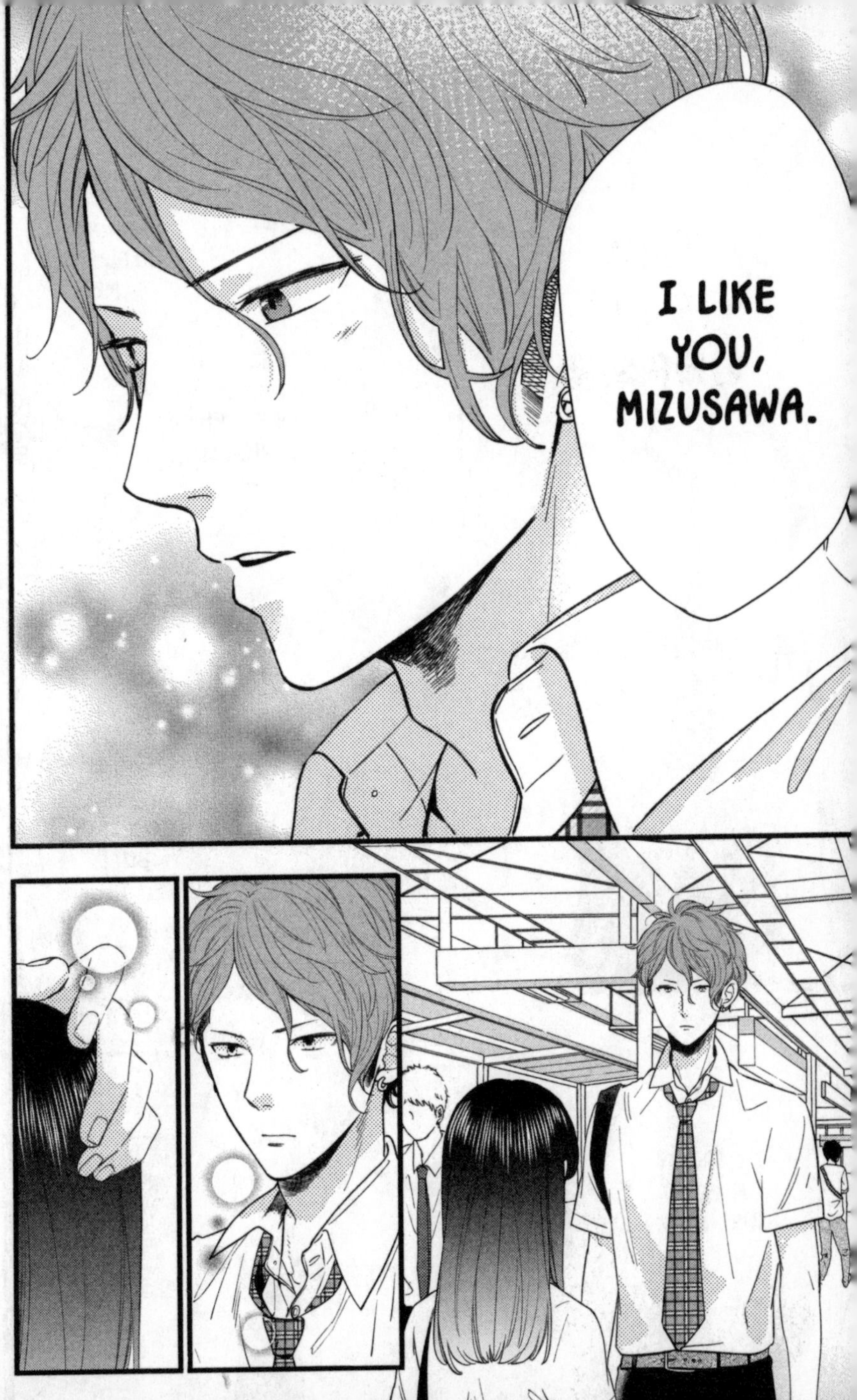
I LIKE YOU, MIZUSAWA.

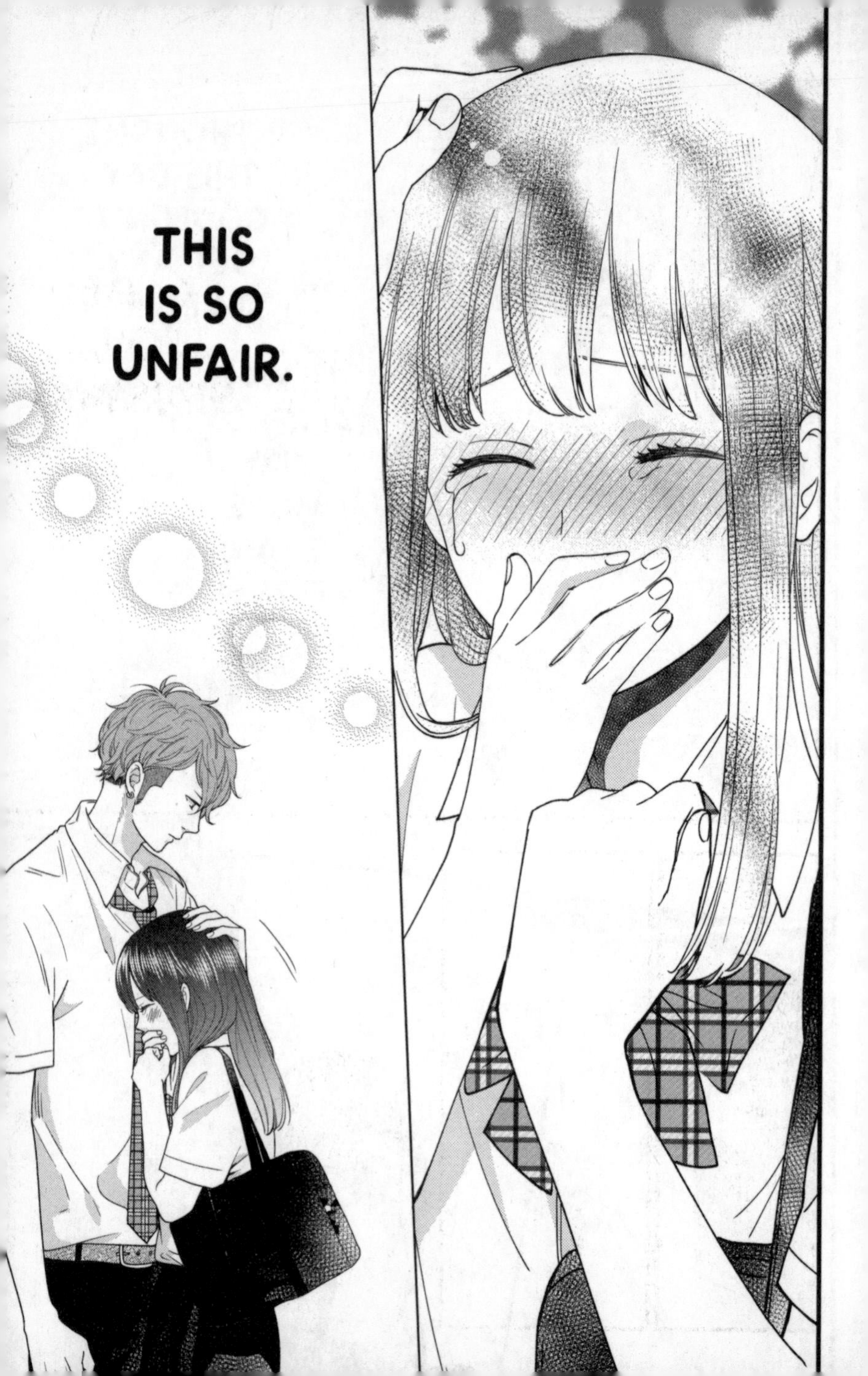
THIS IS SO UNFAIR.

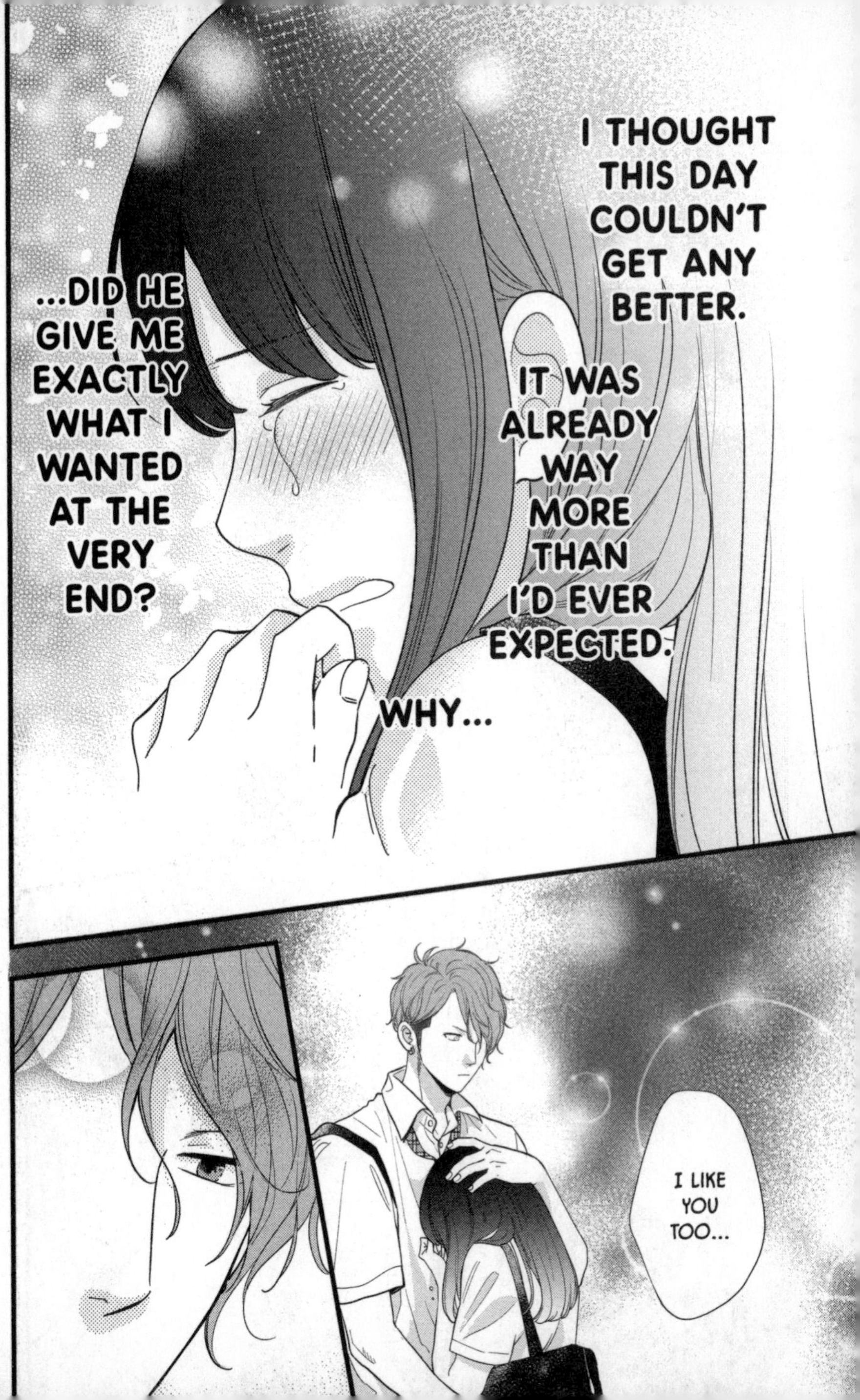
I THOUGHT THIS DAY COULDN'T GET ANY BETTER.
IT WAS ALREADY WAY MORE THAN I'D EVER EXPECTED.
WHY...
...DID HE GIVE ME EXACTLY WHAT I WANTED AT THE VERY END?
I LIKE YOU TOO...

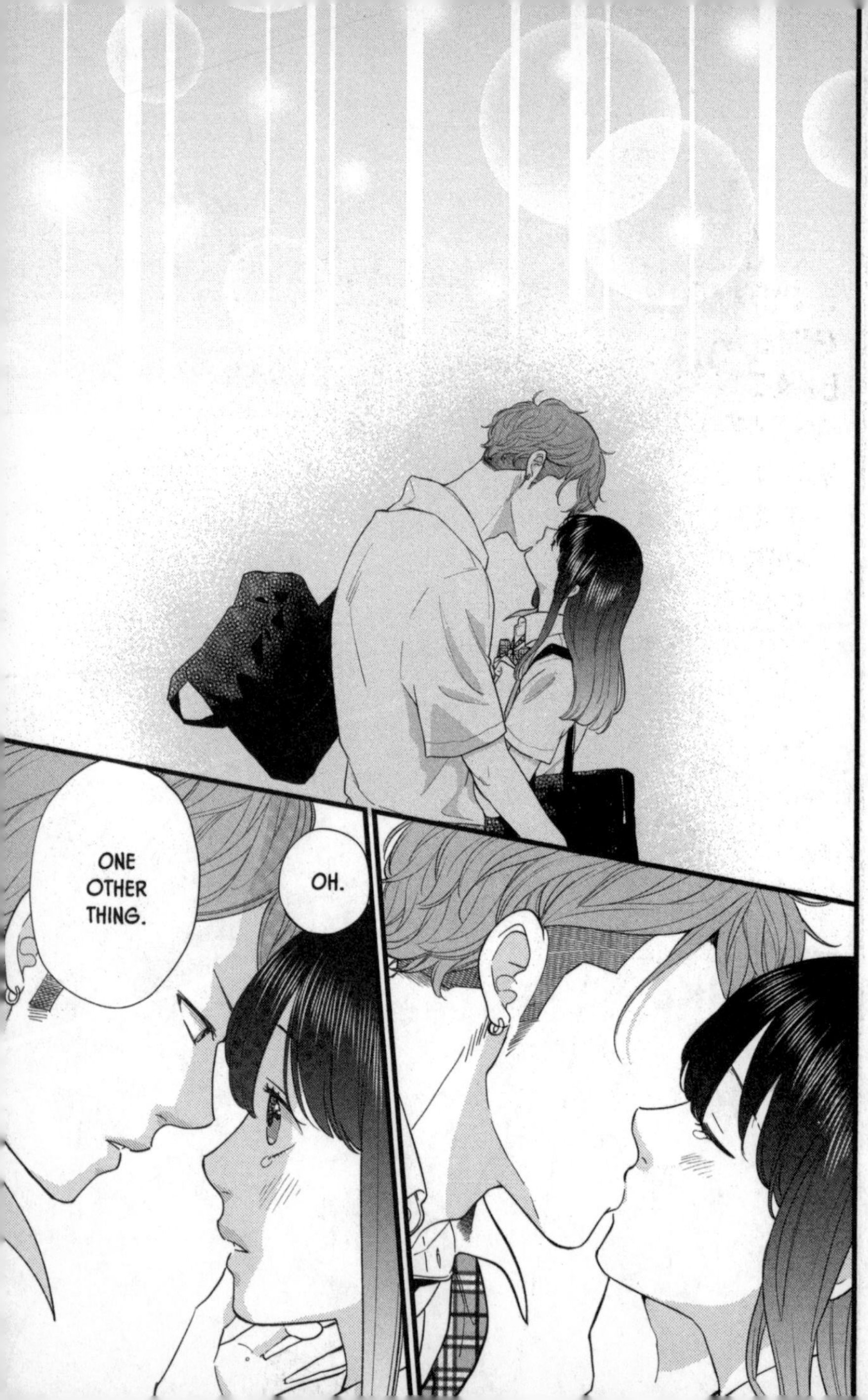
OH.
ONE OTHER THING.

HAPPY BIRTHDAY!
NOW?!
Oh, come to think of it, you never said it.
THANK YOU.
YAGYU...
...I LIKE YOU TOO.
TO BE CONTINUED

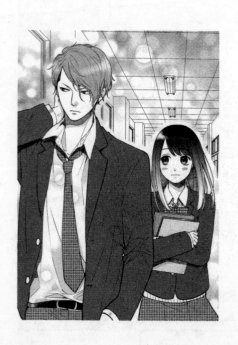

Bonus Manga
Wolf Girl and Dark Prince: Good Spouses Day

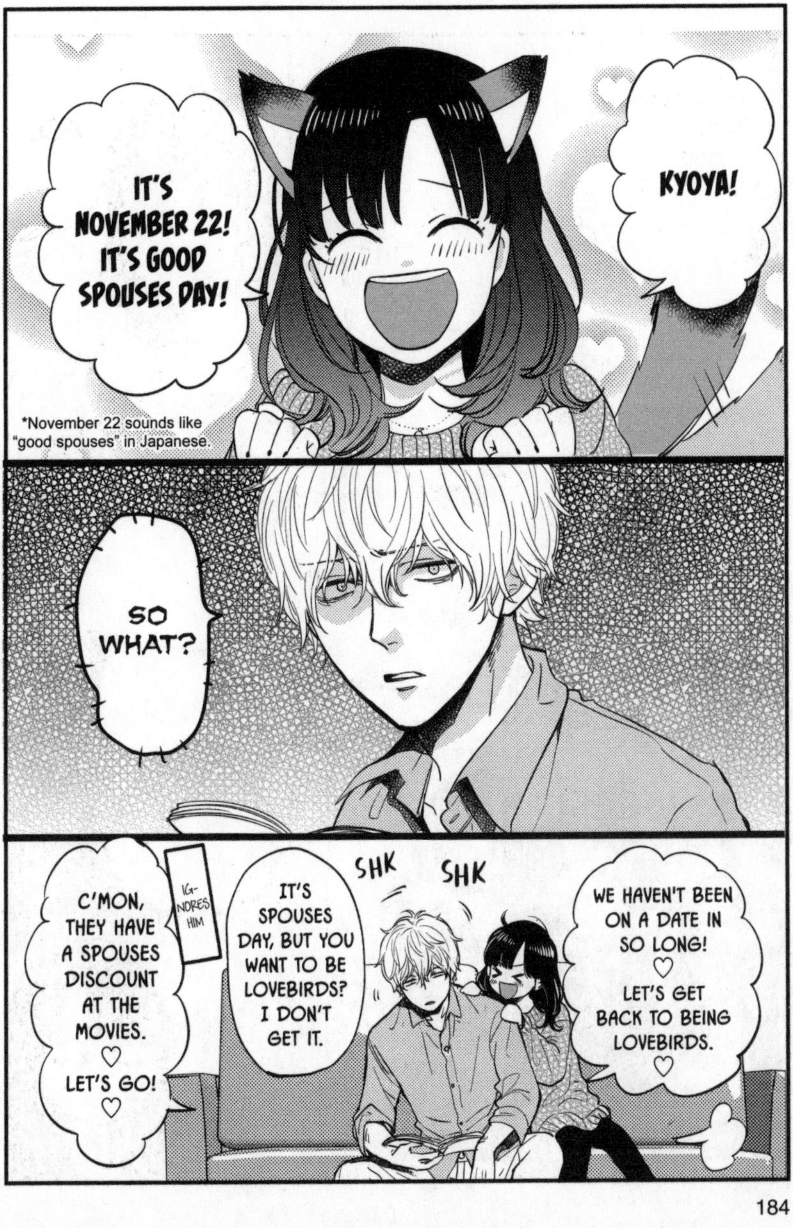
KYOYA!
IT'S NOVEMBER 22! IT'S GOOD SPOUSES DAY!
*November 22 sounds like "good spouses" in Japanese.
SO WHAT?
SHK
SHK
WE HAVEN'T BEEN ON A DATE IN SO LONG! ♡ LET'S GET BACK TO BEING LOVEBIRDS. ♡
IT'S SPOUSES DAY, BUT YOU WANT TO BE LOVEBIRDS? I DON'T GET IT.
IG-NORES HIM
C'MON, THEY HAVE A SPOUSES DISCOUNT AT THE MOVIES. ♡ LET'S GO! ♡

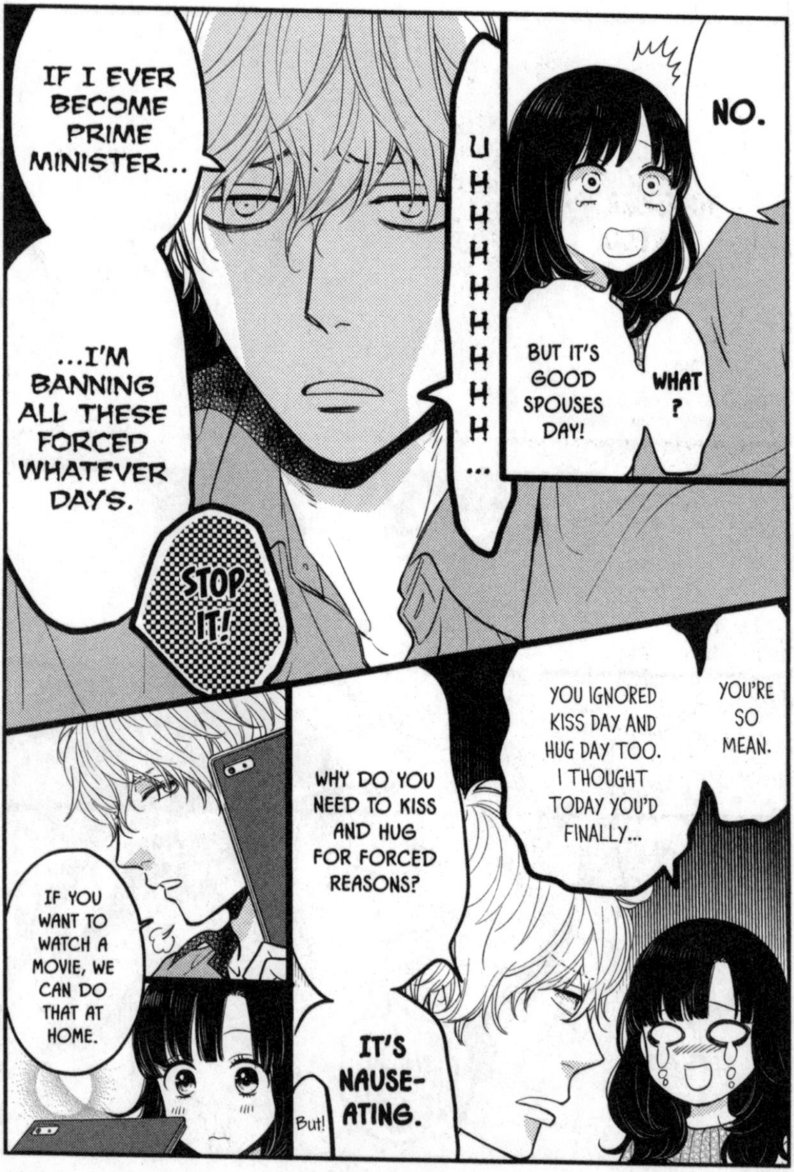
NO.
WHAT?
BUT IT'S GOOD SPOUSES DAY!
UHHHHHHHH...
IF I EVER BECOME PRIME MINISTER...
...I'M BANNING ALL THESE FORCED WHATEVER DAYS.
STOP IT!
YOU'RE SO MEAN.
YOU IGNORED KISS DAY AND HUG DAY TOO. I THOUGHT TODAY YOU'D FINALLY...
WHY DO YOU NEED TO KISS AND HUG FOR FORCED REASONS?
IT'S NAUSE-ATING.
But!
IF YOU WANT TO WATCH A MOVIE, WE CAN DO THAT AT HOME.

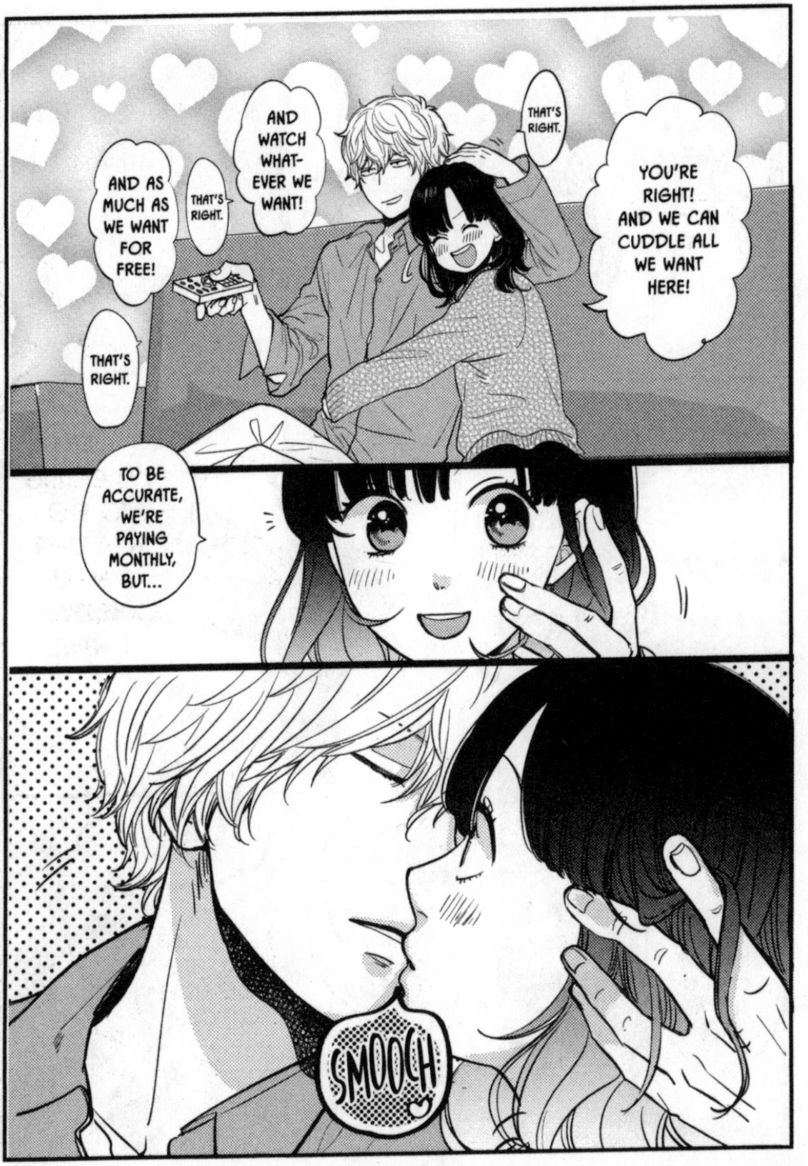
YOU'RE RIGHT! AND WE CAN CUDDLE ALL WE WANT HERE!
THAT'S RIGHT.
AND WATCH WHAT-EVER WE WANT!
THAT'S RIGHT.
AND AS MUCH AS WE WANT FOR FREE!
THAT'S RIGHT.
TO BE ACCURATE, WE'RE PAYING MONTHLY, BUT...
SMOOCH

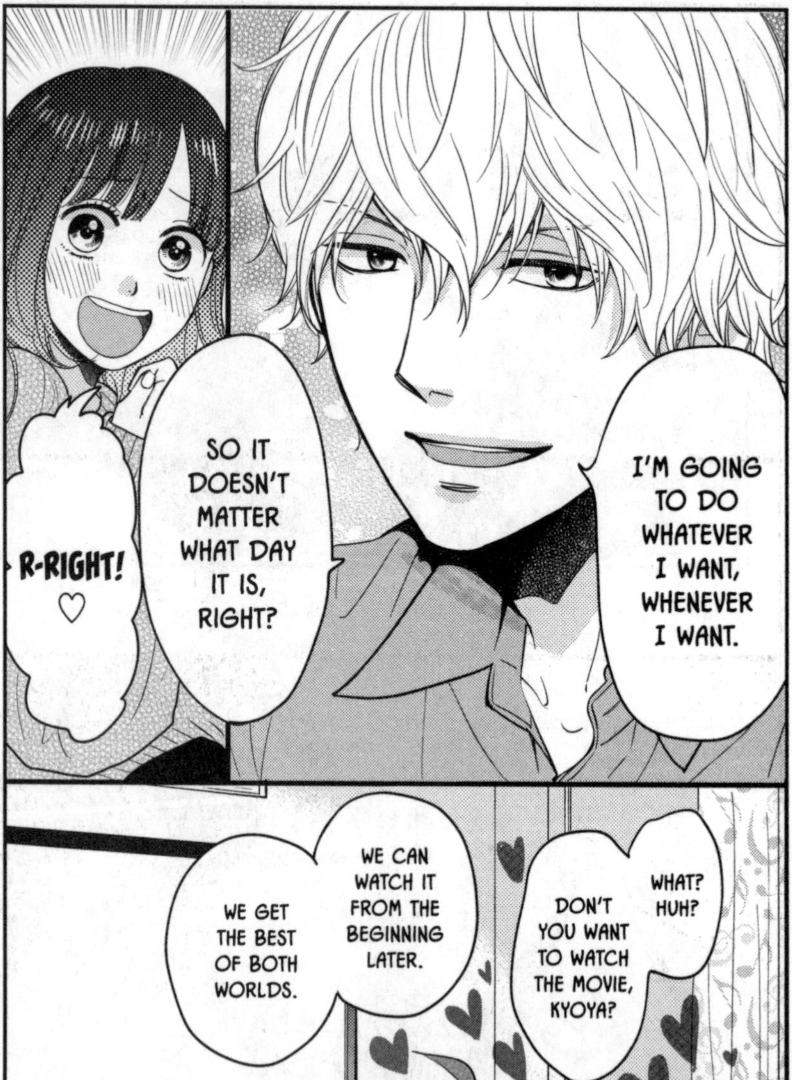
I'M GOING TO DO WHATEVER I WANT, WHENEVER I WANT.
SO IT DOESN'T MATTER WHAT DAY IT IS, RIGHT?
R-RIGHT! ♡
WHAT? HUH?
DON'T YOU WANT TO WATCH THE MOVIE, KYOYA?
WE CAN WATCH IT FROM THE BEGINNING LATER.
WE GET THE BEST OF BOTH WORLDS.

THE END

Sometimes I post some doodles
and work announcements.
I don't tweet much.
I'm flighty, so I appear as suddenly
as I disappear. If you're okay with
that, please follow me. ♥

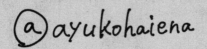
@ayukohaiena

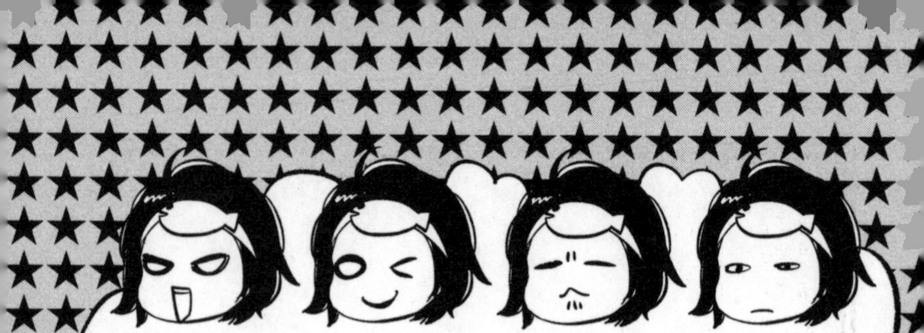

How was it?

Thank you so much for reading all the way to the end! If we were to meet again in the second volume, I would be so happy.

Ayuko Hatta

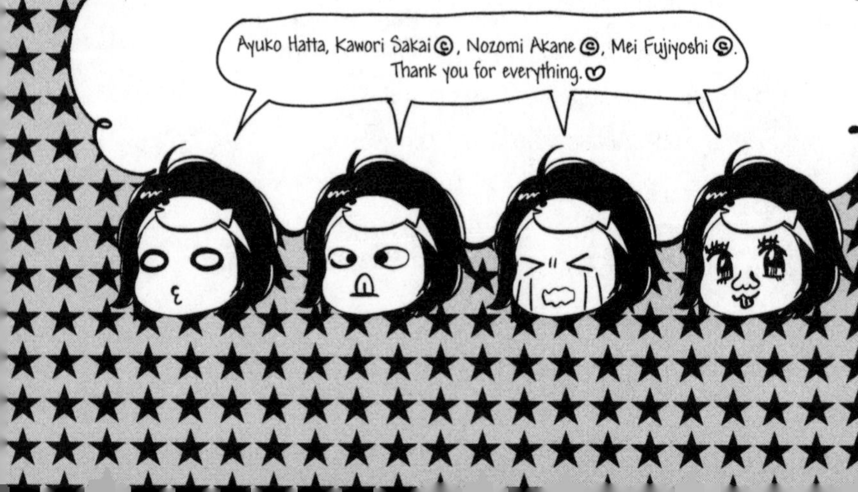
Ayuko Hatta, Kawori Sakai ©, Nozomi Akane ©, Mei Fujiyoshi ©. Thank you for everything. ♡

My parents have a dog at their house...
And it's a toy poodle, but...
Its legs are ridiculously long.
And it always circles me threateningly
when I visit, but...
Its legs are ridiculously long.
It's really cute, but...
Its legs are ridiculously long.

Ayuko Hatta

Ayuko Hatta is a shojo manga artist who resides
in the Kansai region of Japan. She loves playing
games and is generally acknowledged by those
around her to be an innate gamer. She's also
good at cooking and drawing caricatures.

IMA KOI
Now I'm in Love

VOLUME 1 • SHOJO BEAT EDITION

STORY & ART BY
Ayuko Hatta

TRANSLATION & ADAPTATION Jan Mitsuko Cash
TOUCH-UP ART & LETTERING Inori Fukuda Trant
DESIGN Shawn Carrico
EDITOR Nancy Thistlethwaite

IMA, KOIWO SHITEIMASU. © 2019 by Ayuko Hatta
All rights reserved.
First published in Japan in 2019 by SHUEISHA Inc., Tokyo.
English translation rights arranged by SHUEISHA Inc.

The stories, characters, and incidents mentioned
in this publication are entirely fictional.

Printed in Canada

Published by VIZ Media, LLC
P.O. Box 77010
San Francisco, CA 94107

10 9 8 7 6 5 4 3 2 1
First printing, March 2022

VIZ MEDIA
viz.com

Shojo Beat
shojobeat.com

THIS IS
THE LAST PAGE.

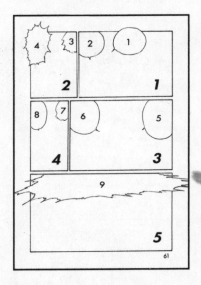

Ima Koi: Now I'm in Love reads from right to
left, starting in the upper-right corner. Japanese
is read from right to left, meaning that action,
sound effects, and word-balloon order are
completely reversed from English order.